THE POLITICIZATION OF SAFETY

FAMILIES, LAW, AND SOCIETY SERIES

General Editor: Nancy E. Dowd

Justice for Kids: Keeping Kids Out of the Juvenile Justice System
Edited by Nancy E. Dowd

Masculinities and the Law: A Multidimensional Approach
Edited by Frank Rudy Cooper and Ann C. McGinley

The New Kinship: Constructing Donor-Conceived Families
Naomi Cahn

What Is Parenthood? Contemporary Debates about the Family
Edited by Linda C. McClain and Daniel Cere

In Our Hands: The Struggle for U.S. Child Care Policy
Elizabeth Palley and Corey S. Shdaimah

The Marriage Buyout: The Troubled Trajectory of U.S. Alimony Law
Cynthia Lee Starnes

Children, Sexuality, and the Law
Edited by Sacha Coupet and Ellen Marrus

A New Juvenile Justice System: Total Reform for a Broken System
Edited by Nancy E. Dowd

Divorced from Reality: Rethinking Family Dispute Resolution
Jane C. Murphy and Jana B. Singer

The Poverty Industry: The Exploitation of America's Most Vulnerable Citizens
Daniel L. Hatcher

Ending Zero Tolerance: The Crisis of Absolute School Discipline
Derek W. Black

Blaming Mothers: American Law and the Risks to Children's Health
Linda C. Fentiman

The Politicization of Safety: Critical Perspectives on Domestic Violence Responses
Edited by Jane K. Stoever

The Politicization of Safety

Critical Perspectives on Domestic Violence Responses

Edited by

Jane K. Stoever

NEW YORK UNIVERSITY PRESS

New York

NEW YORK UNIVERSITY PRESS
New York
www.nyupress.org

References to Internet websites (URLs) were accurate at the time of writing. Neither the author nor New York University Press is responsible for URLs that may have expired or changed since the manuscript was prepared.

Library of Congress Cataloging-in-Publication Data
Names: Stoever, Jane K., editor.
Title: The politicization of safety : critical perspectives on domestic violence responses / edited by Jane K. Stoever.
Description: New York : New York University, 2019. |
Includes bibliographical references and index.
Identifiers: LCCN 2018020945| ISBN 9781479805648 (cl : alk. paper) |
ISBN 9781479806287 (pb : alk. paper)
Subjects: LCSH: Family violence—Law and legislation—United States. |
Family violence—Prevention—United States.
Classification: LCC KF9322 .P65 2019 | DDC 362.82/9270973—dc23
LC record available at https://lccn.loc.gov/2018020945

New York University Press books are printed on acid-free paper, and their binding materials are chosen for strength and durability. We strive to use environmentally responsible suppliers and materials to the greatest extent possible in publishing our books.

Manufactured in the United States of America

10 9 8 7 6 5 4 3 2 1

Also available as an ebook

CONTENTS

Introduction   1
Jane K. Stoever

PART I. THE POLITICS OF SAFETY AND JUSTICE

1. The Coupling and Decoupling of Safety and Crime Control:
   An Anti-Violence Movement Timeline   15
   Mimi E. Kim

2. The Politicization of Domestic Violence   38
   Deborah M. Weissman

3. Empowerment Politics and Access to Justice   62
   Elizabeth L. MacDowell

PART II. MULTIPLE SYSTEMS, STANDARDS,
AND DILEMMAS

4. Battering Court Syndrome: A Structural Critique of
   "Failure to Protect"   91
   Alisa Bierria and Colby Lenz

5. Parental Love and Purposeful Violence   119
   Cynthia Godsoe

6. Specializing Justice for Youth and Families: Intervening in
   Family Violence or Expanding the Carceral Net?   151
   Amy M. Magnus

PART III. INTERSECTIONAL NEEDS FOR SAFETY
AND JUSTICE

7. Feminist Response to Campus Sexual Assault in the
   Republican Era: Crime Logic, Intersectional
   Public Health, and Restorative Justice   171
   Donna Coker

8. A Fraught Pairing: Immigrant Survivors of Intimate Partner
   Violence and Law Enforcement   202
   Natalie Nanasi

   PART IV. MILITARIZATION, FIREARMS, AND
   THE FAMILY

9. Politics, Safety, and Officer-Involved Intimate
   Partner Violence   227
   Leigh Goodmark

10. Playing Politics with Firearms and Family Violence   246
    Jane K. Stoever

11. Preventing Ordinary and Extraordinary Violence   272
    Mary D. Fan

    PART V. MOVING FORWARD WITH A CRITICAL LENS

12. Is Domestic Violence Politicized Too Narrowly?   303
    Jamie R. Abrams

13. Harm Reduction in the Domestic Violence Context   332
    Courtney Cross

14. Developing a National Plan of Action on Violence against
    Women and Gender Violence: A Human Rights Approach   362
    Caroline Bettinger-López

    About the Editor   379
    About the Contributors   381
    Index   387

Introduction

JANE K. STOEVER

The "Politicization of Safety" has multiple meanings and dimensions. This book calls for debate and consideration of some unquestioned and generally bipartisan assumptions, particularly about carceral responses to domestic violence, while maintaining the fundamental right of all people to be free from violence. Some contributors to this volume examine politics in the more traditional partisan sense, using legislative battles to illuminate growing divisions while surfacing values motivating different policies. Others examine politics and tensions within the anti-domestic violence movement and evaluate this movement's position in relation to other social issues and progressive concerns. The feminist movement has championed unity and equality, but has also been marked by tensions and fractures, and differing perspectives and alliances naturally influence policies and practices. The politics of advocacy and narratives surrounding victims/survivors are also implicated, and the book challenges readers to question assumptions, expand perspectives, and consider larger justice issues.

Domestic violence is an issue commonly assumed to be bipartisan and nonpolitical, with politicians of any party seeking headlines saying they are working against domestic abuse. Yet racial and gender politics, the move toward criminalization, reproductive justice concerns, immigration policies, gun control debates, and other factors and political interests increasingly shape responses to domestic violence.

Across party lines, we should agree to work for societal change and healing to prevent and remedy intimate partner violence and sexual violence. In our exploration of the politicization of safety, we may determine that some issues simply should not be up for debate; opposition seems irrational and contrary to our country's safety, justice, and autonomy principles. For example, research shows that firearms in the hands of domestic abusers increase the likelihood of homicide fivefold. Further congressional hearings are not needed, nor should positions about domestic abusers' access to firearms be divided along political lines. Yet as more and more public massacres occur by armed gunmen, almost all of whom have histories of perpetrating domestic violence, the National Rifle Association calls for more guns in the hands of more Americans, while advocates for gun safety and against family violence see the shootings as evidence of firearm danger and problems with ease of access to rapid-fire, high-lethality weapons. Both sides of the gun control debate become further entrenched and our country fails to make meaningful progress regarding these preventable deaths.

At the same time, as several authors in this volume point out, some governmental responses to domestic and sexual violence should be politicized and debated in ways foreign to the dominant political discourse in the United States. For decades, criminalization and use of law enforcement was the default response to social problems across party lines. But intersectional scholarship and grassroots activism have begun to trouble this unquestioned consensus, showing that automatic recourse to law enforcement can be ineffective, traumatic, autonomy-denying, and even dangerous, particularly for people of color and those without secure legal immigration status.

Upon analysis, we see that safety is a political issue, particularly for women and people of color. The question this book poses is: What should the terrain of debate be?

The legislative battle regarding the most recent reauthorization of the Violence Against Women Act (VAWA) provides a prime example of the politicization of safety. First passed in 1994, this landmark federal legislation recognized the scourge of domestic violence; created new legal remedies, including immigration remedies for qualifying abuse survivors; and authorized multiple grant-funding programs. After several bipartisan reauthorizations that expanded immigration remedies and created additional legal protections, VAWA became a source of contention between political parties. During 2012 and 2013, VAWA expired for over 500 days due to U.S. Senate and House differences over whether VAWA would include the protection of Native American abuse survivors; require college campuses to develop responses to sexual assault; and prohibit discrimination against lesbian, gay, bisexual, and transgender domestic violence survivors. These protections should not serve as hot-button flashpoints, but rather should be accepted as basic, necessary, and long overdue in today's world. VAWA again faces reauthorization and expiration in 2018, and the topic of the politicization of safety is more relevant than ever. This is particularly so given the Trump administration's multiple anti-immigrant executive orders, rollbacks of protections for transgender individuals, and the decision to overturn asylum protections for domestic violence victims.

Another example of the politicization of safety concerns teen dating violence education. Teen dating abuse rates are alarmingly high, with one in three teenage girls experiencing physical violence in a dating relationship. This abuse has significant physical, psychological, and sexual health effects on teen victims and causes severe educational and social harm. While the World Health Organization recommends that youth begin receiving education on healthy relationships and teen dating violence prevention and intervention by age eleven, endeavors to introduce the topic in high school curricula have been met with political resistance. For example, in California from 1996 to 2011, of the ten bills regarding teen dating violence that were introduced, only one bill passed. The bill that became law permits teen victims of dating violence to seek civil restraining orders without requiring parental consent; the nine bills that failed all pertained to school-based education.

Engaging in power mapping and seeing hierarchies and axes of power, we can consider who holds the power to make decisions that affect the most intimate aspects of individuals' lives and what they hold most dear. When President George W. Bush's military policies were questioned, he famously dismissed his critics by declaring himself "the decider." Is the current decider of national policy the National Rifle Association, which spent over $30 million to ensure that President Trump was elected? Is it President Trump or Vice President Pence, whose troubling histories of misogyny, homophobia, xenophobia, and religious prejudice alarm many anti-domestic violence advocates? Is it a majority white male Congress? Is the ultimate decider the Supreme Court? What will the composition of the Supreme Court be in the years and decades ahead? It matters, and this book is an attempt to disturb the edges of this map, to illustrate the terms of the debate over safety from violence.

This volume was written during the early months of the Trump era. Survivor-centered domestic violence protections and interventions are understood to be under siege in the Trump White House and with Republican control of the House and Senate. The election cycle featured a video of Trump boasting in vulgar language about sexually assaulting women and the revelation that over twenty gender-discrimination lawsuits have been filed against him. Many other women came forward detailing how he sexually assaulted and harassed them, and reports spanning multiple decades accumulated, documenting instances of Trump using his power, wealth, and celebrity status to control, degrade, and take advantage of women, publicly and privately, all while repeatedly proclaiming, "Nobody respects women more than I do." One of the Trump transition team's first acts was to order the State Department to submit details of programs and jobs that "promote gender equality, such as ending gender-based violence."[1] This act immediately sparked fears of a "witch hunt" and belief that the Trump administration would purge these programs and positions. Indeed, President Trump's first proposed budget eliminated all twenty-five grant programs totaling $480 million currently funded by the Violence Against Women Act. Individuals will differ on funding priorities and ways to prevent and intervene in gender-based violence, but defunding domestic violence services and denying the reality of the problem endangers lives.

While many anti-domestic violence advocates breathed sighs of relief when the budget did not actually cut VAWA funding, Trump's policies and budget exacerbate poverty, prejudice, mass incarceration, and other harms, while limiting access to rights. The movement against gender-based violence must align and partner with other movements to fight these structural conditions that create, reinforce, and entrench intimate partner violence, rather than being complacent.

President Trump, who has the most white-male-heavy cabinet of any president in three decades, took multiple other actions during his first month in office that were an assault on women's rights and advances toward gender equality. In his first week, Trump signed the Global Gag Rule, which ends U.S. foreign aid to organizations that mention the word "abortion" or advise women about where they can obtain safe, legal procedures. This law will almost certainly limit access to family planning methods and HIV treatment, and will increase occurrences of unsafe, sometimes deadly procedures. Tom Price, Trump's choice to lead the Department of Health and Human Services, which oversees Medicaid and Medicare, believes maternity leave should be optional. And, although most Syrian refugees are women and children, the president signed the refugee ban under the pretense that Syrian refugees may be male ISIS terrorists in disguise. The Trump-Pence White House went on to rescind the Affordable Care Act's requirement that employers provide contraception coverage, support proposals to defund Planned Parenthood, and roll back Barack Obama's efforts to close the gender pay gap. The direction the administration is headed is far from advancing gender equality and achieving the right to live free of gender violence and sexual violence. Survivors' needs and proven approaches to abuse prevention should prevail rather than politics and party affiliations, but the Trump administration's actions show the vulnerability of protections from abuse.

While the leaders of our branches of government wield significant power, government actors at the local level also hugely impact the composition of and interventions in households. Consider the Child Protective Services worker who mistakes poverty for neglect and removes children from a loving, non-violent parent; the ICE agent who arrests a domestic violence victim inside a courthouse after her restraining order hearing; the public benefits case worker who fails to offer the Family Violence Option and instead automatically initiates a child support case against an abusive non-custodial parent; or the police officer who makes a dual arrest of a gay couple after receiving a call for help from abuse. We can examine both the laws on the books and forces that motivate them, and how in everyday life, government actors carry out mandates, exercise discretion, and employ state interventions that are helpful or harmful regarding family violence.

The development of current domestic violence responses has a complex history, and the way forward will certainly be politically fraught. Feminist movements of the 1970s that were largely led by white, middle-class women who were able to prioritize one basis of oppression—gender—largely ignored multiple oppressions of racism, homophobia, poverty, religious bias, immigration status, and other axes of oppression and prejudice. Commentators have noted the gap between mainstream feminists and the daily realities of most women in America, with mainstream or elite feminism doing little to address the struggles of poor, rural, or undocumented women. Today's mediagenic feminist priorities too often prioritize middle-class women's concerns, such as workplace harassment, pop culture representation, campus rape, and glass ceilings in professional advancement, with women striving to make individual gains in male-dominated fields. These absolutely are topics of concern to problematize and address, but should not overshadow the ongoing racism, sexism, and violence experienced by masses of Americans. Urgent need for intersectionality in gender-based violence responses remains.

We must remember that the Violence Against Women Act was originally part of the Violent Crime Control and Law Enforcement Act of 1994, in a series of "tough on crime" laws that focused on criminal justice interventions. VAWA's goal of making law enforcement the primary tool to stop domestic violence has been heavily criticized, as we recognize that family violence is not merely a legal problem that can be corrected through arrest and prosecution. While cultural changes in law enforcement, which previously ignored or condoned domestic violence, were necessary, the mandatory arrest and prosecution policies encouraged by VAWA discount the complexity of relationship violence and can be critiqued for essentializing, endangering, and denying the autonomy of abuse survivors. Too often, mandatory arrest policies have increased state control over marginalized abuse survivors and disregarded the many survivors who want the abuse to cease, but do not desire a permanent separation from or criminal justice involvement for their partners. Economic empowerment and housing availability are proven pathways out of domestic violence and are responsive to survivors' needs in comparison to unwanted criminal justice involvement, which has received a disproportionate bulk of funding.

And we create new opportunities to further feminism and foster change. On January 21, 2017, President Trump's first day in office, the "Women's March," the largest single-day protest in U.S. history, occurred at over 400 sites across the nation to send a bold message to the new administration that women's rights are human rights. Worldwide, participation was estimated at five million.

Later in 2017, further uprising occurred through social media with the #MeToo campaign echoing many threads of the 1960s and 70s consciousness-raising circles. The hashtag #MeToo was first started a decade prior by African American activist Tarana Burke as a grass-roots movement to aid sexual assault survivors in underserved communities. Based out of Harlem, she identified the lack of resources and services in her community, and she began a movement of African American women talking to each other and sharing their stories. On October 15, 2017, actor Alyssa Milano popularized this movement with her tweet:

> Me too.
> If all the women who have been sexually harassed or assaulted wrote "Me too" as a status, we might give people a sense of the magnitude of the problem.
> Please copy/paste.

Within the first 24 hours of this posting, there were more than twelve million "me too" Facebook posts, comments, and reactions from 4.7 million people, and nearly half of Facebook users in the United States were friends with someone who had posted "me too." Real solidarity comes from hearing the voices and stories of friends, co-workers, and loved ones that can't be denied; sharing in what we have endured and overcome; and rethinking our societal norms.

We continue to see the expansive reach of the #MeToo campaign online and offline. As the #MeToo movement draws on longstanding feminist movement practices and seeks to create sustained social change, it also displays some of the same privileging, silencing, and infighting. The movement and news reporting initially focused on Hollywood, politicians, and those in the public eye, with multiple complaints against Harvey Weinstein, Matt Lauer, Charlie Rose, Al Franken, Kevin Spacey, Louis CK, Mario Batali, and dozens of other high-profile individuals, leading to their firing or resignation. While less glamorous workplaces and professions were omitted from the early headlines, feminist discussions have since given voice to farmworkers, hotel staff, and other vulnerable individuals in settings with stark power differentials, and news of Dr. Larry Nassar's sexual abuse of gymnasts revealed vast institutional failures. *Time* magazine named "The Silence Breakers" its Person of the Year for 2017, recognizing the actors and artists that launched the #MeToo movement and including fieldworkers, hospital and hotel staff, dishwashers, professors, and journalists among those who created and propelled this movement. Now, the movement must grapple with backlash. The tensions discussed in this book are relevant to the #MeToo movement's challenges and future, including questions of accountability, reckoning, redemption, healing, and forgiveness.

This book aims to encourage critical thinking and generate political discourse and scholarly debate on state interventions in or failures to intervene in family violence, and is relevant to the ongoing work of policymakers, advocates, attorneys, scholars, and individuals who seek to advance gender equality and responses to family violence. Themes that pervade the sections include how government-based funding has prioritized criminalization and criminal justice responses; how dominant narratives about victims privilege certain individuals and make it more difficult for others to gain access to meaningful interventions; and how gendered, hetero-normative, hierarchical state responses to family violence have hindered the development of more survivor-centered, community-based solutions and often have the effect of replacing the abuser's control with state control.

In "The Politics of Safety and Justice," we begin with a critical historical perspective on domestic violence responses. Mimi Kim addresses tensions in the field between criminalization and anti-criminalization advocates, and significantly places this debate within the larger anti-incarceration movement. She describes how the anti-carceral turn that is now redefining the mainstream movement is the result of two decades of resistance and counter-hegemonic movement-building led primarily by women, gender-nonconforming, and trans people of color. Deborah Weissman offers a case study that explores a situation in which domestic violence advocates were positioned in opposition to other progressive concerns, including immigration, labor, and environmental justice. Particularly in today's political environment, with progressives sometimes divided against each other and anti-domestic violence advocacy often isolated from other progressive causes, Weissman's work provokes a critical and pressing discussion. Elizabeth MacDowell reflects on the early battered women's movement's multidimensional empowerment ideals, which are often absent from current self-help approaches, and discusses the need to increase access to justice and promote options and empowerment as the movement further develops.

Central to this project, we grapple with issues of intersectionality, both in terms of the multiple areas of intersectionality and oppression experienced by survivors and the operation of intersecting child welfare and civil and criminal justice systems. The section "Multiple Systems, Standards, and Dilemmas" looks across the separate legal systems pertaining to youth and adults as well as the parties' legal statuses to expand existing legal constructs, and imagines new frameworks.

Alisa Bierria and Colby Lenz, building from the discussion in Part I of the carceral move in domestic violence response, reflect on the criminalization of abuse survivors. They specifically critique "failure to protect" laws and name the spatial continuity of violence these prosecutions create, and propose alternative theorization and defense strategies. Cynthia Godsoe's chapter argues that the underlying mens rea of the parental discipline privilege exception to assault both perpetuates family violence and warps the criminal law's standard approach to punishment, which ordinarily matches culpability with control, and she advocates for the privilege's abolition. Pairing these chapters provokes questions about the role of the state and appropriateness of governmental intervention. Amy Magnus considers youth and families involved in multiple court systems, and critically assesses alternative and specialized justice initiatives, their historical roots, and the potential collateral consequences of specializing justice for crossover youth and families, particularly in light of the punitive and adversarial models from which they derive.

The section "Intersectional Needs for Safety and Justice" explores several particular survivor populations and furthers the examination of policy responses. Donna Coker discusses using restorative justice models to respond to campus sexual assault. Regarding evidence-based proposals, she considers the politics of advocacy against victim-blaming, which has resulted in some advocates' opposition to reducing access to alcohol on campus as a means of reducing sexual assault on campus. A less crime- or blame-focused treatment of violence against women might instead allow a more proactive or preventive approach (i.e., alcohol reduction). Natalie Nanasi focuses on the double-edged U visa program for immigrant victims, which is contingent upon compulsory and continuing cooperation with law enforcement. Such requirements present particular difficulty to immigrant survivors, who are uniquely often unable, fearful, or disinclined to engage with the state. These chapters shed light on systemic and implicit values driving the different policies and question the necessity or efficacy of the values and policies.

The section "Militarization, Firearms, and the Family" considers barriers to intervening in police-perpetrated family violence and the highly politicized nature of addressing firearms and the family. Leigh Goodmark's work on police perpetrators of intimate partner violence raises profound questions about reliance on a criminal legal system that contains a disproportionate number of batterers. I discuss the overt politics surrounding gun control and family abuse, along with the gendered nature of domestic violence, firearm possession, and gun safety advocacy, while also urging policy reforms to protect abuse survivors from gun violence. Mary Fan's chapter discusses the correlation between mass shooters and perpetrators of domestic violence. By linking family violence to public ("random") violence, she strengthens the call for taking family violence as seriously as we take community violence.

In the final section, "Moving Forward with a Critical Lens," Jamie Abrams explores how the traditional focus on internalities is too narrow, frees the state from responsibility for preventing violence, and fails to identify external systemic contributors to risk. Courtney Cross invites a public health-type "harm reduction" approach to judicial consideration of victims' choices. Carrie Bettinger-Lopez utilizes a human rights framework to recommend the development of a National Plan of Action regarding violence against women and gender-based violence. These authors also consider the political resistance to implementing reforms, whether from legislative, criminal- and civil-justice systems, or movement-based perspectives.

The authors include a vibrant range of thought- and movement-leaders and emerging powerful voices from across the nation. They have experience working on behalf of abuse survivors, seeing the law in action, and participating in reform efforts, all while conducting research and writing scholarship, which makes them uniquely qualified to critically explore the politics and future of domestic violence responses.

What is the future of feminism and the movements against gender-based violence, family violence, and domestic violence? The theme, the politicization of safety, invites us to question assumptions about how society and the legal system do and should respond to intimate partner violence, and to challenge the domestic violence field to move beyond old paradigms and contend with larger justice issues. We certainly need nuanced responses that are sensitive to the needs and desires of various communities and individuals. We need to avoid government interventions that are too aggressive and that cause more harm than good. We also need to avoid a failure of moral imagination that accepts family violence and gender subordination as inevitable. I hope we will be both idealistic and pragmatic as we imagine what these movements are and what they can do.

NOTES

1 Mark Landler, *Transition Team's Questions on Gender Equality Raises Concerns at State Dept.*, N.Y. TIMES (Dec. 23, 2016), at A18.

PART I

The Politics of Safety and Justice

1

The Coupling and Decoupling of Safety and Crime Control

An Anti-Violence Movement Timeline

MIMI E. KIM

Introduction

Over the past four decades, the U.S. feminist anti-violence movement addressing domestic violence, sexual assault, and, more recently, stalking and sex trafficking has developed a strong crime control approach. In response, the term "carceral feminism" was coined to describe the close collaboration between feminist social movements and the carceral arm of the state.[1] Critical feminist and legal scholarship now solidly locates the anti-violence movement at the forefront of liberal contributions to the construction of the conditions of "mass incarceration."[2]

By the passage of the Violence Against Women Act (VAWA) as part of the Violent Crime Control and Law Enforcement Act (Crime Bill) of 1994, feminist social movement leaders who helped to craft and support this legislation remained remarkably unaware of the troubling implications of tethering social movement success to the passage of what is now recognized as a draconian crime bill.[3] However, rising and widespread public concern over mass incarceration, mounting critique aimed at feminist complicity with pro-criminalization policies, and internal social movement turmoil over the consequences of its investments in crime control have resulted in significant fissures in the anti-violence movement's pro-criminalization stance. What developed into an unquestioned bulwark of the U.S. feminist anti-violence position has weakened under a confluence of forces that can no longer uphold glib acceptance of crime control as the primary response to gender-based violence.

The selected social movement timeline in Figure 1.1 juxtaposes key events, policies, and organizational innovations within the anti-domestic

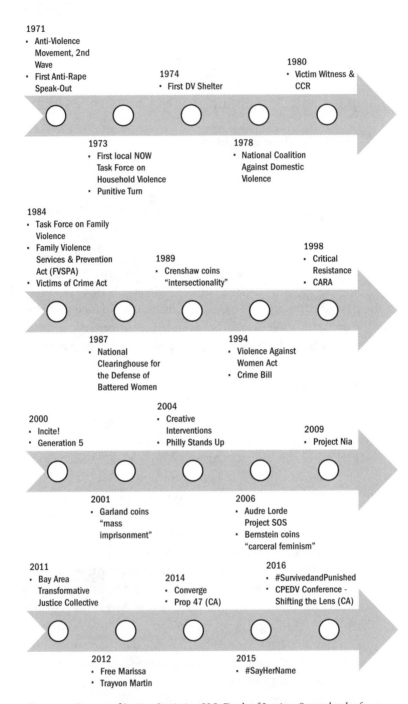

1971
- Anti-Violence Movement, 2nd Wave
- First Anti-Rape Speak-Out

1974
- First DV Shelter

1980
- Victim Witness & CCR

1973
- First local NOW Task Force on Household Violence
- Punitive Turn

1978
- National Coalition Against Domestic Violence

1984
- Task Force on Family Violence
- Family Violence Services & Prevention Act (FVSPA)
- Victims of Crime Act

1989
- Crenshaw coins "intersectionality"

1998
- Critical Resistance
- CARA

1987
- National Clearinghouse for the Defense of Battered Women

1994
- Violence Against Women Act
- Crime Bill

2000
- Incite!
- Generation 5

2004
- Creative Interventions
- Philly Stands Up

2009
- Project Nia

2001
- Garland coins "mass imprisonment"

2006
- Audre Lorde Project SOS
- Bernstein coins "carceral feminism"

2011
- Bay Area Transformative Justice Collective

2014
- Converge
- Prop 47 (CA)

2016
- #SurvivedandPunished
- CPEDV Conference - Shifting the Lens (CA)

2012
- Free Marissa
- Trayvon Martin

2015
- #SayHerName

Figure 1.1. Bureau of Justice Statistics, U.S. Dep't of Justice, *Sourcebook of Criminal Justice Statistics* 500 tbl. 6.28 (Ann L. Pastore and Kathleen Maguire, eds., 2003); E. Ann Carson and William J. Sabol, Bureau of Justice Statistics, *Prisoners in 2011*, at 6 tbl. 6 (2012); E. Ann Carson and Daniela Golinelli, Bureau of Justice Statistics, *Prisoners in 2012–Advance Counts* (2013).

violence movement (top of the timeline) with policy developments more closely associated with the evolving carceral state (bottom of the timeline). The timeline spans the period from the 1970s to the present, beginning with the formation of the anti-rape movement in 1971 and the anti-domestic violence movement in 1973,[4] the latter date coincidentally marking the start of the "punitive turn" and the five-fold rise in U.S. rates of incarceration that would characterize the next four decades.[5] While it is by no means a comprehensive timeline and fails to capture important historical factors that long pre-date the 1970s, the chronology of events reveals insights into the construction and possible dismantling of what we now know as carceral feminism. This chapter traces the evolution of the mainstream feminist anti-violence movement in its relationship to criminalization, the development of an alternative or counter-hegemonic anti-carceral feminist movement, and the intersection between these two movement forces.[6] The narrative that follows refers to events featured on the timeline and expands upon and elucidates some of the contextual factors that contribute to and result from key historical moments.

The Anti-Domestic Violence Movement: Formative Years

Early 1970s: Second Wave Beginnings

The feminist anti-violence movement emerged in the early 1970s, a relative latecomer in a second-wave women's movement that was already in full force in the 1960s.[7] Violence against women emerged as a social problem with the first anti-rape speak-out by a radical feminist group, the Redstockings, in New York City in 1971 and attention to the plight of "household violence" through the formation of a local NOW Task Force on Household Violence in Pennsylvania in 1973.[8] The next year, the first explicitly feminist and organized battered women's shelter began with Women's Advocates in St. Paul after a small group of feminists who had begun a legal crisis line became alarmed by the number of women seeking help for violence suffered at the hands of husbands and boyfriends.[9]

Notably, 1973 also marks the punitive turn in the United States, beginning a dramatic upward rise in rates of incarceration that had remained relatively unchanged for the previous fifty years, from the time when such statistics were first recorded.[10] During the formative years of the anti-domestic violence movement and the carceral build-up, relationships between early shelters and advocacy programs and law enforcement were non-existent, or uneven at best. In the 1970s, law enforcement viewed family violence as a private matter, outside the purview of the law even in the case of physical assault. However, some local programs experienced more sanguine relationships, often based upon personal relationships with a sympathetic police chief or individual law enforcement officer.[11] By the late 1970s, feminist-led litigation against local police departments for "failure to protect" began to pressure policy changes, signaling shifts in police procedure in the case of domestic violence, and to be used to leverage other social movement demands to take violence against women seriously.[12]

Late 1970s: Early Federal Intervention in Domestic Violence

While feminist anti-violence advocates were demanding law enforcement changes on the local level, feminist-identified proponents serving in Congress and populating White House staff positions under the Carter administration began to permeate the federal agenda.[13] The National Coalition Against Domestic Violence (NCADV), the first national organization representing battered women and the anti-domestic violence movement, formed in 1978 by newly identified anti-domestic violence leaders and activists and gathered at a national consultation sponsored by the U.S. Commission on Civil Rights, "Battered Women: A Public Policy."[14]

Around this same time, the Law Enforcement Assistance Administration (LEAA), a former branch of the Department of Justice established under Nixon and continued under Carter, identified the emerging issue of violence against women as one deserving federal attention and resources. With this unprecedented federal attention to violence against women, an issue only gaining feminist attention, some social movement activists warily greeted the advent of Department of Justice funding with the warning that "federal funds have coopted the grassroots, community-based women's groups that initially brought the problem [of violence against women] to the attention of the public."[15] Department of Justice money, in particular, was suspect as the "blood-tinged" nature of law enforcement, and the use of LEAA funding guidelines was seen as a way "to control and subvert battered women's movement to their own interests."[16]

That early caution, published in 1977 in the first collective newsletter of the battered women's movement, the *National Communication Network Newsletter*, reflected the radical racial justice, welfare rights, and anti-war social movement antecedents to the rather late-blooming anti-rape and battered women's movements that emerged in the United States around 1971 and 1973, respectively. However, the opportunity to develop early innovative sexual assault and domestic violence programs under the auspices of a $3 million LEAA initiative that began and ended with the Carter administration proved to be sufficiently compelling, enough so that such warnings were taken as a challenge or were simply dismissed.

Early 1980s: The Emergence of New Carceral Actors and Organizations

Some early feminist leaders sought a more systematic challenge to law enforcement impunity in situations of domestic violence, crafting innovative organizational formations leading to rapidly replicable forms[17] that would go on to significantly change the make-up or constitution of the anti-violence "social movement field." The shift from a social movement almost devoid of law enforcement to one featuring close collaborations between feminist social movement institutions and the criminal justice system rapidly followed the establishment of new organizational forms initiated through social movement demands. The domestic violence-related Victim Witness program, begun in San Francisco in 1980, and the Community Coordinated Response, first developed in Duluth, Minnesota, in that same year, were key innovations crafted by feminist leaders that established formal collaborative relationships with law enforcement.

As a result of formal collaborative organizational forms and their replication, boundaries between social movement actors and institutions within civil society became blurred with those of law enforcement, thereby increasing vulnerability of the feminist social movement to the agenda and institutions of law enforcement. The rapid replication of these hybridized institutional spaces led to the increased occupation of the formerly autonomous feminist social movement with a new set of criminal justice actors and institutions, thereby contributing to the construction of a carceral feminist social movement.[18]

These collaborative initiatives with law enforcement also set into motion some of the enhanced crime control policies that contributed to the sweep of mandatory arrest laws that strengthened the coupling of social concerns about domestic violence with the strong arm of policing. In 1981, the Duluth Project proposed and initiated a mandatory arrest policy that caught the attention of feminist social movement actors, law enforcement officials, legislators, and a newly interested public.[19] In 1984, the Minneapolis Experiment on Mandatory Arrest, carried out by the Minneapolis Police and criminological researchers, conducted a larger-scale experiment on the impact of mandatory arrest on domestic violence outcomes.[20] Despite what would be revealed as inconclusive outcomes regarding the effectiveness and impact of mandatory arrest policies in further studies, the result of the Duluth Model and this first experiment catapulted a sweep of mandatory arrest laws through localities and states across the nation.[21]

Mid-1980s: The Reagan Crime Control Agenda and the Rise of Victim Rights

The Reagan era of the 1980s introduced an invigorated conservative ideology and policy agenda that accelerated the rhetoric of crime control and the reliance upon law enforcement as a foundation of a revised social contract and organization of governance. The first federal domestic violence bill, expected to be passed under the Carter regime but not successfully passed until 1984, the Family Violence Prevention Services Act (FVPSA), was housed under the Department of Health and Human Services.[22] Despite feminist social movement lobbying under the National Coalition Against Domestic Violence (NCADV) to prevent any sections of the bill from diverting funds to law enforcement, the final version of the bill introduced such a component tied to law enforcement funding.[23]

Three days before the rather quiet 1984 passage of FVPSA came the more heralded Victims of Crime Act (VOCA), symbolically elevating victims as new rights-bearing citizens. This bill fortified a structure for providing resources to victims, such as compensation for injuries or loss of wages, that was directly financed by those convicted of federal crimes. The passage of VOCA was preceded by the publication of a Reagan administration report that provided important reframing of crime, even if symbolically, as a federal priority and, hence, national issue. The 1982 final report of the Task Force on Violent Crime highlighted the impact of crime on the lives of everyday innocent U.S. citizens while outlining federal commitment to crime control within the constraints of states' rights with regard to criminal legislation. In contrast to the previous disregard for victims of crime beyond their role as witnesses, crime control proponents began to recognize that advocacy for victim rights complemented demands for harsher punitive measures and the diminishment of defendant rights.[24]

Indeed, the conservative turn in the 1980s set the conditions for a rising victim's rights movement, one that relied heavily upon the energies and advocacy of anti-rape and anti-domestic violence groups. The relationship between mainstream victim's rights advocates, represented by such interest groups as Mothers Against Drunk Driving (MADD) and feminist anti-violence movement leaders, however, was not without antagonisms. Conflicting political values, agendas, stakeholders, and strategies often made these forces appear to be competitors rather than collaborators.[25]

Incensed by the failure of the 1982 Task Force on Violent Crime report to include victims of domestic violence within their scope of innocent victims (rape victims had been included), anti-domestic violence social movement actors demanded attention to victims of domestic violence. The result was a report by the Attorney General's Task Force on Family Violence, established due to the pressure of feminist anti-domestic violence leaders, and published just a month before the passage of FVPSA in September 1984. Deemed a coup by social movement actors, the report also articulated movement demands for family violence to be named a crime, the elevation of victim rights, and a call for coordination with law enforcement.[26]

The Consolidation of a Pro-Criminalization Response

Late 1980s: Feminists Demand Inclusion in Victim's Rights Agenda

Under the Reagan administration, the federal crime control agenda effectively incorporated the feminist anti-domestic violence movement, flexibly replying to demands for inclusion in the roster of innocent victims to be protected by the state against the "epidemic" of violence and what were described as the excesses of previous defendant rights advocacy. While efforts were made by NCADV and other local feminist programs to center feminist advocacy, prioritize shelters as the primary domestic violence institution, and minimize resources to law enforcement, they were engaging with a federal government alert to the benefits of an invigorated victim rights agenda. Feminist protests resulted in the Task Force Against Family Violence sponsored by the office of Attorney General Edwin Meese, a victory with double-edged consequences.[27]

Unique among mainstream feminist efforts was the establishment of the National Clearinghouse for the Defense of Battered Women (NCDBW) in 1987 by Barbara Hart and Sue Osthoff. It advocated on behalf of arrested and incarcerated women who were criminalized for self-defense against gender-based violence. Solid within the set of national domestic violence institutions that will retain governmental funding at least until the time of this publication, NCDBW challenges the facile binary of perpetrator-victim that otherwise characterizes the mainstream anti-domestic violence movement and keeps both victim rights and defendant rights within the scope of anti-domestic violence concerns.

1990s: VAWA 1994 and the Concretization of Carceral Feminism

Ten years after the passage of FVPSA and the publication of the final report of the Task Force on Family Violence, the second federal bill addressing domestic violence, the VAWA of 1994, became law under the Clinton administration. Unlike FVPSA, which was passed under the Child Abuse Amendments of 1984 and was housed under what is now the Department of Health and Human Services, VAWA fell solidly within the Crime Bill of 1994 and concretized the feminist anti-violence movement under the arena of crime control. The Office on Domestic

Violence, briefly housed within the Department of Health, Education and Welfare under Carter but dissolved at the advent of the Reagan era,[28] was revived through the passage of VAWA under a more muscular and well-resourced Office on Violence Against Women (OVW), housed within the Department of Justice.

Countering with an Anti-Carceral Response: The Rise of a Feminist of Color Analysis

1990s: The Articulation of an Anti-Carceral Movement

By the passage of VAWA in 1994, early words of warning all but vanished under the growing acceptance of crime control as the primary strategy of the anti-domestic violence movement, buttressed by expanding criminal justice resources. Legal scholar Kimberlé Crenshaw, though not explicitly critiquing the pro-criminalization stance of anti-violence feminists in her 1989 piece nor in her landmark article of 1991 that coined the term "intersectionality," firmly established the gender, race, class, and immigration-status analysis that would challenge mainstream understandings of gender-based violence and its remedies.

The accolades accompanying the passage of VAWA as part of the Crime Bill muffled any significant dissent from within the anti-violence movement throughout much of the 1990s.[29] However, the concept of intersectionality and the contributions of critical race theory provided a robust analytical framework to de-center the privileged gender essentialist analysis undergirding the mainstream feminist anti-violence movement. The devastating consequences of mass incarceration on communities of color continued to fuel a strengthening feminist of color critique of the anti-violence movement that would emerge more forcefully in the following decade.

On the other hand, with mounting numbers of people of color swept into the criminal justice system, opposition to the carceral build-up and the disproportionate targeting of communities of color gathered strength. It was in 1991 that critical criminologist David Garland coined the term "mass imprisonment" in a book of the same name, as a precursor to what would become a more commonly used term, "mass incarceration."[30] In 1997, Angela Davis coined the term "prison industrial complex," calling attention to the prison build-up as a product of vast intersecting systems of the market and the state.[31] In 1998, Davis and other prison abolitionist activists, led by people currently and formerly incarcerated, held the first Critical Resistance conference in Berkeley, California. Critical Resistance articulated a prison abolitionist politic while providing a national structure to support and connect local organizing around a prison abolitionist agenda.

The New Millennium: Consolidation of Counter-Hegemonic Forces

By the turn of the new millennium, a small but growing force within and at the peripheries of the feminist anti-violence movement, primarily consisting of women of color and lesbian-gay-bisexual-transgender-queer-intersex (LGBTQI) people of color, began to consolidate a counter-hegemonic movement addressing the intersection of gender-based violence and violence perpetrated by the state. In 2000, INCITE! Women of Color Against Violence, now known as INCITE! Women, Gender Non-Conforming and Trans People of Color Against Violence, established as a new social movement organization centering a radical feminist of color analysis.[32]

Critical Resistance and INCITE! formed the foundation of a new cross-sectoral set of social forces. Their joint Critical Resistance-INCITE! statement, written in 2001, articulated both the alignments and tensions between a feminist anti-violence movement that had historically challenged gender-based violence while ignoring its contribution to mass incarceration and a prison abolitionist movement that often paid little attention to violence against women and girls and to the significant and growing numbers of women in jails and prisons.[33]

The establishment of Critical Resistance in 1998, INCITE! in 2000, and generationFIVE, a multi-racial organization committed to liberatory, anti-criminalization strategies to address child sexual abuse founded in 2000, provided a political framework decoupling safety from interpersonal violence and crime control. A diverse set of individuals and organizations—particularly located within the intersection of communities of color, LGBTQI, and immigrant communities—resonated with this anti-carceral turn. While most of the mainstream anti-violence movement would remain unaware of or unconvinced by the critique or its proposed alternative for the next decade or more, the counter-hegemonic movement continued to gain momentum.

2000s: Alternative Local Grassroots Strategies within an Emerging National Network

As this anti-violence/anti-carceral framework began to disseminate widely, a number of local organizations and collaborative initiatives attempted to put this new set of politics into practice. Variably referred to as community-based responses to violence, community accountability, Transformative Justice, alternatives to criminalization, and explicitly prison abolitionist[34] practices, spontaneous and more intentional efforts emerged throughout the first decade of the new millennium. Communities Against Rape and Abuse (CARA) in Seattle, established in 1999, was among the first of such organizations to articulate a new political vision and set of strategies rooted in an understanding of state violence as a primary form of violence endangering communities of color. CARA adopted a community organizing approach as an alternative to the direct service model and began to address specific situations of gender-based violence within communities of color guided by an evolving set of principles aligned with community accountability and prison abolition.[35]

Activists across the city of Chicago were among those in the forefront of collaborative efforts to bring prison abolitionist politics to the issue of violence against girls and women, youth organizing, and campus organizing. Young Women's Empowerment Project, which started in 2002, mobilized young people of color engaged in the sex trade and survival economies, employing strategies of radical self-determination and prison abolition among the city's most vulnerable populations. Females United for Action, founded in 2005, was a leadership development organization taking a multi-issue approach to addressing the pervasiveness of violence in the lives of young women. A strong network of Chicago organizations developed to pursue anti-violence strategies that also challenged policing and other forms of state interference.

Creative Interventions in Oakland,[36] based in communities of color including immigrant and LGBTQI communities, and Philly Stands Up,[37] situated in the punk-anarchist community in Philadelphia, both established in 2004, responded directly to domestic and sexual violence by supporting community-based interventions to violence. Inspired by INCITE! and working in solidarity with other grassroots efforts across the country, Creative Interventions explored practices that brought social networks together to create and carry out interventions to violence. Philly Stands Up supported people in taking responsibility for harming others and in transforming attitudes and behaviors through a process of accountability.

Offering alternative conceptions of accountability that build upon values of care, compassion, and community self-determination, these projects put into practice approaches to accountability that challenge the carceral status quo. For example, Philly Stands Up offered weekly meetings with people who caused harm, supporting them for periods of up to two years. Their approach moved away from initial punitive or shaming tendencies toward a supportive long-term journey emphasizing empathy, responsibility, restitution, and transformation.[38]

Throughout the United States, other organizations similarly began community-based practices that responded to individual acts of harm and to community-level needs for new political vision and innovative options. Like CARA in Seattle, Durham's Ubuntu developed community-based sexual assault organizations within African American communities. Members of Ubuntu, rooted in liberatory practices for healing and violence intervention and prevention, created local community-based responses to violence that were alternative to police intervention.

Sister II Sister, a Black/Latinx organization in Brooklyn, the Harm Free Zone in New York City, and Support New York sought local strategies to replace police responses to gender-based violence and other forms of violence with autonomous community-based interventions. The Audre Lorde Project began a local Brooklyn project that provided community-based strategies for safety for LBGTQI community members called Safe Outside the System (SOS) in 2006. In Durham, Spirit-House developed a rich Harm Free Zone initiative and set of practices to challenge the policing of primarily African American communities and build community-based self-determination to defend against state violence and community-level harms. Other local efforts in Atlanta, Seattle, and Denver emerged to ground Transformative Justice as an alternative vision of violence intervention and prevention.

Mostly operating outside of or at the peripheries of the conventional anti-violence field, these organizations exerted a collective critique of what became known as carceral feminism while building local strategies that formed a more cohesive national movement promoting community accountability and Transformative Justice. INCITE!'s national conferences held in 2000 in Santa Cruz, 2002 in Chicago, 2005 in New Orleans, and again in Chicago in 2015 provided a national platform to share local strategies and strengthen this alternative set of politics and practices. GenerationFIVE also held intensive training sessions and study groups across the United States that articulated Transformative Justice as a response to child sexual abuse.

Late 2000s: Community Accountability and Transformative Justice 2.0

Towards the end of the 2000s and entering into the following decade, a new set of organizations emerged, including Bay Area Transformative Justice Collective (BATJC), created in 2009 out of the activities of generationFIVE. BATJC started an autonomous non-501(c)3 project to develop a Bay Area Transformative Justice network, a deep trust-building infrastructure with the capacity to hold alternative community-based intervention and prevention approaches to child sexual abuse. In 2009, Project Nia launched in Chicago as a project to explicitly bring what they call "participatory community justice," referring to Transformative Justice practices, to shift from the criminal justice system to community-driven forms of justice, particularly in relationship to youth. Both organizations are creating and documenting political analysis, study curricula, and guides to practice based upon their experiences advancing Transformative Justice work.

2010s: The New Rise of Self-Defense Campaigns

The 2012 Florida death of an African America youth, Trayvon Martin, at the hands of George Zimmerman brought national attention to the violent loss of African American lives perpetrated in the name of public safety. It was the criminal justice framing of this act as a justifiable act of self-defense rather than one of wanton homicide that sparked national outrage against injustice embedded within the U.S. system of crime control. In the same city that same year, Marissa Alexander, a young African American woman, just days after the birth of her child, fired a single warning shot in the ceiling to ward off the violence of her abusive husband. Rather than garnering protection from the state for the abuse she suffered, she faced a prison sentence of twenty years.

In 2012, the case of Trayvon Martin sparked the Black Lives Matter movement. In 2015, the recognition of the impact of police targeting of African American girls and women, resulting in lives lost in the wake of law enforcement violence, launched #SayHerName. The imprisonment of Marissa Alexander inspired a companion movement to protect African American lives and the lives of other women, transgender, and gender-nonconforming people of color from criminalization. The campaign to "Free Marissa" mobilized thousands of people across the United States and internationally to advocate for the freedom of Marissa Alexander, but also to recognize the intersection of gender-based violence and racially targeted violence enacted by the criminal justice system.[39]

The incarceration and immigration detention of Nan-Hui Jo, a Korean woman incarcerated for fleeing the country in protection of herself and her daughter, initiated another campaign. "Stand with Nan-Hui" highlighted the criminalization of women of color who use self-defense strategies to protect themselves from gender-based violence. The confluence of the Free Marissa and Stand with Nan-Hui campaigns, and the cross-campaign solidarity forged between those advocating for and with Marissa Alexander, Nan-Hui Jo, and scores of other survivors facing incarceration, launched another organizing initiative called #SurvivedAndPunished in 2016.

In the tradition of self-defense campaigns in support of Joan Little, Inez García, and Yvonne Wanrow in the 1970s,[40] these new initiatives, led primarily by women and gender-nonconforming people of color, advocate for the right to self-defense in the face of gender-based and state violence. In solidarity with many proponents of community accountability and Transformative Justice, those formulating self-defense strategies have expanded the political analysis of a growing counterhegemonic movement. They supported a set of survivors identified three decades earlier by the National Clearinghouse for the Defense of Battered Women and created a reinvigorated organizing strategy prioritizing public self-defense campaigns.

The Mainstream Anti-Violence Movement and the Incorporation of an Anti-Carceral Critique

INCITE! and the Influence of Feminism of Color

Although much of the counter-hegemonic activity has been taking place in social justice spaces outside of the mainstream anti-violence movement, a handful of individuals and organizations associated with these alternatives have been located, at least peripherally, within the more conventional or mainstream anti-violence movement. The dogged persistence and slowly growing prominence of alternative forces coupled with rising internal demands for change served to open and widen fissures within the monolith of individualized direct service and law enforcement responses to violence.

INCITE! was largely founded by women of color who had been longtime veterans of the anti-violence movement but who had also long advocated for a turn away from law enforcement and towards community-based strategies relevant to communities of color, immigrant groups, and LGBTQI communities. Ten years following the introduction of the concept of intersectionality by Crenshaw,[41] Beth Richie,[42] co-founder of INCITE! and longtime veteran of the anti-violence movement, built upon this intersectional analysis to indict the feminist embrace of the criminal justice system. Richie traces how the color-blind *every woman* slogan and ideological category adopted in the 1970s and 1980s by the mainstream anti-violence movement hid the painfully distinct realities for many poor women, girls, and transgender people of color, particularly those within the African American community. While the pursuit of law enforcement protection may have benefited white, middle-class women, it systematically exposed women and transgender survivors of color to heightened surveillance, abuse, and incarceration by the state. This critique by Richie, a movement insider, has had particular influence on the anti-violence movement of which she has been an integral leader.

Others challenged the mainstream anti-violence movement by exploring alternative violence prevention and intervention practices within spaces that invited more conventional anti-violence organizations to co-create radical practice. For example, Creative Interventions, an affiliate organization of INCITE!, founded in Oakland in 2004, established a collaborative project among primarily immigrant anti-violence organizations that were attracted to the tenets and possibilities of community-based responses to violence but felt organizationally tethered to a more conventional approach to violence intervention. The rather unique combination of prison abolitionist and conventional anti-violence advocates within the personnel of Creative Interventions built bridges between generally disconnected social movements with the intention of advancing alternative practices and shifting the mainstream movement.[43]

Mainstream Conferences and the Anti-Carceral Shift

By 2008, the National Coalition Against Domestic Violence invited members of INCITE! to speak at its twentieth anniversary national gathering to revisit a rhetoric that was at one time highly distrustful of law enforcement but that had for at least a decade succumbed to a largely unquestioned adherence to the movement's ties to crime control. Slowly, individual anti-violence organizations, regional meetings, and the occasional state coalition began to introduce the possibility of alternative options and challenges to feminist anti-violence dogma that fueled carceral feminism.

In 2014, activists and engaged scholars from across the U.S. gathered in a national conference sponsored by the Miami School of Law, Converge: Reimagining the Movement to End Gender Violence, which featured proponents of racial justice, restorative justice, and Transformative Justice[44] approaches to addressing and ending gender-based violence.[45] Also in 2014, the funder Blue Shield Against Violence of California gathered its grantees in its annual statewide meeting that featured a keynote conversation with Angela Davis, celebrated radical prison abolitionist activist; Aqeela Sherills, known for his role in negotiating the Crips-Blood truce in Los Angeles; and myself as the founder of Creative Interventions. Two years later, in 2016, the California Partnership to End Domestic Violence featured proponents of restorative justice and Transformative Justice in its statewide conference entitled Shifting the Lens: Transforming Our Approach to Domestic Violence.

Later in 2016, a number of advocates involved in alternative restorative justice and Transformative Justice approaches to domestic violence and sexual assault gathered in an Office of Violence Against Women–sponsored meeting to share strategies and discuss implications for future directions. The Office of Violence Against Women had, since its establishment in 1994, strictly prohibited such violence intervention approaches as antithetical to the form of feminism aligned with a shared mainstream anti-violence movement and Department of Justice agenda. The national gathering represented new federal trends resulting from pressures from influential women of color leaders in the anti-violence movement and the recognition by the Obama administration that conditions leading to mass incarceration needed to shift.

Current Pivots in the Mainstream Anti-Violence Movement

In the days directly following the 2016 California Partnership to End Domestic Violence conference, a national initiative brought together directors and staff of state domestic violence coalitions to discuss what it would take to pivot the mainstream anti-violence movement towards approaches that centered racial justice, turned away from the pro-criminalization trajectory, and moved towards alternative community-based violence intervention and prevention strategies. The gathering was led by Nan Stoops, a veteran activist in the anti-violence movement, longtime executive director of the Washington State Coalition to End Domestic Violence, and leader within the National Network to End Domestic Violence, a national organization representing statewide domestic violence coalitions.

This newly configured collaborative of statewide coalitions collectively committed to this ambitious political agenda. Interested in deepening their knowledge of the counter-hegemonic work developed since 2000, numerous state coalition staff participated in a bilingual English-Spanish language Transformative Justice study group. This work continues in a number of initiatives targeting the mainstream anti-violence movement, sponsored by Move to End Violence.

The Office of Violence Against Women, housed within the Department of Justice, has continued questioning the pro-carceral trajectory concretized with VAWA 1994 by sponsoring research and practice that pushes the edges of its pro-criminalization mandate. Two new initiatives funded in October 2016 by the Office of Violence Against Women explore alternative avenues for the mainstream anti-domestic violence movement and, for the first time, look towards restorative justice, at least as a strategy within the criminal justice system, as a possible diversionary response in cases of domestic violence.

Conclusion

In 1973, the punitive turn leading to a 500% increase in rates of incarceration and the formation of the contemporary feminist anti-violence movement began.[46] From that time, feminists in the formative anti-violence movement increasingly coupled safety with law enforcement. Whether as a genuine effort to bring safety to women and girls experiencing the devastation of gender-based violence, as a strategy to legitimize and garner resources for a social movement, or as a nod to this nation's investment in crime control (and immigration control), the movement has been deeply implicated in its collaboration with the carceral state.

As a response to the limitations of the mainstream feminist anti-violence movement and the build-up of the carceral state, counter-hegemonic forces—consolidated at the time of the new millennium and led primarily by feminists of color—have remained steadfast. Individuals and organizations, largely outside of the conventional anti-violence movement, have created a new world of opportunities through the formation of alternative community structures, informal networks, creative systems of communication, and open-source forms of documentation and dissemination. While these developments have taken place in a largely parallel political and practice space outside of or at the outer edges of the mainstream anti-violence movement, the moment for more productive integration and collaboration has arrived.

In recent years, the counter-hegemonic rhetoric has moved beyond occasional spotlights in mainstream anti-violence conferences, meetings, and workshops towards a more serious attempt to integrate these new visions and practices within the mainstream movement. Many mainstream anti-violence leaders have demonstrated increasingly solid commitments to the very difficult work that lies ahead. Echoing and building upon the political priorities articulated by counter-hegemonic forces, a number of anti-carceral tenets are now being considered by a growing number of mainstream feminist anti-violence individuals and organizations. Recent trends reveal the possibility of a significant shift towards the tenets of intersectional analysis that centers not only gender, but also race, class, sexuality, disability, immigration status, and religion; decriminalizing or decarceration policies; community-based alternatives to criminalization; the freeing of criminalized survivors of violence; and cross-sectoral collaboration that invites non-traditional allies.

Will these opening conversations result in significantly different policy positions, meaningful collaborations with new anti-carceral stakeholders, and innovative practices that break the dominance of the prevailing individualized direct service delivery model? Will the anti-violence movement be able to meaningfully decouple safety and law enforcement? The future trajectory remains unknown.

The profound political shift following the January 2017 presidential inauguration sharply highlights the relevance of these alternative strategies while also presenting uncertainty regarding future conditions and even the existence of the very organizations that now constitute the feminist anti-violence movement. The feminist fortitude driving the #MeToo/#TimesUp movement indicates equally game-changing conditions in the social and political landscape. At this moment, one thing is certain. The need for principled and coordinated strategies in order to create a more liberatory future, free of gender-based violence and state-based violence, has never been more clear.

NOTES

1 Elizabeth Bernstein, *The Sexual Politics of the "New Abolitionism,"* 18 DIFFERENCES: J. FEMINIST CULTURAL STUD. 128 (2007); Elizabeth Bernstein, *Militarized Humanitarianism Meets Carceral Feminism: The Politics of Sex, Rights, and Freedom in Contemporary Antitrafficking Campaigns,* 36 SIGNS 45 (2010).

2 Bernstein 2007, *supra* note 1; Bernstein 2010, *supra* note 1; KRISTIN BUMILLER, IN AN ABUSIVE STATE: HOW NEOLIBERALISM APPROPRIATED THE FEMINIST MOVEMENT AGAINST SEXUAL VIOLENCE (2008); Donna Coker & Ahjane Macquoid, *Why Opposing Hyper-Incarceration Should Be Central to the Work of the Anti-Domestic Violence Movement,* 5 U. MIAMI RACE & SOC. JUST. L. REV. 585 (2015); LEIGH GOODMARK, A TROUBLED MARRIAGE: DOMESTIC VIOLENCE AND THE LEGAL SYSTEM (2012); MARIE GOTTSCHALK,

THE PRISON AND THE GALLOWS: THE POLITICS OF MASS INCARCERA-
TION IN AMERICA (2006); Priya Kandaswamy, *"You Trade in a Man for the
Man": Domestic Violence and the U.S. Welfare State*, 6 AM. Q. 253 (2010); Mimi E.
Kim, *Challenging the Pursuit of Criminalization in an Era of Mass Incarceration*,
43 BRIT. J. SOC. WORK 1276 (2012); BETH E. RICHIE, ARRESTED JUSTICE:
BLACK WOMEN, VIOLENCE AND AMERICA'S PRISON NATION (2012); JONA-
THAN SIMON, GOVERNING THROUGH CRIME: HOW THE WAR ON CRIME
TRANSFORMED AMERICAN DEMOCRACY AND CREATED A CULTURE OF
FEAR (2007).

3 MARI J. MATSUDA, WHERE IS YOUR BODY: AND OTHER ESSAYS ON RACE,
GENDER, AND THE LAW (1996).

4 ELIZABETH PLECK, DOMESTIC TYRANNY: THE MAKING OF AMERICAN
SOCIAL POLICY AGAINST FAMILY VIOLENCE FROM COLONIAL TIMES TO
THE PRESENT (2004).

5 THOMAS P. BONZCAR, PREVALENCE OF IMPRISONMENT IN THE U.S.
POPULATION, 1974–2001 (Bureau of Just. Stat. 2001); ANN CARSON, PRISON-
ERS IN 2014, SPECIAL REPORT (Bureau Just. Stat. 2015); BRUCE WESTERN,
PUNISHMENT AND INEQUALITY IN AMERICA (2006).

6 This chapter employs the term "counter-hegemonic" to refer to feminist anti-
violence social movements that are explicitly opposed to the mainstream movement, particularly in relationship to mainstream tendencies towards gender
essentialism, reliance on an individualized social service delivery model, and its
ties to the criminal justice system. The term "counter-hegemonic" also adopts a
Gramscian analysis of subaltern sources of counter-hegemonic activism, although
Gramsci does not explicitly use this term. This is in contrast to "counter movements," which refer to oppositional sources that may derive from dominant
societal forces, for example, the "men's movement" and its organized backlash
responses to feminist gains.

7 It is now clear that domestic violence and sexual assault do not fall only
within heterosexual relationships but are experienced within same-sex
relationships and gender-nonconforming intimate relationships. At the formative years of the movement and even today, the anti-domestic violence movement has been primarily organized through the lens of presumed heterosexual-
ity and an understanding of domestic violence as perpetrated by cis-gendered
men against cis-gendered women in heterosexual relationships. Many of the
early leaders identified as Lesbian-Gay-Bisexual-Transgender-Queer-Intersex
(LGBTQI), but the inclusion of domestic violence as impacting LGBTQI lives
slowly emerged through the evolution of the movement. As the timeline moves
forward, many of those promoting expanded understandings of the phenomenon of domestic violence, as well as counter-hegemonic strategies to address
and end violence, root their politics and strategies through an explicitly non-
binary lens.

8 PLECK, *supra* note 4.

9 MIMI E. KIM, DANCING THE CARCERAL CREEP: THE ANTI-DOMESTIC
   VIOLENCE MOVEMENT AND THE PARADOXICAL PURSUIT OF CRIMINAL-
   IZATION, 1973–1986 (2014); PLECK, *supra* note 4.

10 BONZCAR, *supra* note 5; MARGERET WERNER CAHALAN, HISTORICAL COR-
   RECTIONS STATISTICS IN THE UNITED STATES, 1850–1984 (Off. of Just.
   Programs 1986); E. ANN CARSON, PRISONERS IN 2014, SPECIAL REPORT
   (Bureau Just. Stat. 2015); WESTERN, *supra* note 5.

11 KIM, *supra* note 9.

12 Pauline Gee, *Ensuring Police Protection for Battered Women: The* Scott v. Hart *Suit*,
   9 SIGNS 554 (1983).

13 KIM, *supra* note 9; LEE ANN BANASZAK, THE WOMEN'S MOVEMENT INSIDE
   AND OUTSIDE THE STATE (2010).

14 SUSAN SCHECHTER, WOMEN AND MALE VIOLENCE: THE VISIONS AND
   STRUGGLES OF THE BATTERED WOMEN'S MOVEMENT (1982).

15 Betsy Karl, *LEAA Funds and Battered Women: The Patriarchal Lure*, 1
   NAT'L. COMM. NETWORK ELIMINATION VIOLENCE AGAINST WOMEN 4
   (1977).

16 *Id.*

17 The innovations were led by the litigious actions of the *Scott v. Hart* lawsuit
   initiated by feminist lawyers of color in 1976 against the Oakland Police Department for "failure to protect" battered women, the establishment of the first
   victim-witness program for battered women in San Francisco in 1980, and the
   creation of the Community Coordinated Response starting in Duluth, Minnesota, in 1980, representing another form of coordinated linkage between
   feminist anti-violence advocates and law enforcement.

18 KIM, *supra* note 9.

19 MICHAEL PAYMAR & GRAHAM BARNES, COUNTERING CONFUSION
   ABOUT THE DULUTH MODEL (Battered Women's Just. Proj. 2007).

20 LAWRENCE W. SHERMAN, POLICING DOMESTIC VIOLENCE: EXPERI-
   MENTS AND DILEMMAS (1992).

21 Holly Maguigan, *Wading into Professor Schneider's "Murky Middle Ground" Between Acceptance and Rejection of Criminal Justice Responses to Domestic Violence*,
   11 AM. U. J. GENDER, SOC. POL'Y. & L. 427 (2002).

22 June Zeitlin, *Domestic Violence: Perspectives from Washington, in* WOMEN IN
   WASHINGTON: ADVOCATES FOR PUBLIC POLICY 265–75 (Irene Tinker ed.,
   1983).

23 KIM, *supra* note 9.

24 *Id.*

25 *Id.*

26 *Id.*

27 *Id.*

28 Zeitlin, *supra* note 22.

29 MATSUDA, *supra* note 3.

30 DAVID GARLAND, MASS IMPRISONMENT: SOCIAL CAUSES AND CONSEQUENCES (2001).

31 ANGELA YVONNE DAVIS & DAVID BARSAMIAN, THE PRISON INDUSTRIAL COMPLEX (1999).

32 INCITE!, *Women of Color Against Violence, in* THE INCITE! ANTHOLOGY (2006).

33 Critical Resistance and Incite!, *Critical Resistance–Incite! Statement on Gender Violence and the Prison-Industrial Complex*, 30 SOC. JUST 141 (2003).

34 These terms are often used interchangeably to refer to intervention and prevention strategies addressing interpersonal violence that: 1) are carried out by community members as opposed to professional or governmental personnel; 2) understand that interpersonal forms of violence are rooted in systemic conditions of oppression; 3) do not engage the state, particularly law enforcement, child welfare, and immigration control; and 4) consider the criminal justice system as perpetrating forms of state violence. With all of these approaches, an emphasis is often, though not always, placed on engaging the person doing harm, using community values of compassion and collective response rather than punishment and coercion. Prison abolitionism prioritizes the dismantling of the criminal justice system as an underlying goal, thereby rejecting reform efforts that legitimize or uphold the criminal justice system.

35 Communities Against Rape and Abuse, *Taking Risks: Implementing Grassroots Community Accountability Strategies, in Color of Violence: The Incite! Anthology* 250–66 (INCITE ed., 2006).

36 Mimi E. Kim, *Moving Beyond Critique: Creative Interventions and Reconstructions of Community Accountability*, 37 SOC. JUST. 14 (2011).

37 Esteban Kelly, *Philly Stands Up: Inside the Politics and Poetics of Transformative Justice and Community Accountability in Sexual Assault Situations*, 37 SOC. JUST. 44–57 (2011).

38 *Id.*

39 Alis Bierria et al., *Free Marissa Now and Stand with Nan-Hui: A Conversation about Parallel Struggles*, FEMINIST WIRE (June 30, 2015), www.thefeministwire. com.

40 Emily Thuma, *Lessons in Self-Defense: Gender Violence, Racial Criminalization, and Anticarceral Feminism*, 43 WOMEN'S STUD. Q. 52 (2015).

41 Kimberlé Crenshaw, *Demarginalizing the Intersection of Race and Sex: A Black Feminist Critique of Antidiscrimination Doctrine, Feminist Theory and Antiracist Politics*, 1989 U. CHI. L. FORUM 139 (1989).

42 RICHIE, *supra* note 2.

43 Kim, *supra* note 36.

44 Restorative Justice in the United States is generally carried out as a diversionary alternative to more retributive or punitive responses to crimes, but is still housed within or in collaboration with the criminal justice system. Transformative Justice responses are carried out as a challenge to the criminal justice system as a whole, and are not engaged in relationships with law enforcement.

45 Donna Coker et al., *CONVERGE: Reimagining the Movement to End Gender Violence*, 5 U. MIAMI RACE & SOC. JUST. L. REV. 248 (2015).

46 BONZCAR, *supra* note 5; WESTERN, *supra* note 5.

2

The Politicization of Domestic Violence

DEBORAH M. WEISSMAN

It has been several decades since scholars and a critical segment of the anti-domestic violence movement first registered their disaffection with mainstream anti-domestic violence strategies—a critique that has deepened in recent years.[1] Critics of the paradigmatic criminal justice response to domestic violence have articulated their concerns in scholarship, conferences, campaigns, and programmatic proposals.[2] Much has been written acknowledging intersectional oppressions and their relationship to the failure of the criminal justice system to meet the needs of many victims of domestic violence.[3] Surveys and interest groups have provided both quantitative and qualitative evidence of the need to turn away from criminal justice responses and towards alternative strategies that better protect domestic violence victims. Activists have argued about the need to oppose the political economy of mass incarceration.[4]

The field of domestic violence advocacy is itself in somewhat of a crisis, particularly because of its relationship with the criminal justice system. Criminal justice interventions have not succeeded in reducing rates of domestic violence; moreover, the dominant law-and-order responses have adversely affected particular social groups.[5] Reliance on the criminal justice system has fractured the domestic violence movement even as it marginalized itself from disenfranchised populations.[6] Critical race theorists and many community activists view the penchant of mainstream domestic violence advocates to rely on law enforcement with wariness. Such relationships, they argue, serve to disempower poor communities and communities of color, increase the rate of incarceration, and impair the ability of communities to develop internal means of social control.[7] Shifting strategies and organizing with other social justice groups by broadening its purpose may help align the anti-domestic violence movement with its good intentions.

This chapter seeks to contribute to the growing critical scholarship that challenges the paradigmatic responses to domestic violence through a case study of an incident that occurred between the sheriff of San Francisco and his wife in December 2011 that drew significant public interest and commentary suggesting that the anti-domestic violence movement is out of touch with community needs. Section I describes an incident that occurred between Ross Mirkarimi and his wife Eliana López and the legal proceedings that ensued. Mirkarimi, then sheriff-elect of the City and County of San Francisco, grabbed his wife's arm during an argument, causing a visible bruise. The incident resulted in domestic violence–related criminal proceedings as well as charges of official misconduct brought by the mayor, who sought to remove Sheriff Mirkarimi from office.

Section II examines theories of victimhood, both generally and as they pertain to domestic violence circumstances, and then applies these theories to the experiences of Eliana López, a Venezuelan actor with immigrant status at the time of the incident. López did not seek and indeed opposed criminal justice intervention, disputed the characterization of the incident as an instance of domestic violence, objected to public officials' designation of her as a reluctant or "minimizing" victim in part due to her immigrant status, and contested all efforts by the mayor to depose Mirkarimi as sheriff.[8]

Section III examines the strong community responses in the case, which extended beyond the courts and city hall to reach into neighborhoods, households, and community centers throughout the city. Mirkarimi had been recently elected sheriff largely as a result of a coalition of marginalized communities, immigrant rights advocates, environmental justice organizations, labor groups, and other progressive organizations. The criminal proceedings, as well as the city's eight-month-long Ethics Commission and Board of Supervisors hearings to determine whether to remove the sheriff, provided ample opportunity for recorded public commentary by interested community members.

Criminal justice scholars have noted that the public capably evaluates the mechanisms of the criminal justice system by assessing whether the requirements of "procedural fairness" have been met.[9] Scholars observe that the public's assessment of procedural fairness is distinct from an evaluation of the lawfulness of criminal justice practices—a judgment generally only made by legal observers.[10] Section III, however, demonstrates that the public not only took measure of procedural justice and the perceived legitimacy of punitive interventions against Mirkarimi, but also scrutinized the issues of the case for substantive fairness. In the public commentary offered in the Mirkarimi-López case, members of the community repudiated a criminal justice response based on racism, xenophobia, and other forms of social violence, challenging the efficacy of the criminal justice system as a means to mitigate the problem of domestic violence. As part of their procedural justice critique, members of the community rebuffed the mainstream domestic violence movement for its default to the mantra of "zero tolerance" and for allowing itself to serve a political agenda hostile to marginalized San Francisco communities and social justice groups. Community viewpoints further provided a substantive critique of the "one-size-fits-all" approach used to determine whether an act of domestic violence occurred and pressed for a more nuanced understanding of intimate partner violence dynamics. Moreover, public commentary reflected concerns regarding a lack of proportionality of the punitive responses and a critique of the substance of "victim's rights."

The hearings ultimately concluded in favor of Mirkarimi, who retained his office after the mayor failed to gain the requisite number of votes to oust him.[11] The outcome reflected the influence of community actors who successfully articulated a critique of the paradigmatic punitive responses to domestic violence. Just as important, the public commentary provides incentive for mainstream domestic violence advocates to find common ground with other social justice movements, particularly those most affected by the apparatus of the carceral state.

I. The Proceedings

A. Ivory Madison vs. Eliana López

On December 31, 2011, Ross Mirkarimi and Eliana López, husband and wife, had an argument. Mirkarimi, a well-known San Francisco politician, had been recently elected as sheriff of San Francisco. López is a successful actor whose theater and television performances are best known in her home country of Venezuela. The specifics of what ensued during that argument are uncontested as recounted by both Mirkarimi and López. During the course of a quarrel while driving to a restaurant for lunch, Mirkarimi refused to stop the vehicle at the restaurant, and instead turned around and headed home. On arrival, when López attempted to get out of the van, Mirkarimi grabbed her arm to keep her from exiting, leaving a visible bruise.[12] López explained that her relationship with Mirkarimi had grown tense over the past several months; he had been busy with his electoral campaign and she had made several month-long trips to Venezuela with their son, Theo.[13]

The next day, López visited with her neighbor, Ivory Madison, and spoke to Madison about the events of the day before and sought her counsel. What transpired between López and Madison is very much in dispute and is at the center of all that ensued in this matter. López stated that she sought legal advice about custody concerns from Madison, whom she knew to be an attorney, recounted the prior day's argument, and showed Madison the bruise.[14] López explained that Madison suggested that in a potential custody suit, López would be at a disadvantage because she was an immigrant, a fact López understood to be true from media accounts about custody determinations adverse to immigrant parents.[15] López stated that Madison advised her to record a video to document the bruise on her arm so that López could use it in the eventuality of a custody battle. López claimed it was for this purpose that she agreed to make such a recording to be used only if she feared losing custody of her son. López further stated that Madison advised her what to say on camera.[16] López understood that the video and the conversation she had with Madison were confidential and protected by attorney-client privilege.[17]

Madison offered her own account. She admitted that she was an attorney, but claimed she was not licensed to practice law and never held herself out as such to López. The sequence of events following the making of the video is also in dispute. Madison admitted that López stated that things had improved following the incident and she was in no fear of physical abuse.[18] Madison nonetheless claimed that she had growing concerns about López's well-being.[19]

What is not in dispute is that López declined Madison's suggestion to call the police, but four days after making the video, without permission from López, Madison called the San Francisco police.[20] The police arrived soon after Madison called, learned from her that she had a video recording of López showing the bruise, and confiscated the video. A police officer confirmed that López repeatedly denied any need for law enforcement assistance, expressed that she was doing well, explained that the video was taken out of context, refused to speak further with the police, and asked them to leave.[21]

B. Criminal Charges

Mirkarimi was elected sheriff on November 8, 2011. The incident took place on December 31, 2011, after the election but prior to his assumed office on January 8, 2012. Mirkarimi had previously served on the Board of Supervisors for District 5 in San Francisco, one of the city's largest low-income African American communities with a disproportionate share of the city's low-income public housing stock. On January 13, 2012, based on the call from Madison and the video she had made, the San Francisco District Attorney's Office brought criminal charges against Mirkarimi. No one from the District Attorney's Office had communicated with López prior to filing the charges. Moreover, without any request by López, prosecutors sought and obtained an emergency protective order (EPO) barring Mirkarimi from any and all contact with López or their son.

At the arraignment on January 19, 2012, before Judge Susan Breall, the prosecutor sought to extend the EPO. López appeared to request that the EPO be dissolved and to state that she was not a victim of domestic violence and wanted no further order separating her husband from herself or her child.[22] Prior to hearing any testimony, Breall stated that she was inclined to issue a "stay away order":

> I understand, from what I read in the newspaper, and that is how I get a lot of my information—. . . . [t]hat Miss L. has only been in this country a couple of years. . . . . She hasn't been in this country very long, although maybe my information is wrong about that. . . . She hasn't been in this country very long. She is an immigrant to this country. She came here without the support of a father or a mother or a brother or sister or family member.
>
>   . . . .

I [ ] think she is in a very difficult position. . . . I think it's difficult
when you come here only two years out and not fluent in English, you are
not fluent in the culture and the laws of this community, you are in a difficult position.[23]

Concerned with her privacy, López unsuccessfully requested that the
court proceed by way of affidavit under seal or in an *in camera* hearing.
Pointing out that the court was treating López like a victim whether she
was one or not, her counsel argued that she was being treated differently from how the court would treat other supposed victims by using
her full name in open court, and she was being denied a victim's right
to "fairness and respect for her privacy and dignity" under California's
Marsy's law.[24] Referring to López as the "complaining witness," although
she was not, Judge Breall nonetheless refused to allow López to provide
testimony except in open court.[25]

When finally provided the opportunity to speak for herself, López
stated:

> . . . I am happy to answer any questions you have. [ ] I want to say that
> this picture, that the little poor immigrant, is a little insulting. I feel that.
> And I feel that in a city like San Francisco, highly diversity, is a little racism.
> I feel that way. So I was really angry listening [to] comments because . . .
> like the little poor immigrant. It's too hard. I came here because of the
> support of my family. I want to request, I want to say that I am 36 years
> old. I am being independent since I am 20 years old. I have been liv-
> ing in Mexico for one year working, I was living in London, I have been
> traveling—I was in Tibet for two months. I was in Europe traveling for
> two months. I have been traveling all around Latin America. . . . I can ex-
> plain myself. I can express myself in Spanish. Maybe I don't have a lot of
> vocabulary in English like in Spanish, but I am able to speak and under-
> stand everything is happening here.[26] . . . . And yes, I think the violence
> against me is that I, I don't have my family together . . . I am not afraid of
> my husband at all. I am not in danger.[27] . . . This country is trying to pull
> my family apart. This is the real violence I am living.[28]

The prosecutor declined to examine López at any time before or during the proceedings and acknowledged that López did not want the

stay-away order and was not in fear. Yet she argued that López was a "reluctant or minimizing victim."[29]

Following a pretrial hearing that included testimony from a domestic violence expert who had never spoken with López, on March 12, 2012, Mirkarimi pled guilty to the charge of false imprisonment. He was sentenced to one day in jail, three years of probation, 52 weeks of domestic violence counseling, community service, and a fine. Mirkarimi also issued a public apology. López (who was never consulted about the plea agreement) and Mirkarimi explained that the plea was the only way the family would be reunited and that the pressure of their legally mandated separation, including spiraling legal costs, was more than they could bear.[30]

C. San Francisco Ethics Commission and Board of Supervisors Hearings

Two days after Mirkarimi pled guilty, the mayor of San Francisco suspended Mirkarimi without pay, filed charges pursuant to the city charter, and initiated proceedings to remove Mirkarimi from elective office.[31] According to the mayor, Mirkarimi's conduct and sentence would interfere with his ability to carry out the functions of the sheriff. The charges were heard in public hearings before the city's Ethics Commission over the course of eight months. López had counsel present, but counsel was denied the opportunity to represent her client's interests. At the end of each hearing, interested residents of the city provided public commentary. As detailed in section III in this chapter, nearly all of the comments offered were in favor of reinstating Mirkarimi to the office of the sheriff.

At the conclusion of the hearings, the Ethics Commission, with one dissenting vote, recommended to the Board of Supervisors that it sustain the charges of official misconduct.[32] The matter then went to final decision by the Board of Supervisors; public commentary was overwhelmingly in favor of Mirkarimi and opposed to his ouster. The mayor failed to gain the requisite number of votes, and Mirkarimi was thus reinstated to the office.[33]

In July 2015, López used her theater and performing arts skills to write and perform a one-woman, bilingual play about her ordeal, "What is the Scandal, ¿Cuál es el Escándolo?" As noted in the media, "After being silenced by the people who were never willing to listen to her story, especially people she said she thought were supposed to support and empower her—such as feminists—López was very happy to give this performance."[34] López sent invitations to leaders of the mainstream domestic violence agencies to attend the play. They did not respond and to the best of her knowledge have not attended any performances.[35]

II. Constructing a Victim

A. *Theories of Victimhood*

A theory of victimhood incorporates several factors: the presence of sufficient harm; harm that is occasioned by the culpable wrong-doing of another person or institution; and a lack of culpability on the part of the person who was harmed.[36] The connotation of victimization implies an imperative to act. The victim must be rescued and repaired; the perpetrator must be punished. Just as important as categorizing the harm that constitutes victimization, the process by which victimhood as a social status is constructed is critical to understanding the political power of identity politics.[37]

"Victims," observed Marie Gottschalk, "became a powerful weapon in the arsenal of proponents of the law-and-order agenda."[38] Courts have expressed concern that the very use of the term "victim" may contribute decisively to determining the guilt of the alleged perpetrator.[39] Federal and state statutes provide those with "victim" status a full range of rights as "full participants in the criminal justice system."[40] California's state constitutional provision (Marsy's Rights) enumerates crime victim rights to include fairness, respect for privacy, and the prevention of the disclosure of confidential or privileged information.[41]

The status of victimhood is not without anomalies. Despite efforts to empower victims through rights of participation in criminal justice proceedings, victims are often expected to assume the demeanor of helplessness, to act as if they are without capacity to exercise their rights independently. Their needs are determined by those in mainstream domestic violence agencies who presume to know or share their circumstances. Although a victim's rights are first and foremost enumerated as rights to dignity, privacy, and compassionate and empathetic treatment, the stories of victims have been fashioned into narratives that act to essentialize victims in ways that are often inaccurate, demeaning, and pathologizing. A victim may thus serve for symbolical purposes; her individuality, will, and strength are effaced as she becomes the stand-in for the weak and subordinated, or for a group with which she is deemed to have affinity although she may have none. In this context, a particularized construct of victimhood has emerged: the domestic violence victim.

B. The Domestic Violence Victim

As the domestic violence movement came to rely on the criminal justice paradigm, so too did it require the construction of a model of victimhood, one that presumes victims are white and heterosexual while matters of class hover as an unaddressed concern.[42] A victim is perceived to be in need of protection from an abusive male partner and thereupon "needs" legal intervention to maintain her victimhood status. She is the ideal victim if she "follows through, leaves the batterer, cooperates with prosecuting the case, and does not provoke violence, take drugs or drink, or abuse children."[43] She must be perceived to have made courageous but unsuccessful efforts to resist. The paradigmatic white victim stands in contrast to the battered woman who may be portrayed as a woman of color, culpable and deemed responsible for (or has otherwise encouraged) the abuse she has endured.

Autonomy, agency, and resiliency further complicate the concept of the model victim. The decision to forego legal remedies to avoid the violence that women experience in the legal system is given little weight in determining her worth as a victim. If she chooses to forego criminal intervention, she forfeits her victim "status" and may be disparaged as pathological without the capacity to act in her own behalf. The legal discourse is not only constitutive of a deserving vs. undeserving victim, but serves to deny agency to self-identify as victim or reject such category based on her own assessment of her circumstances and interests.

Criminal justice policies such as mandatory arrest and mandatory prosecution confer on the police and prosecutors the authority to determine victimhood. On the one hand, advocacy policies give deference to victims' claims and courage in coming forth; evaluation of such claims is discouraged and she is to be believed. On the other, women who fashion an alternative narrative and reject the mantle of victim receive little credibility. It is true that a woman may have been so badly abused as to be denied agency by the very trauma of the violence, but there is little by way of nuanced assessment in the criminal justice system. Women who have experienced some form of violence who do not want to proceed with a legal claim may be deemed disempowered or deemed to suffer from "learned helplessness" or another related mental health deficiency.

Some argue that a battered woman may need the dictates of the criminal justice system to protect her from the perpetrator even if the system's prescriptions deny her autonomy.[44] As Leigh Goodmark points out, "The law disadvantages women who, by virtue of their subordinated status as victims of a patriarchal system, are rarely able to exercise the sort of autonomy contemplated by philosophers."[45] But she notes that victims of domestic violence are very often capable of "rely[ing] on their own knowledge of their abusers and their innate abilities to survive."[46] Some may choose to use the legal system as a means to readjust their relationships and renegotiate power and balance. But women who opt for another course of action deemed to be in their best interests are often denied credibility or respect.

The paradigm of domestic violence victimhood may also affect the collective agency of those concerned with criminal justice issues. The designation of an individual as a victim often influences group emotions, constrains compassion for the perpetrator, and serves to deny important truths about the sources of criminal conduct. Proponents of victim rights deride those who engage in an analysis of perpetrator conduct outside of the premise of patriarchy and individual choice; to do otherwise implies a dangerous form of justification. Sympathy for a defendant whose own circumstances and personal histories of violence or deprivations might otherwise warrant a semblance of compassion is inadmissible, if not blasphemous. The victims' rights movement has endeavored to "recast public sympathies," Martha Minow writes, that might otherwise exist for criminal defendants who also suffer victimization, adding that "there can be victims of the victim-protecting process."[47]

C. The Political Construction of a Domestic Violence Victim: Eliana López

Eliana López was proclaimed a victim of domestic violence: by a neighbor, the police, the mayor, various officials in city government, mainstream domestic violence advocates, and the media. She was *their* victim of domestic violence and objectified through their intervention. Her "injury" demanded their response. The prosecutor and the mayor possessed authority to decide whether and how to proceed; she had none. As one Latina community activist wrote, "No one in the entire chain of people who made decisions on Eliana's behalf offered her any help—besides prosecuting her husband."[48]

The construction of López's victimhood reveals the complexities and contradictions of such status. Ignoring her capacity to represent her own interests, the criminal justice system determined that she was a victim. Victimhood was "established" by an expert who had never spoken with her, lacked firsthand knowledge of events, relied on a "one-size-fits-all" profile of the victim and the perpetrator, and invoked theories about domestic violence, many of which have been repudiated.[49] Her victimhood was embellished through racialized assumptions. The court declared that her immigrant status and her lack of English-language proficiency were evidence of her helplessness and excused her inability to recognize her own victimhood. Thus perceived as a vulnerable immigrant, her understanding of her own circumstances was discredited in favor of an institutional response by those who know better.

It is not only criminal justice actors who exploit victimhood. Women are also denied agency by domestic violence advocates. These are the circumstances López experienced. This was no private matter, no family issue, domestic violence advocates exclaimed in public and on billboards.[50] Domestic violence advocates organized a rally at City Hall in defense of her interests and in the interests of all victims of domestic violence, vowing to "do everything they could to keep her safe."[51] The organizer of the rally, the executive director of the Domestic Violence Consortium, introduced members of the domestic violence community who were present. Ironically, she failed to acknowledge the presence of López because neither she nor other members of the domestic violence alliance knew who she was and did not recognize her.[52]

But that seemed not to matter. If López declined assistance, her "victimhood" was no longer important. A new narrative emerged. "The Mirkarimi case is an anomaly," as one domestic violence advocate noted after referring to López as a survivor, "one in which domestic violence advocates are involved not on behalf of the survivor—usually our only priority—but rather as caretakers of system-wide protections on behalf of the entire community's safety."[53] López served as the means by which domestic violence advocates would make their claim to keep the community safe according to its norms and values associated with punitive responses.

The construction of victimhood also cost López her privacy rights. She made the video reluctantly. She repeatedly requested that the video not be disclosed in any legal proceeding or to the public. She did so prior to the time that Madison contacted the police.[54] She renewed her requests during the criminal and Ethics Commission hearings. She maintained this position while she was in Venezuela with her child, and beyond the reach of her husband.[55] She never authorized its release to any person or entity. But her wishes were not honored. Her desire for privacy and dignity in the matter was paramount to all of her other concerns. This violation of her request for privacy constituted the essential means by which she was made a victim.

Over her objections and without having party status in the criminal proceedings, López was declared a victim by the prosecutor and mayor's office. As a so-called "minimizing victim," López obtained none of the state constitutional victims' rights to fairness and respect for privacy, the prevention of the disclosure of confidential or privileged information, and prompt return of property when no longer needed as evidence.[56]

The López case underscores the complexities raised by the public-private dichotomy and the important goals of the feminist project that challenged the sanctity of the private as a means to condemn domestic violence. But the legal recognition of privacy provides important protections for victims in the realm of the family, and must be weighed against the obligation to limit such protections in domestic violence matters.[57] Privacy and dignity are inextricably related; privacy, too, bears on agency and autonomy.

This is not to suggest a return to the practice of domestic violence as a private matter beyond the public purview. But it does imply the need to avoid a totalizing negation of family privacy and to reconsider an approach that analyzes whether and under what circumstances privacy rights might be relevant and enforceable for victims of domestic violence. As long as the domestic violence movement is captive to the criminal justice system, the public-private dichotomy dilemma may be used for political purposes unrelated to the very needs of those who suffer such violence.

III. Community Assessments: Procedural and Substantive Justice

The public commentary recorded throughout the Mirkarimi-López case suggests that neither defining nor responding to any type of violence is a static social process. Residents who spoke at the hearings provided a critical assessment of the criminal justice response to domestic violence, including a critique of the mainstream domestic violence movement whose members championed a punitive response. Public commentary questioned the very definition of domestic violence for failing to consider the nuances and complexities of intimate partner dynamics and further critiqued the lack of proportionate responses to the distinct forms such acts may take. Moreover, the overwhelming majority of public comments urged that other forms of social violence—including police abuse, environmental degradation, and xenophobia—be addressed as a way to strengthen the fabric of families and communities and address the schism between the anti-domestic violence movement and other forms of social justice activism.

A. Assessing Procedural Fairness

Community supporters drew on their lived experiences and their individual constituent relationships with Mirkarimi while he was their District 5 supervisor in assessing the perceived legitimacy and procedural fairness of the efforts to oust him.[58] Poor people and persons of color who spoke on Mirkarimi's behalf praised his record as their public servant and his enlightened view of state responses to crime. He reflected their beliefs in second chances, restorative justice, and alternatives to incarceration.[59] Indeed, the explicit and implicit message with regard to procedural fairness, particularly given the racial and ethnic identity of those who supported Mirkarimi, was frequently framed around his progressive stance on crime and his support for people of color, immigrants, and the poor in San Francisco.[60]

Religious leaders and social justice groups—including community anti-violence organizations, tenants' organizations, labor unions, LGBT

organizations, progressive lawyers organizations, and the Latino Democratic Club—expressed support for Mirkarimi.[61] He was credited with
creating jobs for disadvantaged neighborhoods and progressive environmental protection legislation.[62] The San Francisco Green Party acknowl-
edged the importance of ending domestic violence, but opposed efforts
to oust Mirkarimi that relied on a punitive approach and urged support
for "redemptive" responses.[63] Its members rallied for Mirkarimi due to
his strong defense of civil rights and the environment. The American
Immigration Lawyers Association emphasized Mirkarimi's importance
to San Francisco's immigrant community.[64]

Mirkarimi was the beneficiary of the community's supportive assessment while those who sought to punish him were not. He was viewed
as someone who acted in their best interests, as opposed to law enforcement, politicians, and members of the mainstream anti-domestic violence movement who were perceived to have little or no legitimacy in
their community.[65] Mirkarimi's supporters criticized the law enforcement and mayor's response to the incident as consistent with the pre-
dilections of the carceral state.[66] Many community members suspected
that the city's effort to remove Mirkarimi was a political maneuver, a
"coup d'état," and a "witch-hunt," a mechanism of voter disenfranchise-
ment targeted at a poor and black district.[67]

This was a political power play to which domestic violence advocates
lent their credibility. Mirkarimi's supporters viewed advocates as ma-
nipulative, self-serving, and allied with the powerful.[68] They rejected any
explanation offered by city officials as well as those domestic violence
advocates who spoke against Mirkarimi that the case demonstrated
city policies by which domestic violence or the needs of women were
taken seriously.[69] It appeared evident to Mirkarimi's supporters that his
prosecution for domestic violence had little to do with the well-being of
women. Instead, the community invoked an emerging critique of a certain brand of feminism, that is, "feminism's appropriation for less than
feminist purposes."[70] The comments reflected the extent to which the
tethering of the mainstream domestic violence movement to systems
of punishment were deemed to be discordant with progressive social
norms and restorative justice approaches, and were particularly at odds
with the interests of those who have suffered the racist reach of the carceral state.[71]

B. Assessing Substantive Fairness

Domestic violence advocates urged city officials to remove Mirkarimi.[72] The paradigm of domestic violence, they argued, allowed little nuance. What had occurred between López and Mirkarimi, domestic violence advocates insisted, was an act of domestic violence to which the criminal justice system was perforce obliged to respond.[73] Community members, however, repudiated this perspective and addressed the issue of Mirkarimi's actions towards López in the context of defining and then responding to domestic violence.

The public opinion voiced throughout the hearings articulated concerns about the over-inclusive definition of domestic violence as a criminal matter. Many argued that the arm grab did not constitute domestic violence and represented nothing exceptional in the realm of family arguments; that it was an unfortunate but commonplace event during a heated dispute between a husband and wife and with which most individuals could identify, and that it did not warrant any intervention.[74] They expressed anger at the way in which the incident was portrayed and criticized the city's attorney for overreaching by claiming that Mirkarimi "beat his wife" or "attacked his wife."[75] Still others believed that the fact that Mirkarimi had taken responsibility for his actions by apologizing to his wife was sufficient mitigation of the "arm grab" in order to move it out of the realm of criminal behavior.[76]

The viewpoints expressed in public commentary are consistent with the studies of many sociologists who have offered more nuanced definitions of domestic abuse that recognize that some forms of violence in relationships are neither abusive nor warrant legal intervention, while others may be so destructive as to warrant criminal sanctions.[77] These researchers differentiate between the former, "situational couple violence,"[78] and the latter, coercive control.[79] Some physical violence between intimate partners, they note, however problematic such behavior may be, does not always fall outside of social norms.[80]

Community speakers not only rejected the characterization of the arm grab as an incident of domestic violence, but also objected to the nature of the consequences that Mirkarimi suffered as a result of having been charged with domestic violence. They challenged the views of the chair of the city's Family Violence Council, who suggested that abusers the world over would be emboldened if Mirkarimi were not punished and removed from office.[81] While mainstream advocates argued that if Mirkarimi were to remain as sheriff, it would send a "message" to perpetrators that domestic violence was readily excused,[82] most public commentators firmly rejected the usefulness of "zero tolerance" by which to address domestic violence and called for a more nuanced approach with an emphasis on redemption and restorative justice consistent with the parameters of situational couple violence.[83] As a rejoinder to the assertions by mainstream program advocates that to allow Mirkarimi to assume his position would serve to terrify domestic violence victims,[84] community members stated that in fact the overblown nature of the response would serve to discourage others from reporting domestic violence.[85]

Insisting that domestic violence could not return to the privacy of the home, advocates demanded that state intervention was needed to prove the state's commitment to protecting women and children.[86] Community members, however, objected to the nature of the consequences that Mirkarimi suffered as a result of being charged with domestic violence. They despaired over the fact that Mirkarimi was not allowed to see his wife and child and was deprived of his pay while suspended, calling it "undemocratic" and "outrageous" and argued that removing him from office was disproportionate to the offense.[87]

Notwithstanding statutory protections for victim rights, many of Mirkarimi's supporters pointed to the harm caused to López—the alleged victim—and her son.[88] According to their understanding of victims' rights, they urged city officials to consider López's perceptions as to whether she was abused and suggested that they cease silencing or ignoring her voice.[89] Community members objected that those domestic violence advocates who spoke in favor of removing Mirkarimi were financially dependent on those city officials seeking to oust him, and thus were exploiting the construct of victimhood.[90] "I feel offended by the domestic violence [advocates] exploiting a family crisis for their own agenda," stated one woman commentator, "which [has] nothing to do with protecting victims."[91]

All in all, over ninety percent of those who offered public commentary at three Ethics Commission hearings and the Board of Supervisors hearing supported Mirkarimi, and it should be added, López.[92] Their critique not only addressed procedural fairness, but also focused on the substantive deficiencies of the laws directed at domestic violence. They further revealed a deepening breach between domestic violence advocates and the social justice movement.

IV. Conclusion

This chapter has sought to examine the ways in which the public evaluates both procedural and substantive fairness and the consequences of reliance on victim politics, criminalization, and punishment as the default remedy to domestic violence. The public discourse throughout the Mirkarimi-López case reflects a "life-as-lived" critique of the domestic violence paradigm. The commentary argues in favor of a redefinition of domestic violence, a reconsideration of rights pertaining to "victimhood" and agency, and a recalibration of the responses to domestic violence without returning to a time when private abuse between intimate partners is considered of little or no socio-political or legal import.

The opinions expressed by community members—most of whom were Black, Latino/a, or had had previous experience with the criminal justice system—confirmed empirical evidence about the inadequacy of criminal justice remedies. The current politics of race and police abuse create an imperative for change and should serve to instill political will among domestic violence advocates to shift both strategy and purpose. Indeed, San Francisco residents who spoke in support of Mirkarimi reflect similar interests as new social movement actors such as #BlackLivesMatter and #SayHerName, which have addressed the deep roots of racism and the historic relationship of the criminal justice system to injustice.

The Mirkarimi-López case is one of many controversies to expose the fissure between those who work in gender-violence advocacy and those concerned with the overreach of the carceral state. Indeed, the case indicates the crisis facing the domestic violence movement and the perception it has garnered as a facilitator of the law-and-order regime. By favoring the criminal justice system as the preferred response, the mainstream anti-domestic violence movement serves to communicate, as Bernard Harcourt has observed, a "political, cultural, racial, and ideological message[ ] . . . about who is in control and about who gets controlled."[93] Such a message all but assures that the movement will remain at the margins of social justice work. That outcome would be detrimental to efforts to end gender-based violence, for it would signal the loss of the knowledge, experience, and dedication that domestic violence advocates possess. A new approach requires domestic violence advocates to engage in the movement to end police brutality both in coalitions and in the courts. Coalitions of these types allow domestic violence advocates to address structural concerns and at the same time attend to issues pertaining to domestic violence.

Author's Note

This chapter is adapted from an article entitled *The Community Politics of Domestic Violence*, 82 BROOKLYN L. REV. 1479 (2017).

NOTES

1 Barbara Fedders, *Lobbying for Mandatory-Arrest Policies: Race, Class, and the Politics of the Battered Women's Movement*, 23 NYU REV. L. & SOC. CHANGE 281, 287 (1997); Adele M. Morrison, *Changing the Domestic Violence (Dis)Course: Moving From White Victim to Multicultural Survivor*, 39 UC DAVIS L. REV. 1063, 1090–91 (2006); PATRICIA ENG, MS. FOUNDATION FOR WOMEN, SAFETY & JUSTICE FOR ALL: EXAMINING THE RELATIONSHIP BETWEEN THE WOMEN'S ANTI-VIOLENCE MOVEMENT AND THE CRIMINAL LEGAL SYSTEM, 1, 15 (2003), www.ncdsv.org [hereinafter SAFETY & JUSTICE]; BETH E. RICHIE, ARRESTED JUSTICE: BLACK WOMEN, VIOLENCE AND AMERICA'S PRISON NATION 2 (2013).

2 *Supra* note 1; Univ. of Miami School of Law Office of External Affairs, *Converge! Reimagining the Movement to End Gender Violence*, http://media.law.miami.edu (last visited Jan. 26, 2018); *Vision*, CREATIVE INTERVENTIONS, www.creative-interventions.org (last visited Jan. 26, 2018); BAY AREA TRANSFORMATIVE JUSTICE COLLECTIVE, https://batjc.wordpress.com (last visited Jan. 26, 2018); ATLANTA TRANSFORMATIVE JUSTICE COLLABORATIVE, http://project south.org (last visited Jan. 28, 2018); GENERATIONFIVE, www.generationfive. org (last visited Jan. 26, 2018).

3 Kimberlé Crenshaw, *Mapping the Margins: Intersectionality, Identity Politics, and Violence Against Women of Color*, 43 STAN. L. REV. 1241, 1257 (1991); Leslye E. Orloff et al., *Battered Immigrant Women's Willingness to Call for Help and Police Response*, 13 UCLA WOMEN'S L.J. 43, 68, 77–79 (2005); Lisi Lord et al., *Lesbian, Gay, Bisexual, and Transgender Communities and Intimate Partner Violence*, 29 FORDHAM URB. L.J. 121 (2001); Donna Coker, *Crime Control and Feminist Law Reform in Domestic Violence Law: A Critical Review*, 4 BUFF. CRIM. L. REV. 801,

852 (2001); Doug Jones, *Domestic Violence Against Women with Disabilities: A Feminist Legal Theory Analysis*, 2 FLA. A&M U. L. REV. 207, 224 (2007) (describing challenges that disabled domestic violence victims face when dealing with police).

4 *See* DONNA COKER ET AL., A.C.L.U., REPONSES FROM THE FIELD: SEXUAL ASSAULT, DOMESTIC VIOLENCE, AND POLICING (2015), www.aclu.org (more than 900 individuals responded); T. K. LOGAN & ROB (ROBERTA) VALENTE, NAT'L DOMESTIC VIOLENCE HOTLINE, WHO WILL HELP ME?: DOMESTIC VIOLENCE SURVIVORS SPEAK OUT ABOUT LAW ENFORCEMENT RESPONSES 4, 8 (2015), www.thehotline.org; AFRICAN AMERICAN POLICY FORUM, SAY HER NAME: RESISTING POLICE BRUTALITY AGAINST BLACK WOMEN (2015), https://fusiondotnet.files.wordpress.com; Olubusola "Shola" Ajayi, *Black Women's Blueprint, Under Siege: The Policing of Women and Girls*, VIMEO (June 16, 2011, 12:42 PM), www.blackwomensblueprint.org; U.S. DEP'T OF JUSTICE, INVESTIGATION OF THE FERGUSON POLICE DEPARTMENT 81 (2015), www.justice.gov.

5 Leigh Goodmark, *Autonomy Feminism: An Anti-Essentialist Critique of Mandatory Interventions in Domestic Violence Cases*, 37 FLA. ST. U. L. REV. 1, 55 (2009) (noting the absence of data that ties criminalization to decreased rates of domestic violence); Deborah M. Weissman, *The Personal Is Political—and Economic: Rethinking Domestic Violence*, 2007 BYU L. REV. 387, 401 (2007). *See generally* MICHELLE ALEXANDER, THE NEW JIM CROW: MASS INCARCERATION IN THE AGE OF COLORBLINDNESS (rev'd ed. 2012).

6 *See generally* SAFETY & JUSTICE, *supra* note 1.

7 *See* Crenshaw, *supra* note 3, at 1241, 1257; Coker, *supra* note 3, at 852–54; Holly Maguigan, *Wading into Professor Schneider's "Murky Middle Ground" Between Acceptance and Rejection of Criminal Justice Responses to Domestic Violence*, 11 AM. U. J. GENDER SOC. POL'Y & L. 427, 432 (2003).

8 Debra J. Saunders, *Ross Mirkarimi Faults Himself, And the System*, S.F. CHRON. (Jan. 3, 2015), www.sfgate.com.

9 Tracey L. Meares et al., *Lawful or Fair?: How Cops and Laypeople Perceive Good Policing*, 105 J. CRIM. L. & CRIMINOLOGY 297, 300 (2015) (suggesting that public judgments about police conduct are shaped by notions of procedural justice evaluations).

10 *Id.*

11 Norimitsu Oshi, *Ross Mirkarimi, San Francisco Sheriff, Reinstated*, N.Y. TIMES (Oct 11, 2012), at A20.

12 Lopèz Decl. 2:16–19, July 2, 2012, available at https://sfethics.org; Mirkarimi Decl. 2:2–4, June 13, 2012, available at https://sfethics.org.

13 Saunders, *supra* note 8.

14 López Decl. 1:26–2:19.

15 López Decl. 2:11–15.

16 López Decl. 2:24–3:2.

17 López Decl. 1:28–2:3, 2:26–27.

18 Madison Decl. 9:27–10:1, 10:7–8, June 15, 2012, available at https://sfethics.org.
19 Madison Decl. 7:9–10.
20 Madison Decl. 13:18–14:6, 15:25–27.
21 Daniele Decl. 2:25–3:5, 3:21–22, 5:1–14, June 7, 2012, available at https://sfethics.org.
22 Arraignment Hr'g Tr., 5–10, Jan. 19, 2012, on file with the author.
23 *Id.* at 14.
24 *Id.* at 24. Marsy's Law refers to the California Constitution, Article I, Sec. 28(b), also known as the California Victim's Bill of Rights.
25 Arraignment Hr'g Tr, *supra* note 22, at 26.
26 *Id.* at 29, 30.
27 *Id.* at 32.
28 *Id.* at 33.
29 *Id.* at 35, 36.
30 Interview with Eliana López in S.F., Cal. (Dec. 14, 2015).
31 Findings of Fact and Recommendation to the Board of Supervisors at 6, Sept. 6, 2012, available at https://sfethics.org.
32 *Id.* at 6.
33 Oshi, *supra* note 11.
34 Rebecca Duran, *Spirited Comedy Unfolds Web of SF Disempowerment*, WESTERN EDITION (Jul. 1, 2015), www.thewesternedition.com.
35 Interview with Eliana López, *supra* note 30.
36 NAT'L CRIME VICTIM LAW INST. AT LEWIS & CLARK LAW SCHOOL, VICTIM LAW BULLETIN: FUNDAMENTALS OF VICTIMS' RIGHTS: AN OVERVIEW OF THE LEGAL DEFINITION OF "CRIME VICTIM" IN THE UNITED STATES (November 2011), https://law.lclark.edu.
37 Tami Amanda Jacoby, *A Theory of Victimhood, Politics, Conflict and the Construction of Victim-Based Identity*, 43 J. OF INT'L. STUD. 511, 513 (2015).
38 MARIE GOTTSCHALK, THE PRISON AND THE GALLOWS, THE POLITICS OF MASS INCARCERATION IN AMERICA 77 (2006); FATIMA NAQVI, LITERARY AND CULTURAL RHETORIC OF VICTIMHOOD: WESTERN EUROPE 1970–2005, at 1 (2007) (observing that the use of victimhood is far more widespread in recent years).
39 *See* Merchants Distributors, Inc. v. Hutchinson, 16 N.C. App. 655, 663 (1982), citing People v. Williams, 17 Cal. 142 (1860).
40 Federal Crime Victims' Rights Act, 18 U.S.C. § 3771; 18 U.S.C. § 3663; Kenna v. U.S. Dist. Ct. for C.D. Cal., 435 F.3d 1011 (2006) (citing 18 U.S.C. § 3771).
41 Cal. Const., art. I, § 28(b)(1), § 28(b)(4), § 28(b)(14); CAL. PENAL CODE § 679.026 (2008).
42 Leigh Goodmark, *When is a Battered Woman Not a Battered Woman? When She Fights Back*, 20 YALE J.L. & FEMINISM 75, 91 (2008); Donna Coker, *Restorative Justice Responses to Sexual Assault on Campus* (forthcoming TEXAS TECH L. REV); Jody Raphael, *Battering Through the Lens of Class*, 11 AM. U. J. GENDER SOC. POL'Y & L. 367, 368 (2003).

43 Sally Engle Merry, *Rights Talk and the Experience of Law: Implementing Women's Human Rights to Protection from Violence*, 25 HUMAN RTS. Q. 343, 353 (2003).

44 MARILYN FRIEDMAN, AUTONOMY, GENDER, POLITICS 150–51 (2003).

45 Goodmark, *supra* note 5, at 24.

46 *Id.* at 27.

47 Martha Minow, *Surviving Victim Talk*, 40 UCLA L. REV. 1411, 1416, 1426 (1993).

48 Myrna Melgar, *Guardian Op-Ed: Domestic Violence, a Latina Feminist Perspective*, GUARDIAN (Mar. 27, 2012), http://sfbgarchive.48hills.org.

49 Lemon Decl., June 18, 2012, available at https://sfethics.org.

50 Joe Eskenazi, *Ross Mirkarimi's Wife Attends Anti–Ross Mirkarimi Rally*, SF WEEKLY (Jan. 12, 2012), www.sfweekly.com.

51 *Id.*; Interview with Eliana López, *supra* note 30.

52 *Id.*; Kat Anderson, *Domestic Violence Consortium Calls for Mirkarimi to Resign, Wife Makes Cameo*, FOGCITYJOURNAL.COM (Jan. 12, 2012), www.fogcityjournal.com.

53 Mallina Kaur, *Domestic Violence Survivors and Allies: We Won't be Silenced*, MS. MAGAZINE BLOG (Oct. 31, 2012), http://msmagazine.com.

54 *See* López Decl.; Madison Decl.

55 Request for Protective Order, May 15, 2012, available at https://sfethics.org.

56 Cal. Const., *supra* note 41.

57 Bert-Jaap Koops et al., *A Typology of Privacy*, 38 U. PA. J. INT'L L. 483, 511, n.89 (2017).

58 *See* Meares et al., *supra* note 9; Special Meeting of the Ethics Comm'n Tr. 87, Aug. 16, 2012, available at https://sfethics.org; Joe Fitzgerald, *Lopez Takes the Stand in Official Misconduct Case Against Suspended Sheriff*, FOGCITYJOURNAL.COM (July 19, 2012), www.fogcityjournal.com (describing overflow crowds at Ethics Commission hearings by supporters of Mirkarimi). Several of the many supportive comments made by San Francisco residents on behalf of Mirkarimi are referenced below. Special Meeting of the Ethics Comm'n Tr. 378–79 (May 29, 2012), available at https://sfethics.org; TR BOS, at 31.

59 Special Meeting of the Ethics Comm'n Tr. 90:16–20 (Apr. 23, 2012) ("people who are in the jails are going to suffer the most" without Mirkarimi) [hereinafter April Meeting Tr.]; *Id.* at 98:11–16 (noting that Mirkarimi "fought for programs that would help serve our community"); *Id.* at 114 (crime victim in support of Mirkarimi). Special Meeting of the Ethics Comm'n Tr. 340–41, 349, 373 (May 29, 2012) [hereinafter May Meeting Tr.]; Special Meeting of the Ethics Comm'n Tr. 119–20, 144, 175, 180 (Aug. 16, 2012) [hereinafter August Meeting Tr.]; TR BOS, at 33 (referring to Mirkarimi as a "jewel") (compassion for prisoners) (at 36) (support for sheriff for his work with "the ones in and out of prison") (at 38); April Meeting Tr. 89:9–15 (commenting that Mirkarimi has been working "in the trenches"); May Meeting Tr. 368; TR BOS, at 32.

60 April Meeting Tr. 102:19–22 (representative of Black media stating Mirkarimi as best for "third-world people"); *Id.* at 112 (statement of support from former Afri-

can American male inmate); May Meeting Tr. 328, 329, 342 (noting Mirkarimi's support for brown, black, and Chinese people); TR BOS (representative of Latino community at San Francisco State, "he stood for us and we should stand for [him]") (at 37); Myrna Melgar, Nov. 2, 2012 (noting that most of the Sheriff's supporters were people of color).

61 April Meeting Tr. 85, 93–94, 105–7; May Meeting Tr. 340, 351, 362, 375 (groups and persons considered to be less than powerful united for sheriff); TR BOS, at 33 (support from community for Mirkarimi's work with marginalized youth); TR BOS (support of Mirkarimi by the American Immigration Lawyers Association) (at 150).

62 April Meeting Tr. 108; May Meeting Tr. 354–55; JOHN-MARC CHANDONIA, SAN FRANCISCO GREEN PARTY, SAN FRANCISCO GREEN PARTY: STATEMENT IN SUPPORT OF SHERIFF ROSS MIRKARIMI REMAINING IN OFFICE AS THE DULY ELECTED SHERIFF OF SAN FRANCISCO (Feb. 7, 2018), http://sfgreenparty.org [hereinafter SAN FRANCISCO GREEN PARTY].

63 SAN FRANCISCO GREEN PARTY, *supra* note 62. Other commentators opposed Mirkarimi's ouster, noting that it was contrary to the city's move toward restorative and redemptive justice. August Meeting Tr. 147.

64 TR BOS, at 151.

65 Meares et al., *supra* note 9, at 304 (procedural fairness determined by whether officials are seen as "legitimate, and their conduct is appropriate, within the communities where they work when exercising their policing authority").

66 August Meeting Tr. 85 (referencing the problem of over-incarceration).

67 April Meeting Tr. 85, 87, 91 (referring to the case against Mirkarimi as a "witch-hunt"); May Meeting Tr. 324, 342, 359, 376; August Meeting Tr. 64, 78–79, 170 (referencing the financing of a billboard against Mirkarimi in order to support his political opponents). The billboard was paid for by domestic violence advocates. *See* Keith Mizuguchi, *Billboard Campaign Launched Against Sheriff Mirkarimi*, 70 SF STATION (Feb. 4, 2012), www.sfstation.com; TR BOS, at 30 (former Mayor of San Francisco warning against overreach) (construing the city's efforts to use the issue of domestic violence for a "political lynching") (at 116); April Meeting Tr. 87, 92, 115 ("I cast my vote"); May Meeting Tr. 338, 339, 348, 351 (noting the will of the people in electing Mirkarimi); *Id.* at 353, 361 ("I want my vote to count"); August Meeting Tr. 17, 156 (pointing out that if the people who elected Mirkarimi so desired to remove him from office because of his actions, they could recall him) (at 24); TR BOS (no authority to "take away my vote") (at 34, 35) ("if we want him out we'll take him out) (at 36) (arguing that removing the Sheriff would send a bad message to immigrants about democracy) (at 43) ("Don't substitute your judgement for the citizens of San Francisco. We elected him.") (at 87).

68 May Meeting Tr. 343; TR BOS, at 35 (criticizing domestic violence advocates for aligning with and taking funds from Mirkarimi's political opponents) (at 39) (critiquing San Francisco's mainstream domestic violence program for using

the incident and others to enrich the organization rather than helping victims) (at 40).

69 May Meeting Tr. 340.

70 *See* Brenda Cossman, *Feminism in Hard Times: From Criticism to Critique, in* FEMINISMS OF DISCONTENT 3, 14 (Ashleigh Barnes ed., 2015).

71 May Meeting Tr. 352, 360; August Meeting Tr. 42, 96; TR BOS, at 54.

72 August Meeting Tr. 45, 112; April Meeting Tr. 119; August Meeting Tr. 29, 30, 43, 73, 104, 109, 106, 114, 117, 121, 122, 123, 185, 130; TR BOS, at 80.

73 August Meeting Tr. 45, 112 (Aug. 16, 2012).

74 April Meeting Tr. 81, 105, 109; May Meeting Tr. at 352, 373; August Meeting Tr. 95, 119, 161, 166; TR BOS, at 75, 98. May Meeting Tr. 331, 334, 335, 337, 364. August Meeting Tr. 14, 26, 51,77, 198; TR BOS, at 79.

75 TR BOS, at 112.

76 May Meeting Tr. 330.

77 Michael P. Johnson & Janet L. Leome, *The Differential Effects of Intimate Terrorism and Situational Couple Violence Findings from the National Violence Against Women Survey*, 26 J. FAM. ISSUES 322, 324 (2005); EVAN STARK, COERCIVE CONTROL: THE ENTRAPMENT OF WOMEN IN PERSONAL LIFE (2007).

78 Johnson & Leome, *supra* note 77.

79 STARK, *supra* note 77.

80 Tamara L. Kuennen, *Stuck on Love*, 91 DENV. U. L. REV. 171, 179 (2013).

81 April Meeting Tr. 119:9 (stating "the world is watching").

82 August Meeting Tr. 29, 106.

83 *See* Johnson & Leome, *supra* note 77; May Meeting Tr. 352 (arguing for diversion in lieu of conviction mechanisms); *Id.* at 360–61 (suggesting domestic violence is not a black and white situation but rather gray); *Id.* at 370; TR BOS, at 33 (commenting on "overkill" reaction to the incident) (excessive reaction to the arm grab) (at 37).

84 August Meeting Tr. 117, 122, 130; *id.* at 121 (arguing that immigrant victims would be afraid to come forth); TR BOS, at 49.

85 TR BOS, at 62.

86 TR BOS, at 80.

87 April Meeting Tr. 85, 93, 96; May Meeting Tr. 372–73 (the loss of a job because of domestic violence would continue the cycle of violence); August Meeting Tr. 24; TR BOS, at 95, 124; May Meeting Tr. 362, 367 ("The issues in this case simply don't come close to warranting termination of employment."); August Meeting Tr. 32 (Aug. 16, 2012); TR BOS, at 131.

88 May Meeting Tr. 339.

89 April Meeting Tr. 96, 99–100; May Meeting Tr. 327, 369; August Meeting Tr. 34, 53; TR BOS, at 108, 137 (expressing concern that López's rights were violated) (at 166).

90 August Meeting Tr. 190; TR BOS (suggesting that case was not about domestic violence and challenging domestic violence advocates to seek a recall instead of

"hid[ing] behind the mayor") (at 55) (referring to domestic violence advocates as "misguided") (at 59).

91 August Meeting Tr. 98; TR BOS (woman speaker criticizing women's groups for professing to speak for everyone when they have no contact with most women) (at 51–52) (arguing that "a moment of family crisis was being transformed ... for illegal and financial gain") (at 168).

92 Over 310 people gave public commentary, with most speaking in support of Mirkarimi. Of these individuals, 94% voiced support for Mirkarimi at the April 2012 Ethics Commission hearing, 100% voiced support at the May 2012 Ethics Commission hearing, 83% voiced support at the August Ethics Commission hearing, and 88% voiced support at the October 2012 Board of Supervisors hearing.

93 Bernard E. Harcourt, *Joel Feinberg on Crime and Punishment: Exploring the Relationship Between the Moral Limits of the Criminal Law and the Expressive Function of Punishment*, 5 BUFF. CRIM. L. REV. 145, 168 (2001).

3

Empowerment Politics and Access to Justice

ELIZABETH L. MACDOWELL

I. Introduction

The concept of empowerment is closely associated with advocacy for gender violence survivors. But what does empowerment really mean, and how does it relate to the delivery of legal services? In the classic formulation of the early battered women's movement, empowerment is a multidimensional process through which a battered woman leaves the isolation of an abusive relationship to join a community of survivors and, ultimately, become an advocate for other battered women.[1] Advocacy in this context is a mechanism for providing the resources and support that survivors need—individually and collectively—for personal and political transformation.[2] However, less expansive accounts of empowerment often inform vital interventions and services relied upon by abuse survivors, including those intended to provide access to justice.[3]

This chapter examines the politics of empowerment and the impacts of shifting conceptualizations of empowerment on survivors who use courthouse self-help programs to access the justice system in civil protection order cases. The chapter first identifies the key components of feminist-informed advocacy, along with challenges to feminist empowerment models. It then reports results from the author's study of self-help programs aiding applicants for civil protection orders. The author previously reported findings from this study demonstrating the ways in which staff members' demeanor toward applicants and the organization of work in self-help programs can limit access to justice.[4] This chapter analyzes data from that study along another dimension: its relationship to empowerment principles. The primary finding is that thin accounts of empowerment dominate the self-help legal services model in these programs, to the detriment of the primarily low-income women of color who utilize self-help protection order services.[5] Given the ongoing expansion of the self-help model in efforts to meet the needs of unrepresented litigants,[6] these results suggest that further research and development of approaches is needed. Legal empowerment models that take a more multidimensional approach to access to justice may be more effective in addressing the legal needs of gender-violence survivors.

II. Empowerment and the Protection Order Process

A. Feminism and Multidimensional Empowerment

The feminist concept of empowerment as articulated within the early battered women's movement is a process characterized by women's increasing agency, political understanding, and community engagement.[7] As described in Susan Schechter's seminal account of the grassroots battered women's movement, empowerment, in this view, operates simultaneously on an individual level and as a "collective power ... validating women's personal experiences [with abuse] as politically oppressive rather than self-caused or 'crazy.'"[8] Schechter explains, "In a feminist political context, empowerment signifies standing together as a community just as it means supportively enabling a person to take risks."[9] Thus, the process of empowerment involves "giving women tools to better control their lives and [join] in collective struggle."[10]

To these ends, feminist-informed advocates used survivor-centered and collaborative methods.[11] For example, collective sharing in support groups was a means through which women would gain understanding of the shared nature of their oppression and its structural causes.[12] The goal was to support women in making their own choices rather than limiting or forcing choices through bureaucratic structures. Hierarchical models were specifically rejected because they were viewed as mimicking the power dynamics between victims and abusers, and thus counter to the project of fostering empowerment. Advocates also sought to address the underpinnings of domestic violence, which were understood as rooted in women's inequality in the family, the workplace, and elsewhere in society.[13] Therefore, advocates worked to facilitate women's social, economic, and political empowerment, including by educating the

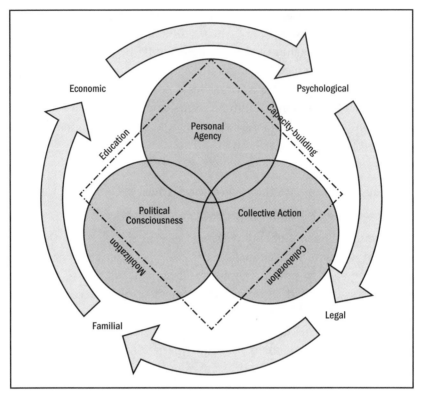

Figure 3.1. Multi-Dimensional Feminist Advocacy

public about the problem of domestic violence and expanding services and legal protections for battered women.[14]

Figure 3.1 depicts the interrelationship of these dynamics operating in feminist advocacy. As shown, empowerment in this view is multidimensional in that it is a process involving multiple, interrelated components (such as personal agency, collective action, and political consciousness) and modes of action (including capacity-building, collaboration, mobilization, and education). Moreover, as a transformative, capacity-building project, empowerment-based advocacy operates in multiple spheres, including the psycho-social and legal spheres, as well as on micro (individual/community) and macro (state/national policy) levels.[15] Protection orders are an example of the interrelated nature of this work.

B. Protection Orders and Empowerment-Informed Advocacy

Lay advocates and lawyer allies in the early battered women's movement worked to make legal systems more responsive to survivors' needs through such efforts as the development of civil protection orders.[16] These efforts were informed by empowerment principles.[17] Protective orders were intended to replace civil injunctions that were available only through divorce actions and were difficult to obtain (especially for unrepresented parties), limited in scope, and hard to enforce.[18] Civil protection orders would be available whether or not the survivor wanted to separate from the abuser or make a criminal report, and were available to married and unmarried women.[19] Protection order legislation was also intended to give survivors more agency and control than was possible through criminal remedies.[20] This was considered especially important for women of color, who might be particularly reticent to seek help from law enforcement and subject partners of color to racist police practices.[21] Moreover, civil protection orders would support women's empowerment by providing relatively quick and simple access to orders for child custody, child and spousal support, and possession of property.[22]

Today, civil protection orders are available in every state and the District of Columbia.[23] With this expansion, engagement with the legal system has become a central experience for survivors of gender violence. Indeed, applying for a protection order has become the most common way survivors seek help for abuse after calling 911.[24] Research shows these encounters with the legal system have the power to de-normalize abuse, and can help women see themselves as legal subjects with capacity to claim rights and get help from the state to address abuse.[25] However, the results are not always positive for survivors, as such encounters can result in re-victimization. For example, state actors may blame survivors for the abuse or impose unwanted and punitive interventions.[26]

Because the legal system plays a pivotal role in shaping the legal consciousness of participants, as well as in providing access to remedies and resources, the nature of survivors' experiences within these systems is critical. This is especially true because survivors are likely to make multiple attempts to leave or renegotiate an abusive relationship.[27] Moreover, advocacy during these system encounters can make an important

difference in outcomes. Specifically, research shows that advocacy practices that respect and support the decision-making of survivors support
positive outcomes, including a decreased likelihood of repeated violence.[28] The next section discusses challenges to empowering survivors,
including during encounters with the legal system.

C. Challenges to Implementing the Feminist Ideal

While the battered women's movement resulted in many achievements,
including social and legal recognition of gender violence as a serious
problem, realization of the feminist ideal of empowerment for gender
violence survivors has faced many challenges. By the time that Schechter's history of the movement was published in 1982, the movement was
already departing from its grassroots ideals. As Schechter describes,
"The goal of sustaining a vision of women's liberation and building
a political movement was lost in the struggle to start, fund, manage,
legitimate, and maintain programs for battered women."[29] Institutionalization of programs led to professionalization of the advocacy role.
In turn, professionalization inhibited the trajectory from victim to
survivor-advocate and threatened survivor-centered advocacy as clinical or service-oriented goals replaced the self-identified goals of abuse
victims.[30] Political scientist Kristin Bumiller and others argue that such
changes recreate the dynamics of abuse and foster dependency rather
than empowerment.[31]

The state systems where survivors are encouraged (and sometimes
required) to obtain assistance impose another set of challenges.[32] The
turn to mandatory arrest and prosecution policies has resulted in more
survivors being arrested for domestic violence and many more losing
the choice of whether to pursue criminal charges against their abusers.[33]
Further, family courts where survivors seek protection orders often react
with hostility to their claims of abuse—especially about related custody
issues. Numerous studies show that women going to family court for
protection orders or raising claims of abuse in divorce and custody proceedings experience hostility and bias from judges and other court personnel.[34] Indeed, in custody cases, reporting domestic violence may in
some instances *reduce* a survivor's chance of receiving an order for full
or joint custody.[35] Survivors going to court may also be exposed to child

welfare reporting requirements and risk being prosecuted for failing to protect their children from abuse, even as they seek help.[36] Moreover, many if not most survivors will be unrepresented by counsel when they go to court;[37] many will also face language and other barriers to access.[38]

These problems are exacerbated by reduced funding and restrictions on legal aid representation. Although legal aid organizations often prioritize casework for survivors of domestic violence or intimate partner abuse, existing resources do not begin to meet the need for attorneys in low-income communities.[39] Additionally, despite the pervasive need for reform, legal aid organizations do not always pursue sorely needed structural reform goals.[40] While lay advocates have long worked to fill gaps in survivor representation by accompanying survivors in court and advocating for them in legal systems, these efforts also present challenges for empowerment goals. The effectiveness of lay advocates is diminished by their lack of legal expertise, as well as by rules against the unauthorized practice of law. Moreover, partnerships with state organizations to address systemic problems, and positions working within courts and state agencies, may erode or compromise advocates' commitments. Ultimately, the priorities of government bureaucracies may replace survivor-centered advocacy, changing advocates more than the system.[41]

Combined with these challenges are barriers to empowerment emanating from race and class dynamics within the anti-violence movement. Women of color have applied an intersectional analysis of both race and gender in efforts to make systems more responsive to survivors' needs.[42] As described above, these insights informed development of protection orders. Too often, however, the failure of middle-class white women within the movement to recognize the intersectional nature of gender violence has led to the exclusion of women of color from vital services and impeded the movement's ability to make positive changes for the most marginalized women.[43] These problems are exacerbated by the general trend away from feminism in advocacy work. While some organizations maintain a feminist orientation, many are focused on service work rather than organizing goals. Some research suggests that, in the absence of feminist frameworks, advocates lose political and intersectional understandings associated with better outcomes for survivors.[44]

Adele Morrison names these circumstances as part of a "(dis)empowerment continuum."[45] Depending on how survivors are treated, their experiences with the legal system can be a process of empowerment or disempowerment. This makes efforts to provide access to justice to survivors an important area of study. Increasingly, these efforts involve assistance for unrepresented litigants through models based on "self-help." As shown in the following sections, the issue is not whether self-help legal services for survivors will be aimed at empowerment, but what theory of empowerment is in play.

III. Self-Help

A. Conceptions of Self-Help

The idea of self-help is embedded in the multidimensional conception of empowerment. For example, Schechter describes empowerment as closely related to self-help, which she defines as "a process through which women, experts about their own lives, learn to know their strength."[46] In this view (and the context of the battered women's movement), the goal is for women to take responsibility for themselves, their children, and their part of the battered women's community—such as the shelter where they are living. However, they do so not in isolation, but within a multidimensional process that includes a supportive community. Similar descriptions of self-help appear in scholarship about social justice lawyering. Gerald Lopez, for example, views teaching self-help as part of a participatory and democratic approach to political life. He describes his perspective on self-help as "a vision where public institutions and professional service providers help people help themselves, in much the same way that people in subordinated communities, at least at their best, have long taken responsibility for themselves and one another."[47] As in the feminist articulation, this view of self-help implies a process of capacity and agency-building within a larger framework of political awareness and care. In this context, self-help legal services have been viewed as a vehicle for social justice aims, as discussed below.

However, these views of self-help exist alongside much thinner accounts of empowerment and more narrowly conceived advocacy practices. Self-help also conjures the trope of pulling one's self up by the bootstraps. This trope suggests that, with sufficient grit and determination, complex, deep-rooted social problems can in fact be dealt with by an individual alone. Similarly, the concept of self-help legal services suggests that, merely provided the right alternatives, individuals are able to take on the legal system without lawyers.

B. Self-Help Legal Services

Self-help in the access-to-justice realm represents efforts to provide legal services to individuals who are not represented by counsel—usually by offering legal information and (in some instances) assistance completing and/or filing forms. Amidst what is frequently called a "pro se crisis," self-help programs have expanded rapidly over the last several decades, often provided through partnerships between nongovernmental organizations and courts.[48] The goal is twofold: to help people who cannot afford or otherwise obtain a lawyer gain access to the courts, and to assist courts in dealing with an increasing deluge of unrepresented parties.[49] Implicit in most self-help models is the idea that generic legal information and (usually) one-time assistance can replace ongoing legal support from a lawyer.

While self-sufficiency is touted as a benefit of self-help, social justice–oriented lawyers have envisioned ways for self-help to meet more multidimensional empowerment goals. For example, lawyers Peter Gabel and Paul Harris envision a self-help model for family law issues in which men and women might engage with one another to challenge limiting gender roles within marriage.[50] However, we know very little about self-help and its implications for empowerment.

As of this writing, there are few published studies of self-help legal services.[51] None of these examine the systemic impacts of services. Like other legal service providers, self-help staff members act as gatekeepers to the legal system.[52] They also help determine the narratives that reach the courts.[53] How self-help staff members perform these functions, and the impacts on survivors and systemic advocacy, are vital questions.

IV. The Study

A. Research Sites

This study examined services provided to protection order applicants at two self-help programs located in metropolitan areas in two western states (Program A and Program B).[54] Program A is managed by a legal aid organization (LAO) in partnership with the county. The LAO provides staff and organizes volunteers for the program, and the county provides space and equipment in several courthouses in the county. Program B, a partnership between the county and a local domestic violence services organization (DVSO), is located in the county's family court complex. The county funds multiple staff positions for the program, including a director; the DVSO funds two positions with the title "advocate."[55] Most applicants using Programs A and B are women of color.[56] Data from Program A shows that most have no college education and have a primary language other than English.[57] Program A assists more than 4,000 applicants annually;[58] Program B assists more than 5,000.[59]

Both programs provide protection order applicants with assistance completing the protection order application, but in different ways.[60] Program A provides one-on-one assistance to applicants in completing the application forms. At this location, a staff member (almost always a non-attorney volunteer or student intern) asks the applicant questions (prompts) to elicit information for the application and completes the forms on a computer or by hand. Once the application is complete, a staff attorney reviews it before it is filed. At Program B, applicants are given the forms and some instructions (both printed and verbal) by front desk staff, and then complete the forms themselves. Applicants can then speak with a staff member, who will review the forms for completeness. There is no attorney involvement at Program B.

Notably, both programs use the term "advocate" to describe staff members. At Program A, all non-attorney staff members are referred to as advocates—for example, in program materials. At Program B, only the two DVSO employees are identified as advocates. These roles are distinguished from advocacy in other settings, however. For example, applicants at Program A are required to initial and sign a form acknowledging that there was no attorney-client relationship and no right to confidentiality based on their use of self-help services.[61] A representative of the DVSO partner at Program B also distinguished advocacy on behalf of DVSO clients from the role of advocates in the program: unlike advocates for clients of the DVSO, she stressed, advocates in the program did not advocate *for* any individual, or evaluate the merit of abuse claims. She believed, nonetheless, that advocacy in the self-help program was consistent with the DVSO's commitment to using empowerment-based advocacy and the goal of empowering survivors. Specifically, she hoped that the information provided by advocates at the self-help program empowered survivors in the legal process—sentiments that were echoed by staff members at these research sites.

B. Method

The research was conducted using qualitative methods, including non-participant observation of interactions between applicants and staff members, and in-depth, semi-structured interviews with program staff members, legal aid attorneys, and advocates. Observations took place at Program A over several months in 2009 and 2010, and at Program B from December 2013 to August 2014.[62] Observations were recorded in field notes,[63] which were later analyzed and coded to identify recurring themes, patterns, and topics for further analysis. The goal was to uncover the ways in which institutional dynamics shape the activities of the programs.[64] Specifically, what is the nature of interactions between staff members and applicants, and how does this relate to the organization of work within the programs? More broadly, how do program activities relate to larger advocacy systems for survivors? And in what ways are these self-help programs involved in creating "the law in action?"[65] Below, the study results are analyzed in relation to the goals and principles of empowerment. As suggested by the title of the section, despite the aspirations of participants, the services at these programs did not meet the criteria suggested by even the thinnest conceptions of empowerment.

V. Self-Help Legal Services as Disempowerment

A. Limiting Access to Legal Remedies

For domestic violence survivors, empowerment occurs in part through gaining access to existing legal remedies—especially those relating to obtaining financial support and restitution from abusers. Yet both programs in this study failed to assist applicants with important economic remedies. Neither program provided any assistance with applications for child support, which the judge could order as part of an extended order of protection. Program A also failed to assist with applications for spousal support, although such orders are available through that jurisdiction's protection order process. Additionally, although orders that the adverse party pay restitution and attorney fees to the applicant were available in both locations, staff members at Program A failed to inform applicants about these remedies. At Program B, where applicants filled out their own forms, the application form contained information about restitution; however, the form said nothing about the availability of attorney fees, and staff members routinely failed to inform applicants that fees were available. These failures of assistance meant that applicants who qualified for support, restitution, or attorney fees would either never learn of these remedies or would need to return to court on another day to complete and file the paperwork supporting their request. Moreover, because the paperwork was not served with the initial protection order application, the hearing on economic issues would have to be continued to allow the adverse party time to respond. Consequently, an applicant would possibly have to incur the expense and inconvenience of multiple trips to court, and any orders requiring payment of economic remedies would be delayed.

Program staff members also limited access to remedies by turning away some applicants and by actively discouraging applicants from seeking disfavored remedies. For example, an applicant from Program A who discovered the availability of restitution after submitting her application returned to ask if she could add a request for reimbursement of costs related to the abuse. Staff members tried to dissuade her from amending her form by arguing that the judge would disapprove of such a request. Despite the existence of a statutory right to restitution, they counseled that restitution was at odds with protecting people, which they opined was the judges' main concern. In this context, they urged, only seeking money needed "for basic survival" was appropriate. When the applicant expressed disbelief and frustration that she could be prevented from seeking relief that was available to her but about which she had not been informed, the staff members simply refused to discuss it further or to contact their supervisor for more information.

Staff members also discouraged applicants who they believed had weak claims from applying. They sometimes did this directly by stating their opinion that they did not believe an order would be granted based on the facts. For example, a staff member at Program A was overheard telling an applicant, "I can guarantee you are not going to get a TPO for something that happened one year ago." They also discouraged applicants in less direct ways. For example, at Program A, staff members sometimes withdrew one-on-one assistance from what they perceived as weak claims, telling the applicants they were too busy to help them with the forms. They also communicated their belief a claim was weak through questioning that emphasized the absence of facts, especially about physical violence.[66] These techniques might not dissuade an applicant from applying, but were likely to be influential given the probability that staff members were perceived as possessing greater knowledge of the court process and decision-makers.[67]

Other features of these programs restricted access to legal remedies as well. Both programs had limited, daytime-only hours. Program A only took applicants for about three hours each day; Program B took applicants for a longer period but stopped taking new applicants several hours before closing, regardless of capacity. The problem of limited hours at these programs was exacerbated by the absence of childcare, which further limited accessibility for applicants with young children. Additionally, both programs had problems providing translation services to applicants who were not proficient in English. Especially at Program B, applicants who needed a translator routinely had to wait longer for assistance. Further, unassisted applicants were not given any resources, even when they were visibly in distress. On several occasions, crying and frightened would-be applicants were simply told to come back the next business day.

B. Restricting Agency

By limiting applicants' access to remedies, staff members also restricted applicants' ability to exercise basic conceptions of agency. Staff members' failure to inform applicants of the availability of remedies obviously limits their ability to make informed and meaningful decisions about legal action. Yet staff members justified decisions to withhold this information with rationales based on protecting applicants. For example, staff members at both programs explained that they did not tell applicants about the availability of attorney fees because if the applicant asked for fees then the adverse party might make the same request and the judge might order them against the applicant.[68] As a practical matter, however, the absence of requests for fees might also prevent some applicants from obtaining a lawyer. If the case was strong and the adverse party was employed, a private attorney might be willing to take the case in hopes of having their fees awarded. But without the knowledge that an order for fees was possible, the applicant might never seek counsel. In any case, the ability of the applicant to weigh these issues and risks was eliminated by the patronizing decision to withhold information.

Similarly, staff members at Program B did not inform applicants that they could seek an order that the adverse party relinquish any guns in their possession. Obtaining such an order is important in the state where Program B is located because there is no mandatory prohibition on gun possession for individuals who are subject to a protection order in that state. Here, the rationale given for not informing the applicant about the availability of such an order was that requesting gun relinquishment might enrage the adverse party and put the applicant at greater risk of additional abuse. Further, there is a question on the application form about whether guns are implicated in the abuse. Administrators reasoned that if applicants provide supporting facts in response to this question, judges will make the order on their own initiative. This reasoning makes dangerous assumptions about what information applicants will provide in response to the prompt, as well how judges will respond, and makes such orders susceptible to due process challenges. Because the presence of guns dramatically increases the risk of serious injury or death in a domestic violence incident,[69] discussing the availability of orders concerning guns is key to lethality assessment and safety planning with applicants.[70] Moreover, if applicants do not request orders for gun relinquishment, then they cannot object if the court fails to grant the order. Thus, an avenue for systemic reform is foreclosed in the event of a problem. Additionally, as with undisclosed financial remedies, withholding this information severely curtails applicants' ability to participate in the decision-making process about their legal needs and how to best meet them.

C. Discouraging the Development of Political Consciousness

The political consciousness of feminist, multidimensional empowerment is inherently counter-hegemonic. It involves learning to understand the often invisible operation of power in everyday life and its role in maintaining subordination. It also includes the insight that one is not alone. Staff members at Programs A and B behaved in ways likely to discourage the development of such insights by treating applicants in an un-empathetic and bureaucratic fashion and by responding negatively to applicants' attempts at self-assertion and self-advocacy.

Specifically, staff members most often treated applicants in a routinized and mechanical manner rather than addressing their individual needs and concerns.[71] This included dispensing generic instructions and advice about the protection order process without screening applicants to determine whether the relief was suitable to their circumstances. For example, at Program B, particularly if it was busy, applicants were screened to determine whether the adverse party was in jail. If the adverse party was in custody, the applicant was redirected to apply for an emergency protection order through a separate process. There was no effort to determine if the applicant would prefer an emergency order, which—while available on an expedited basis—would be in effect for a shorter period than an order obtained in the normal course, and would require a subsequent trip to court to seek an extension. Similarly, applicants were routinely instructed to document the abuse in reverse chronological order and to focus on the recent past, which may make many abuse scenarios hard to recognize—especially stalking or abuse that is episodic in nature.[72]

Staff members' routine failure to provide applicants with appropriate referrals to services and practice of turning applicants away hours before closing even when the program was not busy are examples of treatment that was perfunctory, bureaucratic, and failed to extend dignity and respect to the applicants. Ironically, the most negative treatment by staff members was reserved for applicants who advocated for themselves. Applicants who persisted in seeking disfavored remedies like restitution, or who resisted staff members' admonishments about the weaknesses of their claims, were subject to increasingly disdainful and harsh treatment.[73] In contrast, applicants who responded to staff members in a passive or compliant manner received more positive treatment, even if it was only superficially supportive.[74]

Notably, staff members claimed that their services were "neutral"; they believed that claims were not evaluated for merit and all applicants were treated alike. The administrator of the DVSO partner at Program B indicated that this treatment distinguished self-help advocates from traditional advocates, who evaluated whether clients were victims of abuse. She and staff members at both programs claimed that if the applicant met the criteria for a protection order application (e.g., there was abuse within a qualifying relationship), assistance was available. However, the exchanges observed between staff members and applicants showed that the perception of neutrality was unfounded. Not only did staff members treat applicants differently, the variations in their treatment correspond with the "perfect victim" trope, which characterizes worthy victims as passive and compliant and victims who resist as unworthy.[75] By treating applicants who advocated for themselves more negatively, staff members reinforced rather than challenged these pervasive stereotypes.[76] Even if applicants were unaware of how staff members behaved toward other applicants, their treatment by staff members was unlikely to advance the empowerment goals of developing an awareness of one's oppression and its social and political nature. Indeed, the overall message seemingly sent to many applicants was that they were not worthy, important, or a priority.

The structure of these programs also inhibited the development of a counter-hegemonic political consciousness for applicants by isolating them within individual, case-oriented modes of service delivery. Group interactions and opportunities for storytelling such as those practiced within the early battered women's movement are well recognized as critical to the development of political consciousness. Indeed, feminist consciousness-raising is a quintessential example of the ways in which talking with others who share a subordinated status can lead to the formation of community and an awakened political consciousness.[77] Similarly, lawyers and others working in the social justice tradition incorporate opportunities for group work and group education into their practices to facilitate the development of this critical aspect of empowerment.[78] However, neither of these programs used techniques such as group work in the application process. Volunteer staff members at Program A reported that group work had been used there in the past when a shelter organization ran the program. Staff members reported that applicants had sat together in a circle and completed the application forms with an advocate. After the LAO took over, the program moved to one-on-one assistance. One staff member who had worked under the old model expressed frustration with the current format, which she believed was less efficient and resulted in fewer people getting assistance. Although she favored the group format for efficiency reasons, it would—unlike one-on-one services—tend to encourage the kind of sharing associated with expanding political consciousness.

The development of a counter-hegemonic political consciousness was also curtailed by staff member instructions that limited applicants' narratives of abuse. As described above, applicants were encouraged to focus on physical abuse, although this might discourage applicants who were experiencing other forms of abuse from reporting those incidents. They were also encouraged (especially at Program B) to use a chronological format and focus on recent events, although that might make their narratives less intelligible to the court. In these ways, limiting applicant narratives risked restricting their access to remedies tailored to their situations and safety needs. However, narratives of victimization and survival also have a broader purpose. The protection order process is an opportunity for applicants to tell their stories and to be heard, which may be more important to the survivor than the outcome of the protection order application.[79] Moreover, the application process provides judges with the opportunity to hear stories of abuse that might challenge limited or preconceived notions of abuse and victimization. Ultimately, this might result in a broader spectrum of abuse being recognized as a basis for protection.[80] While staff members may have sought to help applicants shape their stories into forms the court would recognize, they did so in ways that failed to involve applicants in the decision-making process in a meaningful way. Thus, both the applicants and the court were deprived of opportunities for expanding political awareness.

D. Undermining Advocacy Resources

As a practical matter, empowerment requires an objective toward which the process of empowerment is directed. Yet these programs seemingly lacked a vision for substantive change, leading to design weaknesses that diminished advocacy resources and negatively impacted services. For example, both programs promoted themselves as providing advocacy on their websites and in other materials, and partnered in various ways with domestic violence advocates. But their work processes focused nearly exclusively on completing forms. This rendered other assistance—such as safety planning or referrals—peripheral, and likely contributed to the often bureaucratic nature of staff members' demeanor.[81] Additionally, the work environments at both programs lacked privacy. Combined with the lack of childcare, the programs were often crowded and noisy— conditions that inhibited the sharing of sensitive information as well as the development of intimacy or a sense of connection between applicants and staff. Inadequate translation services further diminished the ability of staff members to serve and connect with non-English-speaking applicants, and potentially fueled alienation toward them.[82] Lack of ongoing training on domestic violence issues, inadequate supervision, and a lack of support for the vicarious trauma that can result from working with abuse survivors also likely negatively impacted staff members' ability to provide appropriate support to applicants.[83]

The programs also undermined the development of advocacy resources in the larger community by failing to link self-help services to systemic advocacy or law reform efforts. At Program B, for example, lack of a partnership with a legal aid organization prevented a systemic approach.[84] Moreover, the partnering DVSO had no administrative or programmatic authority, which limited its ability to provide more substantive advocacy services or effectively challenge problematic practices. At Program A, the partnering LAO had primary responsibility for the program, but its leadership prioritized other practice areas over family law, which it saw as unrelated to important systemic change. Therefore, it directed only minimal organizational resources to the program. Additionally, Program A relegated its volunteers who were experienced lay advocates to simply filling out forms, and so did not benefit from the expertise of volunteers who remained from the shelter organization that had previously run the program. These circumstances allowed the court to dominate both partnerships. Furthermore, it also worked to further weaken or lessen existing advocacy resources. At Program A, the legal aid-court partnership replaced a model that was in some respects more effective, in that it assisted more people and used methods associated with counter-hegemonic consciousness. At Program B, DVSO advocates were marooned, separated from education and support they would have received at the DVSO. Meanwhile, their presence in the program siphoned resources from the DVSO.[85]

VI. Implications and Conclusions

The concept of empowerment suggests a continuum of experiences, a process as well as a destination. In this context, the potential for self-help legal services to be empowering can also be viewed as existing on a continuum. Drawing on the concepts of empowerment reviewed in this chapter, Figure 3.2 depicts some possible points of reference on this continuum. On the left are characteristics of a program informed by multidimensional empowerment; on the right are their opposites.

The self-help programs examined for this study fit neatly into the disempowerment side of the continuum. While many applicants who went to these programs for assistance received some form of services, others were turned away or discouraged from filing their applications. Moreover, even those who filed were treated in ways that reinforced negative stereotypes. None received complete information about their legal rights, much less assistance in contextualizing and understanding the nature of abuse or mobilizing for collective action. In the absence of a program design informed by a vision for substantive change, staff members focused on completing paperwork rather than empowering survivors. As a result, these programs redirected scarce resources from partnering organizations that may have been better utilized elsewhere.

This study also has limitations. It was conducted at two locations, so the pervasiveness of these problems remains unknown. It could be that other programs do not share these issues or present different problems. However, the similarity of results in two programs with different histories and types of partnerships, along with the expanding nature of

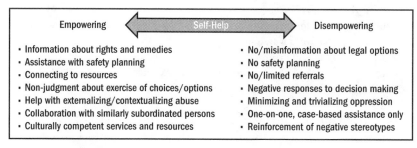

Figure 3.2. Self-Help Empowerment Continuum

self-help legal services, suggests the importance of more research. This should include research about the impact of self-help services on legal consciousness, which was not part of this study and is clearly needed. This requires tracing the ways in which institutions shape power, including specific understandings about abuse, law, and legal rights, and the sense of personal efficacy necessary to use law—not just to file forms but to challenge power relations.[86] Additionally, reformers, advocates, and scholar-activists would do well to look to multidimensional empowerment principles as they seek ways to reinvigorate access-to-justice practices for gender violence survivors.

Author's Note

I am grateful to UNLV for supporting this research with a generous Faculty Opportunity Award in 2013–14, and to Dean Daniel Hamilton and the Boyd School of Law for ongoing research support. Thank you also to Danielle Barraza, Chrislove Igeleke, Amy Mangus, and Brittnie Watkins for excellent research assistance.

NOTES

1 *See* Adele M. Morrison, *Changing the Domestic Violence (Dis)Course: Moving from White Victim to Multi-Cultural Survivor*, 39 UC DAVIS L. REV. 1061, 1087 (2006) (referring to this process as an "empowerment continuum"). The trajectory from victim to advocate is still a common theme in the anti-gender violence movement, and testimonials about it dot the internet landscape. *See, e.g.,* Meghan Mausteller, *From Victim to Survivor to Advocate,* BREAK THE SILENCE AGAINST DOMESTIC VIOLENCE (January 16, 2017), www.breakthesilencedv. org; *Victim to Survivor to Certified Advocate!,* WEAVE, www.weaveinc.org.

2 *See* Elizabeth L. MacDowell, *Reimagining Access to Justice in the Poor People's Courts,* 22 GEO. J. ON POVERTY L. & POL'Y 473, 510–26 (2015) [hereinafter MacDowell, *Reimagining Access to Justice*] (detailing the key features of empowerment-informed advocacy in the social justice lawyering, social work, and lay victim advocacy traditions).

3 *Id.* at 507–10 (describing how conventional access to justice efforts can reinforce hegemonic power relations, including in domestic violence cases).

4 *See* Elizabeth L. MacDowell, *Domestic Violence and the Politics of Self-Help,* 22 WM. & MARY J. WOMEN & L. 203, 207–09 (2016) [hereinafter MacDowell, *Politics of Self-Help*] (establishing a new and expanded typology of demeanor and its impacts on abuse survivors in self-help settings); Elizabeth L. MacDowell, *From Victims to Litigants,* 67 HASTINGS L. J. 1299 (2016) [hereinafter MacDowell,

From Victims to Litigants] (analyzing how the organization of work in self-help programs impacts survivors and advocacy systems).

5 One study of court-community partnerships to provide self-help services in California found that almost two-thirds of people using the services in the study were women, and at least 58% were minorities. ADMIN. OFFICE OF THE COURTS CTR. FOR FAMILIES, CHILDREN & THE COURTS, EQUAL ACCESS FUND: A REPORT TO THE CALIFORNIA LEGISLATURE 54 (2005). In New York City, a survey of unrepresented family court litigants found 45% of respondents were women, 84% were minorities (48% African American and 31% Hispanic), 39% had only a high school–level education, and 53% earned less than $20,000 per year. OFFICE OF THE DEPUTY CHIEF ADMIN. JUDGE FOR JUSTICE INITIA-TIVES, SELF-REPRESENTED LITIGANTS: CHARACTERISTICS, NEEDS, SERVICES: THE RESULTS OF TWO SURVEYS 1, 3–4 (2005).

6 See NAT'L CTR. FOR STATE COURTS, A DIRECTORY OF COURT-BASED SELF HELP PROGRAMS 2 (2006), http://ncsc.contentdm.oclc.org [http://perma.cc/P463-KHJP] (providing a directory of approximately 150 self-help programs in the United States). The American Bar Association estimates that 3.7 million people in the United States use self-help centers annually. AM. BAR ASS'N STANDING COMM. ON THE DELIVERY OF LEGAL SERV.S, THE SELF-HELP CENTER CENSUS: A NATIONAL SURVEY (Aug. 2014).

7 Thus, while personal agency (or autonomy) is sometimes used interchangeably with empowerment, here it is but one aspect of a larger concept of empowerment. For a thoughtful analysis of the relationship between agency and autonomy, see Kathryn Abrams, *From Autonomy to Agency: Feminist Perspectives on Self-Direction*, 40 WM. & MARY L. REV. 805 (1999).

8 SUSAN SCHECHTER, WOMEN AND MALE VIOLENCE: THE VISIONS AND STRUGGLES OF THE BATTERED WOMEN'S MOVEMENT 109 (1982).

9 *Id.*

10 *Id.* This is not to say that all movement participants holding these views understood themselves as feminist and the battered women's movement as a primarily political project. There was also significant diversity of viewpoint among feminists. *See id.* at 43–52; Ellen Pence, *Advocacy on Behalf of Battered Women, in* SOURCEBOOK ON VIOLENCE AGAINST WOMEN 329, 332 (Claire M. Renzetti et al. eds., 2D ED. 2001).

11 Andrea J. Nichols, *Meaning-Making and Domestic Violence Victim Advocacy: An Examination of Feminist Identities, Ideologies, and Practices*, 8 FEMINIST CRIMINOLOGY 177, 178 (2013).

12 SCHECHTER, *supra* note 8, at 110 (discussing the role of support groups in politicizing women).

13 Nichols, *supra* note 11.

14 *See* ELIZABETH PLECK, DOMESTIC TYRANNY: THE MAKING OF AMERICAN SOCIAL POLICY AGAINST FAMILY VIOLENCE FROM COLONIAL TIMES TO THE PRESENT 182 (1987) (detailing the invisibility of domestic violence in the

twentieth century until the 1970s); ELIZABETH M. SCHNEIDER, BATTERED WOMEN & FEMINIST LAWMAKING 44 (2000) (discussing the role of feminist lawmaking in the battered women's movement).

15 See Nanette Page & Cheryl E. Czuba, *Empowerment: What Is It?*, 37 J. EXTEN-SION (Oct. 1999) (describing the multidimensional nature of empowerment).

16 See Margaret Klaw & Mary Scherf, *Feminist Advocacy: The Evolution of Penn-sylvania's Protection from Abuse Act*, 1 U. PA. J.L. & SOC. CHANGE 21 (1993) (describing "collaboration among grassroots women's advocates, legal services attorneys and sensitive legislators"); *see also* SCHECHTER, *supra* note 8, at 162–65 (describing early civil legal reforms for battered women); SCHNEIDER, *supra* note 14 (same). Pennsylvania is generally credited with passing the first domestic violence protection order legislation, as part of the Protection from Abuse Act, now codified at 23 PA. CONS. STAT. ANN. §§ 6101–6122 (West 2015). Protection orders are also known as restraining orders in some states.

17 Interview with Barbara Hart, Director of Strategic Justice Initiatives and Director of Law and Policy, Violence Against Women Initiatives, Muskie School of Public Service, Cutler Institute for Health and Social Policy, University of Southern Maine (Nov. 21, 2013) [hereinafter Hart Interview] (describing motives for seeking passage of first protection order statutes).

18 *Id.* These included "peace bonds," which have been described as "essentially unenforceable." Klaw & Scherf, *supra* note 16, at 21. *See also* SCHECHTER, *supra* note 8, at 162 ("As of 1981, twelve states still granted such injunctions pending only divorce, separation, or custody proceedings.").

19 SCHECHTER, *supra* note 8, at 162 (noting that many women only want the abuse to stop, not to separate from their husbands). *See also id.* at 163 (observing that, absent access to civil protection orders, unmarried women were relegated to criminal remedies); Hart Interview, *supra* note 17.

20 See Klaw & Scherf, *supra* note 16, at 23 ("Filing a civil suit is fundamentally different from pursuing a criminal prosecution because the woman is the plaintiff and is in control of how the case is litigated or settled."); Elizabeth L. MacDowell, *When Courts Collide: Integrated Domestic Violence Courts and Court Pluralism*, 20 TEX. J. WOMEN & L. 95 (2011) [hereinafter MacDowell, *When Courts Collide*] (contrasting the autonomy available through civil as opposed to criminal remedies for domestic violence).

21 Hart Interview, *supra* note 17; SCHECHTER, *supra* note 8, at 163.

22 Klaw & Scherf, *supra* note 16, at 21.

23 See Catherine F. Klein & Leslye E. Orloff, *Providing Legal Protection for Battered Women: An Analysis of State Statutes and Case Law*, 21 HOFSTRA L. REV. 801, 910–1006 (1993) (describing remedies available under civil protective orders in various states). For a state-by-state summary of protection order laws, see WOM-ENSLAW.ORG, www.womenslaw.org.

24 Sally F. Goldfarb, *Reconceiving Civil Protection Orders for Domestic Violence: Can Law Help End the Abuse Without Ending the Relationship?*, 29 CARDOZO L. REV.

1487, 1489 (2008); *See also* Susan Keilitz, *Improving Promises and Risks of Integrated Case Management and Technology Solutions, in* HANDBOOK OF DOMESTIC VIOLENCE INTERVENTION STRATEGIES 147, 149 (Albert R. Roberts ed., 2002) (reporting that survivors are more likely to file for a civil protection order than to file criminal charges).

25 *See* Sally Merry Engle, *Rights Talk and the Experience of Law: Implementing Women's Human Rights to Protection from Violence*, 25 HUM. RTS. Q. 343, 345 (2003).

26 *See* MacDowell, *Politics of Self-Help, supra* note 4, at 216–19 (reviewing the structural and systemic barriers to access to justice for survivors).

27 *See* Jane K. Stoever, *Freedom from Violence: Using the Stages of Change Model to Realize the Promise of Civil Protection Orders*, 72 OHIO ST. L.J. 303, 322–32 (2011) (describing the multiple stages a survivor is likely to go through to address relationship violence over time).

28 *See* Nichols, *supra* note 11, at 179; *see also* JAMES PTACEK, BATTERED WOMEN IN THE COURTROOM: THE POWER OF JUDICIAL RESPONSES 92–111, 177 (1999) (describing the positive role that advocates play for survivors).

29 SCHECHTER, *supra* note 8, at 243; *see also* KRISTIN BUMILLER, IN AN ABUSIVE STATE: HOW NEOLIBERALISM APPROPRIATED THE FEMINIST MOVEMENT AGAINST SEXUAL VIOLENCE 70 (2008) ("Currently, as part of the process of making battered women's shelters more professional, a mandate exists for changing the primary methods by which shelters work—requiring them to move away from encouraging women's transformation through consciousness raising to a more service oriented model that involves administrating clients' needs.").

30 *See* Pence, *supra* note 10, at 339.

31 BUMILLER, *supra* note 29, at 97–98. *See also* Pence, *supra* note 10, at 339 (noting that, as "women coming into shelters became clients [and] advocates became counselors . . . the distinction between the shelter programs and the institutions that regulate women's lives became far less pronounced").

32 *See* MacDowell, *When Courts Collide, supra* note 20, at 119–21 (describing the ways in which a survivor's level of "choice" about accessing civil courts, and level of control once engaged with the court, is conscribed).

33 *See* L. Thomas Winfree Jr. & Christina DeJong, *Police and the War on Women: A Gender-Linked Examination Behind and In Front of the Blue Curtain*, 25 WOMEN & CRIM. JUST. 50, 60 (2015) (concluding that mandatory arrest policies may result in women who fight back being arrested for domestic violence); *see also* LEIGH GOODMARK, A TROUBLED MARRIAGE: DOMESTIC VIOLENCE AND THE LEGAL SYSTEM 113 (2011) ("Hard no drop policies [allowing prosecutors to pursue a case without the survivor's consent] clearly prioritize safety over all other aims, including fostering the agency of women subjected to abuse, and assume that safety can be achieved through prosecution.").

34 *See also* Judith Resnik, *Asking about Gender in Courts*, 21 SIGNS 952 (1996) (bibliography of task force reports). *See generally* Jeannette F. Swent, *Gender Bias at*

the Heart of Justice: An Empirical Study of State Task Forces, 6 S. CAL. REV. L. & WOMEN'S STUD. 1 (1996) (summarizing findings of gender bias from reports of over thirty state court task forces).

35 Survivors seeking custody in states with a presumption in favor of joint custody, and favoring the parent perceived by the court as more open to shared parenting, fare especially poorly when raising abuse claims. *See* Allison C. Morrill et al., *Child Custody and Visitation Decisions When the Father Has Perpetrated Violence Against the Mother*, 11 VIOLENCE AGAINST WOMEN 1076, 1101 (2005) (noting that such presumptions penalize survivors who seek to limit the abusive parent's custody or visitation). But even in states with no presumption for joint custody and with a statutory presumption against awarding custody to batterers, 40% of batterers were still awarded joint custody. *Id.* at 1101.

36 *See generally* Suzanne A. Kim, *Reconstructing Family Privacy*, 57 HASTINGS L.J. 557 (2005) (discussing the punitive impacts of child welfare systems on domestic abuse survivors).

37 In many family courts, 80% or more of litigants are unrepresented. *See* JOHN M. GREACEN, SELF REPRESENTED LITIGANTS AND COURT AND LEGAL SERVICES RESPONSES TO THEIR NEEDS: WHAT WE KNOW 3–6 (2002), www.courts.ca.gov.

38 A study of the thirty-five states with the highest proportion of limited English proficiency (LEP) individuals found that 46% allow courts to deny litigants access to interpreters in some or all civil cases. *See* Laura Abel, *Language Access in State Courts* 1 (Brennan Ctr. for Justice ed., 2009). Eighty percent of these states allow courts to charge LEP litigants for interpreters, despite federal prohibitions on this practice. *Id.* at 1, 17–19.

39 *See* LEGAL SERVS. CORP., DOCUMENTING THE JUSTICE GAP IN AMERICA: THE CURRENT UNMET CIVIL NEEDS OF LOW INCOME AMERICANS 2–3 (2009) (showing that fewer than one in five low-income individuals get the legal help they need); *see also* Rebekah Diller & Emily Savner, *A Call to End Federal Restrictions On Legal Aid For The Poor* 3–4 (Brennan Ctr. for Justice ed., 2009) (describing restrictions on practice by legal aid organizations receiving federal funds).

40 *See* Laura Beth Nielsen & Catherine R. Albiston, *The Organization of Public Interest Practice: 1975–2004*, 84 N.C. L. REV. 1591, 1618 (2006) (reporting that most federally funded public interest law offices focus on individual services, not social change).

41 Pence, *supra* note 10, at 337, 339.

42 *See* Beth E. Richie, *A Black Feminist Reflection on the Anti-Violence Movement*, 25 SIGNS 1133; Andrea Smith et al., *The Color of Violence: Introduction, in* INCITE! WOMEN OF COLOR AGAINST VIOLENCE 1–10 (2006).

43 *See* Kimberlé Crenshaw, *Mapping the Margins: Intersectionality, Identity Politics, and Violence Against Women of Color*, 43 STAN. L. REV. 1241, 1245–50 (1991) (describing failures of the anti-gender violence movement to address the intersection of race and gender).

44 *See* Nichols, *supra* note 11 (reporting study findings showing that advocates who do not identify as feminists lack an understanding of how identity relates to their clients' victimization and are less likely to see the need for structural change to address gender violence).

45 *Cf.* Morrison, *supra* note 1, at 1072 (describing domestic violence "(dis)course" as a vehicle for women to speak their truth, but also as exclusionary).

46 *See* SCHECHTER, *supra* note 8, at 109.

47 GERALD P. LOPEZ, REBELLIOUS LAWYERING: ONE CHICANO'S VISION OF PROGRESSIVE LAW PRACTICE 73 (1992).

48 *See* Russell Engler, *And Justice for All—Including the Unrepresented Poor: Revisiting the Roles of the Judges, Mediators, and Clerks*, 67 FORDHAM L. REV. 1987, 1987 (1999).

49 *See* JUDICIAL COUNCIL OF CALIFORNIA TASK FORCE ON SELF-REPRESENTED LITIGANTS, STATEWIDE ACTION PLAN FOR SERVING SELF-REPRESENTED LITIGANTS 1 (2004) ("Court-based staffed self-help centers, supervised by attorneys, are the optimum way for courts to facilitate the timely and cost-effective processing of cases involving self-represented litigants, to increase access to the courts and improve delivery of justice to the public.").

50 Peter Gabel & Paul Harris, *Building Power and Breaking Images: Critical Legal Theory and the Practice of Law*, 11 NYU REV. L. & SOC. CHANGE 369, 397 (1982–1983).

51 *See also* Jessica Steinberg, *In Pursuit of Justice?: Case Outcomes and the Delivery of Unbundled Legal Services*, 28 GEO. J. ON POVERTY L. & POL'Y 453, 472–74, 482–96 (2001) (discussing previous studies and reporting a comparison of outcomes for unlawful detainer defendants receiving either unbundled legal services from Legal Aid attorneys, full representation from Stanford clinical law students, or no assistance). *See generally* THE EMPIRICAL RESEARCH GROUP: UCLA SCHOOL OF LAW, EVALUATION OF THE VAN NUYS LEGAL SELF-HELP CENTER FINAL REPORT (2001) [hereinafter FINAL REPORT], http:// courts.ca.gov (evaluating services for unrepresented litigants in unlawful detainer and family law matters provided by the Van Nuys Self-Help Center in Van Nuys, California); Michael Millemann et al., *Rethinking the Full-Service Legal Representational Model: A Maryland Experiment*, 30 CLEARINGHOUSE REV. 1178 (1997) (reporting on a study of litigant satisfaction with one-time advice sessions on family law matters with clinical law students from the University of Maryland and the University of Baltimore). I am not including studies of services not characterized as self-help, e.g., legal assistance provided by lay advocates for their clients in shelters, or by institutional advocates working with district attorneys or law enforcement outside of a court partnership.

52 *See* Richard L. Abel, *Law Without Politics: Legal Aid Under Advanced Capitalism*, 32 UCLA L. REV. 474, 577 (1985) (identifying legal aid attorneys as gatekeepers); *see also* Shonna L. Trinch, *The Advocate as Gatekeeper: The Limits of Politeness in Protection Order Interviews with Latina Survivors of Domestic Abuse*, 5 J.

SOCIOLINGUISTICS 475, 476–77 (2001) (discussing the gatekeeping function of advocates who are also institutional service providers).

53 *See* Shonna Trinch & Susan Berk-Seligson, *Narrating in Protective Order Interviews: A Source of Interactional Trouble*, 31 LANGUAGE IN SOC'Y 383, 385 (2002) (discussing the preference within the legal system for linear narratives).

54 To maintain their confidentiality, the programs and persons who participated in this study are not identified.

55 After the data collection period, this was reduced to one staff member due to budget reductions.

56 In 2009, an average of 78% of people who filed a protection order after receiving services at Program A were women; 86.5% were racial/ethnic minorities. Based on data collected at Program B in 2012, protection order applicants were more than four times as likely to be women than men; less than half were white.

57 In 2009, 53% of applicants at Program A spoke a language other than English as a preferred language, and only 26% had attended some college; less than 13% had a college degree. The links between educational attainment and income disparity suggest this group had a relatively low average income. Similar data was not available for Program B.

58 Based on 2009 data drawn from new protection order cases filed at each program location in four one-week periods.

59 Based on 2012 data.

60 Applying for a protection order is a two-step process: First, the applicant files an application form containing allegations of abuse and requested relief. The judge determines whether a temporary protection order (TPO) should be issued without a hearing, usually "ex parte"—without notice to the adverse party. Second, the case is set for a hearing to determine—after notice to the adverse party—whether a lengthier order should be issued.

61 The form does not specify whether no advocate-victim/survivor relationship is established, but arguably this is implied. The state where Program A is located has a qualified privilege for communications between survivors and domestic violence advocates who have completed requisite training. Therefore, survivors using Program A may be waiving a statutory protection otherwise available to them.

62 Observation data totaling eighty-four hours were transcribed from collections in 2009 and 2010 at Program A, and from December 2013 to August 2014 at Program B. An additional 150 hours of data collected from the protection order courtroom and lobby areas outside the courtroom associated with Program B were also transcribed. Observations at Program B were conducted until no new variations were observed. This data was consistent with observation data from Program A.

63 Field notes were recorded in the field using techniques designed not to influence or interrupt observations, such as recording surreptitiously at opportune moments. Notes were augmented if necessary after leaving the field. *See*

W. LAWRENCE NEUMAN, SOCIAL RESEARCH METHODS: QUALITATIVE
AND QUANTITATIVE APPROACHES 443–49 (2009).

64 This study fits into the field of institutional ethnography. *See generally* Marjorie
L. Devault, *Introduction: What is Institutional Ethnography?*, 53 SOC. PROBS.
294 (2006) (describing the field of institutional ethnography). Using texts and
discourses as a starting point, institutional ethnographers seek to uncover how
organizational work process shape the activities and conditions of the every-
day world. For examples, *see* ELIZABETH TOWNSEND, GOOD INTENTIONS
OVERRULED: A CRITIQUE OF EMPOWERMENT IN THE ROUTINE ORGA-
NIZATION OF HEALTH SERVICES (1998); Jane M. Sadusky et al., *The Praxis
Safety and Accountability Audit: Practicing a "Sociology for People,"* 16 VIOLENCE
AGAINST WOMEN, 1031 (2010).

65 *See, e.g.,* Roscoe Pound, *Law in Books and Law in Action*, 44 AM. L. REV. 12, 12–15
(1910).

66 For example, an advocate at Program A repeatedly asked an applicant (who was
reporting voluminous sexual texts messages and unannounced visits to her home
by the adverse party) in a dubious tone, "There hasn't been any violence? But what
about physical violence?"

67 Although no data on this issue was collected systematically at these programs,
other research indicates self-help customers are likely to be first-time court goers.
See, e.g., FINAL REPORT, *supra* note 51, at 3 (reporting that most people using the
self-help center were first-time visitors with no prior court experience).

68 At Program B, this point was reiterated by an administrator at the partnering
DVSO. The pervasive nature of this view may explain why the availability of fees
was omitted from the application form in that jurisdiction as well.

69 *See, e.g.,* Linda L. Dahlberg, Robin M. Ikeda, & Marcie-jo Kresnow, *Guns in
the Home and Risk of a Violent Death in the Home: Findings from a National
Study*, 160 AM. J. EPIDEMIOLOGY 929 (2004) (finding that presence of a gun
in the home is associated with increased risk of firearm-related homicide and
suicide).

70 The only information about safety planning was provided by Program B, where
applicants who had their application reviewed by an advocate were given a hand-
out with the contact information for a local shelter and tips for developing a safety
plan. There was no assistance with safety planning at either program. *See* Stoever,
supra note 27, at 346–53.

71 *See* MacDowell, *Politics of Self-Help*, *supra* note 4, at 236–38 (describing this behavior as bureaucratic demeanor).

72 The application forms at both locations also prompted a reverse chronological
order. However, staff members at Program A typically bypassed this section of
the form and drafted a declaration in a separate document that was later attached
to the application. *See* Deborah M. Weissman, *Gender-Based Violence as Judicial
Anomaly: Between "The Truly National and the Truly Local,"* 42 B.C. L. REV.
1081, 1129 (2001) (describing how forms help reduce domestic violence claims "to

quasi-legal experiences which reinforce the legal system's propensity to prevent them from being presented as formal legal claims at all").

73 *See* MacDowell, *Politics of Self-Help, supra* note 4, at 239–44 (describing staff members' firm or formal, harsh, and patronizing/condescending demeanor).

74 *See id.* at 235–36 (describing token supportive demeanor). *See also id.* at 244–45 (describing the regulatory function of demeanor in the self-help setting).

75 *See* Morrison, *supra* note 1, at 1078–80 (describing the perfect victim trope as a passive, white, heterosexual, and female).

76 *See* MacDowell, *Politics of Self-Help, supra* note 4, at 246 (detailing the inverse relationship between favorable treatment by staff members and applicants' self-advocacy, and its relationship to stereotypes).

77 *See* CATHERINE A. MACKINNON, TOWARD A FEMINIST THEORY OF THE STATE 83–90 (1989) (describing feminist consciousness-raising as a method for perceiving the socially constructed nature of reality).

78 *See* MacDowell, *Reimagining Access to Justice, supra* note 2, at 513 (discussing the use of group work in social justice lawyering traditions).

79 *See* Trinch & Berk-Seligson, *supra* note 53, at 497 (noting how service providers may make survivors' narratives more palatable to judges but frustrate survivors' desire to be heard).

80 *See* Leigh Goodmark, *When Is a Battered Woman Not a Battered Woman? When She Fights Back,* 20 YALE J. L. & FEMINISM 75, 123 (2008) (advocating for finding ways to help abuse survivors tell new narratives and challenge stereotypes).

81 *See* Jill Adams, *The Civil Restraining Order Application Process: Textually Mediated Institutional Case Management,* 10 ETHNOGRAPHY 185, 202–3 (2009) (discussing how the organization of work can limit court personnel's ability to empathize with litigants).

82 *See* MacDowell, *From Victims to Litigants, supra* note 4, at 1321 (reporting that staff members' inability to understand an applicant of limited English proficiency seemingly triggered condescending behavior).

83 *Id.* at 1321–22.

84 Attorneys from a local legal aid organization said they were unsuccessful in even leaving fliers for applicants at the program. Staff members never displayed or distributed them.

85 *See* MacDowell, *From Victims to Litigants, supra* note 4, at 1326–28 (applying a systems analysis to these issues).

86 *See* Susan S. Silbey, *After Legal Consciousness,* 1 ANN. REV. LAW SOC. SCI. 323, 358–61 (2005) (advocating for socially situated, critical approaches to the study of legal consciousness).

PART II

Multiple Systems, Standards, and Dilemmas

4

Battering Court Syndrome

A Structural Critique of "Failure to Protect"

ALISA BIERRIA AND COLBY LENZ

Domestic violence survivors are vulnerable to being targeted for criminalization and incarceration, and researchers have found that the majority of people in women's prisons experienced domestic and/ or sexual violence *before* incarceration.[1] Survivors become targets of policing and prosecution in part because survival action is often criminalized action, including survival strategies such as self-defense, migration to a safer location, or avoiding violence by submitting to coerced illegal activity. Prosecutors also target domestic violence survivors through "failure to protect" laws, or laws that punish survivors for "failing to protect" their children from being exposed to domestic violence or "failing" to prevent their batterers' abuse of their children.[2] "Failure to protect" convictions disproportionately punish mothers;[3] relatively few men have been convicted for this offense.[4] As a strategy, defense attorneys have argued that domestic violence is a "mitigating factor" that should be considered when evaluating whether or not to punish survivors who have "failed to protect." This "mitigating factors" strategy attempts to provide explanatory context for the "failure," while the premise that the survivor has a failure that needs defending remains unchallenged.

Considering two case studies, we argue that the "mitigating factors" approach is often ineffective as a defense for those charged with "failure to protect," ignores the political implications of prosecuting survivors for failing to predict and control their abusers' violent actions, and obscures what Beth Richie has called the "matrix of violence," or a structure in which domestic violence tethers interpersonal and institutional spheres, creating complex systems of battering in which courts are entangled and implicated. We propose Battering Court Syndrome as an alternative model that directly critiques the coupling or transference of culpability from batterer to survivor, clarifies multiple kinds of partnerships between courts and batterers, and foregrounds the role of the criminal legal system in institutionalizing domestic violence and, therefore, failing to protect survivors and their children.

Paradigm Shifts

This section proposes two paradigm shifts from much of the critical thinking on "failure to protect" laws and prosecution. First, we shift the critique of "failure to protect" from a defensive strategy that offers various reasons why survivors should not be blamed for the violence of their abusive partners to a *structural critique* that outlines how the judicial system colludes with battering through "failure to protect" prosecutions. Second, we shift the analytical paradigm for "failure to protect" from an isolated issue of individual responsibility to a *political ideology* that rests on (at least) two ideological foundations: racist heteropatriarchal constructions of "hyper-culpable motherhood," and the trend that began in the mid-90s of increasingly aggressive prosecution that maximizes incarceration.

A Structural Critique of "Failure to Protect"

Critiques of "failure to protect" laws tend to focus on four main strategies that challenge the blameworthiness of survivors when a child witnesses domestic violence or is harmed by an abusive partner. First, theorists have argued that blaming survivors for failing to protect or escape obscures the direct culpability of abusive partners.[5] Second, some discussions have advocated more complex views about survivors' agency, either explaining how survivors' agency becomes compromised due to consequences of domestic violence, such as trauma, duress, or coercive control,[6] or foregrounding how survivors exercise agency through attempts to escape or protect their children from the abuse.[7] The constructs "battered women's syndrome" and "intimate partner battering and its effects" are the most well-known examples of this kind of critique, which asserts a need for expert testimony to explain how domestic violence profoundly influences survivors' deliberations of their situation and their capacity or opportunity for possible action.[8] Third, theorists have argued that the application of "failure to protect" laws is unfair because it disproportionately punishes women,[9] and because survivors of color are particularly targeted due to racist conceptions of "genuine victimhood."[10] Finally, critics have emphasized the lack of sufficient social services and escape options available to survivors.[11] These interventions are important efforts that define a more nuanced and fraught context of violence through which survivors act, helping us to develop an understanding of the complexities of and constraints caused by domestic violence from the perspective of survivors who are also mothers. However, these interventions remain at the level of individual choice and culpability, essentially providing various explanations for why survivors should not be blamed for their abusive partners' violence against their children. Even the final critique addressing inadequate institutional support for survivors is ultimately asserted as a justification for why some survivors "fail" to protect or escape.

Beth Richie proposes a more comprehensive understanding of violence against Black women that contextualizes their experience of domestic and sexual violence within structures of state violence.[12] Her "matrix of violence" framework defines the multidimensionality of violence by proposing a typology of categories of violence and agents of violence, helping us map the nodes of connection across these category "cells." Richie contends that a Black feminist analytical approach to the matrix of violence "demands a more rigorous and in-depth analysis of how state institutions and neoliberal public policies interact with and deepen the harm caused by household and community violence."[13] An analysis of how and why survivors are criminalized by "failure to protect" prosecution must evaluate how their experiences unfold within nodes of connection between the "intimate households" and "state" cells, particularly the cell of the judicial system. A matrix model invites a structural critique of how courts "interact with and deepen the harm" of domestic violence through "failure to protect" cases. This approach should be distinguished from invoking the context of state violence as another "mitigating factor" that further explains survivors' actions. Rather, a structural critique reveals how state violence is part of a matrix that tethers court processes to battering through multiple kinds of partnerships. Therefore, we propose a paradigm shift for critiquing "failure to protect" laws that shifts our focus from "mitigating factors" that trouble individual survivor culpability to a structural critique that exposes judicial collusion with domestic violence.

"Failure to Protect" as Political Ideology

A structural critique of "failure to protect" enables an examination of what powers "failure to protect" prosecutions. "Failure to protect" laws both derive from and further entrench multiple oppressive and racist political ideologies—particularly heteropatriarchy and pro-criminalization—creating powerful ideological pressure that drives court processes, procedures, and discretionary choices. As a heteropatriarchal ideology, "failure to protect" is conspicuously gender-biased towards the punishment of women. As Jeanne Fugate argues, despite the gender-neutral terms of "failure to protect" laws, "the application of failure-to-protect laws is anything but gender-neutral: Defendants charged and convicted with failure to protect are almost exclusively female."[14] Though there is some acknowledgement that "failure to protect" relies on constructions of motherhood that promote disproportionate blame of mothers if children are harmed, gender bias in "failure to protect" prosecutions and convictions tends to be critiqued as evidence of unequal application of the law rather than an indication that the law is itself fundamentally problematic.[15] For example, theorist Sandra Chung has critiqued gender bias in the application of "failure to protect" laws, citing research that asserts, "mothers acting alone tend to be charged alone—but when fathers act alone, mothers are frequently also charged."[16] Chung strongly endorses "failure to protect" laws to ensure parental accountability, but criticizes the lack of gender neutrality in its application: prosecutors and jurors punish women too much and do not punish men enough. With no critical deconstruction of the law itself, this analysis reduces gender bias to a problem of stereotyping that can be corrected with increased self-awareness by jurors, prosecutors, and judges so that they "disregard gender" as a factor.[17]

However, even with increased judicial training about domestic violence, gender bias against mothers remains.[18] Further, Chung's proposed solution to disregard gender when enforcing "failure to protect" statutes is ultimately inadequate because the laws themselves rest on deeply entrenched gendered ideologies of motherhood. As Evelyn Nakano Glenn has argued, claims about the social expectations of mothering (such as those used to justify "failure to protect" laws) must meaningfully contend with the social and political stakes instilled in constructions of "motherhood."[19] In other words, motherhood should be understood as an *ideology*, or a system of beliefs that helps people collectively make sense of the world. Glenn provides a brief inventory of the complex ways motherhood is ideologically constructed, writing,

> Motherhood ideology certainly encompasses multiple contradictions. Mothers are romanticized as life-giving, self-sacrificing, and forgiving, and demonized as smothering, overly involved, and destructive. They are seen as all-powerful—holding the fate of their children and ultimately the future of society in their hands—and as powerless—subordinated to the dictates of nature, instinct, and social forces beyond their ken.[20]

"Failure to protect" prosecutions are both a consequence of the no-win contradictions that define mothering ideology and a juridical extension of this ideology. As an ideology itself, "failure to protect" is remarkably flexible, as prosecutors and judges have used a wide range of actions by survivors—whether understood as passive or active—as evidence of criminal mothering. Survivors have been found guilty if they do not successfully defeat their abusive partner and if they fight back, if they do not escape and if they try to escape, if they take their child to receive medical help and if they try to tend to their children themselves, if judges believe that they are genuinely victims of domestic violence and if judges believe that they are lying about the abuse. Any scenario can be manipulated back into ideological alignment in order to blame mothers for their abusers' actions. The fact that mothers are primarily targeted for prosecution, even when prosecutors recognize that fathers acted *alone*, demonstrates the resilience of "failure to protect" as an ideology based on hyper-culpable motherhood. Further, mothers who are Black, Native, trans or queer, imprisoned, immigrant, or socially marginalized in other ways are particularly vulnerable to being constructed as blameworthy, violent, deviant, criminal, unfit, illegitimate, or otherwise "failed mothers."[21]

Those who defend "failure to protect" prosecutions usually argue that these prosecutions demonstrate a commitment to the safety and well-being of children. However, despite the rhetoric, there is not much evidence demonstrating that "failure to protect" prosecutions are driven by an institutional commitment to the safety of children, nor could we find data suggesting that "failure to protect" prosecutions prevent domestic violence–related child abuse. These prosecutions are not followed by a corresponding increase in funding for services that strengthen survivors' ability to keep their children safe, or even services that directly support the health and safety of children. On the other hand, there is overwhelming evidence that policing, prosecution, prisons, and foster care have had a devastating impact on the lives of child survivors of domestic violence. Eighty-four percent of girls in juvenile detention are survivors of family violence, and recent research has shown that there is a definitive pipeline between girls' experience of sexual and domestic violence and their likelihood of being targeted for prosecution and imprisonment (especially for Black girls and girls who identify as lesbian, bisexual, questioning, gender-nonconforming, and/or trans).[22]

The prosecution of Bresha Meadows, an Ohio-based Black girl who is a survivor of domestic and sexual violence, exemplifies how criminal legal institutions fail to care for and protect child survivors of violence. Bresha was only fourteen years old when she was prosecuted for fatally shooting her father who brutally beat her mother, repeatedly threatened to kill his family, and, according to her accounts, sexually abused Bresha herself.[23] Before the shooting, Bresha reached out to police and others to try to escape the violence, but police regarded her as a runaway and forced her to return home. Also, despite evidence of abuse, Ohio's child protective services did not interview Bresha's mother separately from her father, making it dangerous for her mother to report the abuse.[24] Rather than addressing the state of Ohio's profound failure to protect Bresha and her family, prosecutors laid the full brunt of blame on Bresha herself. The criminalization of child survivors of domestic violence strongly suggests that "failure to protect" prosecutions are not primarily about care for children, but are instead part of a broader pattern of criminalization that punishes both child and adult survivors of domestic and sexual violence. In short, because there appears to be little interest in reconciling prosecutors' contradiction of "caring for" and caging children, we submit that advocates of "failure to protect" laws must contend with the fact that criminalizing survivors fails to *effectively* care for, protect, or prevent violence against children.[25] Despite any personal motivations of individual prosecutors, "failure to protect" undergirds an ideology that promotes the criminalization of mothers who are survivors of domestic violence, and correspondent pro-criminalization forces are targeting child survivors as well.

"Failure to protect" also functions as a *criminalizing* ideology and a theory of law based on the notion that people can and should be punished for the actions of another individual. This inflation of punishable people—or "culpability inflation"—widely implicates criminal legal theory as it operates across an expanding set of laws that include "failure to protect," first- and second-degree murder laws, the felony murder rule, and other accomplice laws that increasingly expand the carceral reach. In the U.S., the rise of "failure to protect" prosecutions in the '70s and '80s occurred in sync with the rise of "law and order" politics and prosecution, fueling mass criminalization and the massive expansion of prisons, jails, and detention centers.[26] "Failure to protect" gained social currency as it was integrated into pro-carceral, pro-law-and-order political ideologies, which gained vast power and legitimacy during this era. Therefore, as the demand to address social issues through incarceration became increasingly normalized, the notion that survivors *ought* to be punished for exposing their children to domestic violence or for their batterers' violence against their children became increasingly taken for granted. Structurally unchallenged, the dominance of "failure to protect" ideology was institutionalized, compounding survivors' vulnerability to being blamed for violence, and opening a wide door to criminalizing survivors for their batterers' actions. "Failure to protect" catalyzes criminal prosecution of survivors charged with child endangerment, abuse, and neglect; accomplice to murder charges using felony murder laws; and first- and second-degree murder charges using "aiding and abetting" or other accomplice laws. All of these laws either construct survivor culpability as if it is bound with abuser action through conflating their respective culpability or openly shifting the bulk of moral responsibility from the batterer to the survivor.

As an example, felony murder laws facilitate carceral entrapment since felony murder convictions require no proof of intent to kill and no need for individual causal action.[27] If prosecutors can somehow link a survivor to the deadly action of an abuser, such as arguing that the survivor was present at the time of the abuser's action, then the abuser's action can be combined with another qualified felony and all parties are *equally* liable for murder. Felony murder convictions are actively pursued by prosecutors because they mandate severe sentences, including life without parole and capital punishment. In first- and second-degree murder "aiding and abetting" cases, the actions of the abuser may *theoretically* be more central, but in fact survivors are often held *equally* culpable, and thus equally punishable.[28] In "aiding and abetting" cases, survivors can be prosecuted for murder because their alleged failure to act is ruled as the "actual and proximate cause" of a child's death when the batterer in fact killed the child. This transference of culpability from batterers to survivors persists even when there is evidence that survivors were attempting to leave the relationship, a survival action that increases lethal risk for survivors and their children.[29]

In the pro-carceral frenzy of criminal prosecution, prosecutors often charge survivors with the highest possible charges. If prosecutions driven by "failure to protect" ideology can secure a child endangerment conviction with a shorter sentence or a first-degree murder conviction with a life sentence, prosecutors will likely charge first-degree murder. Prosecutorial discretion about which charges to pursue is driven by the likeliness of securing convictions, so people of color, poor people, disabled people, immigrants, and queer and trans people tend to face the highest charges and most severe sentences. As John Pfaff notes in his discussion of the systemic roots of contemporary mass incarceration, "At least since 1994, almost all the growth in prison populations has come from prosecutors' decisions to file felony charges."[30] With prosecutors incentivized to secure convictions, the core *systemic* purpose of "failure to protect" is to maximize punishment—including the total number of people convicted and incarcerated, and the total amount of time to which they are sentenced. As a result, survivors who are mothers, and mothers of color in particular, face increasingly severe charges, convictions, and sentences.

The combination of hyper-culpable motherhood with prosecutorial culpability inflation has created a powerful ideological foundation for "failure to protect" laws and prosecutions. Shifting critiques of "failure to protect" from explaining survivors' mitigating circumstances to a structural critique that clarifies the ideologies that drive courts to prosecute and punish survivors helps define the judicial system as an agent acting in concert with rather than against domestic violence. That is, "failure to protect" ideology not only creates justifications for punishing survivors of domestic violence, but also materializes through various forms of judicial complicity in domestic violence. In the next section, we will review two case studies of domestic violence survivors prosecuted for "failure to protect" to illustrate how judicial procedures and prosecutorial arguments ultimately systematize domestic violence, establishing functional partnerships between the judicial system and battering.

Case Studies

The following case studies illuminate how "failure to protect" laws facilitate courts' abusive pattern of merging or transferring culpability from batterer to survivor, which not only echoes dynamics of domestic violence that blame survivors for batterers' violence, but instills institutional legitimacy to domestic violence, ultimately making courts agentic extensions of, and partners with, batterers. To explore how partnerships between courts and battering emerge in the context of "failure to protect" cases, we consider the stories of the following criminalized survivors: Kelly Ann Savage in California and Tondalao Hall in Oklahoma.[31]

Kelly Ann Savage

Kelly Ann Savage is a survivor of severe domestic and sexual violence by her former husband, Mark Savage. Kelly was a twenty-two-year-old, low-income, white mother of two at the time of her arrest and, at the time of this writing, she is serving her twenty-second year in a California prison. In 1995, Kelly's abusive husband killed her four-year-old son, Justin, after she left the house to run errands in preparation to escape with her children. Kelly was following safety plan directives from a domestic violence crisis line she called to seek assistance in escaping the relationship. Prosecutors blamed Kelly for not escaping and saving her children sooner, ignoring the documented dangers associated with attempts to leave an abusive partner. Kelly's trial and conviction rested on the prosecution's exploitation of myths and misconceptions of survivors of abuse. Expert testimony about her husband's severe and continuous violence against her was not allowed in her trial, undermining her defense. Kelly's own lawyer and the trial judge fought her request for a domestic violence expert who could have testified on her behalf. She was convicted of first-degree murder for "aiding and abetting" her abusive husband, and sentenced to Life Without Possibility of Parole. While Kelly was not convicted under California's "failure to protect" statute (California Penal Code § 273(a)), her conviction relied heavily on "failure to protect" ideology that blames mothers for the violent action of their batterers. As we turn to an analysis of one of Kelly's hearings, our intent is not to offer a comprehensive deconstruction of the arguments, but to instead outline how the judicial system colludes with batterers by maintaining the ongoing victimization of survivors.

In 2002, California passed critical legislation allowing a narrow group of domestic violence survivors convicted of killing their batterers—later amended to include any violent felony convictions—to submit a petition for a writ of habeas corpus challenging their original conviction, potentially releasing them from prison.[32] This habeas law only applies to survivors charged with a violent felony that occurred prior to August 29, 1996, because it was justified with the reasoning that, before later reforms, survivors prosecuted for violent felonies were unintentionally restricted from submitting expert testimony about "intimate partner battering and its effects" in their trials. This law was intended as an opportunity for imprisoned survivors to submit expert testimony and correct that procedural injustice. Kelly's husband killed her son in 1995, and the submission of expert testimony about her experience of domestic violence was prevented by the judge, the prosecutor, and her defense attorney in her 1998 trial. Therefore, Kelly's case fit the criteria of eligibility. Because she was sentenced to Life Without Parole, a habeas petition represented a rare opportunity for Kelly to challenge her conviction and potentially not spend the rest of her life behind bars. The judge initially agreed that Kelly's case presented a good contender for habeas consideration. For the hearing, there was no dispute from the judge, prosecution, and defense that 1) Kelly was a victim of physical and emotional abuse by her husband, Mark Savage, and 2) Kelly did not commit specific acts herself that *directly* caused the death of her child.

The prosecutor, however, continued to argue that she directly "aided and abetted" her husband in first-degree murder.[33] The petition provided the judge the option to change Kelly's charge from murder to the more typical "failure to protect" charge of child endangerment, a crime that carries a sentence of up to six years, a significant reduction from the twenty-one years that Kelly had already served by the time she filed the petition. Therefore, to defeat the petition, the prosecution had to establish Kelly's *direct* culpability for her child's death.

A review of arguments used to sustain Kelly's conviction at her habeas petition hearing can help illuminate how a partnership between courts and battering emerges. The prosecutor asserted that the habeas law is not meant to be, in her words, a "catch-all" for all homicides related to intimate partner battering, though the habeas law was *specifically amended in 2005* to broaden eligible convictions from the survivor's homicide of her abuser to all "violent felonies."[34] Though the habeas law applies to all violent felony convictions, the judge was reticent to apply the law to a survivor prosecuted as a consequence of her batterer's killing of her child, therefore reinforcing rather than correcting the prosecution's incorrect understanding of the scope of the law.[35] According to this logic, survivors who did not kill anyone, but whose suffering includes the killing of their child by their batterer, are less likely to receive sentencing reconsideration than survivors who kill their batterers in self-defense. While we strongly support survivors' right to self-defense, this inconsistency highlights the depth of prosecutorial commitment to hold survivors criminally responsible for the actions of their batterers.

While Kelly was never charged with "failure to protect" per se, the judge and the prosecutor continued to use this terminology throughout her 2016 hearing. The judge, in particular, demonstrated a preoccupation with the concept of "failure to protect" in questioning Kelly's culpability, indicating the powerful normalcy of "failure to protect" as a punishment for mothers in particular. When the judge questioned the prosecutor about the jury's understanding of the scope of Kelly's culpability during her 1998 trial, the prosecutor argued that there was no need to distinguish Kelly's culpability from Mark's, asserting, "[Kelly] was found guilty of willful, deliberate, premeditated, first degree murder, and murder by torture. . . . [The jury] did not have to decide which of the two defendants personally committed the murder and which one was aiding and abetting."[36] Despite the fact that only Mark fatally beat Justin, the prosecution asserted that Kelly was equally culpable for his death, effectively merging Mark's and Kelly's culpability and situating them as *interchangeable criminal subjects.*

The prosecution exploited any hint that Kelly was capable of "volitional acts" to make the case that she was *directly responsible* for the death of her child. Thus, any sign of Kelly's capacity for agentic action (presumably including her attempt to escape) was used as an argument that she is guilty of murder. To de-legitimize Kelly's newly submitted expert testimony, the prosecution actively trivialized the violence she endured, at one point stating, "While I can respect that someone has been abused in their life, there are some instances where the law says, I don't want to be heartless, but so what, who cares."[37] Further, in an effort to expand Kelly's culpability, the judge *narrowed* his characterization of the batterer's role in causing the child's death, minimizing Mark's deadly beating of Justin as something that "might have been a final act of abuse."[38]

In a particularly odd twist, the judge argued that Kelly's petition lacked credibility because she relied "on her own declaration given almost 20 years after the fact and an expert's declaration made after meeting with Petitioner [Kelly Ann Savage] many, many years after the fact," essentially asserting that the conditions that make the law necessary also make Kelly less credible.[39] That is, it took the California legislature about ten years to pass the habeas law to correct judicial suppression of expert evidence in trials occurring within a narrow pre-1996 window. Once the law was passed in 2002, expanded in 2005 (making cases like Kelly's eligible for consideration), and finally put into effect, it took years for low-income defendants, such as Kelly, to learn about the new law, secure competent legal counsel to represent them pro bono, undertake the arduous process of preparing the petition itself, and wait for courts to find dates on which multiple hearings can be scheduled (and, often, postponed and rescheduled). The judge's use of "timeliness" as an excuse to reject the petition effectively creates a legal contradiction, rendering the habeas law logically and logistically impossible.

In addition to these issues, the presiding judge relied on weak evidence from the original trial to falsely assert that Kelly was directly violent towards Justin. However, the purpose of the habeas law is that the credibility of this trial, including submitted evidence, is undermined because it failed to account for the evidentiary context of intimate partner battering and its effects. The habeas law challenges the integrity of pre-1996 trials, yet the judge still used, at best, compromised trial evidence to deny the habeas petition, effectively causing a circular contradiction.

This particular problem reveals a vulnerability in the "mitigating circumstances" approach to defending survivors. The domestic violence habeas law was passed to address the repression or omission of domestic violence expert testimony in trials prosecuting survivors. The law states, "If the competent and substantial expert testimony [had] been presented, there is a reasonable probability, sufficient to undermine confidence in the judgment of conviction or sentence, that the result of the proceedings would have been different."[40] There are two ways to interpret the corrective scope of the habeas law. In part because of the legacy of the "mitigating factors" approach—or partial defense model of battered women's syndrome and other "trauma-based" defenses of survivors—one can interpret the statute as implying that the new domestic violence evidence can *only* be understood as mitigating the actions of survivors. This is a narrow interpretation of the statute that projects constraints onto the law that are simply not there.

Alternatively, we submit that there should be a *structural* interpretation of the law's corrective scope in that the statute indicates that the suppression of crucial evidence could "undermine confidence" in the judgment, which can include ways in which the evidence challenges the legitimacy of *multiple procedural and structural elements* of the trial. For example, the suppression of domestic violence evidence:

- blocks the survivor's right to procedural due process, weakening the legitimacy of the trial itself;
- transforms the context in which all trial evidence and arguments are considered, and therefore limits or distorts the jury's and judge's understanding of submitted evidence in competing trial narratives;
- calls into question the credibility or accuracy of testimony, including witnesses who testified without understanding the context of domestic violence, the survivor who may have been threatened into providing responses advantageous to the batterer, and the batterer who may have used the trial as an extension of abuse;

- and, given that "failure to protect" has been evaluated as biased against women, the lack of domestic violence evidence establishes a potential problem of institutional gender bias (and other forms of compounded bias based on identities that intersect with gender) of all court actors, including the defense attorney, prosecutor, judge, and jury.

Further, a structural critique of Kelly Ann Savage's ongoing criminalization helps us understand the culpability slippery slope that continuously expands the domain of prosecutable subjects. Kelly's case reveals extensive judicial investment in narrowing batterer culpability while fictionalizing and expanding survivor culpability. To maximize criminal culpability, court actors mobilize political ideologies that empower and enable "failure to protect" prosecution, including crafting judicial fictions that narrate mothers like Kelly as abusers and, sometimes, *literal* murderers despite the fact that they did not kill anyone.

Tondalao Hall

Tondalao Hall[41] is a domestic violence survivor who has been imprisoned in Oklahoma since 2006.[42] Tondalao was a twenty-two-year-old, low-income, Black mother of three at the time of her trial. Prosecutors charged Tondalao with "failing to protect" her young children from her boyfriend's abuse. Tondalao's abusive boyfriend, Robert Braxton, took his case to trial and ultimately pled guilty to a lesser charge. He was sentenced to ten years in prison, but his sentence was suspended and he was released with two years of time served.[43] Tondalao was issued a "blind plea" deal with an understanding that she would at least receive an equal or lesser sentence than the person who was prosecuted for directly abusing her children. However, the judge and prosecutor exploited Tondalao's identity as a domestic violence survivor and a mother to sentence her to thirty years in prison, while her abuser was freed shortly after the sentencing. Tondalao unsuccessfully attempted to appeal the sentence, and she requested a commutation of her sentence, but was denied. While Kelly's experience of domestic violence was minimized in order to establish her culpability, Tondalao's experience of domestic violence was *leveraged* to argue that she was culpable, suggesting possible racialized differences in how courts manipulate the fact of domestic violence to blame survivors.[44] Like Kelly's case, however, issues highlighted below reflect how the court institutionally extended and intensified Tondalao's experience of domestic violence.

Despite Tondalao's pleading to be transported from jail to court proceedings separately from her abusive boyfriend, they were transported in a van together where he would, in her words, "terrorize" her and tell her she would "spend the rest of [her] life in prison and he would be out with [their] children."[45] The judge and prosecution asserted their belief that Tondalao was intimidated by the batterer while testifying, which they argued was evidence that she was not being truthful and should *therefore* be shown no mercy in sentencing.

The prosecution coupled and conflated survivor and batterer culpability, and *inflated* Tondalao's culpability, arguing that Tondalao is "just as guilty of doing the crimes herself."[46] The prosecutor blamed Tondalao for the state's failure to secure a longer sentence for her boyfriend, arguing that she minimized and denied Robert's violence while on the stand in order to protect herself from domestic violence, which caused the case against him to fall apart, and therefore, Tondalao should be punished. When Tondalao's defense attorney argued that she should at least not be punished more than the person who actually abused her children, the prosecutor countered that she had "a real problem with putting [Tondalao] in the same shoes as [Robert]" with regards to Robert's two-year sentence, suggesting that Tondalao was *more* culpable than Robert for Robert's abuse.[47] This reflects an additional form of culpability inflation as Tondalao was being punished for the failures of *two* people—her batterer's violence against her children and the prosecution's failure to secure a longer sentence for her batterer. The prosecutor also argued that, as the child's mother, Tondalao was the most culpable and thus the most criminal, stating,

> She's their mother. She's responsible for them. She is the one person in this world who should be standing up for them and taking up for them and making sure that they are loved and they are cared for, and she did not do that. They were in harm's way because of what she did, and they were in pain because of what she didn't do, and she should pay for that.[48]

Perhaps one of the most remarkable instances of judicial collusion with domestic violence in Tondalao's case was the judge's appraisal of

Tondalao's body and facial movements, his assignment of narratives of intent to her based on his appraisal, asserting his specific right to do so, and using all of that to conclude that she should receive a thirty-year sentence. He asserted,

> I'm of the opinion, based on my experience and my viewing of Ms. Hall's testimony, her demeanor, her actions and reactions, including not only her body language but the tone of her voice, her facial expressions, and her, what appeared to be lack of candor on many of the questions, that she was holding back. . . . There would be certain questions that would be asked of her where she would look over at the defendant and make direct eye contact with him prior to her taking a moment or two to respond. That tells me something, based on my years of experience. Was she scared of him? Probably. But, again, even weighing that factor into the equation, I'm of the opinion she was less than candid. I think, in my opinion, she lied on some issues under oath. That's just my opinion, which I have a right to have in light of I'm her sentencing judge.[49]

In this passage, the judge visually appraises Tondalao's body as if it were a specimen of information, projecting his own meanings onto her bodily movements, vocal tone, and direction of her gaze. He asserts that his courtroom experience entitles him to conclude which movements are actions and which are reactions, define her agentic intent, and determine the truth of her emotional life. This kind of entitlement is certainly consistent with both a principle enacted in domestic violence that one's body is not one's own, and psychological abuse that enforces the notion that the abusive person is the only person with the authority to determine what things really mean, including the survivor's own actions.

The judge's recounting of Tondalao's body and facial movements as indication of guilt is also reminiscent of the legacy of the violent gaze to which Black women are subject. From enslaved Black women who were experimented on in the founding of gynecology to the public viewings of the so-called "Venus Hottentot," exploitative meaning is constantly projected onto Black women's bodies, making them subject to "expert" claims based on scientific racism.[50] Further, the construction of criminalized subjects is rooted in the legacy of people claiming expertise about the "criminal mind," as we saw in the eugenics movement.[51] The fact that the judge's admitted route to deciding that Tondalao deserved a thirty-year sentence was not through evidence, but through his own assessment of the meaning of her body, shows how these legacies live on in courtrooms.

A "mitigating circumstances" critique of "failure to protect" cannot provide the comprehensive analysis needed to understand the profound violence that courts are enacting in these prosecutions. As Kelly Ann Savage observed after learning that her habeas petition was denied, "Mark *always* wins."[52] There is a deeper collusion between the judicial system and domestic violence that must be unpacked. To understand Tondalao Hall's and Kelly Ann Savage's convictions and the practice of punishing mothers and survivors for being unable to control abusive partners' actions, we need a structural framework that clarifies the integral relationship between the judicial system and domestic violence.

Battering Court Syndrome

These case studies reveal how courts employ "failure to protect" ideology in criminal proceedings and become implicated in the overall trajectory and experience of domestic violence and goals of battering. Therefore, we argue that political analysis of the prosecution of domestic violence survivors, particularly but not exclusively with "failure to protect" cases, should shift from the mitigating circumstances model that explains survivors' actions, such as "battered women's syndrome," to a structural critique model foregrounding the judiciary's role in legitimizing and exacerbating domestic violence, or "battering court syndrome." We define battering court syndrome, or BCS, as judicial collusion with batterers through the criminalization of domestic violence survivors. BCS creates a spatial continuity of violence between domestic space and court space, and the violence of punitivity and confinement becomes violence that is *co-threatened* by the batterer and court actors. BCS also establishes a bureaucracy of battering that officiates domestic violence through ongoing violent punishment of survivors, and it affirms principles of battering as institutionally valid. Examples of battering principles include: survivors do not have the right to self-defense, survivors are inseparable from batterers and should be blamed and punished for batterers' actions, and survivors should be punished for not conforming to racist and sexist social expectations. As a structural diagnosis, BCS clarifies that, when we define "intimate partner battering and its effects," one of the most devastating "effects" for many survivors is being targeted for prosecution and punished through court systems.

BCS manifests through multiple kinds of partnerships between the judicial system and systems of battering, many of which are revealed in the case studies. The following is a working list of those partnerships that reveal nodes of connection and collusion between battering and judicial systems:

- Judicial fictions: To defend criminal coupling or transferring of culpability from batterer to victim, courts distort facts, disregard the law, create legal contradictions, or simply create new narratives about survivors' experiences and intent.
- Carceral pipeline: Survivors of gender violence are vulnerable to being targeted for criminalization, and criminalized survivors are more likely to be targeted for gender violence, either by institutions or individuals. This creates a bidirectional carceral pipeline between courts and gender violence. Further, because of prosecutorial incentive to maximize incarceration, prosecuted survivors are also pipelined into prison, sentencing survivors to a third site of pervasive violence.[53] For example, Tondalao Hall is serving time at the Mabel Bassett Correctional Center, which, according to the Bureau of Justice Statistics, is the women's prison with the highest rate of "sexual victimization" in the nation. Her trajectory is an example of how the institutional extension of domestic violence reaches into prison as well, reflecting the integral relationship between all carceral institutions and domestic and sexual violence.[54]
- Courts "mirror" patterns of domestic violence: Courts, like batterers, isolate, stigmatize, punish, surveil, and control survivors. Mirroring abusive people who blame their targets for the abuse ("It's your fault that I do this . . ."), courts manipulate narratives of culpability and act as if the agency of survivors and of batterers are merged and indistinguishable so that survivors are not allowed an independent identity and truth. Finally, though court actors make discretionary choices to severely punish survivors (such as what charges to pursue or what sentences to order), there is sometimes a performance of regret as if they have no choice, mirroring patterns of regret and continued abuse that is common in cycles of

domestic violence, and making the crisis of the survivor's experience of domestic and carceral violence about court actors and their self-proclaimed ethical dilemmas.[55]

- Courts supplant batterers: Courts produce conditions that extend batterers' abuse and control, which sustains domestic violence even if the batterer is no longer present. This makes it impossible for many imprisoned survivors to escape the abusive relationship because that abuse becomes enacted through judicial and prison systems.

- Gender oppression: Courts adjudicate women based on racialized and classed gender expectations by treating perceived "failure to protect" as transgressive to normative femininity/motherhood, and thus extra punishable. Court actors mobilize mother-blaming ideology to build and sustain these criminalizing narratives, including taking men's violence for granted while acting as if women's "failure to protect" their children from violence is the more egregious transgression.

- Court procedures as institutional tools for batterers: In trials like Kelly Ann Savage's and Tondalao Hall's that conjoin the prosecution of batterer and survivor as co-defendants, batterers use court procedural opportunities to intimidate, coerce, and control survivors either in court or in transit to court proceedings from detention. The court's collusion with battering is most explicit when survivors are prosecuted as co-defendants with their abusers who continue to threaten them during court proceedings.

The criminal trial itself is part of domestic violence victimization, and punishing survivors for violence enacted by batterers essentially institutionalizes domestic violence; judicial systems *become* the batterer. As California-based criminalized survivor Ny Nourn asks, "How many times must I beg for mercy from this system *and* an abusive partner?"[56]

Recommendations

Battering Court Syndrome should be understood as a framework from which to theorize the criminalization of survivors, a political diagnosis of the institutionalization of domestic violence through the judicial system, and a possible legal strategy to defend survivors. Given BCS, we urge feminist organizers, attorneys, and theorists to approach the problem of "failure to protect" prosecutions (and other legal strategies to criminalize survivors) using a structural analysis that directly challenges judicial collusion with domestic violence. To that end, we offer several recommendations.

Political, scholarly, and legal critiques of the criminal legal system must do more to foreground and analyze court brutality as a key system in criminalization. Court violence is as fundamental to the matrix of carceral violence as policing and incarceration. Understanding and exposing court brutality will contribute to a deeper understanding of how carceral systems produce criminalization and punishment, particularly of survivors of domestic and sexual violence. "Failure to protect" laws, broadly defined, offer an alarming and widening pathway for the prosecution and imprisonment of domestic violence survivors. We urge anti-violence and anti-carceral advocates and organizers to address the essential role of the courts, including prosecution, in the carceral pipeline between gender violence and prison. "Prison pipeline" analyses, important as they are, can obscure the role of court violence and blur how professionalized court processes pipe people into prisons, jails, and detention centers. Courtrooms are sites of violence and should therefore be sites of political critique and mobilization.

We recommend that Battering Court Syndrome be explored and developed as part of a potential defense strategy for criminalized survivors. We believe that expert witnesses testifying on behalf of survivors prosecuted for "failure to protect" charges can effectively make the case that batterers are responsible for creating conditions of violence, punitivity, chaos, and control, but that this exists *within* a matrix of institutional and structural violence. Expert witnesses can demonstrate how victims become more vulnerable to criminalization as a consequence of navigating intimate partner battering conditions across domestic and courtroom spaces (duress, etc.), particularly for survivors who are Black, Native, poor, transgender, queer, immigrant, disabled, in the sex industry, etc. For instance, batterers who have multiple encounters with the criminal legal system often become experienced in navigating carceral systems to their advantage, thus developing expertise in using criminal legal systems as tools for battering.[57] Therefore, courts are *implicated* in the overall trajectory and experience of domestic violence and goals of battering, and the trial itself becomes an integral part of domestic violence victimization as court actors begin to supplant batterers. This raises questions about professional ethics, the right to a fair trial, witness intimidation, and the legitimacy of all aspects of the trial, including the choice to prosecute in the first place.

The relative lack of political attention to the violence of "failure to protect" ideology and criminal legal practice is facilitated in part by how it disappears survivors through long-term incarceration. To challenge this disappearance, we recommend that anti-violence organizations prioritize making direct connections with incarcerated survivors convicted under "failure to protect" and other survival-related convictions. Increasing organizational understanding of the criminalization of these survivors and their ongoing subjection to battering within state systems must inform organizational policy to challenge the criminalization of survivors and to strategize how best to provide advocacy services to survivors behind bars. Importantly, these strategies should be developed in concert with formerly and currently incarcerated survivors and advocates with strong experience and understanding of the specific ways power and control unfold within prison conditions. Anti-violence organizations should also examine how funding that is contingent on cooperating with the criminal legal system dangerously compromises organizational autonomy needed to support criminalized survivors.

Coalition building between anti-violence advocates who work with adult survivors and those who advocate for children is urgently needed. In particular, decriminalizing coalitions between children's advocacy and adult survivor advocacy should be developed. Just as the safety of adult and child survivors is interrelated in the context of domestic violence, their fate and safety are interlinked, not oppositional, in the context of carceral violence. Children's advocacy organizations can critique the criminalization of child and adult survivors as part of the broader violence of criminalization, and institute organizational policy and practice to decriminalize survival and support criminalized survivors.

As one strategy for rejecting the ideological premise of "failure to protect" and revealing the impossible standards demanded from survivors, advocates and organizers should shift how criminalized survivors' actions are conceptualized and represented. For example, replacing the phrase "failure to protect children" with "inability to predict and control batterer violence" re-situates culpability for the harm back to the abusive partner and emphasizes the absurd standard of power that survivors who are mothers are expected to have.

We recommend divesting our collective energies from reform efforts that are not based on a strong structural critique of carceral violence and its role in extending deadly battering by individual abusers and state systems. A criminal legal system that promotes oppressive political ideologies, refuses to distinguish survivors from batterers, unethically merges and transfers culpability, and punishes survivors *because* they are survivors, is a *profoundly violent system*. A genuine challenge to the criminalization of survivors must acknowledge the limits and dangers of reforms that strengthen the system's legitimacy without confronting the root political and structural issues for why survivors are being punished. Thus, we recommend that advocates pursue change based on a structural critique of carceral violence, as well as prioritize, develop, and engage strategies that do not rely on the criminal legal system to keep survivors—both children and adults—safe.

Finally, we believe that grassroots political organizing to free survivors is critical for many reasons, including as a complement to legal defense for criminalized survivors. At the time of their initial trials, neither Tondalao nor Kelly had defense campaigns supporting them. However, their current efforts to pursue pathways to freedom are now bolstered by grassroots defense campaigns.[58] These campaigns have also received national attention through Survived and Punished, a national coalition that organizes to free survivors and dismantle the integral relationship between criminal legal systems and sexual and domestic violence. Political grassroots organizing is crucial because both carceral violence and domestic violence systematically disappear survivors from our communities and enact violence behind walls. Openly and politically challenging this violence can strengthen our efforts to defend survivors in court because organizing pushes judicial abuse of survivors into public view, which motivates other survivors and their allies to mobilize and challenge prosecutions and convictions (as we have seen in defense campaigns for Tondalao Hall, Kelly Ann Savage, Nan-Hui Jo, Ky Peterson, Yazmin Obregon, Marissa Alexander, Bresha Meadows, Shantonio Hunter, the historic 1974 campaign to free Joan Little, and many others).[59] We urge anti-violence organizations and feminist attorneys, scholars, and advocates to fearlessly collaborate with grassroots organizers across social justice movements to end the criminalization of survivors and survival.

Authors' Note

The authors greatly appreciate Kelly Ann Savage, Sumayya Coleman, Jakeya Caruthers, all of our partners at Survived and Punished and California Coalition for Women Prisoners, and editors Jane Stoever and Dylan Quigley for their feedback and wisdom that contributed to the development of these ideas.

NOTES

1 Elissa E. Dichter & Sue Osthoff, *Women's Experiences of Abuse as a Risk Factor for Incarceration: A Research Update*, NAT'L RESOURCE CTR. ON DOMESTIC VIOLENCE (NRCDV) (July 2015), http://vawnet.org; BETH E. RICHIE, COMPELLED TO CRIME: THE GENDER ENTRAPMENT OF BATTERED, BLACK WOMEN (1996).

2 We recognize that the static use of the terms "survivors" and "batterers" can be challenging and problematic because, of course, many people who batter have also been victimized by domestic and sexual violence. When we refer to the context of an abusive relationship in this discussion, however, we use "survivor" to refer to the person who is not leading a sustained pattern of violence and control in the relationship, and "batterer" to refer to the person who is. We contend that all survivors should be decriminalized, which includes the development of transformative non-carceral strategies to attend to all people who harm others to work towards genuine safety and accountability. Ana Clarissa Rojas Durazo et al., *Special Issue: Community Accountability: Emerging Movements to Transform Violence*, 37 SOC. JUST. (SPECIAL ISSUE) NO. 4 (2011–2012).

3 There is currently no explicit research that we could find on the prosecutions of transgender people for "failure to protect" children, so for the purposes of this article we are writing about survivors who have been gendered as women and batterers who have been gendered as men in court transcripts, research, etc., which may or may not be inclusive of transgender people. That being said, transgender survivors of domestic and sexual violence experience higher than average rates of criminalization, transgender parenting is stigmatized and criminalized, and research is urgently needed to understand the intersections of these two violent realities in the lives of transgender people.

4 Sandra Chung, *Mama Mia! How Gender Stereotyping May Play a Role in the Prosecution of Child Fatality Cases*, 9 WHITTIER J. OF CHILD & FAM. ADVOC. 205 (2009); Linda C. Fentiman, *Are Mothers Hazardous to Their Children's Health?: Law, Culture, and the Framing of Risk*, 21 VA. J. SOC. POL'Y. & L. 295

(2014) [hereinafter Fentiman, *Mothers*]; Linda C. Fentiman, *Child Abuse by Omission: How American Law Holds Mothers Responsible for Their Partners' Crimes*, TRUTHOUT (Apr. 1, 2017), www.truth-out.org [hereinafter Fentiman, *Child Abuse by Omission*]; Jeanne A. Fugate, *Who's Failing Whom?: A Critical Look at Failure-to-Protect Laws*, 76 NYU L. REV. 272 (2001).

5   "Failure to Protect" Working Group, *Charging Battered Mothers With "Failure To Protect": Still Blaming The Victim*, 27 FORDHAM URB. L.J. 849 (1999); Adele M. Morrison, *Changing the Domestic Violence (Dis)Course: Moving from White Victim to Multi-Cultural Survivor*, 39 UC DAVIS L. REV. 1061 (2006).

6   Evan Stark, *A Failure to Protect: Unravelling "The Battered Mother's Dilemma,"* 27 W. ST. U. L. REV. 29 (2000); JAMES G. WHITE ET AL., CRIMINAL PROSECUTION OF BATTERED NATIVE WOMEN FOR FAILURE TO PROTECT (Southwest Ctr. for L. & Pol'y & US Dep't. of Justice, Off. on Violence Against Women eds., 2005).

7   EDWARD W. GONDOLF & ELLEN R. FISHER, BATTERED WOMEN AS SURVIVORS: AN ALTERNATIVE TO TREATING LEARNED HELPLESSNESS (1988).

8   MARY ANN DUTTON ET AL., UPDATE OF THE "BATTERED WOMAN SYNDROME" CRITIQUE (2009); Kathleen J. Ferraro, *The Words Change, But the Melody Lingers: The Persistence of the Battered Woman Syndrome in Criminal Cases Involving Battered Women*, 9 VIOLENCE AGAINST WOMEN 100 (2003).

9   Chung, *supra* note 4; Fentiman, *Mothers, supra* note 4; Fugate, *supra* note 4.

10 Jacqueline Mabatah, *Blaming the Victim?: The Intersections of Race, Domestic Violence, and Child Neglect Laws*, 8 GEO. J.L. & CRITICAL RACE PERSP. 355 (2016); Morrison, *supra* note 5.

11 V. P. Enos, *Prosecuting Battered Mothers: State Laws' Failure to Protect Battered Women and Abused Children*, 19 HARV. WOMEN'S L.J. 229 (1996).

12 BETH E. RICHIE, ARRESTED JUSTICE: BLACK WOMEN, VIOLENCE, AND AMERICA'S PRISON NATION (2012).

13 *Id.* at 129.

14 Fugate, *supra* note 4, at 274.

15 Chung, *supra* note 4; Marilyn Friedman, *Moral Responsibility for Coerced Wrongdoing: The Case of Abused Women Who "Fail to Protect" Their Children, in* VULNERABILITY: NEW ESSAYS IN ETHICS AND FEMINIST PHILOSOPHY 222 (Catriona Mackenzie et al. eds., 2013).

16 Chung, *supra* note 4, at 212.

17 *Id.* at 223.

18 Leigh Goodmark, *Achieving Batterer Accountability in the Child Protective System*, 93 KY. L.J. 613 (2005).

19 Evelyn Nakano Glenn, *Social Constructions of Mothering: A Thematic Overview, in* MOTHERING: IDEOLOGY, EXPERIENCE, AND AGENCY 1 (Evelyn Nakano Glenn et al. eds., 1994).

20 *Id.* at 11.

21 Barbara Bloom & Marilyn Brown, *Incarcerated Women: Motherhood on the Margins, in* RAZOR WIRE WOMEN: PRISONERS, ACTIVISTS, SCHOLARS

AND ARTISTS 51–66 (Jodie Michelle Lawson & Ashley Lucas eds., 2011); Jake Pyne et al., *Transphobia and Other Stressors Impacting Trans Parents*, 11 J. GLBT FAM. STUD. 107 (2015); Martha Escobar, *ASFA and the Impact on Imprisoned Migrant Women and Their Children, in* RAZOR WIRE WOMEN: PRISONERS, ACTIVISTS, SCHOLARS AND ARTISTS 75–91(Jodie Michelle Lawson & Ashley Lucas eds., 2011); Emily Haney-Caron & Kirk Heilbrun, *Lesbian and Gay Parents and Determination of Child Custody: The Changing Legal Landscape and Implications for Policy and Practice*, 1 PSYCHOL. SEXUAL ORIENTATION & GENDER DIVERSITY 19 (2014); DOROTHY ROBERTS, KILLING THE BLACK BODY: RACE, REPRODUCTION, AND THE MEANING OF LIBERTY (1998); LUABA ROSS, INVENTING THE SAVAGE: THE SOCIAL CONSTRUCTION OF NATIVE AMERICAN CRIMINALITY (1998).

22 MALIKA SAADA SAAR ET AL., THE SEXUAL ABUSE TO PRISON PIPELINE: THE GIRLS' STORY (Mary Bissell et al. eds., 2015); FRANCINE T. SHERMAN & ANNIE BALCK, GENDER INJUSTICE: SYSTEM-LEVEL JUVENILE JUSTICE REFORM FOR GIRLS (Anne Marie Ambrose et al. eds., 2015).

23 Andrea Simakis, *Bresha Meadows to Serve 6-Months in Cleveland Treatment Facility Following Plea Deal in Shooting Death of Her Father*, CLEVELAND (May 22, 2017, 8:30 PM), www.cleveland.com.

24 Victoria Law, *What Bresha Meadows, Arrested for Shooting Her Father after Reported Abuse, Faces Next*, REWIRE (Aug. 25, 2016, 5:41 PM), https://rewire.news.

25 In her landmark work *Killing the Black Body: Race, Reproduction and the Meaning of Liberty* (1998), Dorothy Roberts powerfully makes a similar point about the professed care by pro-life lawmakers and prosecutors who disproportionately prosecute black mothers for "fetal harm." She writes, "When a nation has always closed its eyes to the circumstances of pregnant Black women, its current expression of interest in the health of unborn Black children must be viewed with distrust" (*Id.* at 183). We believe that it could be productive for feminist theorists and legal analysts to place "failure to protect" in the analytical context of efforts to prosecute mothers for criminalized reproduction issues such as abortion, miscarriages, and becoming pregnant while Black, brown, immigrant, Native, queer, or poor.

26 Fentiman, *Child Abuse by Omission, supra* note 4; Palmer v. State, 223 Md. 341 (1969).

27 Felony murder prosecution is dependent on state laws that determine which felonies, in addition to the murder felony, qualify for a felony murder charge. For instance, in Tennessee, Shantonio Hunter was unable to control her abuser's violence towards her child and is being charged with felony murder for the death of her son since "child endangerment" is a qualifying felony in Tennessee. Tenn. Code § 39-15-401 (2010).

28 First-degree murder prosecution for "aiding and abetting" depends on which "aggravating" or "special circumstances" mandate life without parole or death sentencing. For instance, in California, Kelly Ann Savage was charged with the

"special circumstance" of torture, mandating life without parole or the death penalty.

29 Christina Nicolaidis et al., *Could We Have Known?: A Qualitative Analysis of Data from Women Who Have Survived an Attempted Homicide by an Intimate Partner,* 18 J. GEN. INTERNAL MED. 788 (2003).

30 John E. Pfaff, *Waylaid by a Metaphor: A Deeply Problematic Account of Prison Growth,* 111 MICH. L. REV. 1087, 1006 (2013).

31 In the discussion of these case studies, we refer to Kelly Ann Savage and Tondalao Hall by their first names in part to avoid confusion when referring to other members of Kelly Ann Savage's family, but also because the academic and legal distance of referring to subjects of "case studies" by their last name seems discordant with our collaborative relationship with Kelly and other incarcerated survivors who are co-advocating across prison walls to secure survivors' freedom and survival.

32 Cal. Penal Code § 1473.5.

33 Transcript from Habeas Petition Hearing at 35, Kelly Ann Savage vs. The People of the State of California, No. VCF 037179C-96 (Super. Ct. of the State of Cal. in and for the Cty. Of Tulare–Visalia Division, June 3, 2016).

34 *Id.* at 37.

35 In many incarcerated survivor cases presented to California courts, judges and appellate courts have failed to grant habeas relief under Penal Code § 1473.5, in part because judges are extremely hesitant to order new trials or establish new case law where there is very little precedent. This conservative unwillingness to break new ground and apply legal remedy creates an additional barrier for sur- vivor appeals based on laws that aim to correct past erasure of domestic violence evidence.

36 Transcript from Habeas Petition Hearing, *supra* note 33, at 8.

37 *Id.* at 38.

38 Transcript from Judge's Order at 14, Kelly Ann Savage vs. The People of the State of California, VCF 037179C-96 (Super. Ct. of the State of Cal. in and for the Cty. of Tulare–Visalia Division, September 16, 2016).

39 *Id.* at 14.

40 CAL. PENAL CODE § 1473.5.

41 There are multiple spellings of Tondalao Hall's first name in court documents and her own writing. We use the spelling "Tondalao" because that is our understand- ing of her preferred spelling. However, court documents cited here spell her name as "Tondalo."

42 Alex Campbell, *This Battered Woman Wants To Get Out Of Prison,* BUZZFEED NEWS (Nov. 11, 2014, 12:48 PM), www.buzzfeed.com.

43 The State of Oklahoma v. Tondalo Rochelle Hall and Robert Braxton, No. CF- 2004-6403 (Dist. Ct. Oklahoma Cty., State of Okla., 2006); *see also* Petition for Writ of Habeas Corpus at 8, Tondalo Hall v. Debbie Aldridge, No. CV-17-67 (Dist. Ct. Pottawatomi Cty., State of Okla., June 2, 2017).

44 A detailed discussion of racialized differences in how domestic violence is minimized or leveraged to blame survivors for "failure to protect" is beyond the scope of this paper. However, if this difference is indeed a pattern among arguments made in "failure to protect" cases, it suggests that victimhood must be obscured to defend punishing white survivors because the affirmation of white women as genuine victims of violence undermines the claim that they should be punished, while the experience of violence by Black women does not conjure empathy for their victimization, but, perversely, serves as evidence that they *ought* to be punished further. See SARAH HALEY, NO MERCY HERE: GENDER, PUNISHMENT, AND THE MAKING OF JIM CROW MODERNITY (2016) for a vivid historical overview of this racialized dynamic in early-twentieth-century US women's incarceration and Alisa Bierria, *"Where them bloggers at?": Reflections on Rihanna, Accountability, and Subjectivity*, 37 SOC. JUST. 101–25 (2011–2012) for an exploration of how this dynamic unfolds in online efforts to hold Black women "accountable" for being victimized by domestic violence.

45 Application for Commutation of Sentence at 10, State of Oklahoma v. Tondalo Rochelle Hall, No. CF-04-6403 (Dist. Ct. Oklahoma Cty., State of Okla., Nov. 5, 2014).

46 Transcript of Formal Sentencing After Previous Plea of Guilty at 7, State of Oklahoma v. Tondalo Rochelle Hall, No. CF-04-6403 (Dist. Ct. Oklahoma Cty., State of Okla., Dec. 20, 2006).

47 *Id.* at 11.

48 *Id.* at 7, 8.

49 *Id.* at 12, 13.

50 BELL HOOKS, BLACK LOOKS: RACE AND REPRESENTATION (1992); HARRIET A. WASHINGTON, MEDICAL APARTHEID: THE DARK HISTORY OF MEDICAL EXPERIMENTATION ON BLACK AMERICANS FROM COLONIAL TIMES TO THE PRESENT (2006).

51 WASHINGTON, *supra* note 50.

52 Personal communication, Sept. 16, 2016 (on file with author).

53 In addition to facing institutional violence by prison guards once incarcerated, survivors prosecuted for "failure to protect" face increased harassment from other imprisoned people due to the intense stigma attached to cases involving children.

54 ALLEN J. BECK ET AL., U.S. DEPT. OF JUSTICE, SEXUAL VICTIMIZATION IN PRISONS AND JAILS REPORTED BY INMATES, 2011–2012 (Morgan Young & Jill Thomas eds., 2013).

55 For example, in Tondalao's hearing, the prosecutor simultaneously blamed Tondalao for protecting herself from the batterer's threats while also making the problem about her own moral struggle, stating, "I believe that she's still protecting herself, and I believe that, based on her testimony in this courtroom, she is still protecting the co-defendant in this case. So I've really struggled with this case and what the right thing to do is" (Transcript of Formal Sentencing After Previous Plea of Guilty at 6, State of Oklahoma vs Tondalo Rochelle Hall, CF-04-6403 (Dist. Ct. Oklahoma Cty., State of Okla., 2006).

56 Ny Nourn is a California-based Cambodian survivor of domestic violence who was also prosecuted for being unable to control the fatal violence of her abusive partner, and then sentenced to Life Without Parole by her trial judge, who claimed she was *more* culpable than her batterer for her batterer's violence. Anoop Prasad, *She Was Sentenced to Die in Prison Because She Couldn't Control Her Abuser*, MEDIUM (Jan. 4, 2017), https://medium.com.

   Ny Nourn's sentence was overturned on a habeas appeal (CAL. PENAL CODE § 1473.5) and she was re-sentenced to life with the possibility of parole. After serving sixteen years in prison, Ny Nourn was finally granted parole in 2017 in large part due to the advocacy efforts of Asian Americans Advancing Justice—Asian Law Caucus, only to then be sent to immigration detention where she faces possible deportation. Daniela Blei, *Meet Saira Hussain, the Lawyer Fighting for Immigrants' Rights*, TEEN VOGUE (June 20, 2017, 4:11 PM), www.teenvogue.com; Ny Nourn, *Ny's Story*, MEDIUM (June 23, 2017), https://medium.com.

57 Marissa Alexander, Video Presentation for "Incarceration Roundtable" at Office of Violence Against Women, U.S. Dep't of Justice (Sept. 21, 2015).

58 Grassroots organizers in Oklahoma have been mobilizing support for Tondalao Hall's freedom since at least 2015 (more information at freetondalao.com). In 2017, the ACLU agreed to lead a legal effort to secure Tondalao's freedom, arguing that her sentence reflects cruel and unusual punishment. Allie Shinn, *ACLU of Oklahoma Announces Effort to Free Domestic Violence Survivor Imprisoned for Failing to Stop*, FREE TONDALAO HALL (June 15, 2017), www.freetondalaohall.com. Grassroots mobilization for Kelly Ann Savage's freedom has been led by the California Coalition for Women Prisoners, which has raised the profile of her case among anti-domestic violence organizations in California. Kelly's pro bono legal team is requesting a commutation of her sentence. More about Kelly's case and other cases can be found at bit.ly/FreeKelly and survivedandpunished.org.

59 For more information about the history of feminist defense campaigns and more contemporary grassroots campaigns to free survivors of violence, see Emily Thuma, *Lessons in Self-Defense: Gendered Violence, Racial Criminalization, and Anticarceral Feminism*, 43 WSQ 52-71 (Fall–Winter 2015), and the defense campaign organizing toolkit from Love & Protect and Survived and Punished (2017), as well as the Survived and Punished website, survivedandpunished.org.

5

Parental Love and Purposeful Violence

CYNTHIA GODSOE

I. Introduction

The parental discipline privilege is the only remaining status exception to criminal assault and battery. Indeed, William Blackstone's statement of the law in this area is still accurate two hundred and fifty years later: "Battery is, in some cases, justifiable or lawful; as where one who hath authority, a parent or master, gives moderate correction to his child . . . for the benefit of his education."[1] Permissible discipline often goes well beyond the euphemistic term "spanking" to include hair-pulling, beatings with belts or sticks, and even choking.[2] Other once lawful violence, such as the abuse of wives, apprentices, and scholars, has long been criminalized.[3] Corporal punishment even has roots in, and continues to echo, slavery, as one historian of African American history has recently detailed.[4] Despite its anachronistic nature, parental corporal punishment remains surprisingly unquestioned by scholars and reformers alike. One possible explanation is that feminist scholars, the source of so much important work on intrafamilial crime, have largely ignored child abuse because it complicates the gendered picture of domestic violence in that the victimized woman becomes an offender herself, harming an even more vulnerable child.[5] Another is the historic designation of children as parental property, and the echoes of this framework in contemporary law.[6] Whatever the underlying reasons, our society's differential treatment of parental discipline is an important topic for inclusion in this exploration of the politicization of safety.

The parental discipline privilege is a broad and robust exception to the criminalization of interpersonal violence. Every state allows parents to punish their children physically, sometimes to the extreme of any punishment not causing a substantial risk of disfigurement or death.[7] The privilege is a justification, meaning that the conduct is forgiven as non-culpable. Indeed, the legal definition absolves conduct that the Centers for Disease Control and Prevention (CDC) and other experts define as abuse. This privilege subjects many children to a level of permissible violence from those entrusted to care for them that is much greater than that which pet owners may use to discipline or train animals.[8] Corporal punishment has been banned in virtually all other settings, including medical facilities, day cares, and prisons, yet is permitted in the home, where children are supposed to be loved and protected.

The parental discipline exception persists despite the lack of any legitimate, or often even any stated, rationale. The most frequently offered justifications are tradition and parenting folk wisdom, which are contradicted by decades of research and expertise on child development. Experts are virtually unanimous in concluding that corporal punishment is ineffective as a disciplinary tool, and that even mild corporal punishment brings a risk of significant developmental consequences. Its harms include elision into serious child abuse as well as rendering its victims more likely to hit their partners and children as adults, perpetuating the cycle of abuse.

In this chapter, I argue that central to this problematic and anachronistic justification of family violence is the underlying *mens rea*. By forgiving beatings purportedly "intended to benefit a child," or that a parent would reasonably believe was "necessary or appropriate," the privilege inverts the standard *mens rea* framework, which finds greater culpability with greater control. It also gives abusive parents a free pass to take out their anger and frustration on society's most vulnerable, justifying this physical force in the name of its victims. In this way, the privilege equates anger and violence with parental love, just as wife-beating was historically characterized as the duty of a caring husband.[9] Courts ignore or sympathize with parental anger, even forgiving horrific violence including chokings and burnings. This exception is out of step with the evolution of the law to prioritize children's best interests and limit parental choice when it harms children.[10] Criminalization, however, carries substantial costs and potential harm and cannot be viewed as the easy answer, particularly given what is now understood about the domestic violence criminalization experience.

This transformation of hitting into love also normalizes violence against children.[11] Mislabeling assault as discipline obscures the harm and allows the public to approve of it.[12] Corporal punishment also plays out in highly gendered, racialized, and heteronormative ways.[13] Hitting girls while shaming them with names such as "slut" and "bitch" reinforces highly sexualized gender roles while also rendering these girls more likely to be beaten by an intimate partner as an adult. The disproportionate physical discipline against gender-nonconforming and Black children also perpetuates illegitimate power structures.[14] Accordingly, parental discipline can be seen as a kind of "family hate violence"; children internalize harmful messages about their bodies or skin color and the family as a site of societal discrimination, disgust, and the coercive enforcement of power dynamics.

I begin this chapter by charting the vast scope of the parental discipline privilege and documenting its considerable physical, mental, and societal harms. In section III, I turn to the *mens rea*, demonstrating that it diverges from the accepted *mens rea* construction underlying criminal law and problematically equates violence with parental care. Simply put, the empirical evidence makes 'reasonable corporal punishment' an oxymoron. I argue in section IV that the parental discipline privilege renders violence against children, including racialized and gendered violence, standard—or even desirable—from "good" parents. I conclude by calling for the abolition of the parental discipline privilege. To be clear, I do not endorse prosecution, or even criminalization, of all of this behavior. Abolition could take the form of a civil law ban or graduated sanctions. Nonetheless, we do already criminalize some parental corporal punishment and my proposal clarifies the line between permissible and impermissible conduct. I also call for public health and education measures outside of the criminal system to most effectively shift these deeply embedded social norms about parenthood and children's well-being.

II. License to Hit

A. *Parental Discipline Privilege*

Parents in every state are granted the right to physically punish their children with no criminal liability for assault and battery. The parental discipline privilege constitutes the only status-based exception to assault and battery laws. Most jurisdictions have codified the parental discipline privilege either as an affirmative defense or as part of the statutory definition of child abuse; others have recognized the privilege in case law.[15] It is framed as a justification, not an excuse, meaning that the conduct itself is deemed innocent.[16] The privilege historically attached only to fathers, but has since been extended to all legal parents and guardians.[17] Most states also allow custodians or persons acting as parents to assert the privilege.[18] Accordingly, it has a very broad scope—a significant number of people without a legal relationship to the child, such as a mother's boyfriend, are permitted to corporally punish that child with no criminal liability.[19]

Permissible parental discipline goes well beyond the euphemism of "spanking." Parents have been found to be justified in disciplining their children by hitting them with a paddle, pulling their hair, slapping their faces, pinching, choking, and more. Every state law permits parental assault that brings some harm, allowing, for instance, the use of corporal punishment on even very young children and spanking with objects such as wooden spoons and belts. Numerous states, and the influential Model Penal Code, go further and explicitly permit a wide swath of parental discipline as long as the force used is not designed to cause or known to create a "substantial risk of causing death, serious bodily injury, disfigurement, extreme pain or mental distress or gross degradation."[20] Every state permits some physical harm and mental or emotional injury as long as it is not severe or gross.[21] Given this range of permissible assault, it is likely not surprising that corporal punishment is still widely practiced, with over half of adults engaging in it.[22] Parents in the South, fundamentalist Christian parents, and Black parents are significantly more likely to use physical discipline.[23]

This legal definition of acceptable discipline is far broader than any medical definition. Most experts recommend non-physical discipline for its greater effectiveness, and define spanking to include only striking a child with an open hand over clothing on his or her buttocks. They define abuse or maltreatment to include the other acts described here, which are permitted to some degree under every state law. For instance, the American Academy of Pediatrics (AAP) recommends never "striking a child with an object" such as a belt. Other medical experts define child maltreatment to include slapping, hitting with an object, and beating, and define choking and burning—acts courts have given a misdemeanor or no sanction to—as "major physical maltreatment."[24] The CDC defines physical abuse as "the intentional use of physical force against a child that results in, or has the potential to result in, physical injury," including pushing, hitting, and beating. The leading public health agency explicitly states that abuse can result from discipline.[25]

The most common rationales offered for parental corporal punishment are historic, cultural, or personal.[26] Courts continue to cite Blackstone's centuries-old statement of a parent's power to "lawfully correct his child . . . in a reasonable manner; for . . . the benefit of his education."[27] Historic rationales are sometimes coupled with religious justifications; as noted earlier, fundamentalist Christians are significantly more likely than other Americans to support and use corporal punishment.[28] "Spare the rod and spoil the child" remains a frequently, if incorrectly, cited Biblical passage.[29] Indeed, the reliance on tradition rather than empirics or deliberate policy is evident in the fact that about half of states do not cite any rationale for this anachronistic exemption, while those that do have a rationale usually place it in vague and conclusory terms.

Most often, commentators supporting corporal punishment cite their own experiences growing up or their personal beliefs about child rearing. These proponents do not cite any child development research and may even expressly disregard the science. The following two examples are typical: "Regardless of what the experts preach, the undeniable fact is the 'uncivilized' practice of whipping children produced more civilized young people."[30] Or take another: "While some studies have shown the negative effects of spanking, today's disrespectful youth have shown what happens when necessary spanking is forgone. . . . Some kids need it, period. When time-out, talking and taking away toys doesn't work, you have to get that butt."[31]

The parental discipline privilege is the only remaining status-based exculpation for assault, and it has been abolished in almost all settings outside the home. Physical discipline is no longer permitted in juvenile prisons, day cares, and mental health facilities.[32] A majority of states have banned corporal punishment in schools, largely driven by increased knowledge about both the harms of corporal punishment and the effectiveness of non-physical disciplinary methods.[33] In 2016, the Obama administration Secretary of Education called for a nation-wide ban on educational corporal punishment, citing extensive empirical data of its harms, and several jurisdictions are currently working towards this recommendation.[34] Finally, the last decade has demonstrated an international trend towards banning corporal punishment in the home. Sweden was the first country to do so in 1979, and in January 2017, France brought the total to fifty-two worldwide.[35] In doing so, these nations cite the psychological and expressive harms of permitting assault on society's most vulnerable children, as well as international law equating corporal punishment with other physical assaults and torture.[36]

B. Harms of Corporal Punishment

Medical and psychological experts almost unanimously confirm that corporal punishment, even moderate, is not effective at teaching children and is in fact harmful.[37] In addition to physical injury, corporal punishment is correlated with increased risk of thirteen detrimental mental health, behavioral, and cognitive outcomes.[38] Accordingly, since the 1990s, professional organizations such as the American Academy of Pediatrics have issued strong statements against its use.[39] One of the foremost experts on corporal punishment and child abuse, Murray Straus, summarizes the harms: "Corporal punishment can tremendously influence the psychological development of children, increasing the risk of aggressive and anti-social behaviors . . . [and] causing them serious psychological harm."[40]

Also problematic is the elision of corporal punishment into more serious violence against children, and there is a strong correlation between the two. Corporal punishment and abuse are driven by the same root causes; as one expert explains, "The risk of a parent going too far and going out of control is way more if the parent is engaging in corporal punishment in the first place."[41] Tellingly, studies of substantiated cases of physical abuse have found that between 66% and 85% of these cases began as ordinary corporal punishment that escalated.[42]

Moreover, because it legitimizes intra-familial violence, corporal punishment increases the risk that the child will, as an adult, beat his or her partner and/or own child.[43] A recent study published in the *Journal of Pediatrics* found a significant correlation between such violence and corporal punishment (defined only as spanking, not more violent conduct).[44] The researchers controlled for numerous factors, including abuse, thus proving the link between spanking and future intimate partner violence (IPV) which prior studies had been unable to isolate, and determined that spanking alone is predictive of future violence.[45] The increase in risk of IPV came even from infrequent spankings; the study found that a "one unit increase in corporal punishment was associated with a 29% increase in perpetrating dating violence."[46] The researchers concluded that the rhetoric around corporal punishment as "for [children's] own good," as well as the familial relationship between the punisher and the child "confuses the boundaries between love and violence for children" at a key developmental stage, rendering the use of or exposure to violence in future intimate relationships seem "normal."[47]

III. The Fiction of "Parental Purpose"

Despite research proving otherwise, harms associated with corporal punishment continue to be justified as necessary for children's own good—that, somehow, parental love and duty erase the harms of the assault and transform it into a beneficial act. The dominant legal "best interests of the child" standard is not only ignored, but actually perverted, so that a child's best interests are deemed to be met by violence. Despite a thick conception of parental rights, the law has evolved to limit parents' choice to deny the expertise and science on child-rearing when it harms children in the medical and educational arenas.[48] Corporal punishment remains a significant exception to this progression.[49]

The unusual *mens rea* of the parental discipline privilege does a lot of work in this recharacterization of violence as care. *Mens rea* is "the particular mental state provided for in the definition of an offense."[50] Both courts and scholars have noted its centrality to just punishment; as the Supreme Court has declared, "The contention that an injury can amount to a crime only when inflicted by [*mens rea*] is no provincial or transient notion. It is . . . universal and persistent in mature systems of law."[51] Without a *mens rea* element calibrated to culpability and morality, the criminal law is unmoored from notions of societal harm and, accordingly, loses legitimacy.[52]

The *mens rea* for the parental discipline defense differs significantly from that of assault, and is quite unique across criminal law. Almost all states include a parental purpose portion to this defense. Most states require that corporal punishment be for the child's welfare or benefit, sometimes resting on whether the parent reasonably believed that physical discipline was necessary or appropriate.[53] A number of statutes posit a more purely subjective standard, such as whether the punishment's purpose was to "promote" the child's welfare, or whether the force was "intended to benefit the child."[54]

Yet the harms associated with corporal punishment and, even more so, a parent's conduct while administering it, belie a benevolent purpose. At best, it is a misinformed attempt at discipline. The case of NFL star Adrian Peterson, discussed further below, is perhaps an example of this. My argument, however, goes further. I contend that the parental discipline privilege is often asserted to cover assaults driven by anger, stress, or the like rather than a truly well-intended, if ignorant, attempt at parenting. In short, this archaic legal exception allows parents to continue to use children as their whipping posts.

Take the recent case where a father's conviction of assault was reversed after he severely beat his nine-year-old son with a paddle for not eating his dinner, causing severe bruising, some pain, and limited mobility for several days.[55] The appellate court found the parental discipline privilege applied to nullify criminal liability, despite the fact that the father was cursing and screaming at the child throughout the beating. Another court acquitted a father who choked and beat his teenage daughter with a belt for, among other things, disrespecting him and texting with boys.[56] Research and anecdotal evidence confirm that these cases are not unusual; many, if not most, parents administering corporal punishment do so when they are stressed and angry. For instance, one study found that 44% of parents punishing their children "had lost it," with a large majority (85%) experiencing "moderate to high anger, remorse, and agitation."[57] Stress is highly correlated with corporal punishment, further casting doubt on the notion that it is, or even can realistically be, driven purely by concern for a child's welfare and administered in a calm fashion.[58] Finally, the not uncommon elision of corporal punishment into abuse also illustrates that it is often not containable with easily determined boundaries.[59]

Indeed, parental rage and shaming is often a central part of the punishment itself. Commentators urge parents to instill fear in their children so that they "submit to authority regardless of whether or not they agree."[60] In one case, a mother came to her children's school and beat her seven- and eight-year-old sons with a belt, yelling and screaming at them, because she wanted to "embarrass them for their bad behavior."[61] The trend of parents posting their brutal and shaming punishments of their children on the Internet starkly illustrates this reality.[62] The slapping and hair-pulling, accompanied by cursing and derogatory commentary, seem designed not so much to truly educate a child about right and wrong as to gain parents an audience and make them feel powerful.[63]

Nonetheless, courts rarely apply much scrutiny to a parent's true motivations or state of mind at the time of the beating. It is perhaps the only instance of a violent crime where they often rely entirely on the defendant's obviously self-interested statement about his or her state of mind. For instance, the father in one recent case "grabbed his [eleven-year-old son] by the throat" and spanked him over thirty times, causing bruising and pain. The father asserted the parental discipline privilege and reported to police that he "didn't think he was angry" during the punishment.[64] In another case, a father severely burned his five-year-old's hand over an open flame. The judge reduced the father's conviction to a misdemeanor and his sentence to a $100 fine. The judge reasoned that the father was trying to teach the boy not to steal, as the child had taken a pack of gum, and that the father merited less punishment because what he did was "of a corrective nature," even if severe.[65]

Judges sometimes even explicitly condone the anger, disregarding the statutorily prescribed *mens rea* as for a child's benefit. For instance, the judge acquitting the father of the most serious charges in the choking case outlined above praised the father's actions as indicating his care for his children and criticized limitations on parents' physical assaults against their children: "Not only do I believe that you um, had cause[] to discipline her, I do. . . . So, I totally understand why you were as angry as you were, and why you did what you did. Because I'm assuming you were trying to prevent her from living a life you don't want her to live. . . . Um, *unfortunately*, I think we're in this universe now, where parents don't just get to do whatever they want."[66] Finally, courts excuse or minimize the harm when they find the punishment justified by the child's misbehavior and the related parental purpose. Displaying this circular reasoning, the Supreme Court of Hawaii disregarded evidence of week-long bruising and pain that a fourteen-year-old experienced after her mother repeatedly beat her with a brush, a full backpack, and a metal clothes hanger, to reverse the mother's conviction and find her meriting the parental disciplinary defense.[67]

The parental discipline privilege not only confuses hostility with parental care, but also inverts the usual *mens rea* schema. The idea that the more control persons have over their actions, the more culpable they are, runs through criminal law theory and doctrine. Scholars debate free will versus determinism, how neuroscience should inform findings of guilt, and what level of sanctions will deter a rational actor. Rebecca Hollander-Blumoff demonstrates that, despite differences in these philosophical approaches, all three "rest on a shared belief that whether or not individuals have control over their own actions when they engage in criminal acts matters."[68]

This focus on control as increasing culpability underlies other criminal law doctrine as well.[69] The hierarchy of *mens rea* posits purposeful or intentional mindset at the top, followed by knowing actions, and then granting reckless or negligent behavior—that might be characterized as out of control—lower punishment.[70] Other examples include the actus reus requirement,[71] duress doctrine, insanity defense,[72] and Eighth Amendment mitigation based on the greater impulsivity of adolescents.[73] Particularly illustrative is the provocation doctrine, which mitigates murder to manslaughter when the defendant is so emotionally distraught by the victim's actions or supposed actions—infidelity, even nagging—that the defendant (often a man) is deemed to be less culpable and receives a significantly lighter sentence.[74] The Model Penal Code modernized this exception by significantly expanding it. Under this modern rule, "a homicide which would otherwise be murder is committed under the influence of extreme mental or emotional disturbance for which there is reasonable explanation or excuse."[75]

Indeed, proof of a *mens rea*, equivalent to some control over one's actions, is usually a prerequisite for criminal guilt. As criminal theorist Stephen J. Morse notes, "Desert is at least a necessary condition of just punishment, and the fair ascription of criminal culpability thus requires the presence of *mens rea*, which is the indicator of the degree of the defendant's fault."[76] When someone's actions are beyond his or her control, because of youth or insanity or duress, then lesser or no punishment is merited. The *mens rea* hierarchy thus operates to punish deliberate, chosen harm, and to "maximize the power of the individual to determine by his choice his future fate."[77]

Parental corporal punishment, however, is just the opposite—control renders the conduct *less* culpable, not more. The same actions done by a person deemed to be "out of control" are equated with ill will and guilt rather than, as in the general *mens rea* schema, a mitigating or exculpatory factor.[78] For instance, one father's conviction for assault after he spanked his nine-year-old daughter and threw her on her bed turned largely on his failure to "maintain reasonable control over the outcome or physical consequences to the child."[79] Reasoning that throwing a child represents a loss of control that was not present in spanking (even with a belt, presumably), the court affirmed his conviction. The court explicitly connected control to the parental purpose, opining that if one loses control, as by throwing a child, then the force cannot be said to properly prevent or punish misbehavior. The court made this ruling even in the face of the child testifying that she understood her father's actions were to discipline her for her misbehavior.[80] Thus the parent who calmly but severely beats a child, or imposes a lengthier and more painful punishment in a predetermined fashion, is excused, her control frequently deemed the utmost exercise of parental devotion and duty.[81]

In this fashion, the parental purpose transforms corporal punishment from assault to loving child-rearing. Initially, a scheme like this, which equates a parent who appears calm while administering violence with parental purpose and finds that an out-of-control parent suggests other motives, may appear to make sense. Upon further scrutiny, however, this legislative framework both obscures harm and contorts the criminal law. It ignores the anger and frustration accompanying many parental beatings or spankings, allowing parents to inflict harm under the guise of purpose despite the overwhelming evidence that even controlled beatings are not beneficial for discipline or other parenting goals. Anger is framed as for a misbehaving (or not even misbehaving) child's welfare, a type of blame-the-victim mentality that increases the injury.

I have argued here that the parental discipline privilege inverts the standard *mens rea* schema underlying the criminal law, which posits greater culpability as accompanying increased control over one's actions. By forgiving parents who intentionally and deliberately physically punish their children, while sometimes sanctioning those who punish with less forethought, the parental discipline privilege further bolsters this problematic equation of purposeful violence with parental love. In the next section, I theorize that this equation normalizes violence against children and condones its application in gendered and racialized ways to perpetuate illegitimate power hierarchies both within and outside of the family.

IV. Normalizing Violence against Children

This warped *mens rea* schema normalizes familial violence against children. Harm is obscured through exceptional terminology for family members—beating or hitting becomes the much more benign, even caring, "spanking." Tellingly, a recent study revealed that corporal punishment was rated better or worse simply depending on the verb used—"spanking" versus the more accurate terms "beating" or "hitting with a belt."[82] The researchers recommended calling these actions "assault" rather than "spanking," because the latter term minimizes and legitimates violence against children.[83] Harm is transformed into a benefit, into parental care. Scholars have pointed out the dangers of romanticizing parental love in other contexts.[84] The parental discipline privilege is particularly harmful given the extremely widespread use of corporal punishment and its ready elision into abuse. The criminal law has recognized children as some of society's most vulnerable members, and sentencing penalties are often applied to harms committed to them.[85] Yet when the harm is inflicted by those entrusted to care for them, we excuse it in the name of love.

This is sometimes explicit, as demonstrated in the recent controversy over NFL star Adrian Peterson's prosecution for whipping his four-year-old son with a tree branch. Peterson himself, his lawyer, and friends and family all defended the football player as a good father who loved his son and was raising him the same way he had been raised, with physical discipline as an essential component. Peterson's mother put it the most directly: "Most of us disciplined our kids a little more than we meant sometimes. But we were only trying to prepare them for the real world . . . You want to make [your kids] understand that they did wrong . . . *When you whip those you love, it's not about abuse, but love.*"[86]

Other relational exceptions to assault and battery laws have all been abolished, including the freedom to abuse spouses, apprentices, and students.[87] Similar to the parental discipline privilege, these were often justified in the name of love or for the victim's own good, but have since been revealed as paternalistic justifications for criminal violence.[88] Indeed, even animals are protected from the physical discipline parents are permitted in some states. Further demonstrating the archaic nature of the parental discipline privilege is the lack of modern legislative, or often any, rationales for it, as well as the reliance by contemporary courts on Blackstone and other very dated authorities. Tellingly, one appellate court relied heavily on a pre–Civil War case to reverse a man's conviction for severely beating his son with a paddle.[89] That case outlined the "sacred duties of parents to train up and qualify their children, for becoming useful and virtuous members of society . . . to command obedience, to control stubbornness, . . . and to reform bad habits."[90] Reliance on a precedent from a time when slavery, marital rape, and the physical punishment of apprentices were still allowed permits a distortion of the parental role and obscures the significant harms of corporal punishment. Despite massive changes in marital rights and responsibilities, and in knowledge about child development, parenting, and, of course, the immorality and illegality of slavery, the case remains current as to the parental discipline privilege.[91] Indeed, the privilege hearkens to slavery with its assumption that some people can own others, thus fostering violence in the name of instilling proper values and obedience.

Corporal punishment is not applied equally. Instead, it is implemented in a way that perpetuates illegitimate hierarchies within families and society more broadly. Political affiliation, race, and religiosity significantly impact one's likelihood to approve of and engage in corporal punishment, with more conservative groups, including Republicans and evangelical Christians, at the top.[92] (This variation in opinion and the blurry line between permissible corporal punishment and abuse compound the arbitrary and selective enforcement endemic to the criminal justice system, something that was possibly a factor in the Adrian Peterson prosecution.) Children who are particularly vulnerable are more likely to be physically punished by their parents and caregivers. For instance, children with disabilities are more likely to be struck and to be harmed both physically and psychologically.[93] So are gender-nonconforming children and those who identify as adolescents or later as gay, lesbian, or bisexual.[94] Some self-proclaimed parenting authorities even advocate using corporal punishment explicitly to enforce gender roles and heteronormativity. For instance, one popular preacher recommends that a parent whose young boy is acting effeminate "give him a good punch."[95]

Parental punishment is also highly gendered and racialized.[96] Girls are physically punished less frequently than boys, but their punishment is often sexualized in a harmful fashion. Telling a girl, particularly an older one, to remove her pants and skirt and lie down or bend over to be beat on the buttocks has disturbing similarities to sexual assault. One woman describes being physically disciplined as a teenager as "the closest thing to rape as I can imagine . . . punishment masked [as] sadism."[97] Girls are also frequently beaten for behavior deemed unbefitting the "good girl"—dressing in a provocative fashion or engaging in sexual conduct as a teenager—or even derided in misogynist terms for non-sexualized misbehavior.[98] Demonstrating this violent enforcement of femininity and chastity, some parents insult their daughters when hitting them, labeling them as "sluts" and "tricks."[99]

As noted above, corporal punishment is disproportionately used, and approved of, in Black families. Studies reveal that 81% of Black mothers, versus 62% of white or Hispanic mothers, advocate "hard spanking," with smaller but still significant discrepancies in approval ratings between Black and white or Hispanic fathers.[100] Numerous commentators have explained this disproportionality as parents' sometimes desperate attempts to raise Black children to act respectfully towards authority in order to stay safe in a world of endemic discrimination and racialized police violence.[101] For instance, Ta-Nehisi Coates suggests that Black parents spank their children more based on "the perception . . . that black people (class aside) who commit transgressions are subject to [a] higher price . . . black parents carry an extra layer of worry, a sense that mistakes that other kids—especially boys—can write off as the 'folly of youth' actually carry dire consequences for our kids."[102] Others from the Black community agree, as evidenced in the reaction to the Peterson case. Peterson's mother explained that Peterson may have been over-zealous, but "at the end of the day, we [Black parents] want to protect our children."[103] Similarly, NBA star Charles Barkley defended Peterson, who attributed his success in part to being physically disciplined by his own father, noting, "I'm a black guy . . . from the South. Whipping—we do that all the time. Every black parent in the South is going to be in jail under those circumstances."[104]

It is certainly true that Black children, particularly boys, are at greater risk for discrimination, police violence, and other harms in our still-racist society. But even well-intentioned corporal punishment brings great costs and perpetuates the notion that physical force is needed to subdue and "train" boys of color. Take the case described earlier where a judge lessened the father's sentence from incarceration to a misde-meanor fine after he severely burned his five-year-old's hand for taking a pack of gum. In that case involving a Latino boy, the judge relied heavily on the severe punishment's potential role in keeping the five-year-old from a life of crime. Opining that "maybe [the burning] will keep Ju-nior from being one of our customers [i.e., a criminal defendant] down-stream," the judge noted that many juvenile offenders begin with petty thefts.[105] The resolution of the case was as important in teaching the five-year-old son "a lesson" as his father (the one charged with a crime, as the boy was below the age of delinquency jurisdiction).[106]

Indeed, these narratives are deeply entrenched and destructive, and have been connected to slavery.[107] A historian of African American history, Stacey Patton traces the disproportionate use of corporal pun-ishment in Black families in large part to the violence and personhood harms endemic to slavery.[108] Adult slaves, "who endured the trauma of their own beatings, inherited their oppressors' violence and, for centuries, passed down these parenting beliefs."[109] They simultane-ously sought to protect their children from vicious whites by "dis-ciplining" them themselves and expressed their powerlessness, fear, and rage on the only people lower than themselves.[110] Post-slavery, this practice continued, "black parents becoming extensions of the master's lash in order to instill unquestioning obedience to the rules of the Jim Crow system."[111] Although admittedly controversial within the Black community, Patton's claims are not unprecedented. Other scholars, including sociologist Orlando Patterson, have discussed the connection between physical punishment and slavery. In his seminal history of slavery, Patterson highlights the essentiality of violence to maintaining the slave order, noting that "there is no known slaveholding society where the whip was not considered an indispensable instrument."[112] More specifically as to parenthood, Patterson has argued that slave mothers were sometimes cruel to their own children as a displacement of aggression towards the slave masters and overseers who harmed them.[113]

Patton is sympathetic to the historic and contemporary pressures on Black parents, but nonetheless contends that the ongoing use of corporal punishment helps to maintain a racialized hierarchy.[114] She terms this ongoing pattern "one of the saddest untold stories in American history—the way in which victims of racist oppression and violence have hurt the bodies of their own children to protect them from a hostile society. The truth is that white supremacy has done a masterful job of getting black people to continue its trauma work and call it 'love.'"[115] Patton calls for the Black community to stop using corporal punishment because it erodes children's humanity and teaches them blind obedience, when children instead need to learn to object to victimization and resist violence, particularly racialized violence.

Patton and others observe that parental beatings in the name of love convey problematic lessons about obedience, power, and physical force. Being beaten, particularly by someone sworn to care for you, is humiliating and a violation of trust. Although significantly different from slavery, corporal punishment in families conveys some of the degradation characteristic of that system.[116] Moreover, administering beatings while reciting sexist or heterocentric insults leads children to internalize messages about their bodies and skin color: Girls who dress a certain way are worthless and good only for sex, young men who are attracted to other men are deviant, and Black boys are dangerous and bestial, requiring physical force to compel good behavior. Parental violence thus entrenches societal disgust and stigma. It indoctrinates submission rather than teaching self-respect and resilience. As a result, it ends up perpetuating the very societal hierarchy and even violence that parents are attempting to protect their children from. In short, corporal punishment is counterproductive. Girls who are beaten by their fathers or stepfathers may be more likely to submit to intimate partner violence or engage in risky sex, while Black boys who experience parental whippings are arguably more likely to experience violence and discrimination from bosses, police, and other authority figures.[117]

V. Conclusion

The harms of corporal punishment are well documented and significant. Yet parental discipline remains widely practiced and approved of, a very sticky norm. Why are children still seen as appropriate targets for assault, often accompanied by shaming? The few legislators who have tried to limit it have failed, often ridiculed.[118] Why is there so little interest or political will to limit this pervasive intimate violence?

A partial explanation is the low worth put on children in American law, despite the rhetoric of family values.[119] The United States is one of only a handful of nations worldwide not to sign the United Nations Convention on the Rights of the Child, and has the highest rates of child mortality and lowest rates of spending on child health and childcare among industrialized nations. Seen through the lens of children as parental property, child abuse is revealed as not categorically different from parental discipline, but rather as part of the same continuum. The prevalent child-rearing culture is one in which privacy and parental rights are used to justify practices such as corporal punishment, despite their proven ineffectiveness and harms.[120]

The vast realm of parental power, however, has recently begun to be curtailed. To cite just one example, California in 2016 enacted a statute eliminating all exceptions to mandatory vaccination of children, a law that experts have argued will withstand challenges based on religious and parental rights.[121] A scrutiny of parental conduct that may bring harm is particularly important as our knowledge of family and child development changes. Further supporting a ban on corporal punishment is the growing recognition of children as at least partial rights-bearers, as suggested in *Obergefell*.[122] These developments render the parental discipline privilege an illegitimate vestige of a prior era. Like marital rape and the "rule of thumb," this status-based exception to intra-familial violence should be abolished.

This is not to say that every, or even most, parental beatings or slaps should result in prosecution. Criminalization brings great costs and is used far too often in the United States to address complex social problems such as lack of knowledge of and support for appropriate discipline techniques, and family violence. As Jonathan Simon has described, we increasingly "turn to criminalization as a primary tool of social justice," essentially "governing through crime."[123] Overcriminalization is likely the most pressing justice issue of our day, and compounding this concern is the unequal distributional costs of increasing the scope of criminal liability.[124] I have previously critiqued state efforts to intervene to address family behavior, including parenting, as disproportionally punitive to low-income, of color, and other marginalized families.[125]

To address these concerns, the ban on parental corporal punishment could be a violation subject to ticketing rather than severe penalties, or a civil ban bringing fines.[126] As such, it would still educate the public as to the harms of corporal punishment, and hopefully decrease its use. Many European countries banning it have done so via a civil ban, or a criminal ban that is rarely enforced.[127] For instance, Sweden, the first country to ban corporal punishment, "aimed at educating the Swedish public, not at prosecuting parents."[128] Despite virtually no prosecutions of parents under the new law, the national prevalence of corporal punishment declined significantly in the twenty years following the ban.

Despite the costs, I still argue for the abolition of the parental discipline privilege for two primary reasons. First is the significant fact that some parental corporal punishment is already criminalized in every state, and an even wider swath is regulated through the quasi-criminal child protection system.[129] Marginalized families are already subject to disproportionate intervention, as arguably occurred in the high-profile Adrian Peterson case. Yet the current scope of criminalization is a patchwork differing widely across jurisdictions, with no basis in empirics and applied with vast judicial discretion, compounding its disproportionality. One state appellate court recently characterized this area of the law as "the most fraught with subjectivity," and opined that it impedes the notice function of the criminal law given that "one's guilt or innocence depend[s] on how someone else [i.e. the judge or jurors] disciplines his or her children when there is no consensus about what's

appropriate."[130] Eliminating the vague and divergent parental discipline privileges in state law would create a clear line, thereby diluting
discretion and sending a sharp expressive message about appropriate
conduct.

The second reason concerns this expressive message. The criminal
law plays an important role in designating societal norms.[131] It also
communicates the worth, or lack thereof, of victims, and the culpability,
or lack thereof, of offenders.[132] Indeed, efforts to criminalize and punish domestic violence historically, and sometimes still, have centered on
criminalization to convey the wrongness of intimate violence, with "the
social message of domestic violence equated with the level of punishment meted out for the crime."[133] I do not mean to overstate the ability
of laws to shift social norms; the examples of domestic violence and
acquaintance rape demonstrate that legal changes must be accompanied
by, and even be secondary to, other measures in order to shift deeply
embedded social norms.[134]

Accordingly, my conclusion that the parental discipline privilege
should be eliminated warrants a significant caveat. The criminal law
should not be our only, or even our primary, approach to eliminating
corporal punishment, nor should prosecution and punishment maintain their current form. Although I recommend elimination of this
last remaining exception to assault, I strongly endorse public education and other methods to best change this outdated and often misinformed practice.[135] Scholars have called for ongoing criminalization
coupled with education, restorative justice, and other alternative approaches to analogous offenses such as acquaintance rape and intimate
partner violence.[136] Leigh Goodmark, for instance, recently examined
whether domestic violence should be decriminalized. While acknowledging criminalization's significant costs, including its ineffectiveness
and disproportionate impact, she concludes that it is a necessary part
of addressing intimate violence.[137] Goodmark argues that criminalization should, however, be accompanied by non-criminal supports and
services for victims and offenders, and a rethinking of the criminal policies so that families are benefitted, not harmed, and future violence is
better prevented.[138] I would endorse a similar approach to corporal punishment, combining the expressive message that assault, one of the old-
est common law crimes, is not forgiven because of a family relationship,

with the primary use of non-criminal measures to change behavior, and punishment only in the most severe or repeated incidents. This more careful and holistic approach best balances the costs and benefits to children, their families, and our evolving society.

Author's Note

Thanks to Jaime Abrams, Leigh Goodmark, and Kate Mogulescu for helpful comments, Lauren Rayner Davis for valuable research assistance, and, particularly, Jane Stoever for convening this conference and collection of essays. This piece, part of a larger project on the relationship between family status and criminal liability, builds on some arguments raised in prior work. *See* Cynthia Godsoe, *Redrawing the Boundaries of Relational Crime*, 69 ALA. L. REV. 100 (2017) and Cynthia Godsoe, *Redefining Parental Rights: The Case of Corporal Punishment*, 32 CONSTIT. COMM. 281 (2017) (symposium issue).

NOTES

1 3 WILLIAM BLACKSTONE, COMMENTARIES ON THE LAWS OF ENGLAND *120 (1765). Revealing how little the law in this area has evolved, courts continue to cite Blackstone, as well as pre–Civil War era cases, to support parental corporal punishment. *See infra* notes 90–92.

2 I adopt the widely accepted sociological definition of corporal punishment to mean any physical punishment, including spanking with or without objects such as belts and other physical disciplinary tools. *See* Benjamin Shmueli, *Corporal Punishment in the Educational System Versus Corporal Punishment By Parents: A Comparative View*, 73 LAW & CONTEMP. PROBS. 281, 282 (2010).

3 *See, e.g.,* CONN. GEN. STAT. § 46B-38a (2012) (protecting persons who lived together or dated); 23 PA. CONS. STAT. §§ 6102, 6106 (2008) (protecting current spouse, former spouse, or persons who live or have lived together as spouses; parent; child; persons related by blood or marriage; past or present sexual or intimate partners; persons with whom you have a child in common with). Intimate partner violence has also received much more attention from scholars than parent-child assaults. *See, e.g.,* Reva B. Siegel, *"The Rule of Love": Wife Beating as Prerogative and Privacy*, 105 YALE L.J. 2117 (1996); Elizabeth M. Schneider, *The Violence of Privacy*, 23 CONN. L. REV. 973 (1991).

4 STACY PATTON, SPARE THE KIDS: WHY WHUPPING CHILDREN WON'T SAVE BLACK AMERICA 166, 809, 890–95 (2017).

5 *See* Marie Ashe and Naomi R. Cahn, *Child Abuse: A Problem for Feminist Theory*, 2 TEX. J. WOMEN & L. 75, 109–10 (1993) ("It is our belief that most feminist

writers who have attended to the reality of child abuse perpetrated by mothers have minimized the extent of such abuse, ignored its pervasiveness, or attempted to define it away . . ." and calling for feminist theorists to examine these issues "for both theoretical and practical reasons.").

6 Commentators have criticized American law for providing parents with virtual ownership rights over their children. *See* Barbara Bennett Woodhouse, *Who Owns The Child?: Meyer and Pierce and the Child as Property*, 33 WM. & MARY L. REV. 995, 997 (1992) (arguing that the right of parental control, although termed a liberty interest, seems to consider children as parental property); *see also* Akhil Reed Amar & Daniel Widawsky, *Child Abuse as Slavery: A Thirteenth Amendment Response to DeShaney*, 105 HARV. L. REV. 1359, 1361–62 (1992) (arguing that treating children like parental property is unconstitutional).

7 MODEL PENAL CODE § 3.08 cmt. 2 (1985). Demonstrating this equation of parenthood with "good" violence, courts routinely distinguish child abuse from "disciplinary" beatings to reverse a conviction. *See, e.g.*, Gonzalez v. Santa Clara County Dep't of Social Services, 223 Cal. App. 4th 72, 75, 90 (6th Cir. 2014).

8 We have a long history of devaluing children and, concomitantly, normalizing parental violence against children. The American Society for the Prevention of Cruelty to Animals (ASPCA) was founded before the Society for the Protection & Care of Children (SPCC). Compare *History*, ASPCA, www.aspca.org (last visited June 17, 2017) ("The ASPCA was founded in New York City in 1866 to prevent cruelty to animals in the United States."), with *Our History*, SPCC, www.spcc-roch.org (last visited June 17, 2017) ("The story of SPCC began in 1875 with the plight of a small girl named Mary Ellen who lived with abusive caretakers in New York City.").

9 *See* Siegel, *supra* note 3, at 2123.

10 *See, e.g.,* Erwin Chemerinsky & Michele Goodwin, *Compulsory Vaccination Laws Are Constitutional*, 110 NW. U. L. REV. 589, 594, 603–5 (2016) (arguing that a compulsory vaccination law can withstand challenges based on parental rights and religious beliefs, and describing courts' consistent rejection of constitutional challenges to compulsory vaccination laws).

11 Jennifer M. Collins, *Crime and Parenthood: The Uneasy Case for Prosecuting Negligent Parents*, 100 NW. U. L. REV. 807, 812 (2006). See further discussion *infra* section IV.

12 *See* Chloe Kerr, *Mind Your Language*, SUN (Jan. 6, 2017), www.thesun.co.uk (reporting research that people's approval of corporal punishment decreases significantly when the words "hit," "beat," etc. are used instead of "spank").

13 Undoubtedly, prosecution of parental discipline deemed unreasonable also occurs in a disproportionately racial and gendered fashion, as does prosecution more broadly. The high-profile Adrian Peterson case is perhaps an example of this. See discussion *infra* note 18. Yet reasonable or non-criminal corporal punishment also occurs disproportionately among certain communities and enforces stereotypes.

14 To be clear, I do not mean to imply that most parents commit these harms deliberately; in contrast, I think many remain unaware that they are conveying these messages to their children.

15 *See, e.g.,* N.Y. PENAL LAW § 25.10(1) (McKinney's 2015) (affirmative defense, "The use of physical force upon another person which would otherwise constitute an offense is justifiable and not criminal [when] . . . 1. A parent, guardian or other person entrusted with the care and supervision of a person under the age of twenty-one . . . may use physical force, but not deadly physical force, upon such person when and to the extent that he reasonably believes it necessary to maintain discipline or to promote the welfare of such person."); MICH. COMP. LAWS § 750.136b(9) (2015) (part of definition, "This section does not prohibit a parent or guardian, or other person permitted by law or authorized by the parent or guardian, from taking steps to reasonably discipline a child, including the use of reasonable force."); 11 R.I. GEN. LAWS § 11-9-5.3(d) (2015) ("For the purpose of this section, 'other physical injury' is defined as any injury, other than a serious bodily injury, which arises other than from the imposition of nonexcessive corporal punishment.").

16 *See, e.g.,* ALASKA STAT. § 11.81.430 (2016); WIS. STAT. § 939.45(5) (2017); Commonwealth v. Dorvil, 32 N.E.3d 861, 870 (Mass. 2015).

17 Some states still limit it to these categories. LA. STAT. ANN. § 14:18 (2015) ("This defense of justification can be claimed . . . (4) When the offender's conduct is reasonable discipline of minors by their parents. . . .").

18 Forty states allow custodians to assert the privilege, and thirty-four go even further, allowing adults in loco parentis to do so. *See, e.g.,* OHIO REV. CODE § 2151.031(C) (2015) (defining child abuse but excluding "a child exhibiting evidence of corporal punishment or other physical disciplinary measure by a parent, guardian, custodian, person having custody or control, or person in loco parentis").

19 The extremely broad, functional definition in the corporal punishment context stands in sharp contrast to other definitions of parents in the criminal and family law. *See* Cynthia Godsoe, *Redrawing the Boundaries of Relational Crime*, 69 ALA. L. REV. 100 (2017) [hereinafter Godsoe, *Relational Crime*]. This vast sweep increases the harm of corporal punishment by legitimating violence from a large number of adults who are not legally or even functionally parents.

20 MODEL PENAL CODE § 3.08(1) (1985). This standard does not require that the force be reasonable or that the parent reasonably believes the use of force is appropriate. *See id.* § 3.08 cmt. 2. A number of states follow this standard.

21 *See, e.g.,* HAW REV. STAT. § 703-309 (2011) ("The force used [must] not intentionally, knowingly, recklessly, or negligently create a risk of causing substantial bodily injury, disfigurement, extreme pain or mental distress, or neurological damage."). Additionally, corporal punishment statutes in the District of Columbia, Delaware, Hawaii, and Washington attempt to limit harm inflicted by providing categorical exclusions of certain children (i.e., below a certain age such as "nonaccidental injury to a child under the age of 18 months" or "shaking a minor under three

years of age") or particular types of acts (e.g., throwing, kicking, burning, biting, cutting, striking with a closed fist, interfering with breathing, or threatening with a deadly weapon) from the parental privilege. D.C. CODE § 16-2301 (2016); 11 DEL. CODE § 468 (2016); HAW REV. STAT. § 703-309 (2011); WASH. REV. CODE § 9A.16.100 (2012) (harm must not be "greater than transient pain or minor temporary marks").

22 Murray A. Straus, *Prevalence, Societal Causes, and Trends in Corporal Punishment and Parents in World Perspective*, 3 LAW & CONTEMP. PROBS. 1, 3–6 (2010) [hereinafter Straus, *Prevalence*]. Rates are particularly high among babies and toddlers. Elizabeth T. Gershoff & Susan H. Bitensky, *The Case Against Corporal Punishment of Children*, 13 PSYCHOL. PUB. POL'Y & L. 231, 232 (2007). As to public opinion, see Steve Hendrix, *The End of Spanking?*, WASH. POST MAGAZINE (Jan. 3, 2013), www.washingtonpost.com (reporting that 65% to 75% of people believe that "it is okay to occasionally spank a child"). In recent years, support for corporal punishment has declined modestly. *Attitudes Towards Spanking*, CHILD TRENDS DATA BANK (2015), www.childtrends.org (using biannual GSS data).

23 This was the topic of one episode of the popular television show *Black-ish*. See James Poniewozik, *Black-ish Whips Up a Conversation About Spanking*, TIME (Oct. 23, 2014), http://time.com; *see also* Harry Enten, *Americans' Opinions on Spanking Vary By Party, Race, Region and Religion*, FIVETHIRTYEIGHT. COM (Sept. 15, 2014), https://fivethirtyeight.com (using data from 1986–2010 to demonstrate the "large gaps" in opinion between evangelical Christians and other Americans, reporting that African Americans are 11% more likely to support corporal punishment than whites, including Hispanics, and showing that people in the South are 17% more likely to support spanking than those in the Northeast).

24 Heather L. Corliss, Susan D. Cochran, & Vickie M. Mays, *Reports of Parental Maltreatment During Childhood in a United States Population-Based Survey of Homosexual, Bisexual, and Heterosexual Adults*, 26 CHILD ABUSE & NEGLECT 1165 (2002), www.ncbi.nlm.nih.gov.

25 *Child Maltreatment Surveillance: Uniform Definitions for Public Health and Recommended Data Elements*, CDC (2008), www.cdc.gov.

26 *See* Godsoe, *Relational Crime*, *supra* note 19.

27 1 WILLIAM BLACKSTONE, COMMENTARIES *440 (1765). *See also* 3 WILLIAM BLACKSTONE, COMMENTARIES *120 (positing parental discipline as an exception to battery: "battery is, in some cases, justifiable or lawful; as where one who hath authority, a parent or master, gives moderate correction to his child, his scholar, or his apprentice.").

28 *See also* Magazu v. Dep't of Children and Families, 473 Mass. 430, 431 (Sup. Ct. Mass 2016) (parents argued that because physical discipline is an integral aspect of their Christian faith, the department's decision to deny their license as foster parents impermissibly infringed on their constitutional right to the free exercise of religion).

29 *See* MURRAY A. STRAUS, BEATING THE DEVIL OUT OF THEM: CORPORAL PUNISHMENT IN AMERICAN FAMILIES AND ITS EFFECTS ON CHILDREN

183–84 (1994) (detailing the relationship between religion and corporal punishment and noting that this passage refers to a shepherd guiding or redirecting his flock of sheep, not striking them) [hereinafter STRAUS, BEATING THE DEVIL].

30 Walter Williams, *Making a Case for Corporal Punishment*, INSIGHT ON THE NEWS (Sept. 13, 1999), www.questia.com.

31 *See* L. Nicole Williams, *8 Reasons to Spank Your Kids*, MADAME NOIRE (Feb. 8, 2011), http://madamenoire.com.

32 *See* Letter from John B. King, Jr. to Governors and Chief State School Officers (Nov. 22, 2016), www2.ed.gov ("Corporal punishment has also been banned in . . . U.S. prisons and U.S. military training facilities, and most juvenile detention facilities. . . . A long list of education, medical, civil rights, disabilities, and child advocacy groups . . . have also been calling for a ban on this practice.") [hereinafter King letter]; *see also* Melinda D. Anderson, *Where Teachers Are Still Allowed to Spank Students*, ATLANTIC (Dec. 15, 2015), www.theatlantic.com.

33 *State Laws*, GUNDERSEN CENTER FOR EFFECTIVE DISCIPLINE (2017), www .gundersenhealth.org; Hendrix, *supra* note 22, and the vast majority of children "paddled" in schools live in just five states—Mississippi, Texas, Alabama, Arkansas, and Georgia. Anderson, *supra* note 32.

34 King letter, *supra* note 32.

35 *See* Constance Gibbs, *France Says "Non!" to Hitting Kids as it Bans Corporal Punishment*, N.Y. DAILY NEWS (Jan. 4, 2017), www.nydailynews.com (detailing that fifty-two countries worldwide have now banned corporal punishment, including most of Europe); see also *Corporal Punishment Policies Around the World*, CNN. COM (Nov. 9, 2011), www.cnn.com ("Sweden, in 1979, was the first to make it illegal to strike a child as a form of discipline. Since then, many other countries in Europe have also instituted bans, as have New Zealand and some countries in Africa and the Americas.").

36 *See* United Nations, Convention on the Rights of the Child, Res. 44/25, Art. 37(a) (Nov. 20 1989), www.ohchr.org ("No child shall be subjected to torture or other cruel, inhuman or degrading treatment or punishment.").

37 Gershoff & Bitensky, *supra* note 22, at 238–41 (cataloguing research on the harms).

38 Elizabeth T. Gershoff & Andrew Grogan-Kaylor, *Spanking and Child Outcomes: Old Controversies and New Meta-Analyses*, J. FAM. PSYCHOL. 13 (June 2016) (meta-analysis of over one hundred studies on corporal punishment).

39 AAP, *Guidance for Effective Discipline*, 101 PEDIATRICS 4 (1998), http://pediat rics.aappublications.org ("Corporal punishment is of limited effectiveness and has potentially deleterious side effects. The American Academy of Pediatrics recommends that parents be encouraged and assisted in the development of methods other than spanking for managing undesired behavior.").

40 STRAUS, BEATING THE DEVIL, *supra* note 29, at 9. Straus and other researchers have demonstrated that even infrequent and mild corporal punishment can lead to an increased risk of antisocial behavior. *Id.* at 16. Corporal punishment

also has physical effects potentially lasting throughout adulthood and increasing morbidity. *See* Vincent J. Felitti et al., *Relationship of Childhood Abuse and Household Dysfunction to Many of the Leading Causes of Death in Adults*, AM. J. PREVENTATIVE MED. (1998), www.ajpmonline.org (reporting on the CDC Adverse Childhood Experiences [ACE] Study which "found a strong relationship between the number of childhood exposures [to hitting or other physical violence] and the number of health risk factors for leading causes of death in adults").

41 Stephanie Hanes, *To Spank or Not to Spank: Corporal Punishment in the US*, CHRISTIAN SCIENCE MONITOR (Oct. 19, 2014), www.csmonitor.com (quoting Professor Kenneth Dodge).

42 *See* Straus, *Prevalence, supra* note 22, at 21–22 (noting corporal punishment and abuse "share much of the same etiology"); *see also* Elizabeth Thompson Gershoff, *Corporal Punishment by Parents and Associated Child Behaviors and Experiences: A Meta-Analytic and Theoretical Review*, 128 PSYCHOL. BULL. 604 (2002), www .apa.org (physical discipline and abuse are "often at the core the same") [hereinafter Gershoff, *Corporal Punishment*].

43 Gershoff, *Corporal Punishment, supra* note 42, at 539, 541 (finding that every one of the twenty-seven studies she surveyed concluded that corporal punishment is associated with increases in children's aggressive behaviors).

44 *See* Dana Dovey, *Abuse in Relationships: Children Who Are Spanked Grow Up to Hit Their Adult Partners*, NEWSWEEK (Dec. 6, 2017), www.newsweek.com.

45 See also *Study Links Childhood Spanking to Violent Future Relationships*, IFL SCI-ENCE (Dec. 6, 2017) (reporting that the study controlled for sex, age, ethnicity, parental education, and, most importantly, physical abuse).

46 Dovey, *supra* note 44.

47 Sandee Lamotte & Carina Storrs, *Spanking Can Lead to Relationship Violence, Study Says*, ATLANTIC (Dec. 6, 2017), www.theatlantic.com.

48 *See, e.g.,* Erwin Chemerinsky & Michele Goodwin, *Compulsory Vaccination Laws Are Constitutional*, 110 NW. U. L. REV. 589, 594, 603–5 (2016) (arguing that a compulsory vaccination law can withstand challenges based on parental rights and religious beliefs, and describing courts' consistent rejection of constitutional challenges to compulsory vaccination laws); Cynthia Godsoe, *Redefining Parental Rights: The Case of Corporal Punishment*, 32 CONSTIT. COMM. 281 (2017) (symposium issue) [hereinafter Godsoe, *Redefining Parental Rights*] (making this point, but also arguing that parental rights should not be read to support corporal punishment).

49 Jill Hasday has argued that this "progress story" about children's best interests obscures ongoing inequality and overreach of parental rights in family law. She writes, "Divert[ing] attention from examining how family law actually regulates the parent-child relationship and from considering the normative question. . . . Where should family law prioritize parental prerogatives, and where, how, and to what extent does family law's continued deference to parental rights over

children's interests need to be reformed?" JILL ELAINE HASDAY, FAMILY LAW REIMAGINED 148 (2014).

50 JOSHUA DRESSLER, CRIMINAL LAW § 10.02 (6th ed. 2012).

51 Morissete v. United States, 342 U.S. 246, 250 (1952); *see also* United States v. Cordoba-Hincapie, 825 F. Supp. 485, 490 (E.D.N.Y. 1993) (describing *mens rea* as "the criminal law's mantra").

52 Stephen J. Morse, *Inevitable* Mens Rea, 27 HARV. J.L. & PUB. POL'Y 51 (2003) ("The requirement of *mens rea* contributes to the meaning and value of our lives as moral beings.").

53 *See, e.g.,* N.H. REV. STAT. § 627:6 (2016) ("A parent . . . is justified in using force against [a] minor when and to the extent that he [or she] reasonably believes it necessary to prevent or punish such minor's misconduct."). A related limitation on the parental discipline privilege is that the corporal punishment must be reasonable. This reasonableness analysis often explicitly assesses the reason for the discipline, such as what type of misbehavior the child engaged in and how serious it was, as well as the related questions of the parent's frequency of corporal punishment, and other efforts he or she had tried to discipline the child.

54 *See, e.g.,* 11 DEL. CODE § 468 (2016) (allows for two general justifications, either when the "force is used for the purpose of safeguarding or promoting the welfare of the child" or when the "force used is intended to benefit the child"). *See also* NEB. REV. STAT. § 28-1413 (1975) ("for the purpose of safeguarding or promoting the welfare of the minor"); ALASKA STAT. § 11.81.430 (2016) ("to promote the welfare of the child"); ARK. CODE § 5-2-605; CONN. GEN. STAT. ANN. § 53a-18 (2011) ("to promote the welfare of such minor"); N.Y. PENAL LAW § 35.10 (McKinney's 2015) ("to promote the welfare").

55 *Guest Editorial: N.C. Spanking Case Raises Questions on Parental Rights,* WILSON TIMES (March 19, 2017), http://wilsontimes.com [hereinafter *N.C. Spanking Case*]. The case was recently heard by the North Carolina Supreme Court and the decision is pending.

56 Carter v. State, 67 N.E.3d 1041, 1048 (Ct. App. Ind. 2016).

57 Anthony M. Graziano, Jessica L. Hamblen, & Wendy A. Plante, *Subabusive Violence in Child Rearing in Middle-Class American Families,* 98 PEDIATRICS 4 (Oct. 1996), http://pediatrics.aappublications.org.

58 *See* Clay Jones, *Corporal Punishment in the Home: Parenting Tool or Parenting Fail,* SCIENCE-BASED MEDICINE (Jan. 3, 2014), https://sciencebasedmedicine.org.

59 Unfortunately, courts only rarely recognize this. The Massachusetts SJC is one recent exception. It noted that "the [state interest in protecting children] is particularly powerful in the context of corporal punishment, given the risk that the parental privilege defense will be used as a cover for instances of child abuse," but nonetheless affirmed the parental discipline privilege, albeit in more limited form than in many jurisdictions. *See* Commonwealth v. Dorvil, 32 N.E.3d 861, 868 (Mass. 2015).

60 L. Nicole Williams, *supra* note 31 ("To be feared (in the sense of reverence) is to be respected. Your children should be weary [*sic*] of going against your rules.").

61 People v. Thompson, No. 05–2469, 2005 WL 2850915, at *1 (N.Y.City. Ct. Oct. 24, 2005).

62 Sometimes these parents face investigation and prosecution, but often don't. *Compare* Skyler Henry, *Baltimore County Woman in Viral Video Charged with Child Abuse*, ABC 2 NEWS (March 24, 2017, 2:32 PM), www.abc2news.com, *with* Caitlin Nolan, *Mother Streams Beating of Her Daughter on Facebook Live: "I'm Gonna Need Y'All to Send This Viral,"* INSIDE EDITION (July 26, 2016, 9:26 AM), www.insideedition.com.

63 *See* Denene Millner, *The Perils and False Rewards of Parenting in the Era of Digi-Discipline*, NPR (Apr. 7, 2017), www.npr.org.

64 *See* Tess Koppelman, *Family Asserts that Man in Jail for Spanking Child Wasn't Abusing Him*, FOX 4 (Aug. 29, 2013), http://fox4kc.com.

65 Stuart Pfeifer & Jennifer Mena, *Burning Son's Hand: $100 Fine*, L.A. TIMES (Apr. 27, 2002), http://articles.latimes.com.

66 Carter v. State, 67 N.E.3d 1041, 1048 (Ct. App. Ind. 2016) (emphasis added). The judge in *Thompson* described above similarly acquitted the mother who beat her young sons at school, while in a rage. *But see* People v. Devito, 43 Misc.3d 1222(A) (NY. Co. Ct. 2014) (holding that a father's force was unreasonable where he struck his seventeen-year-old daughter in the face while trying to bring her home, in part because "the record establishes that [he] became very angry and upset . . . [and] was motivated by anger, rather than a parental desire to discipline a child. . . ." Significantly, however, that case involved a very public altercation between the father, his daughter, and her teenaged boyfriend, and was witnessed by numerous other adults, unlike most incidents of corporal punishment).

67 State v. Metavale, 166 P.3d 322, 338 (Haw. 2007) (also ignoring the overwhelming empirical research on the harms of corporal punishment to say there was no emotional or psychological harm to the daughter and focusing instead on the daughter's "defiant behavior").

68 Rebecca Hollander-Blumoff, *Crime, Punishment, and the Psychology of Self-Control*, 61 EMORY L.J. 501, 504 (2012).

69 For instance, the *actus reus* requirement also posits control over one's bodily actions as essential to a finding of criminal guilt. *See, e.g.,* People v. Newton, 8 Cal.App.3d 359 (Cal. Ct. App. 1970). As one expert summarizes, it ensures that "a human being—a person—and not simply an organ of a human being, causes the bodily action." DRESSLER, *supra* note 50, § 9.02 at 90.

70 MODEL PENAL CODE § 2.02(2) (1985). Commentators have engaged in robust criticism of strict liability *mens rea* offenses, which require no knowledge, purpose, or disregard of risk, because they punish actors for conduct over which they largely have no control. *See, e.g.,* Stephen J. Schulhofer, *Harm and Punishment: A Critique of Emphasis on the Results of Conduct in the Criminal Law*, 122 U. PA. L. REV. 1497 (1974).

71 *See* discussion *supra* note 69.

72 The MPC definition is: "A person is not responsible for criminal conduct if at the time of such conduct as a result of mental disease or defect [the defendant] lacks substantial capacity either to appreciate the criminality [wrongfulness] of his conduct or to conform his conduct to the requirements of law." MODEL PENAL CODE § 4.01(1) (1985). Mentally ill defendants may also argue that their mental disorder negated *mens rea*. Stephen J. Morse, *Mental Disorder and Criminal Justice*, U. PENN. L. FACULTY SCHOLARSHIP 1751, 21 (Mar. 29, 2017), http://scholarship.law.upenn.edu.

73 *See* Graham v. Florida, 560 U.S. 48 (2010). *See also* Montana v. Egelhoff, 518 U.S. 37 (1996) (voluntary drunkenness).

74 Scholars have critiqued this lesser punishment of homicides prompted by minor, often gendered, behavior. *See, e.g.,* Emily L. Miller, *(Wo)manslaughter: Voluntary Manslaughter, Gender, and the Model Penal Code*, 50 EMORY L.J. 665, 692 (2000).

75 MODEL PENAL CODE § 210.03 (1985).

76 Morse, *supra* note 72, at 34.

77 H.L.A. HART, *Punishment and the Elimination of Responsibility, in* PUNISHMENT AND RESPONSIBILITY, 181–82 (H.L.A. Hart ed., 2008).

78 *See, e.g.,* Newby v. United States, 797 A.2d 1233, 1235 (D.C. Ct. App. 2002) (affirming a conviction of assault against a mother for hitting and kicking her daughter in part because the mother "admitted that she was angry and had lost control of the situation"). One recent decision, however, takes the more pragmatic view that parental control or anger does not change the parental discipline privilege. *See* Dorvil, 32 N.E.3d at 872 ("It is understandable that parents would be angry at a child whose misbehavior necessitates punishment, and we see no reason why such anger should render otherwise reasonable uses of force impermissible.").

79 State v. York, 766 A.2d 570, 575 (Me. 2001).

80 *Id.*

81 Recall the father who burned his son's hand and was granted only a $100 fine despite the physical damage and pain he caused his son.

82 Kerr, *supra* note 12 (describing the report and quoting the researchers). My earlier caveat bears repeating—many parents who corporally punish may not mean to cause their children harm, but the research is clear that they are.

83 *Id.*

84 Jennifer M. Collins, *Lady Madonna, Children at Your Feet: The Criminal Justice System's Romanticization of the Parent-Child Relationship*, 93 IOWA L. REV. 131, 133–34 (2007).

85 Joshua Kleinfeld, *A Theory of Criminal Victimization*, 65 STAN. L. REV. 1087, 1092 (2013) (theorizing that courts "find something still worse about those crimes where the victims are . . . children," because they are "particularly vulnerable or particularly innocent").

86 *Peterson's Mom Comes to His Defense,* ESPN.COM NEWS (Sept. 18, 2014), www
    .espn.com [hereinafter *Peterson's Mom*].

87 Some of these, as with the parental discipline privilege, were justified in the name
    of love or for the victim's own good.

88 *See, e.g.,* Siegel, *supra* note 3.

89 *N.C. Spanking Case, supra* note 55.

90 *Id.*

91 *See also* State v. Taylor, 701 A.2d 389, 393 (Md. 1997) (acknowledging that the privi-
    lege existed "long before the advent of contemporary child abuse legislation").

92 Michael Lipka, *U.S. Religious Groups and Their Political Leanings,* GSS PEW (Feb.
    23, 2016), www.pewresearch.org.

93 Children with disabilities are more likely to be abused by parents, abuse that often
    begins as corporal punishment. *Childhood Maltreatment among Children with
    Disabilities,* CDC, www.cdc.gov (last visited June 17, 2017) ("Children with disabili-
    ties may be at higher risk for abuse or neglect than children without disabilities,"
    because "parents can more easily become stressed with the demands placed on
    them by parenting a child with a disability."). I am also extrapolating from data
    that they are more likely to be physically disciplined in school. Sam Dillon, *Dis-
    abled Students are Spanked More,* N.Y. TIMES (Aug. 10, 2009), www.nytimes.com
    ("Corporal punishment is just not an effective method of punishment, especially
    for disabled children, who may not even understand why they're being hit.")
    (quoting Alice Farmer). Some states appear to recognize this unique vulnerability
    in rendering a child's mental and physical development a factor to consider in
    assessing the reasonableness of punishment. *See, e.g.,* Doriane Lambelet Coleman,
    Kenneth A. Dodge, & Sarah Keeton Campbell, *Where and How to Draw the Line
    Between Reasonable Corporal Punishment and Abuse,* L. & CONTEMP. PROBL.
    (2010), www.ncbi.nlm.nih.gov.

94 *See, e.g.,* Corliss, Cochran, & Mays, *supra* note 24 (summarizing research demon-
    strating that these groups of children are more likely to be physically disciplined
    and abused by their parents).

95 Eric Cain, *North Carolina Pastor Sean Harris Urges Parents to "Man Up" and
    Punch "Effeminate" Children,* FORBES (May 2, 2012), www.forbes.com.

96 This also plays out in intersectional ways, so that, for instance, girls of color may
    be harmed in ways that neither a gender nor a racial lens alone can account
    for. *See* Kimberlé W. Crenshaw, *Mapping the Margins: Intersectionality, Identity
    Politics, and Violence Against Women of Color,* 43 STANFORD L. REV. 1241
    (1991). Black girls experience certain messages about sexuality and promiscuity,
    and black boys receive certain messages about aggression and masculinity. PAT-
    TON, *supra* note 4, at 4265.

97 Melinda Rice, *Experts: Corporal Punishment Harms Girls,* WOMEN'S E-NEWS
    (Sept. 23, 2001), http://womensenews.org (describing corporal punishment in
    schools; the harms are arguably even worse in instances of intrafamilial corporal
    punishment).

98 Cynthia Godsoe, *Contempt, Status and the Criminalization of Non-Conforming Girls*, 35 CARDOZO L. REV. 1091, 1095–96 (2014).

99 *See, e.g.,* State v. Kimberly B., 699 N.W.2d 644, 644 (Ct. App. Wisc. 2005) (describing a case where a mother repeatedly hit her nine-year-old daughter, calling her a "big fat slut"); *see also* Millner, *supra* note 63 (commentators urging parents to "whup that trick," and "beat that [slut] wannabe's ass").

100 *See* Millner, *supra* note 63.

101 *See* Bill Briggs, *Adrian Peterson Case: Some Parents Say Spankings Improved Them*, NBC NEWS (Sept. 19, 2014), www.nbcnews.com; Stacey Patton, *Stop Beating Black Children*, N.Y. TIMES (March 10, 2017), www.nytimes.com ("I've heard many black people attribute their successes, or the fact that they weren't in jail, on drugs or dead, to the beatings they received as children.").

102 *See, e.g.,* Ta-Nehisi Coates, *Race Parenting and Punishment*, ATLANTIC (Jan. 22, 2010), www.theatlantic.com. *See also* Stacey Patton, *Want to Keep Black Kids From Running Away From Home? Stop Hitting Them*, WASH. POST (Apr. 7 2017), www.washingtonpost.com (recalling that her adoptive parents and their Black community described whippings as "love, discipline and protection from the police or white racists").

103 *Peterson's Mom, supra* note 86.

104 Gregory S. McNeal, *Adrian Peterson's Indefensible Abuse of a 4 Year Old Likely Violates Texas Law*, FORBES (Sept. 16, 2014), www.forbes.com.

105 Pfeifer & Mena, *supra* note 65.

106 *Id.*

107 *See also* Elaine Arnold, *The Use of Corporal Punishment in Child Rearing in the West Indies*, 6 CHILD ABUSE & NEGL. 141, 141–45 (1982) (discussing Orlando Patterson).

108 *See* Patton, *supra* note 102 (discussing her book *Spare the Kids, supra* note 4).

109 PATTON, *supra* note 4.

110 PATTON, *supra* note 4, at 166, 809, 890–95 ("[Slave parents] often defended their 'right' to physically discipline children without intrusion by whites because they believed that a whupping at their hands was better than one from a white person. The right to beat a black child is a sacrosanct privilege handed down to black parents from slavery—the only privilege they got from their white masters.").

111 PATTON, *supra* note 4, at 911.

112 ORLANDO PATTERSON, SLAVERY AND SOCIAL DEATH 4 (1982).

113 Arnold, *supra* note 107 (outlining Patterson's argument).

114 PATTON, *supra* note 4, at 109.

115 *Id.*

116 PATTERSON, *supra* note 112, at 93.

117 Experts describe the relationship between parental abuse and intimate partner violence: "The intention of spanking is to cause pain and the causing of pain to girls and then saying 'I love you' is not healthy." Another adds, "Spanking teaches

physical response to problems and immediate obedience. . . . It's all part of a cycle of violence—loss of self-esteem, accepting violent behavior." Rice, *supra* note 97. For racialized submission, see PATTON, *supra* note 4, at 7724, 1783.

118 *See* Hendrix, *supra* note 22 (reporting that recent proposals in California and Maryland to limit more serious corporal punishment were "greeted with howls of nanny-state overreach" and "hooted down"); *see also* Denver Nicks, *Hitting Your Kids is Legal in All 50 States*, TIME MAGAZINE (Sept. 17, 2014), http://time.com.

119 Jamie Abrams, *The Politics of Autono(me) in Reproductive Decision-Making Versus Autono(thee) in Parental Decision-Making*, 44 FLORIDA ST. L. REV. (forthcoming 2017).

120 Godsoe, *Redefining Parental Rights*, *supra* note 48.

121 *See, e.g.,* Chemerinsky & Goodwin, *supra* note 48.

122 Godsoe, *Redrawing the Boundaries of Relational Crime*, *supra* note 19.

123 JONATHAN SIMON, GOVERNING THROUGH CRIME: HOW THE WAR ON CRIME TRANSFORMED AMERICAN DEMOCRACY AND CREATED A CULTURE OF FEAR 159, 180 (2007).

124 The literature on overcriminalization is voluminous, so I cite here just a few iconic examples. *See, e.g.,* William J. Stuntz, *The Pathological Politics of Criminal Law*, 100 MICH. L. REV. 505, 511 (2001) (exploring the abolition of enforcement discretion and "end[ing] legislatures' ability to decide how far criminal law's net should extend" as ways to solve the problem of overcriminalization); Sara Sun Beale, *The Many Faces of Overcriminalization*, 54 AM. U. L. REV. 747, 749 (2005) (listing "excessive unchecked discretion," "disparity among similarly situated persons," "potential to undermine other significant values," and "misdirection of scarce resources" as some of the harms of overcriminalization).

125 *See, e.g.,* Cynthia Godsoe, *Parsing Parenthood*, 17 LEWIS & CLARK L. REV. 113 (2013).

126 This could be similar to the highly successful civil bans on smoking in workplaces and public venues.

127 Joan E. Durrant & Staffan Janson, *Law Reform, Corporal Punishment and Child Abuse: The Case of Sweden*, 12 INT'L. REV. OF VICTIMOLOGY 139, 155–56 (2005). Underenforced laws present their own problems, including being particularly vulnerable to selective or discriminatory enforcement, but they can perform a valuable educational purpose, with examples including mild speeding and teenage alcohol use.

128 *Id.* (quoting Tor Sverne, Chair, Commission on Children's Rights). Sweden banned corporal punishment in 1978.

129 This system, like the criminal justice system, is particularly punitive towards families already marginalized by race and class. *See, e.g.,* Dorothy E. Roberts, *Prison, Foster Care, and the Systematic Punishment of Black Mothers*, 59 UCLA L. REV. 1474 (2012).

130 Carter, 2016 WL 6994203, at *7 (Crone, J., concurring).

131 *See* Dan M. Kahan, *The Secret Ambition of Deterrence*, 113 HARV. L. REV. 413, 420 (1999) ("We can't identify criminal wrongdoing and punishment independently of their social meanings.").

132 *See* Jean Hampton, *Correcting Harms Versus Righting Wrongs: The Goal of Retribution*, 39 UCLA L. REV. 1659, 1686 (1992) (positing that punishment is warranted where a "wrongful action . . . [diminishes] the value of the victim[,]" and that, by injuring the victim, the wrongdoer conveys that the victim is less worthy of dignity and respect than all people intrinsically are and that he is worth more than his victim); *see also* Bennett Capers, *Real Women, Real Rape*, 60 UCLA L. REV. 826, 855 (2013) (discussing the problematic message sent about acquaintance rape offenders and victims in rape shield laws: "Laws are anything but value neutral. They prescribe what behavior is inappropriate, what behavior is orthodox, and what behavior should be rewarded. More importantly, law informs and shapes social mores in ways that are often subtle. This is especially true when it comes to criminal laws.").

133 Leigh Goodmark, *Should Domestic Violence Be Decriminalized?*, 40 HARV. J.L. & GENDER 53, 91 (2017).

134 *See, e.g.*, Aya Gruber, *Rape, Feminism, and the War on Crime*, 84 WASH. L. REV. 581, 584–85 (2009) ("Feminist policies that challenge popular gender constructions and accepted views of criminality are not so well-liked. . . . The feminist effort to send society messages about gender equality through criminal law was drowned out by the din of American criminal justice's ever-louder declaration of the war on crime.").

135 I have previously argued for a similar approach to eradicating the commercial sexual exploitation of minors, based on the limitations of the criminal law. *See* Cynthia Godsoe, *Punishment as Protection*, 52 HOUSTON L. REV. 1313 (2015).

136 *See, e.g.*, Margo Kaplan, *Rape Beyond Crime*, 66 DUKE L.J. 1045 (2017); Angela P. Harris, *Heteropatriarchy Kills: Challenging Gender Violence in a Prison Nation*, 37 WASH. U. J.L. & POL'Y 13, 38 (2011) ("If reliance on the criminal justice system to address violence against women and minorities has reached the end of its usefulness, to where should advocates turn next?").

137 Goodmark, *supra* note 133, at 70–74.

138 *Id.* at 93–94, 102–03 (critiquing, as an example, mandatory arrest policies, and calling for graduated sanctions and punishment that is "secondary to changing behavior and stimulating empathy").

6

Specializing Justice for Youth and Families

Intervening in Family Violence or Expanding the Carceral Net?

AMY M. MAGNUS

From the lobby of the Mountain Crest Juvenile Detention Center,[1] I can view entries to the probation office, children's play area, courtroom, detention center, and corridor to social services. My chair rests against a bubble-gum-pink wall that, when I first entered the facility through double glass doors and metal detectors, made me feel simultaneously comforted and uneasy. The color is at once childlike, approachable, sickeningly sweet, and overcompensating. It is intended to make the lobby feel family friendly, playful, and safe after entrants come through the various security barriers to get there. However, I experience its duality as an aggressive, yet subtle, symbol of what lies in front of it and what exists behind it.

Children play in the designated play area while parents anxiously float between the information window, the courtroom, and the juvenile detention center. The play area emulates a day care or school. Consistent with the pink wall, this space seems to offer a point of refuge for children and their families—a brief escape that, for a moment, allows them to play and laugh and rest without much concern for why they are at Mountain Crest. These moments can be heavy and complicated.

The lobby area shifts between desolate and packed. On a cold winter afternoon as I conduct field research, I observe a man and woman walk through the metal detectors with flushed red cheeks and panicked expressions. This was a particularly busy day at Mountain Crest. People were pacing back and forth, feverishly filling out paperwork, tapping their feet anxiously waiting to be called, and children busy in between all of the adults. Uncertain of their next move, the two people quickly passed through the metal detectors and frantically paced the lobby area in search. Approaching the information window, they demanded to speak with their son. The receptionist was startled and confused, seemingly unfamiliar with their son. The receptionist made a phone call, and within minutes, a detention employee approached the man and woman. With a calm voice, she introduced herself and said, "Please follow me," guiding them to the bubble-gum-pink wall that had once exuded comfort, calmness, and safety. She opened a metal door disguised by the pink paint. They passed through the doorway, and the metal door slammed shut, projecting a jarring and disruptive noise that countered any solace originally provided by the pink wall and play area. The pink wall was no longer comforting. It was a façade that masked the juvenile detention facility behind it.

This chapter highlights two key issues in the study of specialized family and juvenile justice initiatives and alternatives to traditional forms of punishment. The chapter begins with a synopsis of the historical backdrop in which alternatives to the traditional justice system in the United States, such as specialized courts and social justice organizations, came to be formalized and institutionalized. This history significantly relates to contemporary manifestations of specialization and alternatives in the justice system. Second, I complicate the conversation about specialized penal reforms, particularly specialized courts, by raising several concerns: How does the specialized justice model grapple with individuals' multi-system involvement? To what extent does specialization become so specialized that it begins to reproduce inequalities that the alternatives are intended to ameliorate? And to what extent does criminal justice "reach" overwhelm and potentially expand the criminal justice apparatus in ways that are more harmful than helpful? This conversation about alternative or special forms of justice brings some of the most foundational thinking about these initiatives to one place, bridging conversations about race, class, and gender, in particular, in this realm of research and theory. Additionally, I surface some concerns about the expansion of the criminal justice system and the carceral net as a way to ameliorate intersectional experiences of social inequality. I explore contradictions that underlie the specialization of justice, and the chapter concludes by opening a conversation about the future of specialized justice initiatives.

Specializing Justice for Youth and Families

Alternative or "specialized" justice initiatives, such as specialized courts and Family Justice Centers, are rooted in a long history of specializing and socializing justice starting in the late nineteenth century. Alternatives to the traditionally adversarial criminal justice system emerged in light of thinking about social inequality, crime, and justice as social structural phenomena rather than biological or individual phenomena.[2] Instead of viewing issues of crime, deviance, and justice as determined by one's biology, an "enlightened" American society would think of these phenomena as more complex issues coexisting with poverty, education, un- and under-employment, and an increasingly industrialized economy and political system. With this shift in ideology came structural change at a time when the United States was transitioning to a more centralized government, which included courts and other legal institutions. Progressive legal scholars, practitioners, and social scientists argued that with a more "modern" outlook on crime, justice and social and legal institutions should, too, reflect this ideological progress. From this, courts emerged that "aimed not merely to punish offenders but to assist and discipline entire urban populations: to police public health and morals, to reduce child neglect and family dependency, to correct deviant personalities, to teach immigrants good citizenship, and much more."[3] Specialized courts and family justice initiatives are one result of this movement. These initiatives operate under coexisting principles of punishment, legal authority, social service, and public assistance. In this way, an ideological and practical tension exists where the criminal justice system acts as a point of intervention into multi-system involvement, but also as a means for reinforcing the structural impact of the system in families' lives.

In the late 1800s, courts and other specialized initiatives were developed to prevent the erratic, violent treatment of youth in the home. Specialized courts were, and remain, a state intervention designed to protect youth and their families from family violence, child abuse and neglect, and domestic violence. In turn, however, these criminal justice interventions also introduced youth and their families to the criminal justice system or further entangled their involvement in this system. For example, the juvenile court brought youth and their families into the

justice system to simultaneously address youth delinquency while preventing violent punishments from being used in the home. However,
the juvenile justice system increased surveillance and social control over
youth and their families, particularly young women and people of color,
in an effort to correct youth behavior and intervene in different forms
of family violence.

Today, specialized courts, in particular, serve dual purposes of "administering justice" from both a punishment and public service perspective. These courts specialize in addressing particular populations
or social problems. Drug courts, juvenile courts, homelessness courts,
veterans' courts, and domestic violence courts, among others, aim to
uphold the law while also channeling progressive ideals of access to justice,[4] therapeutic jurisprudence,[5] and restorative forms of justice[6] that
the traditional justice system is ill equipped to provide. In this vein, specialized courts function as an intermediary space between social services and the criminal justice system, acting to provide a service to those
in need, but from a position of legal power and authority administered
through the criminal justice system. These principles often become conflated—a phenomenon that complicates their enactment on the ground
and risks simultaneously ameliorating and reproducing the inequalities
they purport to address. In an effort to regulate domestic relations, morals, intersecting inequalities, and young people at the greatest risk of
delinquency, specialized courts were one of the first attempts to socialize
not just the law, but the family.

Good Homes, Good Morals, and Good Kids: Simultaneously Socializing Families and the Law

Domestic relations courts, morals courts, and boys' courts were some
of the first specialized justice initiatives to address social issues the traditional justice system was not equipped to handle.[7] Chicago's court of
domestic relations was among the first to prescribe not only how a family
should and should not operate, but also how society should and should
not operate. Such initiatives formalized and institutionalized a white,
middle-class standard of living, in which predominantly poor families
of color were socialized by white elites about how a "traditional" family
should look and act. Should these families deviate from this prescribed

model, state intervention would "correct" this behavior and "save" those families and their children. These courts, originally designed by powerful legal actors, white purists, and women's rights activists, most of whom were white and middle class, attempted to prevent and rectify "broken" families—those whose husbands and fathers were not upholding the promise of caring for their wives and children properly, single-mother households that needed state intervention to ensure their children were being raised with morals, working-class households with young people who were breaking rules and were perceived to be a future problem for American society if not immediately addressed by the justice system, and households with young women who were sexually delinquent and promiscuous. Gendered, racialized, and classist undertones were thus systemically written into the alternative justice movement and have perpetuated the agendas of those with the power to create said initiatives.

Mary Odem traces the treatment of young women involved with the juvenile justice system by looking to the progressive reformers and advocates of the alternative justice system. Odem finds that through maternal justice—particularly the push for hiring more white women in law enforcement, court positions, social services, and activist roles, and also the expressed charge to "ameliorate the social circumstances that led young women into [sexual] trouble"[8]—young women were to be helped and "saved." Their supposed sexual promiscuity threatened not just their health and well-being, but the social fabric of a society that prided itself on purity, and these young women were to be trained by older women who knew better. The criminal justice system thus adopted the role of socializing young women and their families based on a white, middle-class approach to child-rearing and behaving like a *proper* young woman.

Much of the early efforts to socialize youth and their families were highly racialized. Although white children were perceived as "save-able," with resources more readily accessible to them, the needs of the Black community were neglected.[9] The courts and their advocates recognized the racial disparities experienced by young Black men and women, but the infrastructural and social support to address these disparities was lacking. Geoff Ward calls this issue "institutionalized neglect," in which Black youth were systemically disadvantaged within the specialized juvenile justice system, leading to the entrenchment of racial inequality in the juvenile and family justice systems. Again, stakeholders acknowl-edged this disparity, but the services and advocacy available to this par-ticular group of youth and families were distinctly different from those available to white youth:

> White civic leaders, who exclusively controlled the parental state until the mid-twentieth century, often expressed concern for the well-being of black children and families. In Chicago's early juvenile court commu-nity, black youths remained in detention homes for extended periods of time . . . and were intended for short-term confinement and offered few rehabilitative services. Secular and religious organizations generally re-fused to serve nonwhite dependents and delinquents. . . . Racial discrimi-nation by New York's juvenile court service providers led to prolonged confinement of black girls and boys in shelters and detention facilities that were intended for short-term custody and offered few developmental services.[10]

The socialization taking place both raised concerns about the expe-riences of Black youth and conveyed that these youth were less of a priority—less "save-able"—than white youth. The law and the courts began to acknowledge disparities within the juvenile delinquency and dependency systems, yet continued with a mode of privileging white, middle-class young men, young women, and families over others.

Chicago's Juvenile Court

In the late 1800s, the Municipal Court of Chicago furthered the new path of socializing justice and designing specialized courts in an effort to modernize and orient law around progressive, social justice.[11] Pro-gressivism in late-nineteenth-century and early-twentieth-century Chicago was espoused via "pluralistic, issue-centered politics of social responsibility" and the "ideological commitment to professional-ization, scientific rationalization, and administrative governance."[12] Quickly after the development of specialized courts in Chicago, multi-ple other American cities followed suit, including Philadelphia, Boston, Cleveland, Atlanta, and Kansas City. These cities were influenced by the growing critique around punishment in America, which suggested that the law, its actors, and its institutions must be "socialized" to make any significant impact on crime and delinquency:

> At the turn of the twentieth century, a rising generation of progressive legal academics . . . launched a much broader assault upon the individualistic, rights-based framework of American law and jurisprudence. By the early 1910s, the progressive rhetoric of socialized law had spilled over from the mainstream public discourse. It gave court reformers, clergymen, legal aid activists, social workers, psychiatrists, psychologists, and welfare activists . . . a common and compelling rationale for innovative new governmental approaches to managing urban populations. For legal scholars and social scientists, the new municipal courts served as experimental stations of socialized law.[13]

As previously noted, the changing structure of the American court system happened in tandem with a changing economy and political culture.[14] With this evolving polity and economy came greater centralization of government, resulting in mixed reactions from social scientists, judges, and other legal actors about the subsequent centralization of courts, judicial review, and a potentially intensified version of social control over those under the court's power. By formalizing specialized courts, as Chicago did with the juvenile court, experts from the medical, psychological, and social work fields—among others—deepened their roots and influence in the courts. Self-proclaimed progressive judges and other professionals "quickly established themselves as indispensable personnel of urban socialized courts," which "dealt most aggressively with issues of domestic life, adolescent criminality, and sexual norms."[15] Rooted in this initiative, again, was the belief that "traditional judicial approaches had failed" at addressing the "underlying problems" of people answering to the courts.[16] As a result, the first juvenile court was established in Cook County, Illinois, in 1899, and most states had a juvenile court system soon after.

In an attempt to move away from the erratic treatment of "troublesome" youth and toward greater due process for these youth, the roles of the family and criminal justice system began to merge via the *parens patriae* doctrine. This doctrine emphasizes that the government has a "right," and further, an "obligation," to "care for children who are neglected, delinquent, or in some other way disadvantaged."[17] Two predominant competing interests were at stake when the first juvenile court was established: 1) the juvenile court and its pioneers, particularly Judge Richard Tuthill, believed that children should be treated differently by the justice system and that the juvenile court should have jurisdiction before cases go through the criminal court; and 2) the embeddedness of the *parens patriae* doctrine seemed to be reproducing many of the same inequalities that originally underscored much of why young people and their families were coming before the court. The child-saving movement focused almost exclusively on "wayward" youth who, without early intervention, were perceived as bound for a life of deviance and delinquency—a future problem for society if not addressed early on. These movements predominantly targeted young men and women of color, along with their families, who were thought to be in need of guidance on how to properly parent. The initiatives that followed from this line of thinking cemented a form of social hierarchy, particularly around race, class, and gender, within specialized initiatives impacting families. This is still true today, such that young men and women of color continue to be disproportionately represented in the juvenile justice system.[18]

Addressing Multi-System Involvement: New Alternatives, Same Social Issues

The historical lineage of specialized courts and juvenile justice links youth and their families to specialized justice initiatives, yet the story becomes complicated when considering involvement with multiple state systems. Crossover youth and families, for instance, particularly present need to reevaluate alternative justice initiatives. These youth are those who have been involved with both juvenile dependency and delinquency. The specialized initiatives designed to address multi-system involvement have greatly expanded over the past two decades. The justification for such initiatives often involves principles of access to justice, therapeutic jurisprudence, and restorative justice to validate criminal justice expansion into youth and families' lives. These principles are important to criminal justice reform, yet they often serve as platforms for justifying system expansion and widening the carceral net rather than addressing the core causes of multi-system involvement, discrimination, and inequality within the justice system.

As articulated by Deborah Rhode, the phrase "equal justice under law" is difficult to contest as a principle.[19] The American legal and justice system professes to operate according to this principle; however, the realities are quite different.[20] Access to justice, therapeutic jurisprudence, and restorative justice are bound with progressive assumptions about the ways citizens approach, engage, and understand the criminal justice system and the law. "Access to justice" refers to the increased availability, fairness, efficacy, and efficiency of law and legal institutions for all parties. This concept has been used to describe *pro se* litigation and legal representation,[21] the existence of legal aid and other self-help services,[22] responses to gendered and domestic violence,[23] and responses to poverty,[24] but this concept is also regularly used to understand specialized courts in various contexts.[25] Access to justice, in relation to specialized courts in particular, has, in itself, been used as a platform for expanding the justice system to bolster the justice industrial complex we have come to know in the twenty-first century. This industrial complex extends far beyond the prison system and permeates each layer of the criminal justice system, with courts as no exception.

Judah Schept furthers this line of work in his discussion about a newly proposed "justice campus," where justice can be administered in a one-stop-shop fashion with the intention of increasing access to justice, therapeutic jurisprudence, and restorative justice. Schept delineates the use of progressive rhetoric and ideologies to justify and expand the criminal justice system and justice industrial complex:

> Local officials spoke of the need for more carceral space in terms of therapeutic justice, rehabilitation and treatment, and education, concepts that resurrected Progressive era notions of "penal-social laboratories." In the name of the imagined facility—the justice campus—proponents of expansion harness the collegiate and bucolic image of the community to a call for the largest carceral growth in county history.[26]

Progressive rhetoric possesses undertones of providing more systematic and equal access to justice, assuming that system expansion in the form of specialized courts and greater integration of social services and the criminal justice system will provide said access to justice. However, the principles of therapeutic jurisprudence and restorative justice also aim to justify system expansion for targeted groups of people, such as young people, those who are homeless, and those with substance abuse and mental health concerns.

Therapeutic jurisprudence is articulated as two-fold: the law can serve as an agent of therapeutic resolution, and court actors can use the tenets of therapeutic jurisprudence to make a pro-social change in the lives of people who come before the court. From this progressive rationalization for specialized court expansion, a key theoretical question emerges: considering the general existence of law, justice, and the criminal justice system, why is there a need for specialized justice initiatives for specific groups of people or social problems? In light of the progressive rationalizations articulated for the furtherance of specialized court initiatives, this theoretical question intentionally reads as antagonistic.[27] Specialized courts for juvenile delinquency and child dependency echo the movement toward specialized justice for youth and families in light of access to justice, therapeutic jurisprudence, and restorative justice narratives. Specialized courts are the product of the therapeutic and restorative justice movements, such that cases brought before specialized courts are designed to address the matter in light of "human problems that are responsible for bringing the case to court."[28] So, in an attempt to socialize the law, the coexistence and intersections of social issues such as family violence, poverty, un- and under-employment, and racism entered the picture as human elements that drive much of why individuals find themselves in court.

Historically, we have seen an expansion of punishment ideologies and of the criminal justice system.[29] Throughout the seventeenth and eighteenth centuries, the position of children in society changed drastically. The passage of moral discipline laws, like "stubborn child" and "rebellious child" laws, reflect the first attempt at addressing so-called "wayward youth."[30] Throughout much of the early nineteenth century, youth were treated similarly to adults in the same courts with the same sentencing and punishment guidelines. During this time, the term "delinquent" was used not only to refer to youth who broke the law, but also those who were homeless, abused, and unwanted.[31] With the rise of urbanization, industrialization, and the Progressive Era, youth became an identified population who needed saving as a result of their delinquency and at-risk nature.[32] In this sense, child-saving became deeply entwined with the notion of *parens patriae*.

The child-savers movement was, at face value, designed to facilitate community programs that ultimately led to the development of a formal juvenile justice system, including juvenile courts. As noted by Platt and Ward, however, this process was highly racialized and gendered, and had various collateral consequences for youth and families, including disparate access to community resources for immigrant and Black youth in particular.[33] The child-saving movement was founded upon conservative values and the legitimization of intervening and treating problems.[34] Women were viewed as the "natural caretakers," with higher stakes than men in the welfare of children, which made them prime candidates for leading the movement to save children.[35] The movement toward controlling and treating youth, especially immigrant youth, Black youth, and girls, and the general belief that women were responsible for addressing delinquent youth, reflects the gendered and racialized approach of the child-saving movement.[36] Because of the changing legal regulations on youth and the overlapping referents used to describe them, parents and children alike became governed by the state and were obligated to control their children or bring them before a court as a symbol of answering to a higher authority. The experiences of youth and their families within the juvenile justice system are not monolithic. Rather, the realities of multi-system involvement are overlapping and intersecting in ways that complicate and even exacerbate the inequalities experienced because of multi-system involvement.

Realities of Multi-System Involvement

The Center for Juvenile Justice Reform (CJJR) reports that as many as 30% of youth involved in the foster care system who are aged ten or older become involved in the juvenile justice system at some point. Inversely, as many as 67% of youth involved with the juvenile justice system have also been involved with the child welfare system at some point.

Youth who are dually involved in child welfare and juvenile delinquency are typically referred to as "crossover youth." The common thread for crossover youth is often foster care, and further poor treatment and multiple home placements often exacerbate a youth's likelihood of interacting with the juvenile justice system.[37] These youth are predominantly low-income, female youth of color who have family histories of child abuse and neglect as well as domestic violence.[38] Exposure to these circumstances is known to often result in delinquency, juvenile justice involvement, and crossover status. Approximately half of crossover youth have been arrested at least once and, subsequently, are at an increased risk for incarceration as adults.[39] Much is unknown, however, about the temporal ordering of system involvement, differential impacts of dual involvement on boys and girls, and the overall impact of programs like specialized courts on crossover youth and families. However, recent research does indicate that crossover courts, for example, increase youth and family access to helpful social services, such as drug and alcohol treatment and different forms of therapy.[40]

Youth in juvenile detention, many of whom have crossover status, often experience depression, suicidal thoughts, behavioral issues, and various psychotic disorders.[41] In this same study, responses from these youth further indicate that approximately one-third of them have family members with mental health disorders. More than half of youth in juvenile detention disclose receiving treatment for emotional and behavioral issues, approximately half of youth indicate using violence against a loved one, and slightly less than half of youth indicate being a victim of family violence. Many youth in detention centers also have family members who are experiencing substance abuse challenges, which is theorized by some scholars to have initiated youths' dual-involvement in child welfare and juvenile justice.[42] More than half of children report being exposed to drugs or alcohol abuse by their biological family, increasing their own likelihood of abusing drugs or alcohol.[43] Daining and DePanfilis additionally report that more than half of youth in transition from the child welfare system to early adulthood became a parent during this timeframe.[44] As many of these individuals are leaving the juvenile delinquency and child welfare systems, their ability to succeed is compromised not only by having children at a young age, but also by lacking stable living arrangements upon exiting the system. Daining and DePanfilis find that approximately 30% of the persons in their sample experienced homelessness upon exiting the child welfare system as a young adult.[45] Combined with early pregnancies and parenthood, mental health and substance abuse issues are only some of the studied long-term consequences of system involvement. Further research is needed, however, regarding other challenges that system-involved youth face.

Research is emerging regarding the success of community-based programs, particularly specialized courts, which are geared specifically toward the needs of crossover youth. Ryan, Marshall, Herz, and Hernandez report that restitution-based programs and probation tend to be the most effective at improving youths' life skills and problem-solving skills; however, crossover youth are typically unable to access these programs because of their placement in residential treatment facilities, such as group homes, as a result of their overlapping status with child welfare.[46] From this, crossover youth often do not receive treatment services unique to their needs; their problems are instead exacerbated.[47]

As mentioned previously, much of the scholarship on crossover youth focuses on the short- and long-term outcomes of crossover status rather than the impact and effectiveness of specialized courts providing services to these youth and their families. There is evidence, however, that crossover youth are treated much more punitively than their non-dual-involved counterparts.[48] Procedurally, crossover youth are significantly disadvantaged in juvenile courts because of their dependency on the child welfare system in addition to their involvement with the juvenile justice system.[49] Youth under the supervision of child welfare are much more likely to spend time in detention facilities because of a lack of adequate legal and social representation and absence of a custodial agent who can advocate on the youth's behalf.[50] From these findings regarding procedural disadvantage, research suggests that crossover youth experience unique barriers to justice compared to their juvenile justice counterparts who are not simultaneously involved in the child welfare system. While specialized crossover courts are designed to provide access to justice, treatment, services, and resources to crossover youth, empirical evidence must be expanded regarding the effectiveness of these courts.

Criminal Justice Reach

The term "prison industrial complex" was first coined to describe mass imprisonment and surveillance in the United States. This phenomenon describes not just the act of mass incarceration, but also the economic benefit and business-oriented thread that links each layer of punishment and incarceration, and can be extended to the various other social, financial, political, and legal institutions that intertwine with the criminal justice system. Likewise, the "justice industrial complex" focuses not only on "justice" as fairness or equality, but rather the co-opting of associated terms like "access to justice" to warrant a deepening of social control mechanisms into non-criminal-justice-oriented institutions that inadvertently widen the carceral net.[51] Although interagency collaboration has been found to be useful in yielding greater accessibility to services,[52] the potential collateral consequences of this trend should be more thoroughly and critically considered while taking the history of the juvenile and family justice systems into account.[53]

This is a complex through which the criminal justice system has become so deeply interwoven with and dependent upon social, financial, and political institutions like welfare, health insurance companies, residential treatment centers, private funding agencies, and legislators with political agendas that it is difficult to tease out where the institutions stop and begin. I envision this like the blending of colors on a canvas. Each institution falls somewhere on the canvas, represented by a different color on the spectrum, and the intersection of each color is so evenly blended throughout the transitions that you cannot decipher where one color ends and the other begins. The "justice industrial complex" is the canvas on which the colors have interacted and changed hue. The seamless blending of colors, or rather, institutions, is essential for understanding not just criminal system expansion, but how criminal justice expansion occurs and the subtle ways in which interventions rely upon a problematic deepening of system involvement to achieve their purpose.

Criminal justice professionals and scholars alike argue that system expansion does not breed social justice, but rather extends a deeper reach of the criminal justice system and its tendency toward social control over people's lives.[54] Michael Mann's theory of infrastructural power and "reach" lends itself to understanding how the state has intervened in youth and families' lives through modes of centralized state power.[55] "Reach" is used by Mann to indicate the power and impact of the state throughout its spatial boundaries. "Reach" can further be understood as a state of mind that penetrates much more than just spatial territory. It penetrates a way of life and the extent to which individuals interact with and trust state systems, institutions, and power. From this notion, and as tied to the historical impact of child-saving initiatives and the *parens patriae* doctrine, state power and intervention can be viewed as over-reaching into family relations and thus expanding the justice industrial complex, and consequently the carceral net.

A key concern emerges from this line of thinking: how does system expansion continue to occur, given the well-documented concerns about specialized and alternative justice initiatives? Schept, Ward, Willrich, and Platt illuminate many of the collateral consequences associated with child-saving, net widening, and system expansion with the motivation of helping targeted groups of people, but how does this persist?[56] The historical trajectory of specialized justice not only provided the platform for system expansion and net-widening, it now fosters a co-opting of terms such as "access to justice," "therapeutic jurisprudence," and "restorative justice" to potentially further this line of thought. Whether intentionally or unintentionally, this co-opting process perpetuates system expansion that may consequently lead to a more blurred "canvas" rather than positive social benefits. The notion of the "justice industrial complex" can be utilized to forge a new path for understanding system expansion, net-widening, and the co-opting of progressive rhetoric associated with alternative justice initiatives. Holistically, this is a moment for questioning whether another arm of the criminal justice system can provide services and justice to youth and families without the stigmatization and deeper penetration of system involvement to do so. It is also a moment to critically reflect upon the foundations of the American juvenile justice system to determine if Progressive-Era rhetoric and socialization practices continue to contribute to net-widening and expansion of system reach.

NOTES

1 Personal and institutional names as well as geographic locations have been assigned pseudonyms throughout the text to ensure anonymity of respondents

and field sites. Events and individuals described in the text are often combined and out of chronological order.

2 Tamar M. Meekins, *Specialized Justice: The Over-Emergence of Specialty Courts and the Threat of a New Criminal Defense Paradigm*, 40 SUFFOLK U. L. REV. 1 (2006); MICHAEL WILLRICH, CITY OF COURTS: SOCIALIZING JUSTICE IN PROGRESSIVE ERA CHICAGO 122–23 (2003).

3 WILLRICH, *supra* note 2.

4 Deborah L. Rhode, *Access to Justice*, 69 FORDHAM L. REV. 1785, 1786 (2001) ("access to justice" marks the accessibility of the justice system and the law to everyday people, often provided through services like legal aid).

5 Bruce J. Winick, *Therapeutic Jurisprudence and Problem Solving Courts*, 30 FORDHAM URB. L.J. 1055 (2002) (therapeutic jurisprudence complements access to justice principles; the law has the power to impact people emotionally, behaviorally, and through treatment).

6 HEATHER STRANG & JOHN BRAITHWAITE, RESTORATIVE JUSTICE AND CIVIL SOCIETY (2001) (restorative justice places greater focus on the rebuilding of relationships between victims and offenders in their communities).

7 WILLRICH, *supra* note 2; MARY E. ODEM, DELINQUENT DAUGHTERS: PROTECTING AND POLICING ADOLESCENT FEMALE SEXUALITY IN THE UNITED STATES, 1885–1920 (1995).

8 ODEM, *supra* note 7, at 129.

9 GEOFF K. WARD, THE BLACK CHILD-SAVERS: RACIAL DEMOCRACY AND JUVENILE JUSTICE 110–13 (2012).

10 *Id.*

11 WILLRICH, *supra* note 2.

12 *Id.*

13 *Id.* at 97.

14 *Id.*

15 *Id.* at 122–23.

16 Winick, *supra* note 5, at 1060.

17 LARRY K. GAINES & ROGER L. MILLER, CRIMINAL JUSTICE IN ACTION: THE CORE 365 (7TH ED. 2012).

18 Alex R. Piquero, *Disproportionate Minority Contact*, 18 FUTURE CHILD. 59 (2008).

19 Rhode, *supra* note 4.

20 Jona Goldschmidt, *The Pro Se Litigant's Struggle for Access to Justice*, 40 FAM. CT. REV. 36 (2002).

21 Sande L. Buhai, *Access to Justice for Unrepresented Litigants: A Comparative Perspective*, 42 LOY. L.A. L. REV. 979 (2008); Jona Goldschmidt, *Judicial Ethics and Assistance to Self-Represented Litigants*, 28 JUST. SYS. J. 324 (2007); Goldschmidt, *supra* note 20; Deborah J. Chase, *Pro Se Justice and Unified Family Courts*, 37 FAM. L. Q. 403 (2003); Ronald W. Staudt & Paula L. Hannaford, *Access to Justice for the Self-Represented Litigant: An Interdisciplinary Investigation by Designers and Lawyers*, 52 SYRACUSE L. REV. 1017 (2002).

22 Jim Hilbert, *Educational Workshops on Settlement and Dispute Resolution: Another Tool For Self-Represented Litigants in Family Court*, 43 FAM. L. Q. 545 (2009); Jeff Giddings & Michael Robertson, *Large-scale Map or the A-Z?: The Place of Self-Help Services in Legal Aid*, 30 J.L. & SOC'Y 102 (Jan.–March 2003); Jeff Giddings & Michael Robertson, *Self-Help Legal Aid: Abandoning the Disadvantaged?*, 12 CONSUMER POL. REV. 127 (2002); Jeff Giddings & Michael Robertson, *Informed Litigants with Nowhere to Go*, 26 ALTERNATIVE L.J. 184 (2001).

23 Matthew Desmond & Nicol Valdez, *Unpolicing the Urban Poor: Consequences of Third-Party Policing for Inner-City Women*, 78 AM. SOC. REV. 117 (2012); Cari Fais, *Denying Access to Justice: The Cost of Applying Chronic Nuisance Laws to Domestic Violence*, 108 COLUM. L. REV. 1181 (2008); Rebecca L. Sandefur, *Access to Civil Justice and Race, Class, and Gender Inequality*, 34 ANN. REV. SOC. 339 (2008).

24 Jayanth K. Krishnan & Marc Galanter, *Bread for the Poor: Access to Justice and the Rights of the Needy in India*, 55 HASTINGS L.J. 789 (2004); DEBORAH L. RHODE, ACCESS TO JUSTICE (2004).

25 Meekins, *supra* note 2; Austin Sarat, *Litigation Explosion, Access to Justice, and Court Reform: Examining the Critical Assumptions*, 37 RUTGERS U. L. REV. 319 (1985).

26 JUDAH SCHEPT, PROGRESSIVE PUNISHMENT: JOB LOSS, JAIL GROWTH, AND THE NEOLIBERAL LOGIC OF CARCERAL EXPANSION 7 (2015).

27 WILLRICH, *supra* note 2.

28 Winick, *supra* note 5, at 1055.

29 SCHEPT, *supra* note 26.

30 JOHN R. SUTTON, STUBBORN CHILDREN: CONTROLLING DELINQUENCY IN THE UNITED STATES, 1640–1981 (1988).

31 JOSEPH G. WEIS ET AL., JUVENILE DELINQUENCY READINGS 3 (2001); ANTHONY PLATT, THE CHILD SAVERS: THE INVENTION OF DELINQUENCY (1969).

32 GAINES & MILLER, *supra* note 17, at 36.

33 PLATT, *supra* note 31; WARD, *supra* note 9.

34 PLATT, *supra* note 31.

35 *Id.* at 7–8.

36 WARD, *supra* note 9.

37 Denise Herz et al., *Challenges Facing Crossover Youth: An Examination of Juvenile Justice Decision-Making and Recidivism*, 48 FAM. CT. REV. 305 (2010); MARK E. COURTNEY ET AL., MIDWEST EVALUATION OF THE ADULT FUNCTIONING OF FORMER FOSTER YOUTH: CONDITIONS OF YOUTH PREPARING TO LEAVE STATE CARE 3–60 (2004).

38 Sarah Vidal et al., *Maltreatment, Family Environment, and Social Risk Factors: Determinants of the Child Welfare to Juvenile Justice Transition Among Maltreated Children and Adolescents*, 63 CHILD ABUSE & NEGLECT 7–18 (2017); Kevin T.

Wolff et al., *Maltreatment, Child Welfare, and Recidivism in a Sample of Deep-End Crossover Youth*, 45 J. YOUTH & ADOLESCENCE 625 (2016).

39 M. Jonson-Reid & R. P. Barth, *From Maltreatment Report to Juvenile Incarceration: The Role of Child Welfare Services*, 24 CHILD ABUSE & NEGLECT 505 (2000); COURTNEY ET AL., *supra* note 37.

40 Emily M. Wright et al., *The Importance of Interagency Collaboration for Crossover Youth: A Research Note*, 15 YOUTH VIOLENCE & JUV. JUST. 481 (2016).

41 Michelle Chino et al., *Screening for Mental Health Problems Among Youth in Nevada: Practice in Policy*, 1 NEV. J. PUB. HEALTH 10 (2004).

42 *Id.*

43 *Id.*

44 Clara Daining & Diane DePanfilis, *Resilience of Youth in Transition from Out-of-Home Care to Adulthood*, 29 CHILD. & YOUTH SERVS. REV. 1158 (2007).

45 *Id.* at 44.

46 Joseph P. Ryan et al., *Juvenile Delinquency in Child Welfare: Investigating Group Home Effects*, 30 CHILD. & YOUTH SERVS. REV. 1088 (2008).

47 Herz et al., *supra* note 37.

48 Hui Huang et al., *The Journey of Dually-Involved Youth: The Description and Prediction of Rereporting and Recidivism*, 34 CHILD. & YOUTH SERVS. REV. 254 (2012); Herz et al., *supra* note 37.

49 COURTNEY ET AL., *supra* note 37.

50 DYLAN CONGER & TIMOTHY ROSS, REDUCING THE FOSTER CARE BIAS IN JUVENILE DETENTION DECISIONS: THE IMPACT OF PROJECT CON-FIRM 7–32 (2001).

51 THOMAS G. BLOMBERG, *Penal Reform and the Fate of "Alternatives,"* in PUN-ISHMENT AND SOCIAL CONTROL 417 (Walter de Gruyter, Inc. eds., 2003); DAVID GARLAND, THE CULTURE OF CONTROL 1–192 (2001).

52 Wright et al., *supra* note 40.

53 Jane Stoever, *Mirandizing Family Justice*, 39 HARV. J.L. & GENDER 189 (2016).

54 SCHEPT, *supra* note 26; KAARYN S. GUSTAFSON, CHEATING WELFARE: PUBLIC ASSISTANCE AND THE CRIMINALIZATION OF POVERTY (2011); BLOMBERG, *supra* note 51; WILLRICH, *supra* note 2; GARLAND, *supra* note 51.

55 Michael Mann, *The Autonomous Power of the State: Its Origins, Mechanisms and Results*, 25 EUR. J. SOC. 185 (1984).

56 SCHEPT, *supra* note 26; WARD, *supra* note 9; WILLRICH, *supra* note 2; PLATT, *supra* note 31.

PART III

Intersectional Needs for Safety and Justice

Feminist Response to Campus Sexual Assault in the Republican Era

Crime Logic, Intersectional Public Health, and Restorative Justice

DONNA COKER

The Obama administration brought unprecedented federal attention to the problem of campus sexual assault. This effort included adoption of newly aggressive Department of Education (DOE) guidance and enforcement,[1] initiation of a Department of Justice (DOJ) Campus Climate Survey Validation Study,[2] appointment of a White House Task Force to Protect Students from Sexual Assault that authored two reports,[3] publication of a report by the White House Council on Women and Girls,[4] development of awareness campaigns, provision of substantial resources for colleges and universities,[5] and a significant body of empirical research.[6]

Taken together, these actions created a profound change in university practices. The DOE Office of Civil Rights (OCR) 2011 Dear Colleague Letter (DCL) required that schools adhere to a set of rules for the investigation and determination of claims of sexual assault. Notably, those rules required the adoption of a preponderance of the evidence standard for formal adjudication, allowed schools to use either panels or a single investigator to determine responsibility, and required that both the complainant and the respondent receive equivalent notice.[7] Schools were also mandated to provide interim protection for students who report an assault and to designate a person responsible for investigating allegations of sexual assault.[8] In addition, colleges and universities were encouraged to conduct regular campus climate surveys to gauge the prevalence of sexual assault on campus, the effectiveness of campus services, and student attitudes.[9] The institutions were also encouraged to initiate prevention programs such as bystander intervention programs.[10]

Feminist activism, much of it led by sexual assault survivors, was critically important to the Obama administration's establishment of aggressive enforcement efforts.[11] Several national organizations, including Know Your IX and SurvJustice, grew directly from campus activism, are now well established, and continue to play a significant role in shaping campus response.[12]

These changes elicited significant debate. Conservative Republicans argued that schools should not handle these claims, but rather should hand them over to law enforcement.[13] Critics across the political spectrum raised troubling allegations that campus investigation and adjudication methods were unfair to accused students because of a lack of fair procedures,[14] gender bias against male students,[15] and the preponderance of the evidence standard mandated by the DCL 2011 being insufficiently protective of the right to a fair hearing.[16] Some also noted concerns that racial bias may play a role in the treatment of African American male students accused of sexual assault.[17]

That Was Then, This Is Now

The change in presidential administration has brought a dramatically different set of policies. In September 2017, the DOE announced that it was withdrawing the 2011 DCL and the 2014 Questions and Answers document.[18] The DOE issued interim guidance, titled Q&A on Campus Sexual Assault,[19] and announced that new regulations, subject to notice and comment, would be forthcoming.[20] The move was not unexpected. Candace Jackson, the new Acting Assistant Secretary for Civil Rights, had earlier instructed regional directors to narrow the scope of Title IX investigations related to systemic discrimination.[21] After meetings with advocates for sexual assault survivors and advocates for accused men, Betsy DeVos, Secretary of Education, announced, "This is an issue we're not getting right."[22]

The new guidance withdraws the requirement that schools adopt a preponderance of the evidence standard, allowing schools to elect the higher clear and convincing standard instead.[23] The guidance also allows schools to limit the right of appeal to respondents, rather than require that complainants have equal appeal rights,[24] and does away with the prohibition on mediation.[25]

The impact of the new administration on campus life goes well beyond changes in Title IX policies. Aggressive immigration enforcement,[26] the Muslim travel ban,[27] and an increase in racist and homophobic harassment are significantly impacting individual students and campus climate generally.

Even with weakened federal oversight, universities continue to have strong incentives to respond assertively to sexual assault complaints. Recent popular movements against sexual harassment have intensified as exemplified by the international #MeToo movement.[28] National attention has focused as well on the conviction on multiple counts of sexual abuse of young athletes of former USA Gymnastics team doctor Larry Nassar, a Michigan State medical school faculty member.[29] Michigan State President Lou Anna Simon resigned her position after multiple victims confronted her with the school's failure to respond to earlier reports of Nassar's abuse.[30]

Feminist work to end campus sexual assault should continue to demand that universities respond to reports of sexual abuse and expand support for victims. We should also advocate for policies that respond to the legitimate concerns raised about gender bias and procedural fairness of campus investigations and processes. In addition, we must be responsive to increased racism and intolerance on college campuses. We must also carefully weigh our priorities in a federal landscape hostile to Obama-era policies. In this new political environment, where should we "stay the course" and where should we "course-correct?"

Moving Forward

Stay the Course. Two key areas of the Obama administration's response to campus sexual assault urgently require continued feminist support. The first is a robust defense of the benefits of non-criminal campus investigation and determination of sexual assault claims.[31] Title IX frames the failure of schools to prevent and respond to sexual assault as sex discrimination, foregrounding the importance of the social construction of gender and sex, and underscoring the importance of challenging social supports for gender subordination. The campus setting provides an opportunity to disrupt social supports for gender subordination in ways that are less feasible in the larger community.[32]

The civil rights approach of Title IX is not a second-best option to the criminal justice system; in fact, it has the potential to be better—*much better*.[33] Campus mechanisms provide substantially more support for victims, are substantially more likely to reach a resolution, and through enforcement of campus conduct codes are often able to reach harmful sexual conduct that is non-criminal or that, while criminal, is unlikely to be charged. And because campus mechanisms do not carry the harsh consequences of a criminal conviction, they are preferable for both those accused and for the many victims who would not report to law enforcement because they do not want the person who harmed them to be punished or they do not trust law enforcement.

A second area of feminist focus should be to support the significant federal funding that has enabled universities and colleges to engage in promising, public health-focused prevention efforts and has supported research on sexual assault.[34]

Course Correction. At the same time that we support ongoing public health approaches, research, and the importance of campus-based civil approaches under Title IX, feminists should acknowledge and address serious issues about the fundamental fairness of some of the campus procedures developed under the Obama administration. The new guidance issued by the Trump administration presents challenges, but also offers opportunities to reimagine campus work to prevent and respond to sexual assault. The remainder of this chapter addresses this reimagining project.

I suggest four areas of focus that deserve special attention and that should guide our activism going forward. The first is to reject what I refer to as *Crime Logic*. *Crime Logic* permeates much of our thinking about sexual assault, limiting our ability to pursue meaningful public health measures and creating obstacles to nuanced and creative responses. As I describe more fully below, one of the most dangerous manifestations of *Crime Logic* is the uncritical endorsement of the campus "predator" narrative. The second area of focus is to promote public health responses that interrupt key social factors that increase incidents of male-on-female sexual assault. The third is to deepen our commitment to an intersectional framework. This requires understanding how the campus climate with regard to race, foreign nationals, LGBTQ students, and low-income or first-generation students shapes the climate with regard to sexual assault. An intersectional commitment also requires serious attention to developing processes that mitigate the potential for implicit bias in investigation and adjudication. The fourth focus is to endorse appropriately developed restorative justice processes as part of a larger *intersectional* public health response to campus sexual assault.

I. Reject *Crime Logic*

Crime—crime metaphors, crime control methods, and criminal justice ideology—has come to dominate not only methods of governance, but popular discourse. Jonathan Simon describes this phenomenon as "governing through crime," whereby "crime and the forms of knowledge historically associated with it . . . [have become] powerful tools with which to interpret and frame all forms of social action as a problem for governance."[35]

The discourse regarding campus sexual assault—feminist, popular, and otherwise—is deeply shaped by this larger criminalization discourse and the dominance of criminal justice tactics. I refer to this ideology and rhetoric that shapes responses and popular understanding as *Crime Logic*. *Crime Logic* is reflected in: (1) a focus limited to individual culpability rather than addressing collective accountability; (2) a disdain for policy attention to social determinants of behavior; (3) a preference for narratives that center on bad actors and innocent victims; and (4) a preference for removing individuals who have harmed others as though excising an invasive cancer from the body politic.

Crime Logic presumes that the measure of taking victims' needs seriously is in direct proportion to the pain inflicted on those who harmed them. *Crime Logic* is reflected in a simplistic understanding of individual "choice." This approach resonates with some of the feminist discourse regarding campus sexual assault. For example, in the aftermath of Brock Turner's sexual assault conviction, Stanford University adopted new rules to prevent the type of excessive drinking that both Brock and the victim engaged in on the night he assaulted her. Despite empirical evidence that heavy drinking is associated with sexual assault and that limiting access to alcohol results in fewer sexual assaults,[36] some feminist activists responded negatively to Stanford's new policy.[37] As one activist explained, "Banning hard liquor . . . sends the . . . message that alcohol causes rape . . . . Rapists cause rape, and they use alcohol as a tool to escape culpability."[38]

As Rose Corrigan illustrates, this framing of "choice" echoes second-wave feminist rhetoric that sought to discredit views of rapists as psychological deviants by expressing a simplistic, liberal conception of the rapist who freely "chooses" to rape.[39] This story has political utility, but it makes for bad policy and even worse programs. As Alletta Brenner describes, this simplistic account "fails to account for the ways sex and gender are performative" and how "gender identity and performance" shape sexual behavior.[40] Youth sexual assault is sometimes a calculated attack, but sometimes, "sexually inexperienced [young men] may be especially susceptible to relying on stereotypes about the sexual roles of men and women to interpret situations, and as a result, end up participating in acts of sexual violence."[41]

As described more fully in section II, research on campus sexual aggression finds a more complicated picture. Heavy episodic drinking, male peer networks that support sexual aggression against women, and endorsement of hostile masculinity are strongly correlated with sexual aggression, including sexual assault.[42] Public health responses should focus on interrupting and changing these patterns of masculine identity formation.

Predator Narrative. Further evidence of the application of *Crime Logic* is found in the widespread, uncritical acceptance of the idea that campus sexual assault is committed by a small group of sexual "predators" who cannot be reached or changed and who will remain ongoing threats.[43]

The predator narrative can be traced to the work of psychologist David Lisak. Lisak argues that most rapists are "sophisticated sexual predators who plan their attacks exhaustively and with astonishing cunning."[44] He concludes that

A very small percentage of men—serial sexual predators—are responsible for a vastly disproportionate amount of sexual violence in any community. These men cannot be reached or educated. They must be identified and removed from our communities.[45]

Lisak's conclusions are based on one-time ("snapshot") surveys conducted with college men in which they were asked if they had engaged in behaviorally described sexual conduct that would satisfy the criminal definition of rape.[46] For example, respondents were asked if they had sexual intercourse with an unwilling adult through the use or threatened use of physical force; similarly, whether they had oral sex with an unwilling adult through the use or threatened use of physical force.[47] The instrument measures rape *acts*, not rape *incidents*. The respondent who committed forced sexual intercourse on two different people or who committed forced sexual intercourse on the same person at two different times is counted as a repeat rapist, as he should be. The respondent who committed two different acts of rape against the same victim, at the same time, is also counted as a repeater, when he should not be. In research he conducted with Paul Miller, Lisak reported that 6.4% of a sample of 1,882 college male students reported having engaged in at least one rape act.[48] Within this group, 63% admitted to committing more than one rape act, including 28% who admitted to committing two rape acts. Lisak and Miller identity those who committed two or more rape acts as "repeat rapists."[49] These repeaters committed 90% of the total number of rape acts reported in the study, leading Lisak and Miller to conclude that the majority of rapes were committed by a small number of repeat rapists. In subsequent writing, Lisak claims that these repeaters are "predators" who "cannot be reached or educated."[50]

There are substantial problems with Lisak's interpretation of his data. First, presuming that rape *acts* are rape *incidents* likely over-counts the number of repeat rapists. As described above, a respondent who perpetrated two different rape acts in one incident is rendered a "repeat offender" even if he committed one rape incident. Yet Lisak's claim that these repeaters are predators who will continue to rape turns on this distinction. If the 28% who admitted to committing two rape acts are mislabeled—if in fact this group were guilty of a single rape incident—Lisak's numbers would flip: 35% would be repeaters (not 63%) and 65% would be one-time offenders.[51]

The second problem with Lisak's interpretation of his data is more troubling. Lisak relies on snapshot data—that is, data collected at one time only that is backward-looking information—to predict future behavior. Snapshot research does not capture *individual change over time*.

Yet, Lisak's claim that repeaters are predators who will not respond to interventions rests on the conclusion that *prior* offending is representative of *future* offending. For example, the study does not report information about the time period that separated rape acts, including whether the acts were committed during the respondents' college career or at an earlier time, or how long ago the acts occurred.

Longitudinal research that follows male students through their college careers finds that, contrary to expectations of predatory behavior, the assaultive behaviors of student rapists follow varying trajectories; a substantial number are not repeaters or are repeaters whose assaulting behavior occurs during one time period and then ceases. The largest such study relies on data collected in two prior studies with a combined 1,642 male college student respondents.[52] The first survey assessment in the freshman year gathered data on rape commission since the age of 14, as was the case in Lisak's study. Subsequent annual surveys gathered data on rape commission over the past year (since the last survey.) Focusing on data from the most recent study, the researchers found three groups represented. The majority (92.6%) of respondents were in a "none/low" group.[53] Ninety-two percent of the men in this none/low group did not commit any rape over the course of the study; the remaining 8% of the none/low group committed at least one rape act *but did not repeat offending across yearly assessments.*[54] The second largest group (5.3%) was those who reported committing a rape act at more than one assessment interval but whose level of offending across the assessments *decreased* over time.[55] The smallest group (2.1%) was those whose perpetration *increased* across the intervals.[56] Overall, most of the men (73%) who committed a rape act while attending college did so during *a single academic year,*[57] not consistently across the years as one would predict if the perpetrators were "predator" (serial) rapists.

The benefit of the longitudinal study is to put the findings of repeat rape acts into a timeline perspective. It may be the case that a substantial number of college rapists commit more than one rape,[58] but most do not continue to rape over time. *In other words, rape, like other crimes of youth, is often time-limited.*[59] Contrary to Lisak's claim that most campus rapists are repeaters who cannot be educated or changed, Swartout's data suggest that a substantial number *do in fact change over time.*

These findings, when coupled with research on the social and psychological determinants of campus rape,[60] have important implications for prevention and intervention. Lisak argues that campus prevention work should be concentrated on finding the predator rapists and punishing or expelling those pathological few.[61] Swartout, in contrast, concludes that prevention efforts should recognize the heterogeneity of rapists and counsels against a "one-size-fits-all" approach.[62]

II. Interrupt Key Aspects of Masculinity Performance That Are Correlated with Male-on-Female Campus Sexual Assault

Campus administrators should adopt and feminists should support a public health approach that addresses the social determinants of sexual assault.[63] Three key social determinants emerge from empirical studies of campus male-on-female sexual assault. The first is that heavy drinking is an important correlate with both sexual assault commission and victimization.[64] A college woman who attends a school with a high percentage of students who are "heavy episodic drinkers" has 1.8-fold increased odds of experiencing sexual assault than does a woman who attends a school with a low percentage of heavy drinkers.[65] Studies find that policies that decrease alcohol consumption—for example, taxes that increase alcohol prices—are linked to lowered rates of sexual assault.[66] Similarly, research on campus sexual assault finds that "policies banning alcohol on campus or substance use in residence halls [are] associated with reduced rates of self-reported sexual violence victimization."[67]

A second key finding is that male sexual aggression against women is significantly correlated with the endorsement of sexual dominance, hostility towards women, and hostile masculinity.[68] Sexual dominance is measured by asking respondents the degree to which particular feelings or beliefs are motivations for engaging in sexual acts.[69] Examples of dominance items include "I enjoy the feeling of having someone in my grasp" and "I enjoy the conquest."[70] Hostility towards women is frequently measured by the degree to which respondents agree with statements such as "I feel upset even by slight criticism by a woman."[71] Measures of hostile masculinity capture the degree to which respondents endorse ideas such as "violence is 'manly,'" "men are naturally aggressive and dominant over women," and "the 'sexual conquest' of women is an important aspect of masculinity."[72]

The third key finding is the particularly important role of peer networks in sexual aggression committed by adolescents and young adult men.[73] Male sexual assaulters are more likely to believe that their peers support sexual aggression and hold hostile attitudes towards women.[74] They are also more likely to have friends who pressure them to be sexually active.[75]

> Masculine identity formation in adolescence often involves treating sex as a game or competition. . . . Young men with little sexual experience who are highly motivated to have sex with many women may have a particularly difficult time recognizing the line between seduction and coercion. . . . [T]his suggests that these behaviors may diminish over time as they focus their energies on forming mutually satisfying relationships with women rather than impressing other men.[76]

The interrelationship between individual endorsement of hostile masculinity, peer support for sexual aggression, hostile views of women, and engagement in binge drinking may be critical to understanding the frequent findings of higher rates of sexual aggression in fraternities and male college sports teams.[77] But rather than a universal relationship, research supports a difference between high- and low-risk fraternities and sports teams.[78] Those student organizations that students rate as "high-risk" have significantly higher rates of sexual assault, their members are more likely to endorse hostility towards women, and they are more likely to believe that their peers support sexual aggression. The measures for members of male groups identified by students as "low-risk" for sexual assault were no different from measures for college men who were not group members.[79]

III. Take an Intersectional Approach

Contrary to a slate of recently published criticisms, intersectionality theory is not the equivalent of an oppression sweepstakes,[80] but rather a method of analysis: "a gathering place for open-ended investigations of the overlapping and conflicting dynamics of race, gender, class, sexuality, nation, and other inequalities."[81]

Campus activists have drawn attention to the ways that racial, sexual orientation, and gender identity categories shape differing needs and experiences related to sexual assault.[82] The Obama administration encouraged schools to adopt measures to prevent bias on the basis of sexual orientation and gender identity and to create awareness of sexual assault of LGBT students.[83] Building on these efforts, I argue for a more complete intersectional approach that deepens schools' commitments to responding to the needs of all college students.

I address three implications of a greater intersectional awareness. First, it is critical to understand the ways in which campus climate for marginalized students, more generally, affects campus climate for sexual assault. Second, we should urge support for empirical work that addresses intersectionality. Third, we should support measures in campus investigation, adjudication, and other responses to individual complaints of sexual assault to avoid identity-based bias, particularly implicit bias.

A. Campus Climate

The first lesson to be gained from an intersectional approach is to recognize the ways in which the general campus climate for students of color, LGBTQ students, foreign nationals, immigrants, and low-income students influences the campus climate for sexual assault. This requires recognizing the relevance of a general hostile racial or homophobic campus climate to developing meaningful methods of sexual assault prevention and intervention. It further requires an understanding of how the current political climate affects the campus climate.

Race is the most common basis for campus hate crimes reported to authorities.[84] African American students who attend predominantly white colleges and universities are often the subject of racist remarks from professors and are frequently called upon to validate their intellectual competence.[85] "Many students of color not only have to battle institutional racism, they also have to engage in academic environments that condone microaggressions and stereotyping."[86] Thus, it is not surprising that a recent survey of college freshmen found that African American students were significantly more dissatisfied with their college experience and more likely to report feeling angry and overwhelmed than were white students.[87]

The second most common basis for campus hate crime reports is anti-LGBT bias.[88] LGBT students experience higher rates of harassment, are more likely to report feeling unsafe, and are more likely to be victims of violence than are heterosexual students.[89] Additionally, recent campus research finds significantly high rates of *sexual* assault for LGBT students.[90]

The current political climate, including that which is influenced by newly energized white supremacist groups (the "alt-right") that have targeted campuses, has deepened these campus threats.[91] Hate crimes increased during the 2016 presidential campaign and have remained high.[92] Harassment against Muslims, and those believed to be Muslims, has risen significantly.[93] College administrators report that foreign students are increasingly reluctant to attend U.S. colleges because of President Trump's travel ban and because of the general xenophobic U.S. climate.[94] President Trump's announcement of the end of Deferred Action for Childhood Arrivals (DACA)[95] has left students in fear and distress.[96]

Hostility against marginalized groups of students may have an effect on their vulnerability for sexual assault, as well as their sense of safety. As an African American female student at Columbia University noted, "I feel unsafe at times. I feel that a lot of the stereotypes that come along with being black—we're exoticized and hypersexualized—make me feel targeted a lot."[97] But regardless of the impact on risk for assault, a hostile campus climate has a profound impact on the efficacy of school reporting mechanisms for sexual assault and the likelihood that a report will be handled fairly. Students of color are unlikely to seek assistance from university administrators if they experience the administration as racially hostile. "If I don't trust my institution on issues of racism, why in the event of having been [sexually] assaulted would I trust my institution?"[98]

Awareness of these intersections of potential sites for harassment and risk should guide campus prevention programming and response. For example, while bystander intervention programs frequently teach students to confront misogynist and homophobic beliefs,[99] I have found none that probe the endorsement of racialized gender beliefs such as beliefs that African Americans are "hypersexualized" and violent.[100]

B. Research

Feminist reformers should also support an expanded empirical research agenda that is based in an awareness of intersectionality. Campus climate surveys for sexual assault measure rape myth endorsement, along with capturing data on sexual assault incidents, the accessibility of campus programs, and reporting.[101] The surveys should be expanded to gather data on the intersections of bias. For example, Laurie Cooper Stoll et al. developed a Rape Myth instrument that incorporates rape myths related to race, class, gender, and sexuality, including questions such as:

Rape does not occur in lesbian relationships.
Rape usually occurs in inner city urban areas.
Women of color are more likely than White women to be raped because they
    tend to have more sexual partners.
White women who date men of color are more likely to be raped.
Upper class people have more control over their sexual urges.[102]

A heterosexual framing pervades the majority of the empirical research on campus sexual assault.[103] This is the case first because the vast majority of campus sexual assault studies are of male-on-female assault.[104] Male victims, whether of male- or female-perpetrated assaults, are seldom the subject of research.[105] Research rarely explores the sexuality of the women assaulted by men, creating an implicit assumption that the women are heterosexual.[106] Similarly, studies of male programs and fraternities presume the men to be heterosexual.[107] However, campus studies have found significant rates of sexual assault for LGBT students. A 2016 Campus Climate Survey study sponsored by the DOJ found higher rates of sexual assault of non-heterosexual women compared to heterosexual women.[108] The Association of American Universities' review of survey data from twenty-seven schools found that gay and bisexual men reported higher rates of sexual assault than did heterosexual men: 12.1%, 11.1%, and 3.6%, respectively.[109]

C. Implicit Bias

An intersectional approach requires incorporating protections against implicit bias. Bias may affect the fair treatment of the student who reports sexual assault as well as of the student who is accused of committing sexual assault. Bias may be based in race, ethnicity, class, gender, sexual orientation, gender identity, and the intersections of these categories. Bias is frequently *implicit*—unintentional and unconscious bias that is unrelated to, and may even be in opposition to, explicit attitudes.[110]

1. RACIALIZED GENDER BIAS

Racialized gender bias may affect the treatment of survivors of sexual assault. "The rape myths that undermine survivors' credibility and narratives of harm are not just gendered but are also racialized, and they are especially pernicious in delegitimizing the experiences of women of color."[111] As one activist noted, African American women are viewed as "always wanting, willing, and able [to have sex]."[112] Research finds, for example, significant race-of-the-victim affects in criminal cases,[113] and in hypothetical acquaintance rape scenarios, respondents are more likely to find a Black female victim untruthful or responsible for the rape than a white female victim.[114]

Implicit racial bias may also affect fair treatment of accused male students.[115] As Frank Rudy Cooper describes, a long, bitter racial history promotes the continuing presumptive image of African American men as the "Bad Black Man" who is "animalistic, sexually depraved, and crime-prone."[116] This image "emanates in part from a gender-specific assumption that heterosexual black men are a threat to the sexual security of white women."[117]

Further, the intersection of *class* with race and gender may be important to assessing the risks for bias that accused African American male college athletes face.[118] Those whose class history is substantially poorer than that of other students may experience bias that is gendered, raced, and classed.[119] Racialized class bias is also not limited to students from poor economic backgrounds. White faculty and students frequently presume that African American students are from low-income families.[120] Racialized gender stereotypes of African American men as animalistic and hypersexual[121] intersect with a deeply racialized and classed understanding of who is a "thug."[122]

2. HETERONORMATIVE MALE-ON-FEMALE SOCIAL CONSTRUCTION OF RAPE

Despite gender-neutral language and educational efforts regarding the substantial risk of sexual assault for LGBTQ students, the paradigm around which campus sexual assault policies are organized remains deeply heterosexual.[123] Thus, "rape, as a reality of queer relationships, remains outside of the discourse instilled by these texts—a discourse that constructs men as rapists and women as victims."[124]

3. BIAS IN INVESTIGATION AND ADJUDICATION

Feminist activists should support investigation and adjudication processes that minimize the risk that bias will affect campus investigation and decision-making. The potential for implicit bias may be particularly acute when decision-making rests in the hands of one individual, as is the case when a single investigator determines facts and reaches a conclusion.[125] As Tamara Lave argues, processes that diminish the potential for bias include: 1) the use of panels rather than a single adjudicator to determine responsibility; 2) the separation of the investigation function from the adjudication function; 3) the use of a diverse panel of decision-makers; and 4) training of panel members, investigators, and administrators in implicit bias and confirmation bias.[126]

The 2011 DCL requirement that schools use the preponderance of the evidence (POE) standard in campus adjudication of sexual violence cases has been the subject of enormous controversy. Vocal feminist support for the POE standard argued that it is the standard used in other civil rights contexts, that it fairly balances the interests of both the complainant and the accused student, and that a higher standard would unfairly tip the scales against finding for claimants.[127] Critics argued that the POE standard encourages university decision-makers to find sexual assault on the slimmest of evidence and that supporters fail to address the significant social, psychological, and economic costs of being found "responsible" for having committed sexual assault.[128]

Few commentators on either side of the debate have analyzed the POE question within the context of other campus procedures. This is the approach taken by the ABA Criminal Justice Section Task Force. The task force recommends that the POE standard should be adopted *only* when other safeguards for the accused are in place; when a panel determines responsibility rather than a single investigator; and when the investigatory function is separated from the adjudicatory function.[129] When these protections are not in place, the task force recommends that schools adopt the higher standard of proof: clear and convincing. When accompanied with adequate training on bias, the task force's holistic approach is better calibrated to ensure fairness to the accused student. The withdrawal of the POE requirement by the current DOE OCR allows advocates to push school administrators to adopt this kind of calibrated approach.

IV. Restorative Justice Approaches

[W]e wanted space to explain the devastating and lingering impact [of sexual assault], and we needed to trust that the perpetrators would never violate another person. . . . [R]estorative processes were exactly what my friends and I were asking for. We wanted to hear [the perpetrators] take responsibility for their actions. We wanted to share how we, our parents, our partners, our friends have been impacted by those actions. We wanted to know that they were going to actively and consciously educate and . . . rehabilitate themselves to prevent the creation of more victims. We'd been asking for a restorative process, but we didn't know that one existed. We deserve and deserved better options. . . .[130]

One of the most powerful things I get to see is when a young man makes amends in a sexual harm case. He admits what he has done and looks his victim in the eye and takes responsibility. When he does this, he is not harmed, he is not punished; rather, through the community, through family support, and through understanding the impact of his behavior on his victim, he is made into someone who will never do this again. That is actually to his great benefit and to all of our benefit.[131]

Restorative justice (RJ) can be understood both as a theory of responding to interpersonal harm and as a set of practices. The foundational theory of RJ is a focus on healing for victims and encouragement for those who commit harm to take responsibility for correcting the harms they created.[132] Thus, with both meanings, RJ offers an alternative to policies derived from *Crime Logic* and is consistent with public health measures that aim to change campus culture. Numerous RJ processes are beneficial in the campus context.[133] For example, prevention efforts can benefit from the use of community-building circles. Circles, involving facilitated discussions regarding sexual trauma, provide "a way to surface and explore issues related to sexual norms and behavior" by "rewriting cultural narratives about rape and hegemonic masculinity."[134]

My focus will be on RJ responses to individual complaints and on RJ Conferencing models that have been used successfully to address cases of sexual harm.[135] A growing number of scholars and organizations have endorsed RJ Conferencing as an important tool for handling campus sexual assault.[136]

RJ Conferencing is focused on three central questions: (1) Who has been harmed?; (2) What are their needs?; and (3) Whose obligation is it to meet those needs?[137] RJ practitioner, trainer, and theorist sujatha baliga notes that answering the first two questions requires asking a victim: "How do *you* define the harm? What do you think you need moving forward? What are your safety concerns? What are your material needs? How are you harmed—[in] all the different ways you could be harmed—financially, emotionally, physically, spiritually?"[138]

Several critical preconditions must be met before a conference takes place. First, the facilitator must assess whether an RJ process poses a significant risk to the victim. Research demonstrates that most victims are satisfied with their RJ experience,[139] but if the case involves a significant risk of physical or psychological harm, conferencing should not proceed. Second, both parties must make an *informed* decision to participate. This requires that RJ facilitators explain the process in detail to both claimant and respondent. Both should understand the extent to which evidence gathered in the RJ process may be admissible in any subsequent criminal or civil matter.[140] Both should understand that they can stop the process at any time. The third necessary precondition is that the respondent must admit to the conduct that is at the center of the claimant's claim. When a respondent admits to his or her conduct at the investigatory stage, and if the victim and respondent prefer RJ Conferencing to formal investigation and adjudication, the complaint may go straight to conferencing.[141] Alternatively, a respondent who has been found "responsible" through a campus adjudication process, and who admits to responsibility, may elect to participate in RJ to determine recommendations for the appropriate penalty, subject again to the victim's agreement.

Once these conditions are met, preparation for a conference begins. The facilitator will meet separately with the claimant and the respondent. These meetings include an assessment of any ongoing risk of harm to any party and may include referrals to services.[142] The facilitator will ask the victim what she or he hopes to get from the conference and will prepare the victim for meeting. The facilitator will also meet with supporters who are planning to participate.[143]

The conference is usually a face-to-face meeting with the victim, the respondent, and a trained facilitator; often includes the victim's and respondent's supporters; and sometimes includes professionals (e.g., alcohol treatment providers or school counselors).[144] The respondent begins by describing his or her conduct.[145] The victim follows by describing the impact of the harm.[146] The victim's supporters—family members, teachers, or friends—describe the impact of the respondent's conduct on the victim.[147] The respondent's supporters encourage the respondent to take responsibility for the harm he or she created and to amend his or her conduct, and may also speak to his or her positive qualities.[148] Rules of communication ensure that the victim has adequate communication time, prevent victim blaming, and "avoid excessive verbal shaming of responsible persons."[149]

The process, if successful, ends in a reparative plan.[150] Plans may include victim compensation, rehabilitative measures for the respondent (e.g., counseling or addiction assessment), stay-away provisions, community service, and other disciplinary measures.[151] Reparative plans may incorporate protections that DOE guidance recommends, such as changes in housing or classroom schedules to avoid repeated close contact between the victim and the respondent. RJ program staff will meet regularly with the respondent to ensure that the plan is completed and with the victim to see that she or he is receiving support and has not experienced retaliation.[152] While the concrete provisions of the plan are critical, often "the most valuable outcomes are qualitative. These are more to do with feelings, such as, experiencing a sense of justice, progressing a journey of recovery."[153]

Restorative justice offers sexual assault victims the opportunity to confront the person who harmed them in a safe and controlled environment and to have substantial control in the outcome of the matter.

> For most victims, it is satisfying to be able to express feelings about the offence directly to the offender and to explain fully its consequences. It is even more satisfying to see that the offender properly understands, sincerely apologizes for the offence, and pledges actions to ensure s/he will never behave this way again. . . . [Victims and] others closely connected to the crime . . . usually desire as well some form of censure by the community, a recognition of the wrong which is owed to the victim. They also need the offender to undertake a course of action that signals remorse and underlines the sincerity of the apology. [154]

By broadening the scope of responsibility and action, RJ plans can expand to reach change in the larger campus culture.[155] For example, a respondent whose sexual violence was perpetrated in the context of a high-risk male organization might agree to work with the university to develop new rules for fraternity and sorority life, work to change alcohol use, or assist with student training on gender subordination and sexual assault.

A review of research found that RJ Conferencing produced lower recidivism rates than was true for comparable cases heard in conventional criminal adjudication.[156] Most striking, the recidivism rate differential was strongest for *violent* crimes as compared to property cases.[157] Heather Strang, one of the authors of the study, posits that the difference is explained by the emotional quality of the RJ meetings: victims in the property crime cases "rarely expressed strong emotions," while violent crime victims "brought considerable emotional power" to the conference.[158] In these emotional cases, respondents were faced with the consequences of their actions in a powerful and transformative way, which Strang believes resulted in less repeat offending.[159] Research also finds that victims who participate in an RJ process report higher rates of satisfaction[160] and have lower rates of PTSD[161] than is the case for victims whose cases were addressed in conventional criminal processing.

Conclusion

Feminists should urge colleges and universities to adopt public health responses to sexual assault that are informed by insights regarding the importance of intersectional experiences and intersectional subordination. The evidence that many young men who sexually assault women do so for a limited period of time suggests the critical importance of university interventions to curtail assault. The interactive role of peer support, problem drinking, and hostile masculinity points to opportunities for universities to disrupt patterns of sexual aggression.[162] For schools to take advantage of this opportunity, universities and feminist activists must abandon *Crime Logic* reasoning and instead look to change the social structures that encourage and support campus sexual assault.[163] In addition to current bystander intervention programs, schools should adopt other public health measures, including, when appropriate, alcohol control measures.[164] An intersectional lens also means taking seriously concerns for procedural safeguards for both complainants and those accused of committing sexual harm. The debate over the appropriate standard of proof should expand to an examination of the entire process. Those schools that adopt less protective procedures (e.g., single investigatory models) should create other procedures that mitigate the risks for unfair decision-making, including the influence of implicit racial and other bias.

RJ Conferencing will be useful in developing the nuanced and flexible response required to meet the different experiences described and can helpfully change the social circumstances that promote sexual assault. RJ processes have the potential to interrupt peer networks that support hostile masculinity and problem drinking in the life of the individual student who perpetuates sexual aggression. The integration of RJ into a larger public health/intersectional response to campus sexual assault may provide an alternative that is better for many victims, more likely to lead to real changes in the behavior of the assaulter, and more likely to change campus life.

Author's Note

This chapter draws in substantial part from Donna Coker, *Crime Logic, Campus Sexual Assault, and Restorative Justice*, 49 TEXAS TECH L. REV. 147 (2016). I am grateful for the invaluable comments given me by Carrie Bettinger-Lopez, Marc Fajer, Leigh Goodmark, David Karp, Martha Mahoney, Carly Starkey, Jane Stoever, Thomas Voracek, and Deborah Weissman, as well as the participants in the Politicization of Safety conference.

NOTES

1 *See* U.S. DEP'T EDUC., OFFICE FOR CIVIL RIGHTS, DEAR COLLEAGUE LETTER FROM ASSISTANT SECRETARY FOR CIVIL RIGHTS RUSSLYNN ALI (2011) [hereinafter DCL 2011]; U.S. DEP'T EDUC., OFFICE FOR CIVIL RIGHTS, QUESTIONS AND ANSWERS ON TITLE IX AND SEXUAL VIOLENCE (2014); U.S. DEP'T EDUC., OFFICE FOR CIVIL RIGHTS, RESOURCE GUIDE FOR TITLE IX COORDINATORS (2015).

2 CHRISTOPHER KREBS ET AL., CAMPUS CLIMATE SURVEY VALIDATION STUDY: FINAL TECHNICAL REPORT 60 (2016).

3 *See* Press Release, White House Office of the Press Sec'y, Memorandum—Establishing a White House Task Force to Protect Students from Sexual Assault (2014); NOT ALONE: THE FIRST REPORT OF THE WHITE HOUSE TASK FORCE TO PROTECT STUDENTS FROM SEXUAL ASSAULT (2014); THE SECOND REPORT OF THE WHITE HOUSE TASK FORCE TO PROTECT STUDENTS FROM SEXUAL ASSAULT (2017) [hereinafter SECOND REPORT OF W.H. TASK FORCE].

4 *See* THE WHITE HOUSE COUNCIL ON WOMEN & GIRLS AND THE OFFICE OF THE VICE PRESIDENT, RAPE AND SEXUAL ASSAULT: A RENEWED CALL TO ACTION (2014).

5 *See, e.g.,* Press Release, White House Office of the Press Sec'y, Fact Sheet: Launch of the "It's On Us" Public Awareness Campaign to Help Prevent Campus Sexual Assault (September 19, 2014), https://obamawhitehouse.archives.gov.

6 *See, e.g.,* SECOND REPORT OF W.H. TASK FORCE, *supra* note 3, at 29.

7 DCL 2011, *supra* note 1.

8 *Id.*

9 See *Protecting Students from Sexual Assault*, U.S. DEP'T JUSTICE, www.justice. gov (last updated November 23, 2016) (providing a model campus climate survey). "Rape myths" are "false beliefs about rape shaped by sexism and other prejudices." Sarah McMahon & G. Lawrence Farmer, *An Updated Measure for Assessing Subtle Rape Myths*, 35 SOC. WORK RESEARCH 71, 71 (2011).

10 *See, e.g.,* Ann L. Coker et al., *Evaluation of Green Dot: An Active Bystander Intervention to Reduce Sexual Violence on College Campuses,* 17 VIOLENCE AGAINST WOMEN 777, 791 (2011).

11 *See* Nancy Chi Cantalupo, *Institution-Specific Victimization Surveys: Addressing Legal and Practical Disincentives to Gender-Based Violence Reporting on College Campuses,* 15 TRAUMA VIOLENCE & ABUSE 227, 231 (2014) (describing the influence of the *IX Network* and *Know Your IX*); Ruth Milkman, *A New Political Generation: Millennials and the Post-2008 Wave of Protest,* 82 AM. SOC. REV. 1 (2017) (describing the importance of the advocacy organization SurvJustice).

12 Cantalupo, *supra* note 11; Milkman, *supra* note 11.

13 *See* Republican Party Platform, 2016, at https://prod-cdn-static.gop.com; Memorandum from Attorney General Sessions to Heads of Department Components and United States Attorneys Supporting Federal, State, Local and Tribal Law Enforcement (April 3, 2017), available at www.justice.gov.

14 *See, e.g.,* Tamara Rice Lave, *Ready, Fire, Aim: How Universities Are Failing the Constitution in Sexual Assault Cases,* 48 ARIZ. L.J. 637 (2016); Jacob Gersen & Jeannie Suk, *The Sex Bureaucracy,* 104 CALIF. L. REV. 881, 900–01 (2016); Janet Halley, *Trading the Megaphone for the Gavel in Title IX Enforcement,* 128 HARV. L. REV. F. 103, 106–08 (2015); Jeannie Suk, *Shutting Down Conversations About Rape at Harvard Law,* NEW YORKER (December 11, 2015).

15 *See, e.g.,* Cathy Young, *Betsy DeVos Is Right: Sexual Assault Policy Is Broken,* Op-Ed, N.Y. TIMES (July 21, 2017), www.nytimes.com; Max Kutner, *The Other Side of the College Sexual Assault Crisis,* NEWSWEEK (Dec. 10, 2015, 5:33 AM), www.newsweek.com.

16 *See, e.g.,* Lave, *supra* note 14.

17 Suk, *supra* note 14.

18 *See* Office for Civil Rights, *Dear Colleague Letter from Acting Assistant Secretary for Civil Rights Candice Jackson,* U.S. DEP'T EDUC. (Sept. 22, 2017) [hereinafter DCL 2017].

19 *See* Office for Civil Rights, *Q&A on Campus Sexual Misconduct,* U.S. DEP'T EDUC. (Sept. 2017) [hereinafter Q&A 2017].

20 DCL 2017, *supra* note 18.

21 *See* Letter from Thirty-Four U.S. Senators to The Honorable Betsy DeVos, Secretary, U.S. Department of Education (June 27, 2017) (expressing disappointment and alarm at DeVos's decisions affecting Title IX enforcement).

22 Benjamin Wemund, *DeVos Vows Changes on Campus Sexual Assault Policy,* POLITICO (July 13, 2017), www.politico.com.

23 Q&A 2017, *supra* note 19, at 5.

24 *Id.* at 7.

25 *Id.* at 4.

26 Exec. Order No. 13767, 82 Fed. Reg. 8793 (Jan. 30, 2017) (*Border Security and Immigration Enforcement Improvements*); Exec. Order No. 13768, 82 Fed.

Reg. 8799 (Jan. 25, 2017) (*Enhancing Public Safety in the Interior of the United States*).

27 Proclamation No. 9645, 82 Fed. Reg. 45161 (2017) (*Enhancing Vetting Capabilities and Processes for Detecting Attempted Entry Into the United States by Terrorists or Other Public-Safety Threats*). In June 2018, the U.S. Supreme Court upheld the ban as modified in the 2017 Proclamation in Trump v. Hawaii, 585 U.S. __, 138 S.Ct. 2392 (2018).

28 *See* Stephanie Zacharek, Eliana Dockterman, & Haley Sweetland Edwards, *Person of the Year: The Silence Breakers, The Voices that Launched a Movement*, TIME MAGAZINE (Dec. 18, 2017), http://time.com.

29 *See* Steve Kolowich & Andy Thomason, *An Army of Survivors Topples a President*, 64 CHRON. HIGHER EDUC. A14 (2018).

30 *Id.*

31 The DCL 2017 letter criticizes the 2011 DCL for disallowing schools to rely on law-enforcement investigations. *See* DCL 2017, *supra* note 18, at 1.

32 *See* Donna Coker, *Crime Logic, Campus Sexual Assault, and Restorative Justice*, 49 TEXAS TECH L. REV. 147 (2016).

33 *See, e.g.,* Katharine K. Baker, *Why Rape Should Not (Always) Be a Crime*, 100 MINN. L. REV. 221, 223 (2015).

34 *See* Margo Kaplan, *Rape Beyond Crime*, 66 DUKE L.J. 102, 104 (2017) (describing the critical need for public health research on sexual assault); *see* SECOND REPORT OF W.H. TASK FORCE, *supra* note 3 (describing the significant research accomplished with federal funds under the Obama administration).

35 *See* JONATHAN SIMON, GOVERNING THROUGH CRIME: HOW THE WAR ON CRIME TRANSFORMED AMERICAN DEMOCRACY AND CREATED A CULTURE OF FEAR 17 (2007); *see also* BETH E. RICHIE, ARRESTED JUSTICE: BLACK WOMEN, VIOLENCE, AND AMERICA'S PRISON NATION (2012).

36 *See, e.g.,* Caroline Lippy & Sarah DeGue, *Exploring Alcohol Policy Approaches to Prevent Sexual Violence Perpetration*, 17 TRAUMA VIOLENCE & ABUSE 26, 27 (2016).

37 *See, e.g.,* Irin Carmon, *What Advocates Are Doing to End Sexual Assault on Campus*, NBC NEWS (Sept. 4, 2016, 5:20 PM), www.nbcnews.com.

38 *Id.* (quoting campus activist Wagatwe Wanjuki).

39 *See, e.g.,* ROSE CORRIGAN, UP AGAINST A WALL: RAPE REFORM AND THE FAILURE OF SUCCESS 9, 35 (2013).

40 Alletta Brenner, *Resisting Simple Dichotomies: Critiquing Narratives of Victims, Perpetrators, and Harm in Feminist Theories of Rape*, 36 HARV. J.L. & GENDER 503, 517–19 (2013). For a discussion of the harmful effects on feminism of the increasing feminist focus on criminal justice approaches to rape, *see* Aya Gruber, *Rape, Feminism, and the War on Crime*, 84 WASH. L. REV. 581, 624 (2009); CORRIGAN, *supra* note 39.

41 Brenner, *supra* note 40, at 519.

42 *See infra* section III.

43 There is a growing recognition of the problems with presuming that most campus sexual assaulters are unrepentant predators. *See, e.g.,* SECOND REPORT OF W.H. TASK FORCE, *supra* note 3, at 22 (noting the conflicting interpretation of data on the matter and urging more research).

44 DAVID LISAK, PREDATORS: UNCOMFORTABLE TRUTHS ABOUT CAMPUS RAPISTS 19 (2004), http://files.eric.ed.gov.

45 *Id.*

46 David Lisak & Paul M. Miller, *Repeat Rape and Multiple Offending Among Undetected Rapists,* 17 VIOLENCE & VICTIMS 73 (2002).

47 *Id.* at 77–78. Follow up questions ask the number of times the respondent engaged in the rape act and whether he committed the rape act against "another person," but these questions do not address the distinctions described in the text. *Id.* at 78.

48 *Id.*

49 *Id.*

50 LISAK, *supra* note 44.

51 See Lisak & Miller, *supra* note 46.

52 Kevin M. Swartout et al., *Trajectory Analysis of the Campus Serial Rapist Assumption,* 169 JAMA PEDIATRICS 1148, 1149 (2015).

53 *Id.* at 1150.

54 *Id.* at 1151.

55 *Id.* at 1152.

56 *Id.*

57 *Id.*

58 Kevin Swartout & Andra Teten Tharp, *Rethinking Serial Perpetration of Sexual Violence: Implications for Prevention,* PREVENTCONNECT (Sept. 15, 2015), www.preventconnect.org (a substantial number of the Swartout et al. sample committed multiple rape *acts* in numbers that are comparable to those found by Lisak and Miller).

59 *See, e.g.,* Antonio Abbey et al., *Patterns of Sexual Aggression in a Community Sample of Men: Risk Factors Associated with Persistence, Desistance, and Initiation Over a 1-Year Interval,* 2 PSYCHOL. VIOLENCE 1, 4 (2011).

60 *See* discussion *infra* section III.

61 *See* LISAK, *supra* note 44, at 24.

62 Swartout & Tharp, *supra* note 58.

63 For a more thorough description of the benefits of a public health approach, *see* Kaplan, *supra* note 34.

64 *See* Lippy & DeGue, *supra* note 36, at 27; Antonia Abbey, *Alcohol's Role in Sexual Violence Perpetration: Theoretical Explanations, Existing Evidence and Future Directions,* 30 DRUG & ALCOHOL REV. 481, 486 (2011).

65 Meichun Mohler-Kuo et al., *Correlates of Rape While Intoxicated in a National Sample of College Women,* 65 J. STUD. ON ALCOHOL 37, 40–41 (2004).

66 Lippy & DeGue, *supra* note 36, at 31.

67 *Id.* at 11.

68 Leah E. Adams-Curtis & Gordon B. Forbes, *College Women's Experiences of Sexual Coercion: A Review of Cultural, Perpetrator, Victim, and Situational Variables*, 5 TRAUMA VIOLENCE & ABUSE 91 (2004); Neil M. Malamuth & Nancy Wilmsen Thornhill, *Hostile Masculinity, Sexual Aggression, and Gender-Biased Domineeringness in Conversations*, 20 AGGRESSIVE BEHAV. 185, 186 (1994).

69 Malamuth & Thornhill, *supra* note 68, at 189.

70 *Id.*

71 *Id.*

72 Sarah K. Murnen & Marla H. Kohlman, *Athletic Participation, Fraternity Membership, and Sexual Aggression Among College Men: A Meta-Analytic Review*, 57 SEX ROLES 145, 146 (2007).

73 *See id.* at 148.

74 *See, e.g.,* Adams-Curtis & Forbes, *supra* note 68, at 105.

75 *Id.* at 105.

76 Abbey et al., *supra* note 59, at 11.

77 *See* Murnen & Kohlman, *supra* note 72, at 155.

78 Stephen E. Humphrey & Arnold S. Kahn, *Fraternities, Athletic Teams, and Rape: Importance of Identification with a Risky Group*, 15 J. INTERPERSONAL VIOLENCE 1313, 1315–16 (2000).

79 *Id.*

80 *See, e.g.,* Andrew Sullivan, *Is Intersectionality a Religion?*, N.Y. MAGAZINE (March 10, 2017); James Kirchick, *How Intersectionality Makes You Stupid*, TABLET MAGAZINE (January 21, 2016).

81 Sumi Cho, Kimberlé Williams Crenshaw, and Leslie McCall, *Toward a Field of Intersectionality Studies: Theory, Applications, and Praxis*, 38 SIGNS 758, 788 (2013).

82 *See, e.g.,* Milkman, *supra* note 11, at 2 (millennial left activists involved in anti-sexual assault work embrace intersectionality, "viewing race, gender, sexuality, and class as inextricably intertwined"); the website for *Know Your IX* describes the difficulties for "survivors from marginalized communities" who "often face additional obstacles to pursuing justice both for our own cases and as organizers" and offers assistance for "address[ing] discrimination by school officials and in activist spaces," available at www.knowyourix.org.

83 See *Protecting Students from Sexual Assault*, *supra* note 9.

84 SIMONE ROBERS ET AL., INDICATORS OF SCHOOL CRIME AND SAFETY: 2014 170–71 (2015).

85 *See, e.g.,* Shaun R. Harper, *Nine Themes in Campus Racial Climates and Implications for Institutional Transformation*, NEW DIRECTIONS FOR STUDENT SERVICES (Winter 2007), available at www.interscience.wiley.com, DOI: 10.1002/ss.254; Deborah Weissman, *Domestic Violence, Differences, and Intersectionality: Responses to Campus Sexual Assault* (unpublished manuscript, on file with author).

86 Adrienne Green, *The Cost of Balancing Academia and Racism*, THE ATLANTIC (Jan. 21, 2016), www.theatlantic.com.

87 *See* THE JED FOUND., JORDAN PORCO FOUND., & P'SHIP FOR DRUG-FREE KIDS, THE FIRST-YEAR COLLEGE EXPERIENCE: A LOOK INTO STUDENTS' CHALLENGES AND TRIUMPHS DURING THEIR FIRST TERM AT COLLEGE (2015), www.settogo.org.

88 ROBERS ET AL., *supra* note 84; *see also* SUSAN R. RANKIN, CAMPUS CLIMATE FOR GAY, LESBIAN, BISEXUAL, AND TRANSGENDER PEOPLE: A NATIONAL PERSPECTIVE (2003).

89 Elizabeth Reed et al., *Alcohol and Drug Use and Related Consequences Among Gay, Lesbian and Bisexual College Students: Role of Experiencing Violence, Feeling Safe on Campus, and Perceived Stress*, 35 ADDICTIVE BEHAVIORS 168, 169 (2010); RANKIN, *supra* note 88.

90 See KREBS ET AL., *supra* note 2, at 78.

91 See *ADL: White Supremacists Making Unprecedented Effort on U.S. College Campuses to Spread Their Message, Recruit*, ANTI-DEFAMATION LEAGUE (April 24, 2017), www.adl.org.

92 *See* Reuters, *U.S. Hate Crimes Up 20 Percent in 2016, Fueled by Election Campaign: Report*, NBC NEWS (Mar 14, 2017), www.nbcnews.com.

93 *See* Janice Williams, *Under Trump, Anti-Muslim Hate Crimes Have Increased at an Alarming Rate*, NEWSWEEK (July 17, 2017), www.newsweek.com.

94 *See* Karin Fischer, *Foreign Students Avoid Partly Reinstated Travel Ban*, CHRON. HIGHER EDUC. A24 (July 7, 2017).

95 *See* Katherine Mangan, *Trump Will End DACA in 6 Months, Confirming Dreamers' Fears and Putting Onus on Congress*, CHRON. OF HIGHER EDUC. (Sept. 5, 2017), www.chronicle.com.

96 *Id.*

97 *See, e.g.*, Darializa Avila-Chevalier, *Sister Outsider*, COLUM. SPECTATOR: THE EYE (Oct. 16, 2014, 1:38 AM), http://columbiaspectator.com.

98 Colleen Murphy, *Still Another Challenge on Campus Sexual Assaults: Getting Minority Students to Report Them*, CHRON. OF HIGHER EDUC. A15 (June 26, 2015) (quoting Kathleen Wong, Director of the Southwest Center for Human Relations Studies at the University of Oklahoma).

99 Donna Coker & Ahjané Macquoid, *Alternative U.S. Responses to Intimate Partner Violence, in* COMPARATIVE APPROACHES TO DOMESTIC VIOLENCE: LESSONS FROM EFFORTS WORLDWIDE (Rashmi Goel & Leigh Goodmark eds., 2015) (describing various bystander education models).

100 Frank Rudy Cooper, *Against Bipolar Black Masculinity: Intersectionality, Assimilation, Identity Performance, and Hierarchy*, 39 UC DAVIS L. REV. 853, 857 (2006).

101 McMahon & Farmer, *supra* note 9.

102 Laurie Cooper Stoll, Terry Glenn Lilley, and Kelly Pinter, *Gender-Blind Sexism and Rape Myth Acceptance*, 23 VIOLENCE AGAINST WOMEN 28, 34 (2017).

103 *See* Sara Carrigan Wooten, *Heterosexist Discourses: How Feminist Theory Shaped Campus Sexual Violence Policy, in* THE CRISIS OF CAMPUS SEXUAL VIOLENCE: CRITICAL PERSPECTIVES ON PREVENTION AND RESPONSE 33, 39

(Sara Carrigan Wooten & Roland W. Mitchell eds., 2016). Unlike the majority of campus research, Campus Climate surveys promoted by the Obama Administration gathered data on anti-LGBT bias and incident rates for LGBT students. *See* KREBS ET AL., *supra* note 2.

104 *Id.* at 48.

105 *See* Denise A. Hines et al., *Gender Differences in Sexual Assault Victimization Among College Students*, 27 VIOLENCE & VICTIMS 922, 923 (2012).

106 Wooten, *supra* note 103, at 47.

107 *Id.*

108 KREBS ET AL., *supra* note 2, at 78.

109 DAVID CANTOR ET AL., REPORT ON THE AAU CAMPUS CLIMATE SURVEY ON SEXUAL ASSAULT AND SEXUAL MISCONDUCT 86 (2015).

110 *See* L. Song Richardson & Phillip Atiba Goff, *Interrogating Racial Violence*, 12 OHIO ST. J. CRIM. L. 115, 120 (2014).

111 Deborah L. Brake, *Fighting the Rape Culture Wars Through the Preponderance of the Evidence Standard*, 78 MONTANA L. REV. 109, 138 (2017); *see also* DONNA COKER ET AL., RESPONSES FROM THE FIELD: SEXUAL ASSAULT, DOMESTIC VIOLENCE, AND POLICING (2015), http://academicworks.cuny.edu.

112 Murphy, *supra* note 98 (quoting Aishah Shahidah Simmons, activist and documentary filmmaker).

113 *See, e.g.,* Edward L. Glaeser & Bruce Sacerdote, *Sentencing in Homicide Cases and the Role of Vengeance*, 32 J. LEGAL STUD. 363 (2003) (offenders who kill blacks receive significantly shorter sentences than those who kill whites); Cassia Spohn, *Crime & the Social Control of Blacks: Offender/Victim Race & the Sentencing of Violent Offenders*, *in* INEQUALITY, CRIME, AND SOCIAL CONTROL 249, 264 (George S. Bridges & Martha A. Myers eds., 1994) (Blacks who sexually assaulted whites were significantly more likely to face incarceration and received longer sentences than did Blacks who assaulted Blacks or whites who assaulted Blacks).

114 Cynthia E. Willis, *The Effect of Sex Role Stereotype, Victim and Defendant Race, and Prior Relationship on Race Culpability Attributions*, 26 SEX ROLES 213 (1992).

115 *See, e.g.,* L. Song Richardson, *Cognitive Bias, Police Character, and the Fourth Amendment*, 44 ARIZ. ST. L.J. 267, 271–72 (2012).

116 Cooper, *supra* note 100, at 857.

117 *Id.* at 860–61.

118 Shaun R. Harper, *Am I My Brother's Teacher?: Black Undergraduates, Racial Socialization, and Peer Pedagogies in Predominantly White Postsecondary Contexts*, 37 REV. RESEARCH EDUC. 183, 192 (2013) (Black men, especially those who are athletes, are presumed to not be serious about their education).

119 *See* Gersen & Suk, *supra* note 14, at 900–01; Donna Coker, *"Stand Your Ground" in Context: Race, Gender, and Politics*, 68 U. MIAMI L. REV. 943 (2014).

120 Harper, *supra* note 118, at 192.

121 Cooper, *supra* note 100, at 857.

122 *See* D. Marvin Jones, *"He's A Black Male . . . Something Is Wrong with Him!": The Role of Race in the Stand Your Ground Debate*, 68 U. MIAMI L. REV. 1025, 1033 (2014) ("The same moral panic, which once targeted all blacks, has refocused on black males in urban areas with saggy pants and hoodies" who are seen as "urban thugs.")

123 *See* Wooten, *supra* note 103; *see also* Rebecca Ropers-Huilman, Kaaren M. Williamsen, & Garrett Drew Hoffman, *Afterword: Questioning the Scripts of Sexual Misconduct, in* THE CRISIS OF CAMPUS SEXUAL VIOLENCE: CRITICAL PERSPECTIVES ON PREVENTION AND RESPONSE 185, 188 (Sara Carrigan Wooten & Roland W. Mitchell eds., 2016) ("Does the 'gendered script' adopted by Title IX coordinators prevent male-identified, trans, and genderqueer students from seeing the support and response structures as means of assistance . . . ?").

124 Wooten, *supra* note 103, at 45; *see also* Bennett Capers, *Real Rape Too*, 99 CAL. L. REV. 1259, 1273–74 (2011).

125 Lave, *supra* note 14.

126 *Id. Know Your IX*, a leading victim advocacy organization founded by survivors of campus sexual assault, recommends a similar combination of safeguards: panels rather than single investigators, creating diverse panels, and separating the investigation from the adjudication function. *See* Know Your IX, STATE POLICY PLAYBOOK, www.knowyourix.org (last visited Feb. 1, 2018).

127 *See, e.g.,* Katherine K. Baker et al., *Title IX & the Preponderance of the Evidence: A White Paper* (2016), www.feministlawprofessors.com (published by a group of law professors); Brake, *supra* note 111; Nancy Chi Cantalupo, *"Preponderance of Evidence" Is the Correct Standard for College Sexual Violence Case*, NYT Opinion Pages: Room for Debate, N.Y. TIMES (Jan. 4, 2017), www.nytimes.com.

128 *See, e.g.,* Bobbie Wilson, *Hanover: A Mother Shares Her Son's Persecution & His TIX Injustice Over False Accusation*, SAVE OUR SONS (July 17, 2017), http://helpsaveoursons.com; Erica L. Green and Sheryl Gay Stolberg, *Campus Rape Policies Get a New Look as the Accused Get DeVos's Ear*, N.Y. TIMES (July 12, 2017).

129 ABA CRIMINAL JUSTICE SECTION TASK FORCE ON COLLEGE DUE PROCESS RIGHTS AND VICTIM PROTECTIONS: RECOMMENDATIONS FOR COLLEGES AND UNIVERSITIES IN RESOLVING ALLEGATIONS OF CAMPUS SEXUAL MISCONDUCT (June 2017), www.americanbar.org [hereinafter ABA Criminal Justice].

130 Jasmyn Story, *Reflection by Jasmyn Story, Recent Skidmore College Alumna and Current RJ Facilitator, in* PRISM, *Campus Interest in Adding Restorative Justice as an Option for Campus Response to Sexual Misconduct* (Oct. 2016) (on file with author).

131 *See* Donna Coker et al., Transcript, *Plenary 3—Harms of Criminalization and Promising Alternatives*, 5 U. MIAMI RACE & SOC. JUST. L. REV. 369, 376 (2015) (sujatha baliga describing her RJ practice).

132 *See generally* Jennifer J. Llewellyn et al., *Report from the Restorative Justice Process at the Dalhousie University Faculty of Dentistry* (2015), https://www.dal.ca/con tent/dam/dalhousie/ pdf/cultureofrespect/RJ2015-Report.pdf.

133 *See, e.g.,* Mary P. Koss et al., *Campus Sexual Misconduct: Restorative Justice Approaches to Enhance Compliance with Title IX Guidance,* 15 TRAUMA VIOLENCE & ABUSE 242 (2014); DAVID R. KARP ET AL., A REPORT ON PROMOTING RESTORATIVE INITIATIVES FOR SEXUAL MISCONDUCT ON COLLEGE CAMPUSES 2, 3 (2016), www.skidmore.edu; David Karp, *Restorative Justice and Responsive Regulation in Higher Education: The Complex Web of Campus Sexual Assault Policy in the United States and a Restorative Alternative, in* RESTORATIVE AND RESPONSIVE HUMAN SERVICES (Gale Buford, Valerie Braithwaite, & John Braithwaite eds.) (forthcoming).

134 KARP ET AL., *supra* note 133.

135 *See, e.g.,* Mary P. Koss, *The RESTORE Program of Restorative Justice for Sex Crimes: Vision, Process, and Outcomes,* 20 J. INTERPERSONAL VIOLENCE 1623 (2014); KARP ET AL., *supra* note 133; SHIRLEY JÜLICH, JOHN BUTTLE, CHRISTINE CUMMINS, & ERIN V. FREEBORN, AUT UNIVERSITY, PROJECT RESTORE: AN EXPLORATORY STUDY OF RESTORATIVE JUSTICE AND SEXUAL VIOLENCE (2010); Kathleen Daly, *Restorative Justice and Sexual Assault: An Archival Study of Court and Conference Cases,* 46 BRIT. J. CRIMINOL. 334 (2006).

136 *See, e.g.,* Koss et al., *supra* note 133; Leigh Goodmark, *"Law and Justice Are Not Always the Same": Creating Community-Based Justice Forums for People Subjected to Intimate Partner Abuse,* 42 FLA. ST. U. L. REV. 707, 722–23 (2015); Angela P. Harris, *Heteropatriarchy Kills: Challenging Gender Violence in a Prison Nation,* 37 WASH. U. J.L. & POL'Y 13 (2011); Deborah M. Weissman, *The Personal Is Political—and Economic: Rethinking Domestic Violence,* BYU L. REV. 387, 443–44 (2007); Alletta Brenner, *Transforming Campus Culture to Prevent Rape: The Possibility and Promise of Restorative Justice as a Response to Campus Sexual Violence,* HARV. J.L. & GENDER 1, 15 (2013); Lois Presser & Emily Gaarder, *Can Restorative Justice Reduce Battering?: Some Preliminary Considerations,* 27 SOC. JUST. 175 (2000); Tamara Rice Lave, *Campus Sexual Assault Adjudication: Why Universities Should Reject the Dear Colleague Letter,* 64 U. KAN. L. REV. 915 (2016); *See generally* RESTORATIVE JUSTICE AND VIOLENCE AGAINST WOMEN (James Ptacek ed., 2010); Margo Kaplan, *Restorative Justice and Campus Sexual Assault,* 89 TEMPLE L. REV. 701 (2017); Brake, *supra* note 111.

137 *See generally* HOWARD ZEHR, CHANGING LENSES: A NEW FOCUS FOR CRIME AND JUSTICE (3rd ed. 2005).

138 Coker et al., *supra* note 131.

139 HEATHER STRANG ET AL., CAMPBELL SYSTEMATIC REVIEWS, RESTORATIVE JUSTICE CONFERENCING (RJC) USING FACE-TO-FACE MEETINGS

OF OFFENDERS AND VICTIMS: EFFECTS ON OFFENDER RECIDIVISM AND VICTIM SATISFACTION: A SYSTEMATIC REVIEW 12 (2012).

140 Restorative justice programs often have a use-immunity agreement with the local prosecutor that protects against the criminal use of evidence gathered in a restorative justice process and a few states provide similar protection by statute. Absent such protections, students should be informed that their statements could be admissible in future legal proceedings. The same is true for *all* Title IX proceedings and investigations, and campus administrators should inform students of this possibility in all cases. Coker, *supra* note 32.

141 Koss et al., *supra* note 133.

142 *Id.*

143 *Id.*

144 Donna Coker, *Enhancing Autonomy for Battered Women: Lessons from Navajo Peacemaking*, 47 UCLA L. REV. 1 (1999).

145 Mary P. Koss, *Restorative Justice for Acquaintance Rape and Misdemeanor Sex Crimes, in* RESTORATIVE JUSTICE AND VIOLENCE AGAINST WOMEN 220 (James Ptacek ed., 2010).

146 *Id.*

147 *Id.*

148 *Id.*

149 Koss, *supra* note 135, at 1631.

150 *Id.*; VALLI KALEI KANUHA, FINAL REPORT: W. E. B. DU BOIS RESEARCH FELLOWSHIP 19 (2007), www.ncjrs.gov.

151 Koss, *supra* note 135. All reparative plans used by the RJ program RESTORE included a "stipulation that the offender be evaluated by a state licensed sexual offender treatment provider and, if indicated, undergo treatment targeting deviant arousal patterns, alcohol/drug use, and anger." *Id.* at 1631.

152 *Id.* at 1632.

153 Heather Strang, *Is Restorative Justice Imposing Its Agenda on Victims?, in* CRITICAL ISSUES IN RESTORATIVE JUSTICE 95, 102 (Howard Zehr & Barb Toews eds., 2004).

154 *Id.* at 102.

155 David R. Karp, *Introducing Restorative Justice to the Campus Community, in* RESTORATIVE JUSTICE ON THE COLLEGE CAMPUS: PROMOTING STUDENT GROWTH AND RESPONSIBILITY, AND REAWAKENING THE SPIRIT OF CAMPUS COMMUNITY 5 (David R. Karp & Thom Allena eds., 2004).

156 Lawrence W. Sherman, Heather Strang, Evan Mayo-Wilson, Daniel J. Woods, and Barak Ariel, *Are Restorative Justice Conferences Effective in Reducing Repeat Offending?: Findings from a Campbell Systematic Review*, 31 J QUANT. CRIMINOL. (2014).

157 *Id.* at 12.

158 Strang, *supra* note 153, at 99–100.

159 *Id.* at 100–101.

160 STRANG ET AL., *supra* note 139.

161 Caroline M. Angel et al., *Short-term Effects of Restorative Justice Conferences on Post-Traumatic Stress Symptoms Among Robbery and Burglary Victims: A Randomized Controlled Trial*, 10 J EXP. CRIMINOL. 291 (2014).

162 *See* Antonia Abbey et al., *Review of Survey and Experimental Research That Examines the Relationship Between Alcohol Consumption and Men's Sexual Aggression Perpetration*, 15 TRAUMA VIOLENCE & ABUSE 265, 275–78 (2014); Humphrey & Kahn, *supra* note 78, at 1318–19 (2000) ("Changes in perceptions of peer norms condoning forced sex, frequency of casual sexual relationships, and drinking in these sexual situations may be tied to changes in sexual aggression status.").

163 Kaplan, *supra* note 34, at 104–10.

164 *See* Jenny Dills et al., CTRS. FOR DISEASE CONTROL & PREVENTION (CDC), SEXUAL VIOLENCE ON CAMPUS: STRATEGIES FOR PREVENTION 10, 16 (2016) (schools should partner sexual assault prevention efforts with drug and alcohol abuse prevention programs).

8

A Fraught Pairing

*Immigrant Survivors of Intimate Partner Violence
and Law Enforcement*

NATALIE NANASI

I. Introduction

The relationship between immigrant communities and law enforcement
has long been complicated and fraught. But the Trump administration's
growing emphasis on criminalization and detention of immigrants
makes understanding and navigating the complexities increasingly critical, in no small part because the effects of immigration enforcement
in the Trump era have been particularly devastating for vulnerable
populations. A domestic violence survivor was recently apprehended
by immigration authorities in a Texas courthouse as she sought a protective order against her abusive partner, and similar arrests have been
made in New York's Human Trafficking Court.[1] Reports confirm that
non-citizen victims are afraid to report crimes to police for fear of
deportation.[2] And a 2017 survey of over 700 advocates working with
victims of intimate partner violence, sexual abuse, and human trafficking revealed that 43% had dropped a civil or criminal case due to fear of
immigration enforcement.[3] This is thus a critical time to examine both
the nuances of the relationship between immigrant survivors and law
enforcement as well as the legal structures put into place to serve both
groups.

This chapter embarks upon that examination by analyzing the U visa,
a form of immigration relief that provides crime victims, including survivors of intimate partner violence, a path to lawful status. Enacted by
Congress in 2000, the U visa has two stated aims. First, it provides legal
status to certain immigrant victims in recognition of the unique harms

they face and overcome in the aftermath of their abuse in the United States. A visa allows these survivors to "come out of the shadows" and into safety. Along with this humanitarian aim, the U visa aids law enforcement agencies in their efforts to investigate and prosecute crime, premised on the notion that non-citizen victims might otherwise be too fearful of deportation to identify themselves and report offenses to the police. The cooperation of immigrant victims, which would ideally lead to the identification, arrest, and eventual prosecution of the dangerous criminals who sought to harm them, would thus assist both the state and public at large.

Although the visa's two goals were purportedly coequal, in practice, the benefits to police and prosecutors are achieved at the expense of the victims Congress sought to protect. Receipt of U nonimmigrant status is conditioned upon compulsory and continuing cooperation with law enforcement, and the desire to engage with the state in this manner does not reflect the reality of the lives of many immigrant survivors of intimate partner violence. In fact, as this chapter will detail, requiring battered immigrants to cooperate with law enforcement in order to receive the U visa has ironically exacerbated the very vulnerabilities the U visa was intended to address.

This chapter will describe the specific ways in which the challenges immigrant survivors of intimate partner violence face make them uniquely unable, fearful, or disinclined to engage with law enforcement as required by the U visa. It also proposes novel solutions that mitigate the harmful effects of the U visa application process and restore the congressionally intended balance between protection of victims and benefit to law enforcement.

II. The U Visa

The U visa, or U nonimmigrant status, is a form of immigration relief available to an individual who is the victim of one or more enumerated crimes in the United States and has suffered "substantial physical or mental abuse" as a result of his or her victimization.[4] To be eligible, the victim must possess information about the crime and demonstrate that he or she has been helpful, is currently being helpful, or is likely to be helpful in investigating or prosecuting the criminal activity.

The crimes that make one eligible for a U visa are mostly violent offenses against another person in violation of federal, state, or local criminal law; the list of crimes includes offenses such as domestic violence, rape and sexual assault, stalking, abduction, false imprisonment, manslaughter, and murder.[5] An individual who experienced an offense similar to any of the enumerated crimes, or an attempt, conspiracy, or solicitation to commit any of the enumerated crimes, can also be U visa eligible.

To prove the "helpfulness" prong of the requirements, an applicant for a U visa must submit a certification form—USCIS Form I-918 Supplement B—signed by a federal, state, or local law enforcement official, prosecutor, judge, or any other entity that has criminal investigative jurisdiction over a specific U visa crime (e.g., the Equal Employment Opportunity Commission [EEOC] for workplace crimes or Child Protective Services for crimes committed against children).[6] The I-918 Supplement B form can be signed by either the head of the agency or a "designated certifier" who has been appointed by the agency head.

Although the U visa certification form is only one part of a U visa application, it is an essential part; the U.S. Citizenship and Immigration Services (USCIS) will not grant U nonimmigrant status without it, which highlights the significant weight adjudicators place on law enforcement cooperation. Other requirements throughout the U visa application process also underscore the importance of this cooperation. For example, even after the certification form is signed, the victim of a crime has an ongoing obligation to assist police and prosecutors.[7] Engagement with law enforcement is deemed so critical that a certification can be revoked if an individual ceases to cooperate.[8] Lastly, when a U visa holder seeks to adjust his or her status to that of lawful permanent resident, she must once again demonstrate to USCIS that she has continued to provide any assistance that a law enforcement agency has requested.[9]

A victim of a crime can seek a U visa not only for his or herself, but also for certain family members. An applicant who is under twenty-one years of age can include her spouse, minor children, parents, and unmarried siblings under the age of eighteen on her petition. An applicant who is twenty-one years of age or older can include her spouse and minor children. An individual who has been granted U nonimmigrant status is eligible to receive work authorization. The work permit and U visa are valid for four years,[10] but after three years, a U nonimmigrant can apply to adjust his or her status to that of lawful permanent resident, or Green Card holder. There is an annual cap of 10,000 visas per fiscal year.[11]

III. The U Visa as a Remedy for Survivors of Intimate Partner Violence

Although the U visa is available to victims of a wide range of crimes, the deep connection between the visa and the fight against intimate partner violence is unambiguous. From its origin, the U visa has been understood, and likely even intended, as a mechanism to protect survivors of gender-based violence, specifically domestic or sexual violence. The most readily apparent proof is in the titles of the enacting legislation. The specific provision creating U nonimmigrant status was entitled the Battered Immigrant Women Protection Act of 2000 (BIWPA).[12] The BIWPA was a part of the Victims of Trafficking and Violence Prevention Act (TVPA), the 2000 reauthorization of the Violence Against Women Act. The legislative history is replete with references to and statistics concerning domestic violence generally as well as the disproportionate impact intimate partner abuse has on immigrant populations.[13] At the hearing on the TVPA, Representative Sam Gejdenson referred to the U visa as a "new visa for battered immigrant women," cementing a link that continues to this day.[14]

Protections for immigration survivors were enacted because although intimate partner abuse impacts women regardless of their racial group, socio-economic status, or country of origin, immigrant women are uniquely vulnerable to intra-family violence and are more likely to face intimate partner abuse than members of the general population. The interplay and intersection of immigration laws, language barriers, social and familial isolation, financial constraints, and cultural issues leave many immigrant women vulnerable to exploitation with few options to remedy their situations.

In fact, gender-based violence is one of the most common forms of victimization experienced by immigrants.[15] Studies have shown that "between 34 and 49.8% of immigrant women in the United States experience domestic violence in their lifetimes."[16] The incidence of intimate partner violence in immigrant communities is so significant that experts have labeled it a "pandemic."[17] And it appears that the immigrant experience itself can be isolated as a cause of increased abuse; in one study, 48% of Latinas reported that the violence they had faced in their home countries increased upon their immigration to the United States.[18]

Not only do immigrant women experience intimate partner abuse more frequently than their native-born counterparts, they also face an increased level of danger from the violence they suffer. Research has shown that "where there is immigration-related abuse in [a] relationship, it usually coexists with physical and emotional abuse and appears to be a predictor of the lethality of abuse in those relationships."[19]

Lastly, and significantly to the drafters and proponents of the U visa, immigrant survivors of crime—including domestic violence—are often reluctant to seek assistance from law enforcement.[20] In a national survey of law enforcement officials, 67% of respondents agreed that recent immigrants report crimes less frequently than other victims.[21] These officials also believed that domestic violence was the crime least reported to authorities.[22]

The U visa was therefore intended to protect victims of intimate partner violence by removing a significant barrier to reporting—fear of deportation. However, requiring interaction with authorities as a condition of receiving the U visa has had many unintended consequences, and the most vulnerable victims are often left without necessary protections or, paradoxically, are placed in increasingly precarious situations as a result of their involvement with law enforcement.

IV. Immigrant Survivors of Intimate Partner Violence Are Reluctant to Engage with Law Enforcement

While U.S.-born abuse survivors may be hesitant to involve law enforcement—or the state generally—in their lives, battered immigrant women face unique challenges and obstacles. Cultural, economic, political, linguistic,[23] social, and legal considerations may make immigrant survivors unwilling, or sometimes even unable, to report abuse to law enforcement (or continue to cooperate after a report has been made). And as receipt of the U visa is conditioned upon such cooperation with law enforcement, the precise population the visa seeks to protect is often left without recourse.

A. Fear or Distrust of Law Enforcement

Many immigrants have complex feelings about, and complicated relationships with, law enforcement. Their experiences, both in their home countries and in the United States, affect how they understand domestic violence and the resources available to escape it.

Immigrants may come from countries where domestic violence is not considered a crime, or is even condoned.[24] If a victim's home country did not have criminal or social service systems in place to respond to intimate partner violence, if calls for help were routinely ignored, and shelters or safe homes were not available, she would have no context for seeking such services in the United States. Moreover, even if a battered immigrant woman was aware of the potential assistance law enforcement could provide, she may still be reluctant to seek help due to negative associations with official state actors in her home country.

With this background, it should perhaps be unsurprising that the police are not seen as a positive force in many immigrants' lives. As the International Association of Chiefs of Police explains, immigrants from developing countries have an image of law enforcement that is

> drastically different than that within the United States. Often the police in some of these countries are perceived as violent, corrupt and ineffective. These perceptions are often transferred to the immigrants' perception of the American police as well, creating a general reluctance to seek law enforcement assistance. These tenets also influence crime underreporting within immigrant communities, particularly domestic violence, sexual assault and gang activities.[25]

Although experiences with law enforcement in immigrants' home countries can sometimes explain their reluctance to engage with officials in the United States, our domestic police force is not without culpability. Many immigrants simply do not trust the police because they see official actors engaging in racial bias, discrimination, and mistreatment in their communities. Non-citizen victims, particularly men and women of color, may therefore be hesitant or even afraid to report crime to law enforcement because of "legitimate concerns that they will be subjected to differential treatment because of their ethnicity, gender, and immigration status."[26]

A troubling example of hostility towards immigrants by law enforcement is the experience of a woman of Asian descent who called the police when her husband violated the restraining order she had obtained against him. When an officer arrived, he refused to assist her, telling her that she should instead "go back to where she belongs."[27] Facing the possibility that a call to police will not result in help or will lead to their deportation, many immigrant survivors of intimate partner violence understandably never pick up the phone.

B. Fear of Deportation

Unsurprisingly, fear of deportation is significant in immigrant communities. For many non-citizens, local police are indistinguishable from immigration enforcement; concerns that they will be asked about their immigration status when reporting a crime cause non-citizens to remain silent and in dangerous situations. Such anxieties are particularly acute today, as the Trump administration quickly signaled its intent to increase immigration enforcement and reliance on programs such as 287(g)[28] and Secure Communities,[29] which deputize local law enforcement as federal immigration agents.[30] Immediately after taking office, President Trump issued a January 25, 2017, Executive Order, which included language that blocked federal funding for so-called "Sanctuary Cities" that refuse to cooperate with the federal government's immigration enforcement efforts.[31] States such as Texas were quick to follow suit with their own Sanctuary City bans.[32]

Fear of deportation is felt in most immigrant communities, but victims of intimate partner violence, whom the U visa is primarily intended to protect, may be especially afraid. Deportation and immigration enforcement have been identified "as either the first or second most intimidating factors that kept battered immigrants from seeking the services they needed" to escape abuse.[33] Batterers "often use their partner's immigration status, fear of law enforcement and misinformation about the U.S. legal system as tools to exert power and coerce the partner into staying in the situation."[34] The "Immigrant Power and Control Wheel," a tool widely used by domestic violence advocates, details various immigration- and deportation-related forms of abuse from the most direct, such as "threatening . . . to get her deported," to those with roots in economic abuse, such as "threatening to report her if she 'works under the table,'" or forms of control, such as "withdrawing or threatening to withdraw papers filed for her residency."[35]

If an abusive partner has lawful immigration status but the victim does not, the status imbalance leads to a power imbalance. As an official with the legacy Immigration and Naturalization Service (INS) explained, immigration can be a powerful weapon of abuse that "can be misused in many ways: threatening to report a family member to the INS, making false promises to file a petition some time in the future, withdrawing a petition that has already been filed, withholding important documentation, or refusing to appear for the scheduled interview with INS."[36]

Of course, a true disparity in status need not even exist for immigration status to be used as a tool of abuse. A client I represented in a petition for relief under the Violence Against Women Act, which requires that the victim of intimate partner violence be married to either a U.S. citizen or lawful permanent resident, was certain that her abuser was lawfully in the U.S. because he regularly mocked her after beatings, challenging her to call the police, who, he said, would not arrest him but instead deport her for being "illegal." We submitted her application, but it was ultimately denied because my client's husband was in fact undocumented himself. His abuse and deception knew no bounds—he had even shown her a fraudulent "Green Card." More broadly, this example demonstrates the power that threats of deportation can wield in an abusive relationship.

Although the U visa was created to address fear of deportation, the risk associated with seeking help from the police may exceed the potential benefit. The consequences of deportation are dire—separation from one's home, family, and children, potentially indefinitely, as well as a loss of income and the possibility of increased violence in one's home country. Alerting law enforcement to a crime, on the other hand, does not necessarily guarantee that one will be able to remain in the United States. Officers in a particularly hostile or anti-immigrant jurisdiction may detain and turn a victim over to Immigration and Customs Enforcement (ICE) without notifying her of potential eligibility for U nonimmigrant status (as they are under no obligation to do so) or providing her with the opportunity to apply. An agency is not required to sign U visa certification forms even if a victim reports and is fully cooperative with any ensuing investigation or prosecution (in fact, many jurisdictions have either opted out or passed onerous limitations on certification),[37] making her vulnerable to deportation by self-identifying to law enforcement. And if a victim ceases to cooperate at any time—even if she does so due to threats of retaliatory harm by the batterer—the agency can either refuse to sign a U visa certification or withdraw a previously signed one. Lastly, although an unsuccessful U visa petition did not previously pose a significant risk of deportation, a June 2018 USCIS Policy Memorandum greatly expanded the agency's enforcement authority.[38] The memo authorizes USCIS, whose primary mandate has long been issuing immigration benefits, to place individuals into removal proceedings, thereby significantly increasing the likelihood that a survivor applying for a U visa will be deported.

For the many reasons described above, when they experience domestic violence, immigrant survivors may either be unable or unwilling to reach out to police, or to continue cooperating with police who become involved in their lives. Their fear and distrust of law enforcement and deportation, however rational, may leave them without critical legal and social protections. And although they are bona fide victims of intimate partner abuse, in declining to engage with law enforcement, they are also ineligible under current law to benefit from immigration protections created with such victims in mind.

C. Family Fracturing, Economic Consequences, and Isolation

Even if she believes that the police will help and not turn her over to immigration authorities, an immigrant woman may be unwilling to report intimate partner abuse because of the potential impact that engagement with law enforcement may have on her partner and family. Domestic violence and other crimes against women, such as stalking, protective order violations, or sexual violence, are deportable offenses.[39] Thus, if a woman reports an abusive spouse with the goal of making the violence stop, or perhaps even having him receive a prison

sentence as punishment for his actions, calling her abuser to the attention of authorities could initiate a process that leads to deportation,
the potentially permanent loss of a woman's partner and her children's
father, and the ensuing fracturing of a family and the victim's economic
instability.

Scholars have described immigrant women as experiencing a "double
bind" wherein they are forced to achieve "empowerment through the
disempowerment of a male member of the community."[40] In a study
of undocumented Chinese, Filipina, and Latina survivors, researchers
found that only six out of 413 women surveyed had called the police for
help; the primary reason given for their silence was that "they [did] not
want to cause their husband or partner's deportation."[41] The study's authors described the double bind as not only adversely impacting a survivor's perceptions of her role in the community, but also affecting her
on an individual and personal level, "cutting her off from vital economic
support, confronting her sense of cultural solidarity and undermining
traditional value systems."[42]

If the abuser is the primary breadwinner in a family—which may
often be the case where the exertion of power and control takes the form
of economic abuse—his absence can be highly damaging for a survivor
and her children. Studies have shown that there is a 50% chance that an
abuse survivor will fall below the poverty line if she leaves her abuser.[43]
Domestic violence has also been revealed as the leading cause of homelessness for women.[44] Thus, if a survivor sees her options as choosing
between abuse and poverty, she may ultimately decide that the former
provides greater safety and security for herself and her children. Experts
have discovered that many women make precisely this calculation. A
study of immigrant Latinas who had experienced physical and sexual
abuse at the hands of their partners found that "the single greatest barrier to leaving an abusive relationship was lack of money."[45]

An immigrant woman may be particularly dependent on an abusive
partner for money, childcare, housing, transportation, healthcare, and
other critical needs. Foreign-born women are more likely to be lacking
in formal education or employment skills and may be unable to work
due to their immigration status.[46] Moreover, without access to a welfare
safety net, separation can threaten immigrant women's "tenuous hold on
economic viability."[47]

Ultimately, because of the nature of both intimate partner abuse and the immigrant experience, as well as the intersection of the two, "interventions that encourage battered women to take action based on a perspective of individual rights may be culturally incongruent and subsequently ineffective . . ."[48] An abused immigrant woman may value her community, along with the economic and social stability that it provides, over her personal safety. She may make a rational determination that she and her children are safer and more secure with her abuser than without him. This perspective challenges the basic tenets of the U visa, which is focused on individual protection stemming from public action that may be incompatible with the greater needs of a family or community.

D. Separation Violence

Perhaps the most troubling aspect of conditioning receipt of the U visa on cooperation with law enforcement is that the immigration relief intended to protect victims of intimate partner violence is based upon the flawed assumption that the separation from an abusive partner that results from arrest and prosecution will increase safety. In fact, reporting domestic abuse to the police can place a victim in greater danger.

Because intimate partner violence is, at its core, about one person's desire to exercise power and control over another, a challenge to that dynamic will often cause the abuser to lash out and retaliate against a survivor who asserts herself by, for example, seeking external protection against violence. This phenomenon, known as "separation violence" or "separation assault," has been defined by Martha Mahoney as

> the attack on the woman's body and volition in which her partner seeks to prevent her from leaving, retaliate for the separation, or force her to return. It aims at overbearing her will as to where and with whom she will live, and coercing her in order to enforce connection in a relationship.[49]

Engaging with law enforcement sends a clear signal that a victim will no longer tolerate abuse or the batterer's control, and can therefore be a significant triggering event for separation assault. An arrest can also provide a batterer with an excuse to perpetuate further harm. He may blame the victim for his incarceration and seek retribution in the form of increased violence. He may seek to injure or kill her to prevent her from testifying. Retaliatory violence may even "be motivated by knowledge of supportive or protective resources for women, particularly in men who believe such services deprive them of their rightful authority or control in intimate relationships."[50]

Separation violence is indisputably prevalent and dangerous. At least half of women who leave their abusers are stalked, harassed, or further attacked by them.[51] Moreover, the majority of domestic violence homicides occur when a victim leaves a relationship,[52] and experts have found that a battered woman is 75% more likely to be murdered when she tries to flee or has fled than when she stays.[53]

The stories behind the statistics are expectedly chilling. In Louisiana, a woman was gunned down by her abusive husband outside of the courthouse where she had just filed for a protective order and divorce.[54] The murder of a Dallas woman by her ex-husband was captured on a 911 call; as he strangled her, he demanded repeatedly, "Did you call the police?"[55] After a Las Vegas woman filed for divorce, her estranged husband regularly harassed and threatened her. She sought a protective order, which was denied, and three weeks later, he shot and killed her, their three children, and himself.[56]

Significantly here, cooperation with the authorities is a major cause of separation abuse. And violence has been documented at nearly every stage of the legal process. A study revealed that 25% of men arrested for domestic abuse re-assaulted their partner before the original criminal case was resolved in court.[57] The same study found that allowing a victim to drop charges against her abuser resulted in the lowest rate of pre-settlement violence.[58] In contrast, the prosecution of protective order violations is associated with increased homicide rates.[59] Lack of funding for witness protection programs further exacerbates these risks. And women in abusive relationships are keenly aware of this danger; in a comprehensive study, "fear of batterer" was listed as the number one reason abuse victims were unwilling to cooperate with the government.[60]

For these numerous reasons, the criminal justice system is not capable of securing the safety of many victims. Survivors therefore often make the rational decision to remain with their abusive partners, who are at least a known danger, or they seek safety without involving the criminal justice system, an apparatus that may lead them to experience more violence. Sadly, this choice necessarily costs non-citizen victims security in their immigration status, an imbalanced tradeoff that was not envisioned by those who created the U visa to protect battered immigrant women.

V. Proposed Solutions

Potential solutions to the problems raised by the U visa's requirement of cooperation with law enforcement can be easily discerned by looking to other immigration remedies that are available to survivors of gender-based harms, such as intimate partner violence and human trafficking. For example, the immigration benefits conferred by the Violence Against Women Act (VAWA) require a survivor of domestic violence to demonstrate that he or she entered into a good faith marriage with either a U.S. citizen or lawful permanent resident and was subjected to battery or extreme cruelty in that relationship.[61] The grant of immigration status under VAWA is not conditioned on assistance to or cooperation with law enforcement; a survivor is entitled to relief based solely upon proof that he or she has suffered domestic violence.

VAWA's immigration provisions demonstrate that precedent exists for a solely humanitarian conferral of benefits to survivors of abuse, i.e., relief that is not dependent upon a victim's engagement with law enforcement. As such, simply removing law enforcement certification from the U visa eligibility requirements would not only be consistent with current immigration law, but also allow the humanitarian aims of the U visa to be achieved without any of the attendant costs entailed in engagement with the state. Eliminating proof of cooperation with law enforcement would still leave in place the other U visa eligibility criteria detailed in section II, namely, proof that one is a victim of an enumerated crime as well as evidence of substantial harm as a result of that victimization. As such, measures would remain in place to ensure that only true victims of intimate partner violence would be granted U nonimmigrant status.

Alternatively, the T visa, immigration relief for survivors of human trafficking that was contemporaneously enacted with the U visa in the Victims of Trafficking and Violence Prevention Act, is an example of an immigration remedy that achieves the appropriate balance between humanitarian and law enforcement aims. Like the U visa, an applicant for a T visa must demonstrate to USCIS that he or she has "complied with any reasonable requests for assistance in the Federal, State, or local investigation or prosecution of acts of trafficking."[62] However, unlike U nonimmigrant status, T nonimmigrant status contains an opt-out provision for minors as well as those who are unable to cooperate due to physical or psychological trauma.[63]

Comparable accommodations exist when a U visa holder applies for lawful permanent resident status. In the Green Card application process, a survivor must demonstrate to USCIS that he or she has "not unreasonably refused to provide assistance to . . . a law enforcement agency . . . after [he or she] was granted U nonimmigrant status."[64] The abused individual can establish this continuing assistance by providing a newly executed I-918B Certification Form. However, USCIS will also accept alternative forms of proof, including an affidavit describing efforts to obtain a new law enforcement certification "or other evidence describing whether or not the [applicant] received any request to provide assistance in a criminal investigation or prosecution, and the [applicant's] response to any such request."[65] Additionally, the regulations do not automatically disqualify applicants who refused to comply with law enforcement's requests for assistance from eligibility for adjustment of status, instead allowing survivors to provide USCIS with an explanation for their lack of cooperation and their belief that the requests for assistance were unreasonable.

The U visa requirements could be rewritten to incorporate exceptions, similar to those that exist for the T visa and the U visa's lawful permanent resident application, for survivors who are too traumatized to engage with law enforcement, for those whose safety or security would be compromised by reporting or cooperating, or for victims who can demonstrate that a law enforcement agency arbitrarily or unreasonably refused to sign a certification form. Allowing survivors who fall into these limited categories to be eligible for a U visa without submitting the law enforcement certification form would be an appropriate mechanism for allowing victims of intimate partner violence who deem it too dangerous to work with the police or prosecutors to receive immigration relief and protection. And because the opt-out would be an exception as opposed to the rule, the appropriate balance envisioned by Congress could still be achieved: benefits would accrue to law enforcement in the majority of cases, while genuine victims for whom engagement with authorities is impossible would still receive justice.

Even if the U visa retains the law enforcement certification requirement, there are ways to mitigate its negative impacts. The U.S. Citizenship and Immigration Services currently provides resources and information to law enforcement about the U visa, but while it encourages local agencies to participate in the U visa program, it does not require them to do so. The federal government could instead mandate the participation of law enforcement agencies. While USCIS could likely not force local officials to sign individual U visa certifications, as such a determination is best left in the hands of those who are most familiar with a victim's helpfulness and cooperation, it could require localities to designate certifiers within their relevant agencies, direct that the certifiers receive appropriate education training, and maintain a national database of these certifiers. The issuance of new or updated Department of Homeland Security (DHS) policy memoranda would also go a long way in providing additional guidance to agencies. Although these proposals would not solve all of the problems discussed in this chapter, ensuring that an adequately trained official conducts a fair review of a law enforcement certification request would provide a level of certainty to applicants and eliminate some risk of arrest and deportation for survivors.

Finally, states can step in if the federal government does not take action. In fact, some jurisdictions have already begun to do so. In 2015, California signed into law S.B. 674, which mandates the participation of law enforcement agencies in the U visa certification process.[66] The law requires agencies to provide certifications to victims who meet the federal standard of helpfulness, establishes a rebuttable presumption that victims who have not refused to provide information or assistance have met the requisite level of helpfulness for certification, and requires requests for certifications to be processed within ninety days. The law also requires law enforcement agencies to provide information to the legislature on the number of certifications signed and the number of certification requests denied each year.

Other state legislatures have introduced similar bills, including Maryland,[67] Minnesota,[68] and Washington.[69] The Nebraska legislature passed a resolution to study law enforcement policies and practices in that state and determine whether any legislation is needed to encourage or require agencies to certify victims.[70] Local governments have done their part as well. For example, in an effort to ensure consistency for victims, the City of New York promulgated a rule that details the process for requesting certifications, provides a timetable within which requests are processed, and specifies the process for appeals.[71]

VI. Conclusion

Requiring cooperation with law enforcement as a condition of U visa eligibility has adversely impacted the very victims the visa was created to assist. Yet the immigration system is not unique in its arguably misguided effort to aid victims of intimate partner violence by demanding interaction with the criminal justice system. As such, the U visa's law enforcement certification requirement cannot be properly understood outside the broader historical context of "mandatory interventions" in cases of intimate partner violence in the United States.

For centuries, the state refused to intervene in incidents of intimate partner abuse, or what was then deemed a "private family matter." If a woman called the police to seek protection from her partner's attacks, such calls were regularly ignored. And if officers did arrive, they often did not provide the victim with the safety and security she sought. As a result, jurisdictions enacted policies such as mandatory arrest, which compel police officers to effectuate an arrest once probable cause of domestic violence has been established, and no-drop prosecution, pursuant to which prosecutors do not dismiss criminal charges in a domestic violence case, even if the victim does not want to cooperate with the prosecution or see it proceed.

There are certainly some real and symbolic benefits of mandatory interventions. Requiring officers to arrest perpetrators of intimate partner violence deprives law enforcement of the discretion to not treat intimate partner violence as a crime. Moreover, both mandatory arrest and no-drop prosecution policies send a message about the gravity of domestic violence and the fact that intra-family violence will not be tolerated. In requiring arrest and prosecution for domestic violence, abuse of one's spouse or intimate partner is treated comparably to violence against a stranger, a parity that has long been the goal of advocates.

However, many scholars and advocates have critiqued mandatory interventions. They argue that the pendulum has swung too far and that forced interaction with the legal system can be extraordinarily harmful to those who have experienced intimate partner abuse. Some survivors, particularly those from minority or marginalized communities, may not want to be involved with a criminal justice system that they view with suspicion or distrust. Victims' decisions to avoid interactions with the police and courts are often rational calculations, "made based on past experiences and with intimate knowledge of their partners, their resources, their political views, their family concerns—in short, based on the lives that they seek to fashion."[72]

Moreover, once a survivor is forced to work within a system against her will, with official actors she believes are not acting in her best interest and who achieve results that are not necessarily beneficial to her life or safety, she may be reluctant to seek help in the future. This can in turn potentially increase the level of risk and danger she faces in her relationship.

Lastly, if the primary goal of domestic violence advocates is to empower victims who have been subjected to abusive power and control, the stripping of agency from survivors through either mandatory or coercive interaction with law enforcement is troubling. Forced engagement with law enforcement does not allow a survivor of intimate partner violence to control the means in which she extricates herself from an abusive relationship or to determine her own goals and priorities and assess her own risk. As such, mandatory engagement with the criminal justice system can be described as disempowering at best, and at worst, dangerous for a survivor of intimate partner abuse.

Despite warnings about the harms of mandatory justice system interventions, the U visa fell into the familiar trap of requiring survivors to engage with law enforcement to achieve safety. Although immigrant victims retain the choice of whether to seek the U visa (and engage with law enforcement) or to remain in the shadows without lawful immigration status, it can certainly be described as a coerced choice that is in the spirit of the mandatory interventions that preceded it.

Since the 1970s, there has been a significant positive cultural shift in the recognition of the severity of the problem of domestic violence. Both the general public and law enforcement have made great strides in understanding that intimate partner abuse is not simply a family matter but as serious as any other assaultive or violent crime. As society has achieved a more sophisticated understanding, it is now time to scale back the mandatory interventions that were originally enacted to ensure equity for victims. The protections provided by police, prosecutors, and the legal system can be lifesaving for many victims, but such intervention is not appropriate for all, especially immigrant survivors. As such, it is time to question not only continued adherence to mandatory interventions, but perpetuation of analogous ideas into new areas, such as U visa eligibility.

Author's Note

Thanks go to Joanna Grossman for her endless supply of patience, wisdom, and guidance as well as Jane Stoever for this opportunity.

NOTES

1 Tom Dart, *Undocumented Texas Woman Arrested While Seeking Domestic Violence Help*, GUARDIAN (Feb. 16, 2017), www.theguardian.com.

2 James Queally, *Latinos Are Reporting Fewer Sexual Assaults Amid a Climate of Fear, LAPD says*, L.A. TIMES (Mar. 21, 2017), www.latimes.com.

3 KEY FINDINGS: ADVOCATE AND LEGAL SERVICE SURVEY REGARDING IMMIGRANT SURVIVORS (2017), www.tahirih.org.

4 8 U.S.C § 1101(a)(15)(U)(i) (2014).

5 8 U.S.C § 1101(a)(15)(U)(iii). A complete list of U visa crimes is as follows: rape, torture, trafficking, incest, domestic violence, sexual assault, abusive sexual contact, prostitution, sexual exploitation, stalking, female genital mutilation, being held hostage, peonage, involuntary servitude, slave trade, kidnapping, abduction, unlawful criminal restraint, false imprisonment, blackmail, extortion, manslaughter, murder, felonious assault, witness tampering, obstruction of justice, perjury, and fraud in foreign labor contracting.

6 U.S. CITIZENSHIP AND IMMIGRATION SERVICES, I-198, Petition for U Nonimmigrant Status, www.uscis.gov.

7 8 C.F.R. § 214.14(b)(3) (2013).

8 8 C.F.R. § 214.14(h)(2).

9 8 U.S.C. § 1255(m).

10 8 U.S.C. § 1184(p) (2015), INA § 214(p)(6).

11 8 U.S.C. § 1184(p), INA § 214(p)(2). Demand for U visas has far exceeded their availability. In fiscal year 2014, the cap was reached in December 13, 2013, two and a half months into the fiscal year. In fiscal year 2015, as a result of the backlogged

visas from 2014, the cap was reached on October 1, the day the fiscal year began. Although USCIS continues to adjudicate applications once the cap is reached, and grants individuals deferred action as well as work authorization while they wait for their visas to be approved, the backlog continues to grow. 63,762 applications remained pending at the end of fiscal year 2015 (*see* U.S. CITIZENSHIP AND IMMIGRATION SERVICES, NUMBER OF I-918 PETITIONS FOR U NONIMMI-GRANT STATUS (VICTIM OF CERTAIN CRIMINAL ACTIVITIES AND FAM-ILY MEMBERS) BY FISCAL YEAR, QUARTER, AND CASE STATUS 2009–2016 (2016), www.uscis.gov), a backlog which would take six years to clear. Only Congress can raise the cap, and while advocates have called for this change, any increase in benefits to immigrants in today's political climate is unlikely.

12 This chapter will use the female pronoun to refer to survivors of domestic violence because although both men and women experience intimate partner abuse, women are impacted at a significantly higher rate. One in four women have been the victim of severe physical violence by a partner, as opposed to one in seven men. CTRS. FOR DISEASE CONTROL & PREVENTION, NATIONAL DATA ON INTIMATE PARTNER VIOLENCE, SEXUAL VIOLENCE, AND STALKING (2014), www.cdc. gov. In fact, between 1994 and 2010, four in five victims of domestic violence were female. *Statistics*, NAT'L DOMESTIC VIOLENCE HOTLINE, www.thehotline.org. Other sources indicate that as many as 85% of victims of domestic violence are women. CRYSTAL WICK, NAT'L CTR. ON DOMESTIC & SEXUAL VIOLENCE, FAQ ON DOMESTIC VIOLENCE 1 (Jan. 2004), www.ncdsv.org.

13 For example, Senator Boxer explained her support of the Trafficking Victims Protection Act by describing the unique vulnerabilities of immigrant victims and stating, "[w]e also, for the first time, look at battered immigrants. . . . They need to understand their rights, that their bodies don't belong to anyone else, and they have a right to cry out if they are abused." At the same hearing, the late Senator Kennedy described the importance of the U visa in equalizing access to justice for all survivors: "These and other important measures will do a great deal to protect battered immigrants and their children from domestic violence and free them from the fear that often prevents them from prosecuting these crimes. Congress enacted the Violence Against Women Act in 1994 to help all victims of domestic violence, regardless of their citizenship." *Trafficking Victims Protection Act of 2000—Conference Report*, 146 Cong. Rec. S. 10164 (Oct. 11, 2000).

14 *Conference Report on H.R. 3244, Victims of Trafficking and Violence Prevention Act of 2000*, 146 Cong. Rec. H. 9029 (Oct. 6, 2000).

15 ROBERT C. DAVIS & EDNA EREZ, U.S. DEP'T OF JUSTICE, IMMIGRANT POPULATIONS AS VICTIMS: TOWARD A MULTICULTURAL CRIMINAL JUS-TICE SYSTEM (1998), www.ncdsv.org.

16 *Battered Immigrant Women Protection Act of 1999: Hearing Before the Subcommittee on Immigration and Claims of the H. Comm. On the Judiciary*, 106th Cong. 135 (2000) (statement of Leslye Orloff, Director, Immigrant Women Program, NOW Legal Defense and Education Fund) [hereinafter *BIWPA Hearing*].

17 Anita Raj & Jay Silverman, *The Roles of Culture, Context, and Legal Immigrant Status on Intimate Partner Violence*, 8 VIOLENCE AGAINST WOMEN 367, 369 (2002).

18 CHRIS HOGELAND & KAREN ROSEN, COALITION FOR IMMIGRANT AND REFUGEE RIGHTS AND SERVICES, DREAMS LOST, DREAMS FOUND: UN-DOCUMENTED WOMEN IN THE LAND OF OPPORTUNITY (1990).

19 *BIWPA Hearing, supra* note 16.

20 *See* INT'L ASS'N OF CHIEFS OF POLICE, POLICE CHIEFS GUIDE TO IMMIGRATION ISSUES 11 (2007), www.theiacp.org ("In particular [undocumented] immigrants are often afraid to report crime to local authorities, making them easy targets for those with criminal intentions.").

21 DAVIS & EREZ, *supra* note 15.

22 *Id.*

23 Language barriers pose a significant obstacle for immigrant survivors of intimate partner violence who seek to extricate themselves from violent situations. If a victim does not speak English, she may be unaware of the resources available to her or unable to access the resources of which she knows. Experts have identified language barriers as posing the greatest hardship to immigrant victims' reporting of crimes to law enforcement. And even if immigrant survivors of domestic violence are aware of available services, they are often unable to utilize them to the same extent as English-speaking survivors. The lack of bilingual shelters as well as certified interpreters who can provide access to 911, the police, and the court system can be a substantial impediment.

24 Raj & Silverman, *supra* note 17, at 370.

25 INT'L ASS'N OF CHIEFS OF POLICE, *supra* note 20, at 21.

26 Edna Erez & Carolyn Copps Hartley, *Battered Immigrant Women and the Legal System: A Therapeutic Jurisprudence Perspective*, 4 WESTERN CRIMINOL. REV. 155–69 (2003).

27 Linda Kelly, *Stories from the Front: Seeking Refuge for Battered Immigrants in the Violence Against Women Act*, 92 NW. U. L. REV. 665, 679 (1998).

28 U.S.C. § 1357(g), INA § 287(g). Under the 287(g) program, Immigration and Customs Enforcement (ICE) delegates power over immigration enforcement to a state or local agency. The agency is then empowered to ascertain immigration status, arrest and detain undocumented immigrants, and transfer undocumented immigrants to ICE custody to initiate deportation proceedings. See *Delegation of Immigration Authority Section 287(g) Immigration and Nationality Act*, U.S. IMMIGRATION AND CUSTOMS ENFORCEMENT, www.ice.gov.

29 Secure Communities is a Department of Homeland Security (DHS) program designed to identify immigrants in U.S. jails who are deportable under immigration law. See *Secure Communities*, U.S. IMMIGRATION AND CUSTOMS ENFORCEMENT, www.ice.gov.

30 See *Executive Order: Enhancing Public Safety in the Interior of the United States*, THE WHITE HOUSE, www.whitehouse.gov (Section 8(a) of the Executive Order,

entitled "Federal-State Agreements," states, "In furtherance of this policy, the Secretary shall immediately take appropriate action to engage with the Governors of the States, as well as local officials, for the purpose of preparing to enter into agreements under section 287(g) of the INA (8 U.S.C. 1357(g))." Section 8(b) states, "To the extent permitted by law and with the consent of State or local officials, as appropriate, the Secretary shall take appropriate action . . . to authorize State and local law enforcement officials . . . to perform the functions of immigration officers in relation to the investigation, apprehension, or detention of aliens in the United States. . . . Such authorization shall be in addition to, rather than in place of, Federal performance of these duties.").

31 *Id.*

32 Niraj Chokshi, *Texas Governor Signs a Ban on Sanctuary Cities*, N.Y. TIMES (May 7, 2017), www.nytimes.com.

33 *Id.*

34 INT'L ASS'N OF CHIEFS OF POLICE, *supra* note 20, at 29.

35 NATI'L CTR. ON DOMESTIC & SEXUAL VIOLENCE, IMMIGRANT POWER AND CONTROL WHEEL (2009), www.ncdsv.org. The Power and Control Wheel organizes and describes the most common abusive tactics used in domestic violence relationships. It is regularly used by counselors and advocates to help survivors identify how batterers utilize each behavior identified on the wheel to perpetrate abuse. Since the original wheel was developed in 1984, it has been adapted for specific communities of survivors (e.g., immigrants, people with disabilities, gays and lesbians, Muslims) in order to identify the unique vulnerabilities presented by those statuses.

36 *BIWPA Hearing, supra* note 16, at 94 (statement of Barbara Strack, Acting Executive Associate Commissioner for Policy and Planning, Immigration and Naturalization Service).

37 Empirical studies reveal a shocking lack of uniformity and consistency among U visa certification processes nationwide. The reports demonstrate that law enforcement agencies across the United States have both formal and informal policies that are not in keeping with Congress's intent to provide immigration relief to victims who have assisted at various stages of investigations and prosecutions. The discretion that rests with law enforcement agencies has resulted in what advocates have termed "geographic roulette," wherein victims in identical circumstances are either granted or denied certification depending on the location of the agency from which they seek it (*See* UNC SCHOOL OF LAW IMMIGRATION/HUMAN RIGHTS POLICY CLINIC, THE POLITICAL GEOGRAPHY OF THE U VISA: ELIGIBILITY AS A MATTER OF LOCALE 22, www.law.unc. edu). Some jurisdictions refuse to execute certification forms for victims under any circumstances, while others have arbitrarily limited certification policies. As a result, legitimate victims are capriciously denied the opportunity to seek U visa relief.

38 U.S. Citizenship & Immigration Services, Updated Guidance for the Referral of Cases and Issuance of Notices to Appear (NTAs) in Cases Involving Inadmissible and Deportable Aliens, www.uscis.gov.

39 8 U.S.C. §1227(a)(2)(E)(i), INA §237(a)(2)(E)(i) ("Any alien who at any time after admission is convicted of a crime of domestic violence, a crime of stalking, or a crime of child abuse, child neglect, or child abandonment is deportable."); 8 U.S.C. §1227(a)(2)(E)(ii), INA §237(a)(2)(E)(ii) ("Any alien who at any time after admission is enjoined under a protection order issued by a court and whom the court determines has engaged in conduct that violates the portion of a protection order that involves protection against credible threats of violence, repeated harassment, or bodily injury to the person or persons for whom the protection order was issued is deportable.").

40 Jenny Rivera, *Domestic Violence Against Latinas by Latino Males: An Analysis of Race, National Origin, and Gender Differentials*, 14 B.C. THIRD WORLD L.J. 231, 248 (1994). *See also* Michael Kagan, *Immigrant Victims, Immigrant Accusers*, 48 U. MICH. J.L. REFORM 915 (2015).

41 HOGELAND & ROSEN, *supra* note 18, at 61.

42 *Id.*

43 Lisa Marie De Sanctis, *Bridging the Gap Between the Rules of Evidence & Justice for Victims of Domestic Violence*, 8 YALE J.L. & FEMINISM 359, 368 (1996).

44 Dublas E. Beloof & Joel Shapiro, *Let the Truth Be Told: Proposed Hearsay Exceptions to Admit Domestic Violence Victims' Out of Court Statements as Substantive Evidence*, 11 COLUM. J. GENDER & L. 1, 4 (2002).

45 Mary Ann Dutton, Leslye E. Orloff, & Giselle Aguilar Hass, *Characteristics of Help-Seeking Behaviors, Resources and Service Needs of Battered Immigrant Latinas: Legal and Policy Implications*, 7 GEO. J. POVERTY L. & POL'Y, 245, 295 (2000). *See also* Richard J. Gelles, *Through a Sociological Lens: Social Structure and Family Violence*, *in* CURRENT CONTROVERSIES ON FAMILY VIOLENCE 31, 33–35 (Donileen R. Loseke & Richard J. Gelles eds., 1993) (reporting that wives with fewer resources were more likely to stay with violent husbands).

46 *See* HOGELAND & ROSEN, *supra* note 18 (noting that most working Latinas were only working part time, and of the immigrant Latina women who were not working, 53% reported that they were being supported by their husbands).

47 Donna Coker, *Shifting Power for Battered Women: Law, Material Resources, and Poor Women of Color*, 33 UC DAVIS L. REV. 1009, 1017–18 (2000).

48 Erez & Hartley, *supra* note 26, at 155–69.

49 Martha R. Mahoney, *Legal Images of Battered Women: Redefining the Issue of Separation*, 90 MICH. L. REV. 1, 65–66 (1991).

50 Laura Durgan, Daniel S. Nagin, & Richard Rosenfeld, *Exposure Reduction or Retaliation?: The Effects of Domestic Violence Resources on Intimate-Partner Homicide*, 37 LAW & SOC'Y REV. 169 (2003).

51 Mahoney, *supra* note 49, at 64.

52 Tom Lininger, *Prosecuting Batterers After Crawford*, 91 VA. L. REV. 747, 769 (2005).

53 Sara Buel, *Fifty Obstacles to Leaving, a.k.a., Why Abuse Victims Stay*, THE COLO. LAW. 19 (Oct. 1999) (citing Hart, *National Estimates and Facts About Domestic Violence*, NCADV VOICE 12 [Winter 1989]).

54 Hearing on S.B. 9846 (October 4, 2000) (statement of Senator Mary Landrieu), www.congress.gov.

55 Tanya Eiserer, *911 Tape Reveals Horrific Last Minutes for Murdered Dallas Woman*, DALLAS MORNING NEWS (Mar. 2013), www.dallasnews.com.

56 Travis Gettys, *Las Vegas Woman Denied Protection Order 3 Weeks Before Husband Killed Her and Their Three Children*, RAW STORY (July 2016), www.rawstory.com.

57 David A. Ford, *Preventing and Provoking Wife Battery Through Criminal Sanctioning: A Look at the Risks*, in ABUSED AND BATTERED: SOCIAL AND LEGAL RESPONSES TO FAMILY VIOLENCE 191, 198 (Dean D. Knudsen & JoAnn L. Miller eds. 1991).

58 David A. Ford & Mary Jean Regoli, *The Preventive Impacts of Policies for Prosecuting Wife Batterers*, in DOMESTIC VIOLENCE: THE CHANGING CRIMINAL RESPONSE 181, 195 (Eve S. Buzawa & Carl G. Buzawa eds. 1992).

59 *See* Durgan, Nagin, & Rosenfeld, *supra* note 50, at 194.

60 Edna Erez and Joanne Belknap, *In their Own Words: Battered Women's Assessment of the Criminal Processing System's Responses*, 13 VIOLENCE & VICTIMS 251, 260 (1998).

61 Survivors of domestic violence can obtain immigration relief under two distinct but related provisions of the Violence Against Women Act—the Self Petition process (8 U.S.C.A. § 1154(a)) and the Battered Spouse Waiver (8 U.S.C. § 1186a(c) (4)(C)).

62 8 U.S.C. § 1101(a)(15)(T)(III)(aa) (2014).

63 8 U.S.C. § 1101(a)(15)(T)(III)(bb)-(cc).

64 8 C.F.R. § 245.24(b)(5) (2013).

65 8 C.F.R. § 245.24(e)(2).

66 S.B. 674 (Cal. 2015); codified at Cal. Penal Code § 679.10.

67 S.B. 1023 (Md. 2016).

68 S.B. 3331, 2015-16 Leg. 89th Sess. (Minn. 2016); H.F. 3656, 2015-16 Leg. 89th Sess. (Minn. 2016).

69 H.B. 2895, 64th Leg. (Wash. 2016); H.B. 2912, 64th Leg. (Wash. 2016).

70 Leg. Res. 549, 104th Leg. 2d Sess. (Neb. 2016).

71 *Requesting Certifications for U Nonimmigrant Status (U Certifications)*, N.Y.C. RULES, https://rules.cityofnewyork.us.

72 Leigh Goodmark, *Autonomy Feminism: An Anti-Essentialist Critique of Mandatory Interventions in Domestic Violence Cases*, 37 FLA. ST. U. L. REV. 1, 38 (2009).

PART IV

Militarization, Firearms, and the Family

9

Politics, Safety, and Officer-Involved Intimate Partner Violence

LEIGH GOODMARK

The United States relies heavily—some would argue dispropor-tionately[1]—on law enforcement in its response to intimate partner violence. The desire to ensure the safety of people subjected to abuse has been used to justify the decision to prioritize law enforcement intervention in intimate partner violence law and policy. While that decision may seem natural, given the prevailing beliefs that intimate partner violence is, above all, a crime, and only law enforcement can protect citizens from crime, the decision is also a political one, with consequences along three dimensions. First, prioritizing the law enforcement response has precluded the development of other policy responses; in the zero-sum world of funding, resources devoted to law enforcement are not available for other policy initiatives. Fun-neling resources through law enforcement also creates incentives that undermine the efficacy of victim services. Second, by channel-ing money into law enforcement, policymakers and the anti-violence advocates championing those policies facilitated the expansion of a hypermasculine, militarized environment, one in which, ironically, violence against women flourishes. Finally, the decision to rely upon law enforcement to respond to intimate partner violence requires policymakers to ignore more than twenty years' worth of research and anecdotal data on the propensity of police officers to commit intimate partner violence in their own relationships. Given the high rates of officer-involved intimate partner violence, there is a signifi-cant chance that the officer responding to a domestic violence call has used violence against a partner, calling into question the effectiveness of police interventions. These political decisions have had profound consequences for all people subjected to intimate partner violence, but one group whose stories are not often told suffers uniquely from these political decisions: the partners of police officers.

I. Criminalizing Intimate Partner Violence

Although the state's willingness to intervene in situations involving intimate partner violence has waxed and waned over time, in the 1960s and '70s, the criminal legal system was reluctant to become involved in what it viewed as private family disputes. Police were trained in "arrest avoidance" and told to advise abusive men to take a walk around the block rather than bring them into custody.[2] Arrest and prosecution were rare, conviction rarer, and incarceration for intimate partner violence almost unheard of. In the late 1970s, however, anti-violence advocates began challenging this non-interventionist stance in litigation, arguing that the failure of police and prosecutors to vigorously investigate, arrest, charge, and prosecute intimate partner violence cases violated the rights of the victims of those crimes. Those cases, as well as research suggesting that arrest was associated with lower rates of recidivism among men who used violence, helped to spur the adoption of policies requiring a more robust law enforcement response to intimate partner violence. By 1984, when the United States Attorney General's Task Force on Family Violence declared that intimate partner violence was a criminal problem that required a criminal law solution, many state governments and anti-violence advocates strongly concurred.

By 1994, a number of states had adopted laws and policies strengthening the criminal legal response to intimate partner violence. The Violence Against Women Act (VAWA) created additional attractive financial incentives for states to invest fully in criminalizing intimate partner violence. Part of the Omnibus Crime Act of 1994, VAWA authorizes and distributes hundreds of millions of dollars each year in grant funding to police, prosecutors, courts, and community-based agencies; in fiscal year 2016, the Office on Violence Against Women requested $243 million for its two largest grant programs, the Service-Training-Officers-Prosecutors (STOP) Program and the Improving Criminal Justice Responses to Sexual Assault, Domestic Violence, Dating Violence, and Stalking Program (formerly known as the Grants to Encourage

Arrests Program).[3] Since its passage, VAWA has funneled approximately $5.7 billion to the states. In 1994, 62% of VAWA funding went to the criminal legal system; by 2013, that figure had risen to 85%.[4]

The criminal legal system is now the primary response to intimate partner violence in the United States. Necessarily, police are at the center of the criminal legal response. Police serve as first responders to emergency calls for assistance, determine whether probable cause to arrest exists, make arrests in cases involving intimate partner abuse, gather evidence that can be used during prosecution, and serve as witnesses in intimate partner violence trials. Any person subjected to abuse hoping for a successful criminal prosecution of their partner is utterly dependent upon the police for that outcome.

The preference for law enforcement has had an impact on the anti-violence service sector as well. The Violence Against Women Act encourages, and in some cases requires, linkages between police and anti-violence advocates. VAWA's Improving Criminal Justice Responses to Sexual Assault, Domestic Violence, Dating Violence, and Stalking Program and STOP grants, for example, mandate collaboration between law enforcement and advocacy groups as a condition of funding. The Improving Criminal Justice Responses Program calls for formal collaborations between law enforcement and nonprofit, nongovernmental service providers, who must be involved in both the development and implementation of grant-funded activities.[5] An applicant's STOP planning committee must include representatives of state domestic violence coalitions, law enforcement, prosecutors, state and local courts, and victim service providers, among others.[6] Given the substantial federal resources made available through these two programs, the incentives to create and maintain collaborative relationships between law enforcement and service providers are significant.

Additionally, VAWA has encouraged closer ties between law enforcement and advocates through its support for the development of coordinated community response programs.[7] Coordinated community responses generally include law enforcement (police, prosecutors, probation officers), advocates for people subjected to abuse, counselors, and courts, and focus on "developing and implementing policies and procedures that improve interagency coordination and lead to more uniform responses to domestic violence cases."[8] A coordinated community response often includes pro-arrest or mandatory arrest policies, support and advocacy for people subjected to abuse, pro-prosecution policies, monitoring of probation, enhanced civil remedies, and system-wide monitoring.[9] STOP grant funds can be used to support "formal and informal statewide, multidisciplinary efforts . . . to coordinate the response of state law enforcement agencies, prosecutors, courts, victim services agencies, and other state agencies and departments, to violent crimes against women. . . ."[10]

VAWA has also provided support for Family Justice Centers, which bring together a number of community actors, including law enforcement and service providers, in a single, centralized location.[11] Family Justice Centers have been touted as providing many of the same benefits as coordinated community response programs, but with the added advantage of being a "one-stop-shop" for people subjected to abuse. Family Justice Centers emphasize the importance of the law enforcement response, seeing pro- or mandatory arrest policies and aggressive prosecution as essential in combatting intimate partner violence.[12]

Most recently, law enforcement and advocates for people subjected to abuse have partnered in the development of lethality assessment programs. Lethality assessment programs provide law enforcement with risk assessment tools to measure the level of danger that a person subjected to abuse may be experiencing.[13] The assessment involves a standard set of questions asked in a particular order; the responses help law enforcement determine the level of danger and make appropriate referrals. The stated goal of lethality assessment is to provide people subjected to abuse with some understanding of their current risk levels and to connect high-risk individuals with domestic violence services.[14] In addition, lethality assessment is explicitly designed to increase collaboration between law enforcement and domestic violence service providers.[15] As one advocate noted following a lethality assessment program, "Big relationship building [between advocates and police officers] went on at the training!"[16] Partnering agencies are encouraged to enter into memoranda of understanding, detailing the various roles and responsibilities within the collaboration.[17] The success of lethality assessment programs relies in part on the development of relationships between law enforcement and service providers; police officers must be convinced of the value of these partnerships, which decreases disincentives to calling service providers from the scene of an incident. While other system actors may be involved in lethality assessment programs, the core relationship upon which the program is built is the relationship between law enforcement and intimate partner violence service providers. But achieving law enforcement buy-in has been a challenge for some lethality assessment programs, which may create pressure for anti-violence service providers to work as seamlessly and harmoniously as possible with law enforcement.

In theory, all of these collaborations between law enforcement and anti-violence advocates are a positive development. Such partnerships recognize both the expertise of victim service providers in shaping law and policy responses to domestic violence and the need to ensure that intervention by law enforcement is not the only option provided to people subjected to abuse. In its evaluation reports on the STOP grant, the Office on Violence Against Women touts the improved collaboration between law enforcement and other system actors as one of the benefits of the program.[18] In practice, though, such collaborations have also led to what one advocate characterized as "co-optation and collusion."[19] Through collaboration, service providers develop personal and professional relationships with law enforcement officers that make it difficult to criticize their behavior. Such criticism not only has the potential to jeopardize those personal relationships, it could also affect the assistance provided to clients. Moreover, given that federal funding is focused on law enforcement, and that victim services funding comes through programs with an explicit law enforcement focus, advocates may find it challenging to raise issues involving law enforcement—including officer-involved intimate partner violence—without imperiling their funding.

II. Supporting the Hypermasculine Environment of Policing

VAWA funding supports an environment that is hypermasculine, militarized, and hostile to women. The history of policing reveals that policing has always been, and continues to be, gendered male.[20] Policing shares a number of attributes with all-male institutions like sports teams and single-sex schools: a need for dominance, an emphasis on masculine solidarity and the insistence that others within the group be protected "especially when they are in the wrong,"[21] a focus on physical courage, and the glamorization of violence.[22] Machismo is central to police culture.[23] Criminologist Susan Miller describes gatherings of police officers where "the conversation revolved around 'guy stuff,' such as joking about guns or other weapons, talking about surveillance work, and pretending to pull out one's gun. Their language was full of expletives, with some version of 'f—k' being the most common. . . . These topics reinforced the tough, masculine, crimefighting image of policing."[24]

Policing has been called a "pure form" of hegemonic masculinity.[25] Among the features of hegemonic masculinity ascribed to police officers are combative personalities, resistance to management, a propensity towards violence, and use of weapons.[26] Police officers are trained to be "stoic, hard[,] . . . decisive, unemotional, strong, dominating, and in control."[27] Studies show that police officers embrace a number of "rigidly masculine beliefs;"[28] to preserve their authority, police officers are quick to punish what they perceive as disrespect, seeing challenges to their authority as assaults on their masculinity.[29] Law professor Angela Harris describes policing as hypermasculine, embracing a form of masculinity "in which the strictures against femininity and homosexuality are especially intense and in which physical strength and aggressiveness are paramount."[30]

Violence and the denigration of women are endemic in hypermasculine settings.[31] From the minute they enter the police academy, even when the training seems to be gender neutral, police officers are expected to adhere to a form of masculinity that devalues and objectifies women.[32] In their study of a law enforcement training academy, sociologists Anastasia Prokos and Irina Padavic found that male recruits regularly belittled and objectified women, adopting the phrase "There oughta be a law against bitches" as their mantra when joking about female police recruits and women generally.[33] Male recruits also downplayed the seriousness of violence against women, ignoring the content of a domestic violence training film in favor of rating the attractiveness of the actresses playing roles in that film.[34] This type of verbal degradation continues after officers leave the academy; criminologist Susan Miller found that in a progressive, diverse law enforcement agency, female officers were "still privately classified as 'bitch,' 'whore,' 'dyke,' or 'prude,' and never seen as just another officer."[35]

The attitudes and actions associated with hegemonic masculinity carry over into officers' personal lives, making them particularly dangerous to their partners. As Jennifer Brown and Frances Heidensohn have argued, policing and abuse have a great deal in common: they are both structures within which "men maintain control by being patronizing, violent, or paternalistic. . . . The structural realities of a male majority in control of resources within the police mirror those in domestic relationships."[36]

Police officers not only operate in a hypermasculine setting, but in a militarized masculine setting as well. Criminologist Peter Kraska defines militarism as "an ideology that stresses aggressiveness, the use of force, and the glorification of military power, weaponry, and technology as the means to solve problems."[37]

Militarism and masculinity are deeply intertwined. As sociologist Paul Higate and social worker John Hopton explain,

> Militarism is the major means by which the values and beliefs associated with the ideologies of hegemonic masculinity are eroticized and institutionalized. Although there are alternative contexts in which traditional masculine virtues are valorized and eroticized, they lack the potential to link masculinity with the political concerns of the state.[38]

Militarism glorifies men as warriors, and, equally importantly, warriors as men.[39] Women fare less well in a militarized system, [40] where militarized masculinity defines itself in opposition to femininity and relies on the denigration of the feminine.[41] Militarism shares important characteristics with hegemonic masculinity: sexism, glorification of aggression, and the need for domination.[42] Hypermasculinity is, Kraska argues, essential to militarism, the combination of masculinity and militarism creating a cultural foundation justifying the use of violence by militarized actors.[43]

Feminist scholars have posited a relationship between militarism and violence against women. Militarism's embrace of hypermasculinity, with its focus on dominance, control, and violence, creates a climate within which violence against women flourishes.[44] Militarism entrenches patriarchal gender hierarchies that dictate appropriate roles for men (as dominant) and women (as subservient).[45] Men working within militarized settings may have difficulty maintaining boundaries between the expressions of masculinity expected in work settings and their behavior in their relationships with their partners. As cultural anthropologist

Madelaine Adelman explains, "Militarized men, unable to contain their soldiering, unable to become civilianized, bring home military norms of domination and violence to enforce compliance with, protect the integrity of, and quash women's resistance to their regime of domestic power."[46] The very difficulty that such men seem to have in leaving their work at work highlights the problematic connection between militarism and violence against women.[47]

Militarized men rely on the belief that they are maintaining the natural (patriarchal) order to justify their violence against their partners.[48] Such men use their status and their skills to abuse their partners, relying upon knowledge of military systems and exploiting economic and social vulnerability to entrap their partners, and using military-issued weapons to reinforce their threats.[49] The partners of militarized men are urged to remain silent about the abuse for fear of devaluing the status of their "heroes" and are told that to leave their military partner is to neglect their duty to their country.[50]

The line between military service and policing is increasingly blurry. Although police forces were constructed within a "quasi-military" framework,[51] the distinctions between policing and military service were clear until the last several decades. The language of war found its way into policing first with the inception of the "war against crime" announced by President Lyndon B. Johnson in 1965[52] and the "war on drugs" of the 1970s.[53] Although policing and military service both reinforce the power of the state[54] and enable those representing the state to use force in certain situations, some military tactics now regularly employed by law enforcement agencies had long been reserved for use against foreign aggressors, not United States citizens.

The blurring of the line between police and military manifests itself in a number of ways. The hierarchical structure found in most law enforcement agencies resembles that used in the military. Recruits are trained military-style, using techniques like those deployed in boot camp training to "remold[] the individual to take on a new identity."[55] Police increasingly use paramilitary tactics on the streets.[56] Police officers "dress in commando black, instead of the traditional blue. [Police forces] own military-grade weapons, armored personnel carriers, helicopters, and Humvees. Their training is military. Their approach is military. They are in a war against crime and violence and terror that never ends."[57]

The militarization of policing on the state and local levels has been exacerbated by federal policy. Since its creation in 1990, the Department of Defense's Excess Property (or 1033) Program has transferred equipment worth hundreds of millions of dollars, including weapons, field packs, and medical supplies, to law enforcement agencies.[58] Moreover, since September 11, 2001, billions of dollars in funding for military-style equipment has been provided to state and local police through Department of Justice and Department of Homeland Security programs to fight terrorism.[59] Police SWAT teams patrol the streets in battle dress uniforms, carrying automatic weapons and attempting to restore order through their presence.[60] Officers carry combat knives, sport military-style haircuts, and wear army fatigues and t-shirts that memorialize their campaigns.[61]

Individual officers may not subscribe to the militarized hypermasculinity found in many police departments. But the notion of what it means to be a police officer is shaped by a militarized hypermasculine environment, which is particularly dangerous for the partners of officers who ascribe to those norms.[62] Given the attitudes and beliefs of those who become police officers, as well as the context within which they perform their duties, the high levels of intimate partner violence among police officers are hardly surprising. Anti-violence advocates and policymakers have contributed to a culture in which officer-involved intimate partner violence flourishes by directing funding to, and encouraging the expansion of, militarized hypermasculine law enforcement agencies.

III. Officer-Involved Intimate Partner Violence

Reports of officer-perpetrated intimate partner violence are increasingly common, and studies have repeatedly shown elevated rates of intimate partner abuse among police officers,[63] although much of this data is now dated. In 1991, Dr. Leanor Johnson testified before the United States Congress that more than 40% of the 728 officers she surveyed had been abusive towards a spouse in the last six months.[64] Ten percent of the 479 spouses she surveyed reported having been physically abused.[65] Sixty percent of the spouses were subjected to verbal abuse by their officer spouses.[66] Seeking to replicate the results, a 1992 study found that 28% of male officers reported physically abusing their spouses; 25% of their spouses reported having been physically abused.[67] Twenty-seven percent of female officers reported using minor violence in their relationships.[68]

Later studies show officers reporting lower rates of abuse. Seven percent of Baltimore City police officers in a 1999 study admitted to "getting physical" (pushing, shoving, grabbing, and/or hitting) with a partner.[69] A 2000 study of seven law enforcement agencies in the Southeast and Midwest United States found 10% of officers reporting that they had slapped, punched, or otherwise injured their partners.[70] Fifty-four percent of the officers knew someone in their department who had been involved in an abusive relationship, 45% knew of an officer who had been reported for engaging in abusive behavior, and 16% knew of abusive incidents that were not reported to their departments.[71] The lower rates of self-reporting in later studies may be related to a number of factors, including increased enforcement of domestic violence laws and the passage of the Lautenberg Amendment, which restricts access to firearms for those who have been convicted of intimate partner violence or are subject to a protective order.

Independent investigations of police departments have also unearthed significant evidence of intimate partner abuse among police officers. In 1997, after the media reported that the Los Angeles Police Department (LAPD) failed to seriously address cases of intimate partner abuse by its officers, the LAPD's inspector general reported that the department's handling of those cases was problematic at best. Two hundred twenty-seven cases of intimate partner abuse by officers were reported to the LAPD between 1990 and 1997.[72] Many of the investigations involved the same officers: 30 officers were responsible for 71 (31%) of the 227 matters investigated, almost one-third of the allegations of abuse that were sustained. Allegations of intimate partner violence were not factored into officers' evaluations or considered when they sought promotions, even when the reports were substantiated. A supervisor praised an LAPD officer who was suspended for grabbing a woman by the hair, pushing her to the ground, and punching her with a closed fist; the supervisor said the officer had "consistently displayed a calm and professional demeanor even when dealing with the most highly agitated and stressful situations."[73] Another officer, described by supervisors as "problem-free," received a fifteen-day suspension for slapping his wife. About 30% of the officers who had been the subject of complaints were

promoted notwithstanding those allegations. When officers were punished for their actions, those punishments were minor. An officer who
drove after drinking was involved in a hit-and-run accident and hit his
wife and broke her nose while he attempted to push his car away from
the scene. "Despite being drunk in public, assaulting his wife, fleeing an
accident scene and failing to have his car insured,"[74] the officer was suspended for just ten days. Although the LAPD substantiated the claims
of abuse in about 40% of the cases, criminal charges were filed in very
few, even when the officers were repeatedly abusive. One officer who received an official reprimand after the LAPD found that he had raped his
girlfriend was again reprimanded later that same year after the department found that he had "insert[ed] a 9-millimeter handgun into [his]
girlfriend's vagina without her consent." The officer was not criminally
charged for either incident.[75]

More recent investigations by the United States Department of Justice
confirm that intimate partner abuse remains a serious problem in police
families. In its 2011 report on the Puerto Rico Police Department, the Department of Justice wrote, "Domestic violence infects the ranks of PRPD
and interferes with the ability of PRPD to provide police services in a
constitutional manner."[76] Between 2005 and 2010, 1,459 civilians alleged
that officers committed intimate partner abuse. "Disciplinary or corrective action" was recommended in 1,018 of those cases. Between 2007 and
2010, ninety-eight officers were arrested more than once on charges involving intimate partner abuse; eighty-four of those officers, including
commanders, were still on active duty in 2011 when the Department of
Justice investigation was completed,[77] notwithstanding a finding by the
Puerto Rico Supreme Court that engaging in intimate partner abuse is
inconsistent with the ability to carry out one's duties as a police officer.[78]
Three PRPD officers shot their partners or former partners before killing themselves in 2010; one of the officers, Heriberto Rivera Hernández,
was under electronic monitoring stemming from previous intimate partner violence and weapons charges at the time he murdered his ex-wife.
Although the PRPD had reportedly dismissed Rivera Hernández and
confiscated his service weapon at the time of his initial arrest, Rivera
Hernández used a PRPD firearm to kill his ex-wife.[79]

The data on intimate partner abuse by police officers are both dated
and potentially flawed, but in ways that make it likely that abuse is

being under- rather than overreported. Most of the studies rely on self-reporting by police officers to establish prevalence of abuse. Self-reporting is a notoriously unreliable measure; as one study noted, "The issue of the reliability of self-report[ed] data is problematic when considering any socially undesirable behavior."[80] Intimate partner abuse is frequently underreported, both by those who experience it and those who commit it. Underreporting is likely to be particularly prevalent among law enforcement officers "who fear, even when anonymity is assured, that admitting their own or their colleagues' abusive behavior may jeopardize careers and break up families."[81]

Additionally, most of the studies focus on physical abuse, ignoring the many other types of abuse that police officers use. With the exception of Johnson, Todd, and Subramanian's finding that 60% of police spouses reported verbal abuse,[82] no study measures emotional, verbal, or any other form of abuse by police officers. Definitions of intimate partner abuse vary among the studies: the definition of abuse used in Johnson's 1991 study, which found that 40% of officers were abusive, is unknown.[83] Neidig asked in 1992 about minor and severe, but only physical, violence.[84] Gershon's 2000 data involved rates of physical aggression.[85] Ryan's 2000 study focused on officers slapping, punching, or otherwise injuring their partners.[86] Physical violence is both illegal and detrimental to the person subjected to abuse; clearly, police officers should not physically abuse their partners. But this focus on physical abuse obscures the other forms of abuse that some women experience as even more harmful.

Even with flawed data, there is reason to believe that police officers are committing intimate partner abuse at rates greater than the general population. But if the rates of intimate partner abuse among police officers were consistent with the rates for the general population, there would still be reason for concern. As retired Nashville Police Lieutenant Mark Wynn notes, "If we believe that 10 to 15 percent of the population in this country is involved in domestic violence . . . we at least have a 10 to 15 percent chance of getting someone in uniform who's an abuser."[87] Given the training and weapons with which the state arms police officers, even those lower rates of abuse should be reason for real concern.

Some would argue that intimate partner abuse is an assertion of power and control by the police officer over his partner, in line with the longstanding feminist understanding of what causes intimate partner abuse. Central to the feminist narrative is the idea that men who abuse are not generally angry or violent; rather, they only abuse their partners as a means of asserting power and control. But intimate partner abuse by police officers may follow another narrative altogether—a narrative of unfocused, generalized violence. In their study of media reports of officer-involved intimate partner violence between 2005 and 2007, Philip Stinson and John Liederbach found that almost 22% of the officers accused of intimate partner violence had also been named as defendants in federal civil rights police misconduct claims.[88] In 2017, a Pittsburgh police officer captured in a cell phone video kicking and kneeing a suspect had only recently returned to duty from paid administrative leave; the officer had been on leave as a result of intimate partner violence charges in another state.[89]

Policing tends to attract individuals with authoritarian personalities. Among the characteristics of an authoritarian personality are narrow-mindedness, violence, suspicion, and an unwillingness to tolerate the failure to submit.[90] For some subset of police officers, that authoritarian personality may be manifested in the use of violence whenever the officer is angry or feels challenged in some way, whether by a partner or by a member of the general public.[91]

Given the studies on intimate partner violence among police officers, as well as the propensity of some officers to use violence in multiple spheres, one might question whether continued reliance upon police officers to safeguard people subjected to abuse is wise. But policymakers have not acknowledged the dangers of officer-involved intimate partner violence or the structural underpinnings of the problem. Officers who commit intimate partner violence are seen as "bad apples," the problem one of individuals, not of policing more generally. Few law enforcement agencies even have policies addressing intimate partner violence perpetrated by officers. The decision to ignore the prevalence and causes of intimate partner violence among police officers is a political decision, which may be driven in part by the unwillingness to consider other responses to intimate partner violence. But criminalizing intimate partner violence cannot be an effective policy response when those policing the crime and those committing it are often the same person.

IV. Conclusion

Increased victim safety is touted as one of the results of prioritizing a law enforcement response to intimate partner violence. But the data suggest that the law enforcement response has not been as effective as policymakers might have hoped. Between 1994 and 2000, rates of intimate partner violence fell in the United States, but at a rate commensurate with the drop in the overall crime rate. Between 2000 and 2010, rates of intimate partner violence declined less than the continued decrease in the overall crime rate, notwithstanding the hundreds of millions of dollars law enforcement was receiving under the Violence Against Women Act. And for one group of victims, increasing the role of law enforcement has had particularly problematic consequences. The partners of law enforcement officers (who are more likely to experience abuse than those in the general population) find themselves with few options for intervention; most, if not all, of the services to which they might turn are allied in some way with their partners. Keeping people subjected to intimate partner violence safe (however those people define safety) is a laudable goal. But investing in a hypermasculine, militarized law enforcement system—an environment that breeds violence—will not make victims of violence safer.

Author's Note

This chapter is adapted from Leigh Goodmark, *Hands Up at Home: Militarized Masculinity and Police Officers Who Commit Intimate Partner Abuse*, 2015 B.Y.U. L. REV. 1183 (2015).

NOTES

1 Leigh Goodmark, *Should Domestic Violence Be Decriminalized?*, 40 HARV. J.L. & GENDER 53 (2017).

2 SUSAN SCHECHTER, WOMEN AND MALE VIOLENCE (1982).

3 U.S. DEP'T OF JUSTICE, OFFICE ON VIOLENCE AGAINST WOMEN, FY 2016 CONG. BUDGET SUBMISSION 12–14 (Feb. 2015), www.justice.gov [https://perma.cc/96GE-57PX].

4 Jill Theresa Messing et al., *The State of Intimate Partner Violence Intervention: Progress and Continuing Challenges*, 60 SOCIAL WORK 305, 306 (2015).

5 U.S. DEP'T OF JUSTICE, OFFICE ON VIOLENCE AGAINST WOMEN, OVW FISCAL YEAR 2014 GRANTS TO ENCOURAGE ARREST POLICIES AND

ENFORCEMENT OF PROTECTION ORDERS PROGRAM SOLICITATION 14 (Jan. 7, 2013) [hereinafter OFFICE ON VIOLENCE AGAINST WOMEN, ARREST PROGRAM SOLICITATION].

6 *Id.* at 19.

7 Brenda K. Uekert, *The Value of Coordinated Community Responses*, 3 CRIMINOL. & PUB. POL'Y 133, 134 (2003) (explaining that most coordinated community response programs emerged as a result of VAWA funding).

8 Melanie Shepard et al., *Enhancing Coordinated Community Responses to Reduce Recidivism in Cases of Domestic Violence*, 17 J. INTERPERSONAL VIOLENCE 551–52 (2002).

9 *Id.*

10 OFFICE ON VIOLENCE AGAINST WOMEN, STOP PROGRAM 2012 REPORT, PART A, at 4 (2012) www.justice.gov [hereinafter OFFICE ON VIOLENCE AGAINST WOMEN, 2012 REPORT].

11 OFFICE ON VIOLENCE AGAINST WOMEN, ARREST PROGRAM SOLICITA-TION, *supra* note 5, at 12.

12 Casey Gwinn et al., *The Family Justice Center Collaborative Model*, 27 ST. LOUIS UNIV. PUB. L. REV. 79, 83, 89 (2007); *see also* Jane K. Stoever, *Mirandizing Family Justice*, 39 HARV. J.L. & GENDER 189 (2016).

13 DEP'T OF CRIMINAL JUSTICE SERVICES (VIRGINIA), REVIEW OF LE-THALITY ASSESSMENT PROGRAMS (LAP) 2 (2013).

14 Margaret E. Johnson, *Balancing Liberty, Dignity, and Safety: The Impact of Domestic Violence Lethality Screening*, 32 CARDOZO L. REV. 519, 532 (2010).

15 *What is LAP?*, MARYLAND NETWORK AGAINST DOMESTIC VIOLENCE, http://mnadv.org/ (last visited Mar. 3, 2015); *see also* DEP'T OF CRIMINAL JUS-TICE SERVICES (VIRGINIA), *supra* note 13, at 13–14.

16 *Lethality Assessment Program: The Maryland Model Can Save Lives*, MARYLAND NETWORK AGAINST DOMESTIC VIOLENCE, www.ncdsv.org (last visited Mar. 3, 2015) (quoting advocate Meg Kuhne).

17 DEP'T OF CRIMINAL JUSTICE SERVICES (VIRGINIA), *supra* note 13, at 7.

18 *See, e.g.,* OFFICE ON VIOLENCE AGAINST WOMEN, 2012 REPORT, *supra* note 10, Pt. A at 19–21; U.S. DEP'T OF JUSTICE, OFFICE ON VIOLENCE AGAINST WOMEN, STOP PROGRAM: SERVICES, TRAINING, OFFICERS, PROSECU-TORS 2010 REPORT 22–23 (2010).

19 Remarks of Diane Fleet, Assistant Director, Greenhouse 17, May 15, 2014 (notes on file with the author).

20 Susan Broomhall & David G. Barrie, *Introduction, in* A HISTORY OF POLICE AND MASCULINITIES, 1700–2010, at 22 (David G. Barrie & Susan Broomhall eds., 2012); JENNIFER BROWN & FRANCES HEIDENSOHN, GENDER AND PO-LICING: COMPARATIVE PERSPECTIVES 14 (2000); Frank Rudy Cooper, *"Who's the Man?": Masculinity Studies, Terry Stops, and Police Training*, 18 COLUM. J. GENDER & L. 671, 679 (2009); SUSAN L. MILLER, GENDER AND COMMU-NITY POLICING: WALKING THE LINE 3 (1999); LOUISE WESTMARLAND,

GENDER AND POLICING: SEX, POWER AND POLICE CULTURE 133 (2001). Susan Broomhall and David Barrie note that policing's association with masculinity has remained constant even as the traits associated with masculinity have changed over time. Broomhall & Barrie, *supra*.

21 WESTMARLAND, *supra* note 20, at 93–94.

22 *Id.*

23 BROWN & HEIDENSOHN, *supra* note 20, at 29; Nigel Fielding, *Cop Canteen Culture, in* JUST BOYS DOING BUSINESS 47 (Tim Newburn & Elizabeth A. Stanko eds., 1994).

24 MILLER, *supra* note 20, at 175.

25 Fielding, *supra* note 23, at 47.

26 Anastasia Prokos & Irene Padavic, *"There Oughtta be a Law Against Bitches": Masculinity Lessons in Police Academy Training,* 9 GENDER WORK & ORG. 439, 442 (2002).

27 Thomas Nolan, *Behind the Blue Wall of Silence,* 12 MEN & MASCULINITIES 250, 253 (2009).

28 Anne O'Dell, *Why Do Police Arrest Victims of Domestic Violence?: The Need for Comprehensive Training and Investigative Protocols,* 15 J. AGGRESSION MALTREATMENT & TRAUMA 53, 56 (2007).

29 Cooper, *supra* note 20, at 697.

30 Angela Harris, *Gender, Violence, Race, and Criminal Justice,* 52 STAN. L. REV. 777, 793 (2000); *see also* Cooper, *supra* note 20, at 692.

31 Marisa Silvestri, *Managerial Masculinity: An Insight into the Twenty-First-Century Police Leader, in* A HISTORY OF POLICE AND MASCULINITIES, 1700–2010, at 236 (David G. Barrie & Susan Broomhall eds., 2012).

32 Prokos & Padavic, *supra* note 26, at 440, 446.

33 *Id.* at 439. The phrase was taken from an episode of the television show *COPS* used during police academy training, spoken by a man who was arrested after his girlfriend called the police. *Id.*

34 *Id.* at 452.

35 MILLER, *supra* note 20, at 177.

36 BROWN & HEIDENSOHN, *supra* note 20, at 155.

37 Peter B. Kraska, *Playing War: Masculinity, Militarism, and Their Real-World Consequences, in* MILITARIZING THE AMERICAN CRIMINAL JUSTICE SYSTEM: THE CHANGING ROLES OF THE ARMED FORCES AND THE POLICE 141, 153 (Peter B. Kraska ed., 2001).

38 Paul Higate & John Hopton, *War, Militarism, and Masculinities, in* HANDBOOK OF STUDIES ON MEN & MASCULINITIES 436 (Michael S. Kimmel, Jeff Hearn, & R. W. Connell eds., 2005).

39 JOSHUA GOLDSTEIN, WAR AND GENDER: HOW GENDER SHAPES THE WAR SYSTEM AND VICE VERSA (2001); *see also* Jamie R. Abrams, *The Collateral Consequences of Masculinizing Violence,* 16 WM. & MARY J. WOMEN & L. 703, 718 (2010).

40 Susan L. Caulfield, *Militarism, Feminism, and Criminal Justice: Challenging Institutionalized Ideologies, in* MILITARIZING THE AMERICAN CRIMINAL JUSTICE SYSTEM: THE CHANGING ROLES OF THE ARMED FORCES AND THE POLICE 137 (Peter B. Kraska ed., 2001).

41 Valerie Vojdik, *Sexual Abuse and Exploitation of Women and Girls by U.N. Peacekeeping Troops*, 15 MICH. ST. J. INT'L L. 157, 163 (2007). *But see* bell hooks, *Feminism and Militarism: A Comment*, 23 WOMEN'S STUD. Q. 58, 59 (1995).

42 Higate & Hopton, *supra* note 38, at 443.

43 Kraska, *supra* note 37, at 154.

44 Madelaine Adelman, *The Military, Militarism, and the Militarization of Domestic Violence*, 9 VIOLENCE AGAINST WOMEN 1118, 1132; Caulfield, *supra* note 40, at 126, 134; Vojdik, *supra* note 41, at 158.

45 Caulfield, *supra* note 40, at 124.

46 Adelman, *supra* note 44, at 1134–35.

47 Caulfield, *supra* note 40, at 125.

48 *Id.*

49 Adelman, *supra* note 44, at 1143.

50 *Id.*

51 WESTMARLAND, *supra* note 20, at 183.

52 Katherine Beckett & Theodore Sasson, *The Origins of the Current Conservative Discourse on Law and Order, in* DEFENDING JUSTICE: AN ACTIVIST RESOURCE KIT 47 (Palak Shah ed., 2005), www.publiceye.org.

53 Nolan, *supra* note 27, at 255; *see also* JAMES P. GRAY, WHY OUR DRUG LAWS HAVE FAILED AND WHAT WE CAN DO ABOUT IT: A JUDICIAL INDICTMENT OF THE WAR ON DRUGS 27 (2001) (crediting Nixon as "the first U.S. president to declare the nation's 'War on Drugs'").

54 Gerda W. Ray, *Science and Surveillance: Masculinity and the New York State Police, 1945–1980, in* A HISTORY OF POLICE AND MASCULINITIES, 1700–2010, at 217, 218 (David G. Barrie & Susan Broomhall eds., 2012).

55 Amanda L. Robinson, *The Effect of a Domestic Violence Policy Change on Police Officers' Schemata*, 27 CRIM. JUSTICE & BEHAV. 600, 605 (2000).

56 Higate & Hopton, *supra* note 38, at 435; O'Dell, *supra* note 28, at 55.

57 Editor's Note, *Warring Against Crime*, ABA J. 43 (July 2013) (responding to Radley Balko, *How Did America's Police Become a Military Force on the Streets?*, featured on the same page).

58 Dan Bauman, *On Campus, Grenade Launchers, M-16s, and Armored Vehicles*, CHRON. HIGHER EDUC. (Sept. 11, 2014), http://chronicle.com.

59 Niraj Chokshi, *Militarized Police in Ferguson Unsettles Some; Pentagon Gives Cities Equipment*, WASH. POST (Aug. 14, 2014), www.washingtonpost.com.

60 Kraska, *supra* note 37, at 7–8.

61 *Id.* at 144 (observing that one off-duty police officer "wore a T-shirt that carried a picture of a burning city with gunship helicopters flying overhead and the caption 'Operation Ghetto Storm'").

62 Caulfield, *supra* note 40, at 129.

63 It is difficult to make a direct comparison between the rates of perpetration of intimate partner abuse by police officer and the rates of perpetration in the general population. Because perpetrators frequently deny or underestimate their abuse, self-reporting data from perpetrators is considered suspect. *See, e.g.,* Russell P. Dobash et al., *Separate and Intersecting Realities: A Comparison of Men's and Women's Accounts of Violence Against Women*, 4 VIOLENCE AGAINST WOMEN 382, 405–06 (1998) (reporting significant differences in men's and women's reporting of violence in their relationships, with men underreporting a number of types of severe and controlling violence); L. Kevin Hamberger & Clare E. Guse, *Men's and Women's Use of Intimate Partner Violence in Clinical Samples*, 8 VIOLENCE AGAINST WOMEN 1301, 1322–23 (2002) (explaining that men tend to significantly underreport their own violence); Michael Kimmel, *Gender Symmetry in Domestic Violence*, 8 VIOLENCE AGAINST WOMEN 1332, 1345 (2002) (same). Researchers therefore tend to rely on data reported by victims. For example, the 2010 National Intimate Partner and Sexual Violence Survey found that 35.6% of women and 28.5% of men in the United States reported rape, physical violence, and/or stalking in their lifetimes; 24.3% of women and 13.8% of men reported severe physical violence at the hands of an intimate partner. CDC, NAT'L CTR. FOR INJURY PREVENTION & CONTROL, NATIONAL INTIMATE PARTNER AND SEXUAL VIOLENCE SURVEY 2010 SUMMARY REPORT: EXECUTIVE SUMMARY 2 (2011). Data from official sources like the National Intimate Partner and Sexual Violence Survey is also problematic, however, given that it only "capture[s] a small proportion of violent offenses." Hamberger & Guse, *supra*, at 1323.

64 *On the Front Lines: Police Stress and Family Well-Being, Hearing Before the H. Select Comm. On Children, Youth, and Families*, 102d Cong., 1st Sess. 32, 42 (1991) (testimony of Leanor Boulin Johnson, Associate Professor, Arizona State University); *see also* Leanor Boulin Johnson et al., *Violence in Police Families: Work-Family Spillover*, 20 J. FAM. VIOLENCE 3 (2005). Johnson's testimony did not define "abuse," making it impossible to determine whether the officers were describing physical, emotional, verbal, or some other form of abuse. Peter H. Neidig et al., *Interspousal Aggression in Law Enforcement Families: A Preliminary Investigation*, 15 POLICE STUD. 31 (1992).

65 Neidig et al., *supra* note 64, at 31.

66 Johnson et al., *supra* note 64, at 4.

67 Neidig et al., *supra* note 64, at 32.

68 *Id.*

69 Robyn R. M. Gershon et al., *Mental, Physical, and Behavioral Outcomes Associated with Perceived Work Stress in Police Officers*, 36 J. CRIM. JUST. & BEHAV. 275, 282 (2009).

70 Andrew H. Ryan, *The Prevalence of Domestic Violence in Police Families, in* DOMESTIC VIOLENCE BY POLICE OFFICERS 297, 301 (Donald C. Sheehan ed., 2000).

71 *Id.*

72 HUMAN RIGHTS WATCH, SHIELDED FROM JUSTICE: POLICE BRUTALITY AND ACCOUNTABILITY IN THE UNITED STATES (1998), http://columbia.edu.

73 *Id.*

74 Matt Lait, *LAPD Abuse Probes of Its Officers Called Lax*, L.A. TIMES (July 20, 1997), http://articles.latimes.com.

75 *Id.*

76 CIVIL RIGHTS DIV., U.S. DEP'T OF JUSTICE, INVESTIGATION OF THE PUERTO RICO POLICE DEPARTMENT 16 (2011), www.justice.gov.

77 *Id.*

78 San Vicente Frau v. Policía, 142 D.P.R. 1, 1 (1996).

79 CIVIL RIGHTS DIVISION, *supra* note 76, at 17.

80 Neidig et al., *supra* note 64, at 33; *see also* Philip M. Stinson & John Liederbach, *Fox in the Henhouse: A Study of Police Officers Arrested for Crimes Associated with Domestic and/or Family Violence*, 4 CRIM. JUST. POL'Y REV. 601 (2013); Sandra M. Stith, *Police Response to Domestic Violence: The Influence of Individual and Familial Factors*, 5 VIOLENCE & VICTIMS 37, 47 (1990).

81 Anita S. Anderson & Celia C. Lo, *Intimate Partner Violence Within Law Enforcement Families*, 26 J. INTERPERS. VIOLENCE 1176, 1188 (2011); *see also* Neidig et al., *supra* note 64, at 33 ("It seems reasonable to be particularly cautious in relying on self reports of marital aggression by law enforcement officers as they may be expected to be sensitive to potentially adverse consequences to reputation and career, even when assurances of anonymity are given.")

82 Johnson et al., *supra* note 64, at 4.

83 Neidig et al., *supra* note 64, at 31.

84 *Id.* at 32.

85 Gershon et al., *supra* note 69, at 7.

86 Ryan, *supra* note 70, at 300–1.

87 Sarah Moughty, *How to Combat Officer-Involved Domestic Violence*, FRONTLINE (Nov. 23, 2013), www.pbs.org.

88 Stinson & Liederbach, *supra* note 80, at 615, 619.

89 Ralph Iannotti, *Sources: Officer Involved in South Side Fight Previously Faced Domestic Violence Charges*, CBS PITTSBURGH (May 10, 2017), http://pittsburgh.cbslocal.com.

90 Anita S. Anderson & Celia C. Lo, *Intimate Partner Violence Within Law Enforcement Families*, 26 J. INTERPERSONAL VIOLENCE 1176, 1178 (2011).

91 Stinson & Liederbach, *supra* note 80, at 604.

10

Playing Politics with Firearms and Family Violence

JANE K. STOEVER

The gun lobby argues that firearms don't kill people—people kill people. Survivors of domestic violence, however, will tell you that they fear both the abuser and the abuser's access to firearms. Indeed, abusers' access to firearms is "strongly associated with intimate partner femicide," and research shows that domestic abusers are five times more likely to murder their intimate partners when they have access to guns.[1] As the late Senator Frank Lautenberg (D-NJ), a strong advocate for anti-domestic violence efforts, stated, "The difference between a murdered wife and a battered wife is often the presence of a gun."[2]

Alarming numbers of women and children are murdered by family members with firearms each year in the United States, but this national emergency has a solution. Many domestic violence fatalities could be prevented through reasonable gun laws, such as requiring background checks, which have been proven to reduce domestic violence gun murders by 47%.[3] Unfortunately, safety as related to firearms and family violence has become highly politicized, with the National Rifle Association (NRA), one of the most politically powerful advocacy groups in the United States, funding political campaigns and lobbying without regard for research findings on public health and safety.

This chapter examines the politics of firearms in the context of the highly gendered nature of: (1) victimization within intimate relationships, (2) firearm ownership, and (3) the firearms debate, including considerations of how women are portrayed and the gender identities of the most prominent voices for "gun rights" and gun control. The chapter concludes with recommended reforms that would receive bipartisan support if politicians resolve to stop playing politics with the deadly combination of firearms and family violence.

I. Family Violence and Firearms

Both women and men experience domestic violence, but women account for approximately 80% of individuals abused by an intimate partner.[4] Nationally and globally, nearly one in three women is assaulted by an intimate partner in her lifetime, and the home remains the most dangerous place in the world for a woman. Rather than a gun in the home increasing the household's safety, a domestic abuser is likely to use the firearm to perpetrate abuse against an intimate partner and children. One well-known study found that in nearly three-quarters of battered women's households that contained a gun, the abusive partner had used the firearm against the abuse victim, whether by threatening to shoot and kill her or by actually shooting at her.[5]

Firearm injuries in the United States reveal an "endemic public health threat," since rates of injuries have remained stable over time.[6] Despite societal fear of danger posed by strangers, "intimate partners with guns present the greatest fatal risk to women."[7] In recent decades, the number of women killed by strangers has decreased while homicides by intimates with firearms have actually increased.[8] Indeed, the majority of women murdered with guns in the United States are killed by intimate partners or family members, women are nearly six times more likely than male homicide victims to have been killed by an intimate partner,[9] and guns are used in fatal domestic violence more than any other weapon.[10] Accidental and intentional gun deaths involving children also present all-too-common tragedies in the United States.

Regarding lethality predictors, access to a firearm is the primary predictor, and prior threats with a weapon are correlated with increased femicide risk.[11] Jealousy, separation violence, and children are also associated with heightened lethality by firearm. One study found that when the most severe incident of abuse was triggered by the abuser's jealousy or by the victim leaving the abuser for another partner, there was a nearly five-fold increase in femicide risk.[12] Additionally, having a child in the home who is not the abusive partner's biological child more than doubles the femicide risk.[13]

II. Firearm Ownership

About one-third of U.S. homes contain a firearm and one-fifth contain a handgun.[14] Research suggests three subcultures of gun owners: protection-minded owners who acquire firearms for defense of self, family, or property; sport- or hunting-oriented owners who engage in target shooting or hunting; and individuals who obtain firearms for criminal purposes.[15] Attitudes about local and personal danger, along with feelings about the government's ability to provide security, predict firearm ownership.[16] Researchers have also determined that "racial prejudice interacts with aggressive attitudes to produce higher levels of ownership."[17]

In what the gun industry refers to as "political sales," political moments are used to provoke fear, and gun sales are timed to the political process. For example, demand for ammunition increased leading up to the 2016 presidential election,[18] and during President Barack Obama's leadership, the gun industry more than doubled gun production due to fear of the imposition of restrictions on gun sales if another Democrat were elected.[19] Firearm and ammunition purchases also spike immediately following mass shootings, as occurred following the October 2017 Las Vegas massacre.[20]

A. The Gendered Nature of Ownership

The majority of gun owners are white men,[21] even accounting for increases in female gun ownership in the South.[22] The armed forces are predominately male, and men participate in "gun sports" and hunting significantly more than women. Sharpshooter Annie Oakley distinguished herself by pushing the boundaries of expected gender roles and discourses, and wrote, "When I began shooting in public, it was considered almost shameful for a woman to shoot. That was a man's business."[23] Regarding the interplay of income and firearms, homes of white affluent individuals are more likely to contain firearms, as compared with homes of other populations, although ownership decreases at the highest economic levels.[24]

Masculinity theorists have explored links between dominant modes of masculinity and violence, and have considered how socially endorsed and normative ideals of male behavior legitimize male domination over women and other men. Domestic violence is widely understood to be about power and control, and masculinity that emphasizes dominance and control valorizes violence as a way to prove self-worth and positions women and LGBT individuals as inferior.

A recent example of dominance masculinity, domestic violence, and firearms concerns Omar Mateen, the mass murderer who killed forty-nine people and wounded fifty-three others in a mass shooting at Pulse, a gay nightclub in Orlando, Florida, in June 2016.[25] Mateen had a history of perpetrating domestic violence and frequently expressed his disgust for homosexuality, was included in the Terrorist Screening Database twice, and purchased an assault rifle and handgun days before committing the massacre.[26]

Handguns "function as props for doing masculinity" by allowing men to feel they both adopt the role of protector and can overtake threats posed by other men, regardless of age and physical prowess.[27] The gun lobby has used social images of masculinity, including "frontier masculinity," to promote gun use, and has mythologized rare stories of private citizens defending vulnerable individuals with guns. White men who feel marginalized by gains made by women and African Americans during recent decades are particularly drawn to the "frontier masculinity" portrayal.[28]

Men are considerably more likely to purchase firearms than women and to store these firearms. Research of heterosexual married couples shows that husbands are four to five times more likely to personally own a gun than their wives.[29] In one survey of gun-owning couples with young children in the home, 82% of men and 17% of women claimed to own the firearms in the home.[30] In most families, "a gun is viewed by all concerned as the private property of a particular family member."[31] This notion is supported by a Gallup survey telephone interview of over 1,000 adults, which found that "only 5.4% of respondents who reported guns in their home indicated that there was joint ownership for one or more of them."[32] Furthermore, in homes with firearms, 80% of men and women reported that storing the guns was solely the man's responsibility.[33]

B. Gender Gap in Knowledge of Guns in the Home

Many men fail to disclose to their partners that there are guns in the home.[34] Given the elevated rates of homicide, suicide, and fatal firearm-related accidents when guns are in the home, knowledge about household gun ownership and firearm access is significant. It also turns out to be highly gendered. Multiple national surveys have established that women are often unaware of the existence of guns in the home and, if they are aware that a firearm is in the home, studies consistently find that husbands report more guns in the home than wives do.[35] Moreover, studies show a gender gap in knowledge among couples with young children in the home regarding the type and number of guns in the home and how firearms are stored.[36]

Women may falsely believe there are no guns in their home or that the guns are safely stored, and this gender gap in knowledge compromises women's ability to participate in decision-making regarding firearms in the home and to ensure the safety of those in the home. Mothers more often take their children to doctors' appointments, at which doctors may inquire and offer counsel about gun storage practices, particularly now that the "docs vs. glocks" ban on doctors inquiring about firearms has been overruled,[37] but men are more likely to actually have control over storage.[38] Likewise, public health campaigns have recently encouraged parents to inquire about guns in the home when making play dates for their children, and the efficacy of the exercise depends on household members having knowledge about whether there are guns in the home and how they are stored.

Given the gender disparity in ownership and use, the gun industry saw an opportunity to target women's fears to encourage firearm ownership for protective purposes. Beginning in the 1980s, pro-gun groups targeted women in their membership drives and launched campaigns to urge women to arm themselves for self-protection. They played on cognitive bias to spectacularly inflate the danger of strangers and likelihood of guns to provide protection, even though sexual and physical assaults perpetrated by strangers are statistically far less likely to occur than those perpetrated by intimate partners.[39] The industry even designed guns especially for women, including pink purse handguns.[40] The 1990s campaign "Refuse to Be a Victim"[41] equated gun ownership with empowerment and characterized female gun possession as the "last frontier of feminism."[42] Despite these efforts, ownership of firearms among women did not increase and the gender gap did not close. Most female gun owners are married women living outside large cities who participate in hunting rather than being unmarried women in urban areas who fear crime or have experienced victimization.[43] Regardless of the NRA's attempts otherwise, the market for guns is still mostly male.

C. Teen Dating Violence Implications

The gender gap between women and men owning guns and being aware of whether there are guns in the home extends to adolescents. While there is little "age gap" in reporting, there is a significant gender discrepancy between boys and girls in marital and non-marital homes regarding knowledge of firearms in the house.[44] There is also a gender gap in personal experience with guns, with boys three times as likely to report handling firearms than girls.[45]

Although individuals under age eighteen are generally prohibited from possessing a handgun,[46] surprisingly high percentages of youth possess or have access to firearms. Approximately one in sixteen high school students in the United States report having carried a firearm in the past thirty days,[47] with adolescents stating self-defense as the most common reason for carrying a gun.[48]

Most firearms possessed by youth are obtained outside of legal channels through illegal, unregistered sales to minors, making minimizing illegal firearm access key to fatality prevention efforts.[49] In a study of nearly 700 assault-injured youth (aged fourteen to twenty-four) appearing at emergency departments, 23% reported firearm possession in the past six months, and this study excluded any firearm used for hunting, target shooting, or a sporting activity.[50] Only 17% of the firearms were obtained through plausibly legal channels (e.g., accessed from family members who legally obtained the weapons), with the remaining 83% of firearms acquired illegally. In this study, 22% of youth reporting firearm possession owned highly lethal, rapid-fire, large-clip automatic or semi-automatic weapons.

Youth is a potent characteristic when considering lethality, as people under age eighteen are more likely to use a firearm to kill someone else or to commit suicide than older individuals.[51] Issues with impulsivity, fighting, and a lack of dispute resolution skills increase lethality risks for youth,[52] and firearm possession is also highly associated with teen dating violence, as detailed below.

Youth firearm possession has been found to correlate with male gender, illicit drug use, binge drinking, recent serious fights, and retaliatory attitudes. Furthermore, researchers conclude that dating violence or intimate partner violence is "highly associated with firearm possession."[53] The study of emergency departments found that youths with firearms were more likely to commit dating violence, to have been in a recent serious physical fight, and to endorse aggressive attitudes that increase risk for retaliatory violence. While this study considered subjects who were seeking medical care for injury-causing assaults, making this a "high-risk" sample of youth, the ease of access to illegally obtained, highly lethal weapons and the connection between firearms and dating violence demand action. Future efforts to reduce illegal firearm access are needed, along with hospital- and community-based initiatives that utilize behavioral interventions regarding aggressive attitudes.

The closely drawn relationship between firearms and masculinity is socially construed from a young age. Society has created a culture around firearms that promotes male desire for dominance and control, and the gun lobby has been adept at tapping into that fear and using it for political gain.

III. Gendered Nature of Advocacy

Various groups have taken on the nation's 30,000 annual firearm deaths, and this advocacy is also frequently gendered. Women are "more likely than men to be anti-gun."[54] Men are far less likely than women to support gun control measures, and they are more likely to believe that keeping a gun is necessary for self-defense.[55]

Moms Demand Action for Gun Sense in America (MDA) formed in response to the Sandy Hook Elementary School shooting and quickly launched in all fifty states.[56] It modeled itself after Mothers Against Drunk Driving (MADD), the pioneering grassroots movement of the 1980s that battled cultural resignation about alcohol-related automobile deaths and rewrote laws, with MDA seeking to be a "MADD for guns." MDA also built from efforts by the Million Mom March that occurred in the wake of the 1999 Columbine shooting.[57]

MDA lobbied for Facebook to prohibit private, unlicensed sales on its platform, and persuaded companies such as Target, Starbucks, and

Chipotle to stop allowing guns to be brought into their stores.[58] When open-carry groups, such as Open Carry Texas, conducted demonstrations at Target stores, MDA responded by stating, "American moms will not shop where our children and families, including our teens who work at Target, are not safe."[59]

In 2013, MDA called for a nationwide boycott—"Skip Starbucks Saturday"—to successfully pressure the company to change its policy.[60] In forty-three states (where allowed by state law at that time), Starbucks had permitted individuals to carry loaded weapons in its stores, and gun owners were increasingly using the coffee shops as gathering places, even sponsoring a "Starbucks Appreciation Day" on which customers toted guns into Starbucks stores.[61]

MDA members use their identities as mothers to suggest moral authority, calling for gun safety measures under the mantle of motherhood. Shannon Watts, founder of MDA, says, "Moms showing up en masse and speaking to lawmakers is powerful."[62] Of her "army" of moms, she states, "There is no stronger force in the world than a mother protecting her child."[63] Regarding open-carry demonstrations at the sites of MDA meetings, Watts issued the statement, "Sadly, these bullies are attempting to use guns to intimidate moms and children and to infringe on our constitutional right to free speech."[64] MDA members identify as protectors of children and increasingly of women because women disproportionately experience intimate partner violence and intimate homicides, and heightened attention has been given to the realization that most perpetrators of mass shootings have histories of committing domestic violence.

Open Carry Texas, in turn, makes the MDA members' gender the target of their threats and attacks. The "high-stakes political performance"[65] of open carrying is explicitly gendered, and Open Carry Texas members describe the MDA members as "thugs with jugs."[66] In March 2014, Open Carry Texas held an event at a firing range at which participants shot at mannequins, mimicking the military exercise of "mad minutes," but titling it "Mad Mom," which is how Open Carry members describe MDA members.[67]

Members of Open Carry Texas have also convened with weapons to protest MDA meetings, with the armed group frightening members of MDA and other members of the public. Gun rights advocates increasingly gather in public with their firearms in efforts to normalize open carry and decrease alarm, but these displays of weapons elicit fear and are problematic for the police and city officials.[68]

While reliable NRA membership statistics are difficult to ascertain, the majority of its leadership and members are male, the NRA is largely a racially singular organization, and persons of color tend not to join the NRA. Naturally, there are exceptions to demographic norms: Whoopi Goldberg, for example, is an outspoken NRA member, just as there are prominent men who champion gun reform, such as New York City Mayor Michael Bloomberg.

Even following many mass shootings by individuals with histories of committing family violence and school shootings perpetrated almost entirely by middle-class white men, the gun lobby has resisted reforms favored even by the majority of gun owners and NRA members. The sides are more entrenched than ever.

IV. Public Opinion

Public opinion on gun control varies based on the type of question posed.[69] When voters are asked about specific gun safety measures, most support these policies. However, when asked whether they would prioritize gun ownership or gun control, a majority of voters prioritize gun ownership.

A Pew Research Center study of public opinion on guns during the 2016 campaign found the following about voters: 83% support "background checks for private and gun show sales," 81% support preventing "people with mental illness from purchasing guns," 74% support "barring gun purchases by people on the federal no-fly or watch lists," 66% support "a federal database to track gun sales," 54% support a ban on "high-capacity ammunition clips," and 54% support a ban on "assault-style weapons."[70] This survey of voters suggests broad support for gun control, but when the same Pew survey asked whether it is more important to control gun ownership or protect the right of Americans to own guns, most voters supported gun ownership over gun control. Fifty-two percent of the general public in 2016 said it is more important to protect the right to own guns, while 46% said it is more important to control guns.[71] This follows a significant downward trend of overall support for gun control since 2000, when 66% of the general public prioritized controlling gun ownership over protecting gun owners' rights, and only 29% of the general public said it was more important to prioritize gun ownership.[72]

This study also found that support for prioritizing gun control among registered Democratic voters held steady at about 66% from 2000 to 2012, but there was a noticeable uptick in support by Democrats in 2016 when 79% said they prioritized gun control over ownership.[73] In contrast, Republican voters dramatically shifted opinions, moving from 46% of Republican voters in 2000 prioritizing gun control over gun ownership down to 21% in 2012, and then down to only 9% in 2016.[74] Moreover, despite evidence to the contrary, a "majority of the general public (58%) says that gun ownership does more to protect people from crime than to put them at risk."[75]

Therefore, although most voters support many specific gun control policies, Republican voters support prioritizing gun ownership over gun control so overwhelmingly that there has been an overall downward trend in the general public's support for prioritizing gun control. Even following the October 2017 mass shooting at a Las Vegas country-music concert in which a single gunman killed fifty-eight people and wounded 540, divided opinions on gun control persist.[76] Focusing on specific policies could result in greater bipartisan support for the passage of gun safety measures, particularly if members of Congress place their constituents' concerns above allegiance to the NRA.

V. Party Politics and Trends in Gun Control Policy

Opposition to gun control largely comes from Republican legislators,[77] gun rights activists,[78] and Republican voters.[79] The National Rifle Association spent over $30 million supporting President Donald Trump's election.[80] He campaigned on a pro-gun platform, among other issues, vowing, "I will get rid of gun-free zones in schools."[81] Having poured so many millions of dollars into efforts to elect Trump, the NRA is set on getting what it paid for.

Republican-controlled legislatures at the federal and state levels have achieved numerous victories in rolling back gun control and passing laws protecting gun owners' rights,[82] leaving dangerous gaps in the law that proliferate gun ownership, including by those known to be violent. The primary trend in state law over the past thirty years has favored gun owners' access to and ability to carry firearms, including legislation to make guns easier to obtain and to more broadly permit the concealed carrying of firearms.[83] When new gun laws are enacted, they typically make guns more accessible instead of making them harder to obtain.[84] For example, in 2013, of the 109 state laws passed regarding firearms, seventy loosened gun restrictions while thirty-nine added safety measures.[85]

Some gun-control victories quickly lead to setbacks. In Colorado, for example, soon after tighter gun control legislation was passed, two state legislators were recalled in a special election pushed by gun rights groups, and another resigned to avoid the same fate.[86] Democrats increasingly fear political repercussions from the gun lobby and have blocked background checks from coming to a vote due to such fear.[87] As a result of the 2010 elections and the subsequent reapportionment of state legislative districts, the balance of power in many state legislatures shifted to favor conservative voters who are opposed to firearm regulation and federal authority.[88] This balance of power is not expected to appreciably change to favor firearm control legislation before reapportionment following the 2020 census.[89]

Despite public outcry following school shootings and greater attention to familial firearm homicides, gun control at the federal level has remained "essentially unchanged" for the past two decades.[90] The Gun Control Act (GCA) of 1968, enacted after the assassination of President John F. Kennedy, remains the primary federal statute governing the sales and possession of firearms. Nearly two decades later, the Firearm Owners' Protection Act (FOPA) was passed in 1986, limiting the GCA. FOPA reduced the crime of firearm records falsification from a felony to a misdemeanor and prohibited the federal government from creating a gun registration system. The last significant federal gun control law was the Brady Law enacted in 1993, requiring a waiting period and criminal background check before a gun dealer can sell a firearm. Gun rights groups even opposed domestic violence–related gun control such as the Lautenberg Amendment.[91]

Mass shootings lead to a significant increase in the number of firearm bills proposed in state legislatures, and massacres that result in more fatalities have larger effects on gun legislation, with each additional death leading to a 2.5% increase in the number of gun-related bills introduced.[92] The gun bills that actually pass in state legislatures following mass shootings, however, depend greatly on whether Republicans or Democrats are in the majority.[93] Following mass shootings, Republican-controlled legislatures pass firearm laws that loosen gun control, and Democrat-controlled legislatures generally fail to pass more gun laws of any kind.[94] Thus, mass shootings have served as an impetus for Republican legislators to pass laws to make guns more accessible, creating more dangerous gaps in the law.

State governments are the primary regulators of firearms,[95] but strict gun control measures routinely fail, as occurred in Massachusetts and California,[96] and the U.S. Supreme Court struck down the District of Columbia's handgun ban as violating the Second Amendment in *District of Columbia v. Heller*.[97] In *McDonald v. City of Chicago*, the Court further held that the Second Amendment is incorporated under the Fourteenth Amendment, thus protecting the right of an individual to "keep and bear arms" from infringement by local governments.[98] A wave of "shall issue" statutes, which give applicants a right to a concealed-carry permit unless they are prohibited from possessing a firearm, swept across states in the 1990s.[99] More recent examples include Georgia's passage of a "guns everywhere" law in 2014 that allows individuals to carry firearms in bars, airports, government buildings, and churches.[100] In August 2016, soon after the notorious biker brawl in Waco, Texas passed a law that allowed open carry in most places and concealed carry on college campuses.[101] Twenty-three states have also adopted "stand your ground" laws that allow individuals to use their weapons when they feel threatened.[102]

Although gun rights advocates achieved significant momentum in the courts following the Supreme Court's *Heller* decision, two recent decisions favored gun control.[103] The Ninth Circuit recently upheld restrictions on concealed-carry weapons in two California counties as constitutional.[104] A panel of the D.C. Circuit similarly upheld a concealed-carry ban, signaling that concealed-carry laws may be difficult for gun rights advocates to challenge in court.[105] However, under the Trump administration and in light of Justice Anthony Kennedy's retirement, the balance of the Supreme Court will tip more heavily toward gun rights. The current Congress has introduced a concealed-carry reciprocity bill to enable individuals to take their concealed weapons into any jurisdiction in the United States if they have received a permit from their home state, along with legislation to make silencers more readily available.[106]

Examples of the politicization of safety as related to firearms abound, with recent instances in the domestic violence, medical, and mental health contexts illustrating opposition to approaches proven to reduce lethality.

Regarding the recent politicization of safety as related to firearms and domestic violence victims, on the heels of the National Rifle Association's endorsement of President Donald Trump, New Jersey Governor Chris Christie again vetoed legislation that would have put gun control measures in place for domestic abusers whom courts have deemed dangerous.[107] The New Jersey bill contains many reasonable ways to remove firearms from highly dangerous domestic violence situations and provide abuse survivors with needed safety information. For example, the New Jersey bill would require law enforcement authorities to consult a registry of domestic violence offenders before issuing gun permits, require individuals subject to restraining orders to surrender firearms not confiscated by police, create a question on restraining order petitions about the abuser's access to firearms, and inform victims of their ability to seek the revocation of an abuser's firearms permit before confiscated guns are returned. These types of practical and judicious steps have been proven to save lives. Christie instead proposed to expedite abuse victims' access to firearms, a move destined to increase lethality to victims, abusers, and their children.

Similarly, an Indiana bill allows domestic violence protection order recipients to obtain a firearm without a license, background check, or training.[108] Indiana legislators initially tried to give a free gun to everyone who obtained a protective order at taxpayer expense through this bill. The Indiana Coalition Against Domestic Violence forcefully opposed each iteration of the bill, recognizing the increased lethality outcomes to abuse survivors, their children, and the broader community.[109]

Concerning public health, although the medical profession largely agrees that firearm violence is a serious public health threat and that doctors should counsel patients about responsible gun ownership, multiple states, including Minnesota,[110] Missouri,[111] and Montana,[112] have passed laws regarding medical professionals and firearms. A recent area of dispute concerned a 2011 Florida law the NRA lobbied for called the Firearms Owners' Privacy Act (FOPA, not to be confused with the 1986 Firearm Owners' Protection Act mentioned earlier), which barred medical professionals from asking patients whether they owned guns based on the idea that Second Amendment freedoms prohibit doctors from discussing firearm ownership with their patients. Medical associations, the Brady Campaign to Prevent Gun Violence, Moms Demand Action, and Everytown for Gun Safety argued that the law interfered with doctors' ability to provide medical advice to patients. The American Medical Association, American College of Physicians, and other medical groups encourage their members to inquire about firearms in the household as a routine part of childproofing the home and educating patients about the dangers of unsecured firearms,[113] but a majority of doctors still do not ask about firearms due to their discomfort with the conversation.[114] Studies show that physician counseling produces results; for example, one study found that 60% of families in a predominantly Latino pediatric clinic who received gun safety counseling either removed all guns from the home or improved gun-storage safety practices.[115]

Under the 2011 FOPA, doctors who inquired about firearm ownership as part of household safety counseling could be disciplined by the Florida Board of Medicine, with punishment including permanent licensure revocation, suspension, probation, compulsory remedial education, or a $10,000 fine. After lengthy legal battles, including a three-judge panel upholding the law, in 2017 the Eleventh Circuit Court of Appeals struck down key portions of the law that has come to be known as "Docs vs. Glocks," on the ground that it violates medical professionals' First Amendment free speech rights.[116]

Gun control efforts often target individuals thought to present the greatest danger to society, such as those with diagnosed severe mental illness or domestic violence convictions. Mental health provisions provide another recent example of the partisan nature of gun legislation. During Obama's final days in office, his administration instituted a regulation requiring the Social Security Administration to disclose to the national gun background check system information about individuals with mental illness. The Republican-controlled Congress, using the

Congressional Review Act to roll back regulations instituted by President Obama, quickly repealed this regulation, and Trump signed this NRA-backed measure.[117] Notably, Congresswoman Gabrielle ("Gabby") Giffords was shot by a man with untreated mental illness; the current representative of Giffords's Arizona district, Congresswomen Martha McSally, voted to repeal this regulation.

Congress could make it harder for suspected terrorists to obtain firearms by closing the so-called "terror gap." Such a bill, which again failed in 2016, was based on a Bush administration proposal, but Republicans voted it down. Under this legislation, gun sales are blocked only after proof that a prospective gun buyer on the watch list is known or suspected to be involved in terrorism, and if blocked, the individual can challenge the denial in federal court.

VI. Recommended Reforms That Should Receive Bipartisan Support

"America is absolutely awash with easily obtainable firearms. So what are you waiting for?" the spokesman for Al Qaeda invites in a 2011 recruitment video.[118] Politicians should be concerned about America's routine gun violence, and cultural values that support carrying firearms for protection shouldn't take priority over daily evidence of the harm caused by wielding weapons. Given the stark and brutal realities of firearms and family violence, politicians across the ideological spectrum should readily agree that people who violently attack or threaten family members should be subject to practical and measured restrictions on their access to firearms.

Risk factors for gun violence are known, and research shows that certain types of policies are particularly effective in addressing gun violence, but gaps in the law exist where ineffectual policies or no policies are in place. Most Americans, including gun owners and NRA members, are in favor of universal background checks, and a majority of Americans also want to prevent gun sales to suspected terrorists and prohibit high-capacity magazines. Instead, the NRA rejects these positions and maintains that "a heavily-armed populace is the best way to keep America safe."[119] Contrary to pro-gun messaging, proliferation of firearm ownership causes gun owners to be at a higher risk of homicide rather than providing the meaningful protection they seek.[120] Although many people feel that having a gun in the home provides protection, instead it dramatically increases risks of death or injury, while using the firearm to shoot someone who endangers the household is far less common.[121]

A. Universal Background Checks

Enacting policies that require all firearm sales—including sales by unlicensed sellers—to be subject to background checks, and enforcing these policies against all firearm sellers, would more effectively keep guns out of the hands of individuals subject to gun bans.[122] Studies have shown that relatively few offenders (only 3.9%) commit crimes with firearms purchased directly from licensed firearms dealers,[123] and the current lack of regulation of unlicensed firearms sellers significantly limits the government's ability to keep firearms from prohibited individuals.[124]

B. National Registry

Unlike motor vehicle registration and licensing for drivers, firearm purchases are prohibited from being recorded in an on-going national database.[125] In states that do have firearms registration systems, compliance is believed to be poor.[126] Furthermore, the Affordable Care Act prohibits medical professionals from collecting information about the presence or storage of firearms in a patient's home. Legislators should reconsider the multiple laws that inhibit the ability to track firearms.

C. Domestic Violence Restrictions and Reforms to the Violence Against Women Act and Lautenberg Amendment

Given the strong association between domestic violence, firearm ownership, and domestic fatalities, laws that make guns more accessible endanger individuals vulnerable to domestic violence, whereas domestic violence–related gun control can effectively reduce violence.[127] Policies that keep individuals subject to restraining orders, felons, and misdemeanants from purchasing firearms are quite effective in reducing homicides.[128] Furthermore, laws that require medical professionals to investigate potential domestic violence involving gun usage or threats can reduce intimate homicides.[129]

Because firearm possession is correlated with high rates of perpetrating domestic violence and intimate fatalities, restrictions on abuse perpetrators' access to firearms is an important gun control measure.[130] Firearm possession bans for individuals subject to restraining orders result in significantly lower rates of total intimate partner homicides.[131] Because a significant portion of law enforcement fatalities occur while responding to domestic disturbance calls in states with high rates of gun ownership, evidence of law enforcement homicides could persuade legislators.[132]

The Violence Against Women Act (VAWA) imposed some restrictions on domestic violence perpetrators, but the act suffers from gaps in the law and lack of enforcement. Although VAWA prohibits the possession of firearms by individuals who (1) are subject to restraining orders issued after hearings and with notice or (2) have been convicted of misdemeanor crimes of domestic violence, immense gaps in domestic violence–related gun control remain.[133] VAWA prohibits possession but not purchase, which leaves a significant gap in the law, and VAWA does not apply to *ex parte* domestic violence restraining orders, which courts may order upon a finding of imminent bodily harm and past abuse.[134] VAWA and many states do not include the most effective gun policies: prohibitions on purchase of firearms by individuals subject to all forms of protective orders, including *ex parte* orders. Furthermore, the troubling lack of enforcement of the domestic violence–related gun laws on the books must be addressed.

One study found that state laws imposing firearm restrictions during restraining orders were correlated with a significant reduction in family homicide rates.[135] Another study elaborated on the magnitude of these effects by finding a 9% reduction in the rate of intimate partner homicides committed with firearms.[136] This study found that states with purchase restrictions have a significant reduction in intimate partner homicides, as opposed to states that merely include a restriction on possession,[137] a distinction that can be attributed to the easier enforcement of firearm restrictions at the point of purchase than ascertaining ownership and possession.[138] Additionally, keeping a registry of all firearm owners would be necessary to increase the effectiveness of the current laws prohibiting possession.[139]

The "boyfriend loophole" also needs to be remedied. Currently, the Lautenberg Amendment's restrictions on firearm possession only cover batterers who lived with their spouses or had children with them, not individuals who were merely dating without children. F.B.I. data, however, shows that a boyfriend is nearly as likely as a husband to be a perpetrator of firearm homicide of an intimate. As one sheriff testified before Congress, "Dangerous boyfriends can be just as scary as dangerous husbands, they hit just as hard and they fire their guns with the same deadly force."[140] Some states offer more protective laws that encompass such categories, providing ready examples for doing so.

Gun rights proponents, including law enforcement organizations, object to firearms restrictions on people subject to temporary restraining orders, arguing that temporary restraining orders are granted too quickly and often do not allow the respondent to present evidence.[141] One study examined the conflicting interests in regards to the Lautenberg Amendment that added the gun ban for domestic violence misdemeanants to VAWA: "Law enforcement organizations and Second Amendment advocates have formed a powerful alliance to oppose the law."[142] These groups that promote gun rights opposed the Lautenberg Amendment and sought to challenge it in court because they viewed the law as unfair and overly broad.[143]

Framing and contextualizing issues can help overcome opposition to gun safety measures. For example, it may be effective to explain to law enforcement organizations the associations between gun ownership and homicide rates, particularly homicide rates of law enforcement officers when responding to domestic violence calls in areas with high gun ownership rates. Research has shown that higher rates of gun ownership—and not higher rates of crime—lead to higher rates of homicide of law enforcement officers.[144] Law enforcement officers are three times as likely to be killed in the line of duty in states with high rates of gun ownership, as compared to states with low rates of gun ownership.[145] Framing domestic violence–related gun safety policies as saving the lives of law enforcement, and therefore building a narrative that these policies are pro-law enforcement, could engender support from law enforcement organizations and Republican voters who otherwise generally oppose gun control policies.

Limits on magazine capacity are also needed, as assault rifles can fire thirty-round clips as fast as a person can pull the trigger, instantly causing mass homicides.

D. Enforcement Efforts

Currently, many states lack effective domestic violence gun policies, and the poor enforcement of current laws further endangers vulnerable individuals.[146] Six states have no gun control laws at all regarding domestic violence: Georgia, Kansas, Mississippi, Missouri, New Mexico, and Wyoming. Only twenty states have laws authorizing courts to issue gun bans for individuals subject to *ex parte* protective orders: Arizona, California, Colorado, Connecticut, Hawai'i, Illinois, Indiana, Massachusetts, Michigan, Montana, Nebraska, New Hampshire, New York, North Carolina, North Dakota, Pennsylvania, Texas, Utah, Virginia, and West Virginia. Furthermore, only six states allow courts to issue gun bans in relation to domestic violence crimes in other contexts that go beyond VAWA: California, Kentucky, Maine, Minnesota, New Jersey, and North Dakota. Kentucky, New Jersey, and North Dakota allow courts to impose gun bans on those accused of domestic violence crimes before they have actually been convicted, whereas California, Maine, and Minnesota allow for gun bans for misdemeanors not specifically related to family violence. In addition, not all states require officers to remove firearms at the scene of domestic violence incidents, and even some of those that do only allow removal of firearms used in the commission of the crime. Enormous gaps at the state level prevent meaningful domestic violence gun control policy.

Lack of enforcement of existing domestic violence gun laws is the norm. The weakness of VAWA's gun ban enforcement is reflected in the high numbers of individuals supposedly restrained by protective orders who still murder intimate partners with firearms.[147] Because there is no mechanism in VAWA to remove guns, it is most often not enforced.[148] States often rely on the "honor system" for abusers to surrender their guns because officers are not required to confiscate or remove guns.[149] Only seventeen states have laws that actually require the abusers subject to domestic violence restraining orders to surrender their guns: Arizona, California, Colorado, Connecticut, Hawai'i, Illinois, Iowa, Maryland,

Massachusetts, Minnesota, New Hampshire, New York, North Carolina, Tennessee, Washington, West Virginia, and Wisconsin. To enforce the already-enacted laws, weapon surrender should be required and pursued.

Legislators offer prayers and moments of silence, but their silence regarding gun safety reforms kills. Even given the challenge of enforcing gun laws, experts estimate that a serious effort to reduce gun violence in the United States could reduce the death toll by one-third, with over 10,000 lives saved per year.[150]

Gun safety should not be a Republican or Democrat issue, and people of any party affiliation should be determined to remedy the senseless firearm fatalities that are of epidemic proportions in America. We should be able to enact measures proven to keep guns out of the hands of domestic abusers, such as requiring background checks for all purchases, permitting firearm confiscation when a judge determines someone has committed domestic violence and presents a threat of imminent harm, and enforcing existing laws. We know that the combination of domestic violence and firearms is too often lethal, and that practical and reasonable measures can limit abusers' access to firearms. These data-driven solutions are supported by the majority of Americans, including gun owners, and lawmakers should have the courage to take direction from their constituents, not the NRA.

Author's Note

The author wishes to thank Dylan Quigley, Michael McConnell, and Franklin Thomas for their research assistance.

NOTES

1 Jacquelyn C. Campbell et al., *Risk Factors for Femicide in Abusive Relationships: Results from a Multistate Case Control Study*, 93 AM. J. PUB. HEALTH 1089, 1090 (2003).

2 142 Cong. Rec. 1, 25002 (daily ed. Sept. 26, 1996) (statement of Sen. Lautenberg).

3 *Background Checks*, EVERYTOWN FOR GUN SAFETY ACTION FUND, https://everytown.org (last visited Oct. 26, 2017).

4 JENNIFER L. TRUMAN & RACHEL E. MORGAN, NONFATAL DOMESTIC VIOLENCE, 2003–2012, at 5 (U.S. Dep't of Justice, Apr. 2014); CALLIE MARIE RENNISON, U.S. DEP'T OF JUSTICE, INTIMATE PARTNER VIOLENCE, 1993–2001, at 1 (2003).

5   Susan Sorenson, *Firearm Use in Intimate Partner Violence: A Brief Overview*, 30 EVALUATION REV. 229, 235 (2006).

6   Katherine Kaufer Christoffel, *Firearms Injuries: Endemic Then, Endemic Now*, 97 AM. J. PUB. HEALTH 626, 626–29 (2007).

7   Sorenson, *supra* note 5, at 232.

8   *Id.*

9   ALEXIA COOPER & ERICA L. SMITH, U.S. DEP'T OF JUSTICE, HOMICIDE TRENDS IN THE UNITED STATES, 1980–2008, at 10 (2011), www.bjs.gov.

10 *Id.*

11 Campbell et al., *supra* note 1, at 1091.

12 *Id.* at 1090–91.

13 *Id.* at 1090.

14 Susan B. Sorenson & Philip J. Cook, *"We've Got a Gun?": Comparing Reports of Adolescents and Their Parents About Household Firearms*, 36 J. COMMUNITY PSYCHOL. 1, 3 (2008) (quoting TOM W. SMITH, UNIV. OF CHI., 2001 NATIONAL GUN POLICY SURVEY OF THE NATIONAL OPINION RESEARCH CENTER: RESEARCH FINDINGS (2001), www.norc.org).

15 Brian R. Wyant & Ralph B. Taylor, *Size of Household Firearm Collections: Implications for Subcultures and Gender*, 45 CRIMINOLOGY 519, 520 (2007).

16 *Id.* at 523.

17 William B. Bankston et al., *The Influence of Fear of Crime, Gender, and Southern Culture on Carrying Firearms for Protection*, 31 SOC. Q. 287, 298 (1990).

18 Aaron Mendelson, *Politics, Gun-Control Anxiety Cited for California's Record 2016 Gun Sales*, 89.3 KPCC (Mar. 15, 2017), www.scpr.org; T. Rees Shapiro & Katie Zezima, *Gun Sales Have Dropped Since Trump's Election, Except Among People Scared of His Administration*, WASH. POST (Mar. 5, 2017), www.washingtonpost.com.

19 Morgan Chalfant, *Gun Manufacturing Skyrockets 140% on Obama's Watch*, WASH. POST (July 24, 2015) (citing U.S. DEP'T OF JUSTICE, BUREAU OF ALCOHOL, TOBACCO, FIREARMS & EXPLOSIVES, FIREARMS COMMERCE IN THE UNITED STATES: ANNUAL STATISTICAL UPDATE (2015), www.atf.gov), www.washingtonpost.com.

20 Polly Mosendz & Kyle Stock, *Las Vegas Horror Drives All-Too-Predictable Gun Stock Rally*, BLOOMBERG (Oct. 2, 2017), www.bloomberg.com.

21 Wyant & Taylor, *supra* note 15, at 522.

22 Bankston et al., *supra* note 17, at 288.

23 ANNIE OAKLEY, THE AUTOBIOGRAPHY OF ANNIE OAKLEY 49 (Marilyn Robbins ed., 2006).

24 Sorenson & Cook, *supra* note 14, at 3.

25 Kevin Sullivan & William Wan, *Troubled. Quiet. Macho. Angry. The Volatile Life of the Orlando Shooter*, WASH. POST (June 17, 2016), www.washingtonpost.com.

26 *Id.*; Soraya Chemaly, *In Orlando, as Usual, Domestic Violence Was Ignored Red Flag*, ROLLING STONE (June 13, 2016), www.rollingstone.com.

27 Angela Stroud, *Good Guys with Guns: Hegemonic Masculinity and Concealed Handguns*, 26 GENDER & SOC'Y 216, 227 (2012).

28 SCOTT MELZER, GUN CRUSADERS: THE NRA'S CULTURE WAR 222 (2009).

29 Jens Ludwig et al., *The Gender Gap in Reporting Household Gun Ownership*, 88 AM. J. PUB. HEALTH 1715, 1717 (1998).

30 *Women in Dark on Men's Storage Habits*, USA TODAY 7 (Aug. 2006) (citing UNC Chapel Hill study by Tamera Coyne-Beasley, Associate Professor of Pediatrics and Internal Medicine).

31 Ludwig et al., *supra* note 29, at 1716–17.

32 *Id.*

33 *Women in Dark on Men's Storage Habits*, *supra* note 30, at 7.

34 *Id.*

35 Ludwig et al., *supra* note 29, at 1717.

36 *Women in Dark on Men's Storage Habits*, *supra* note 30, at 7.

37 Wollschlaeger v. Governor, Florida, 848 F.3d 1293 (11th Cir. 2017).

38 *Women in Dark on Men's Storage Habits*, *supra* note 30, at 7.

39 Tom W. Smith & Robert J. Smith, *Changes in Firearms Ownership Among Women, 1980–1994*, 86 J. CRIM. L. & CRIMINOLOGY 133, 133, 136 (1995).

40 *Id.*

41 *Id.* at 137.

42 Erik Larson, *Armed Force: Paxton Quigley Shows Her Women Students How to Shoot a Man*, WALL ST. J. (Feb. 4, 1993), at A1.

43 Smith & Smith, *supra* note 39, at 145.

44 Philip J. Cook & Susan B. Sorenson, *The Gender Gap Among Teen Survey Respondents: Why Are Boys More Likely to Report a Gun in the Home than Girls?*, 22 J. QUANTITATIVE CRIMINOLOGY 61, 61 (2006); Sorenson & Cook, *supra* note 14, at 2 (confirming applicability to non-marital households).

45 Cook & Sorenson, *supra* note 44, at 61; Sorenson & Cook, *supra* note 14, at 2 (confirming applicability to non-marital households).

46 18 U.S.C. § 922 (2015).

47 J. A. Grunbaum et al., *Youth Risk Behavior Surveillance—United States, 2003*, MORBIDITY & MORTALITY WKY. REP. 53 (SS-2) (2004).

48 Philip J. Cook & Jens Ludwig, *Does Gun Prevalence Affect Teen Gun Carrying After All?*, 42 CRIMINOLOGY 27–54 (2004).

49 Patrick M. Carter et al., *Firearm Possession Among Adolescents Presenting to an Urban Emergency Department for Assault*, 132 PEDIATRICS 213, 213 (2013).

50 *Id.*

51 Sorenson & Cook, *supra* note 14, at 2.

52 Richard Spano, *First Time Gun Carrying and the Primary Prevention of Youth Gun Violence for African American Youth Living in Extreme Poverty*, 17 AGGRESSION & VIOLENT BEHAVIOR 83, 84 (2012).

53 Carter et al., *supra* note 49, at 218.

54 Ludwig et al., *supra* note 29, at 1717.

55 Cook & Sorenson, *supra* note 44, at 62.

56 Mark Follman, *Mothers in Arms*, MOTHER JONES 29, 29 (Sept.–Oct. 2014).

57 *Id.*; Mark Follman, *These Women Are the NRA's Worst Nightmare*, MOTHER JONES (Sept.–Oct. 2014).

58 Natalie DiBlasio, *Facebook Takes Aim at Gun Posts*, USA TODAY (Mar. 6, 2014), at 4a.

59 Doug Stanglin, *Moms Ask Target to Holster Guns Policy*, USA TODAY 1b (June 5, 2014).

60 Bruce Horovitz, *Gun-Control Group Organizes "Skip Starbucks Saturday,"* USA TODAY (Aug. 22, 2013), at 2b ("Many moms are unaware that if they take their children to Starbucks, their children may be standing next to a customer who has a loaded weapon.") (quoting Shannon Watts, founder of MDA).

61 *Id.*

62 KC Baker, *Mom on a Mission*, PEOPLE 66 (Jan. 9, 2017).

63 *Id.*

64 Manny Fernandez, *A Face-Off Outside Dallas in the Escalating Battle Over Texas' Gun Culture*, N.Y. TIMES (Nov. 11. 2013), at A14.

65 Chloe Johnston, *Open Carry, Critical Acts*, 59 DRAMA REV. 176, 177 (2015).

66 *Id.*

67 *Id.* at 178.

68 Fernandez, *supra* note 64, at A14.

69 *Opinions on Gun Policy and the 2016 Campaign*, PEW RESEARCH CENTER 1–2 (Aug. 26, 2016).

70 *Id.* at 1.

71 *Id.* at 2.

72 *Id.*

73 *Id.*

74 *Id.*

75 *Id.* at 3.

76 Lisa Marie Pane & Emily Swanson, *Poll Shows Little Societal Change Over Gun Control After Las Vegas Shooting*, CHRISTIAN SCI. MONITOR (Oct. 20, 2017), www.csmonitor.com.

77 William J. Vizzard, *The Current and Future State of Gun Policy in the United States*, 104 J. CRIM. L. & CRIMINOLOGY 879, 879 (2015).

78 Ashby Jones, *Gun-Control Backers Turn Their Focus to Domestic Violence*, WALL ST. J. (Feb. 13, 2015), www.wsj.com.

79 *Opinions on Gun Policy and the 2016 Campaign*, *supra* note 69, at 1–2.

80 Peter Stone & Ben Wieder, *NRA Spent More Than Reported During 2016 Election*, MIAMI HERALD (Oct. 5, 2017), www.miamiherald.com (citing data from the Federal Election Commission and the Center for Public Integrity).

81 Morgan Winson, *Trump's Gun Views in Spotlight Amid String of Accidental School Shootings*, ABC NEWS (May 24, 2016), www.abcnews.com.

82 Noah Feldman, *Two Wins for Gun Control Buck the U.S. Legal Trend*, BLOOMBERG (June 12, 2016), www.bloomberg.com.

83 Firmin DeBrabander, *New Gun Laws Pass Often in the United States. But They Usually Make Guns Easier to Get*, WASH. POST (Oct. 6, 2015), www.washington post.com.

84 *Id.*

85 Jay Newton-Small, *Gun Control Activists Seek to Reboot After Newtown Shooting Momentum Fades*, TIME 1 (Dec. 13, 2013) (citing Karen Yourish et al., *State Gun Laws Enacted in the Year After Newton*, N.Y. TIMES (Dec. 10, 2013), www.nytimes .com).

86 *Id.*

87 *Id.*

88 Vizzard, *supra* note 77, at 885.

89 *Id.*

90 *Id.* at 879.

91 *Id.* at 884.

92 Michael Luca et al., *The Impact of Mass Shootings on Gun Policy* 10 (Harvard Business School, Working Paper No. 16-126, 2016).

93 *Id.*

94 *Id.*

95 *Id.* at 4.

96 Vizzard, *supra* note 77, at 884.

97 District of Columbia v. Heller, 554 U.S. 570, 635 (2008).

98 McDonald v. City of Chicago, 561 U.S. 742 (2010).

99 Vizzard, *supra* note 77, at 885.

100 *Id.*; GA. CODE ANN. § 16-11-137 (2014).

101 DeBrabander, *supra* note 83; TEX. GOV'T CODE ANN. § 411.2031 (2016).

102 DeBrabander, *supra* note 83.

103 Feldman, *supra* note 82.

104 Peruta v. Cnty. of San Diego, 824 F.3d 919, 924 (9th Cir. 2016).

105 Wrenn v. D.C., 179 F. Supp. 3d 135, 141 (D.C. Cir. 2016).

106 H.R. 38, 115th Cong. (1st Sess. 2017); H.R. 367, 115th Cong. (1st Sess. 2017); Carolyn Lochhead, *Pair of Pro-Gun Bills on Move in House*, S.F. CHRON. (Oct. 1, 2017).

107 S. 805 (N.J. 2016).

108 H.B. 1071 (Ind. 2017).

109 Devan Filchak, *Local Advocate Opposes Domestic Violence Gun Bill*, THE HER-ALD BULL. (Mar. 16, 2017), www.heraldbulletin.com; Brenna Donnelly, *Indiana Domestic Violence Survivor Gun Law Goes Into Effect*, WISHTV.COM (July 7, 2017), http://wishtv.com.

110 MINN. STAT. ANN. § 155.05 (repealed 2017); MINN. STAT. ANN. § 62V.06 (2013).

111 MO. ANN. STAT. § 571.012 (2014).

112 MONT. CODE ANN. § 50-16-108 (2017).

113 Renee Butkus et al., *Reducing Firearm-Related Injuries and Deaths in the United States: Executive Summary of a Policy Position Paper from the American College of Physicians*, 160 ANNALS INTERNAL MED. 585 (2014), http://annals.org.

114 Renee Butkus & Arleen Weissman, *Internists' Attitudes Toward Prevention of Firearm Injury*, 160 ANNALS INTERNAL MED. 821, 821–27 (2014), http://annals.org.

115 Paul S. Carbone et al., *Effectiveness of Gun-Safety Counseling and a Gun Lock Giveaway in a Hispanic Community*, 159 ARCHIVES PEDIATRIC & ADOLESCENT MED. 1049, 1049–54 (2005).

116 Wollschlaeger v. Gov., Fl., 848 F.3d 1293 (2017).

117 Merrit Kennedy, *Trump Repeals Rule Designed to Block Gun Sales to Certain Mentally Ill People*, NPR (Feb. 28, 2017, 6:34 PM), www.npr.org.

118 Editorial, *The N.R.A.'s Complicity in Terrorism*, N.Y. TIMES (June 16, 2016), at A22.

119 *Id.*

120 Puneet Narang et al., *Do Guns Provide Safety? At What Cost?*, 103 SOUTHERN MED. J., 151, 151 (2010).

121 *Id.*; Lisa M. Hepburn & David Hemenway, *Firearm Availability and Homicide: A Review of the Literature*, 9 AGGRESSION & VIOLENT BEHAVIOR 417, 437–38 (2004); David I. Swedler, *Firearm Prevalence and Homicides of Law Enforcement Officers in the United States*, 105 AM. J. PUB. HEALTH 2042, 2046 (2015); Eric W. Fleegler et al., *Firearm Legislation and Firearm-Related Fatalities in the United States*, 173 JAMA INT'L MED. 732, 736 (2013).

122 Katherine A. Vittes, *Legal Status and Source of Offenders' Firearms in States with the Least Stringent Criteria for Gun Ownership*, 19 INJURY PREVENTION 26, 26 (2013).

123 *Id.* at 30.

124 *Id.*

125 Consolidated Appropriations Act of 2004, Pub. L. No. 108-199, 118 Stat. 3.

126 Sorenson & Cook, *supra* note 14, at 3.

127 Narang et al., *supra* note 120, at 153.

128 Elizabeth Richardson Vigdor & James A. Mercy, *Do Laws Restricting Access to Firearms by Domestic Violence Offenders Prevent Intimate Partner Homicide?*, 30 EVALUATION REV. 313, 332 (2006).

129 Campbell et al., *supra* note 1, at 1094.

130 Narang et al., *supra* note 120, at 153.

131 Vigdor & Mercy, *supra* note 128, at 332.

132 Swedler, *supra* note 121, at 2046.

133 18 U.S.C. § 922(g)(8)–(9) (2015).

134 *Id.*

135 F. Stephen Bridges et al., *Domestic Violence Statutes and Rates of Intimate Partner and Family Homicide*, 19 CRIM. JUST. POL'Y REV. 117, 127 (2008).

136 *Id.*

137 Vigdor & Mercy, *supra* note 128, at 333.

138 *Id.*

139 *Id.* at 337.

140 *Boyfriends Can Kill, Too*, N.Y. TIMES (Dec. 19, 2017), www.nytimes.com.

141 *Id.*

142 Suzanne Morgan et al., *Domestic Violence Gun Ban: An Analysis of Interest-Group Conflict*, 13 AFFILIA 474, 485 (1998).

143 *Id.*

144 Swedler, *supra* note 121, at 2046.

145 *Id.*

146 Brooke Adams & Jason Bergreen, *Firearms Law Often Shirked*, SALT LAKE TRI-BUNE (Jan. 21, 2008), www.sltrib.com.

147 Carrie LeFevre Sillito & Sonia Salari, *Child Outcomes and Risk Factors in U.S. Homicide-Suicide Cases 1999–2004*, 26 J. FAM. VIOL. 285, 285 (2011).

148 Adams & Bergreen, *supra* note 146.

149 *Id.*

150 Nicholas Kristof, *Some Extremists Fire Guns and Other Extremists Promote Guns*, N.Y. TIMES (June 16, 2016), at A23.

11

Preventing Ordinary and Extraordinary Violence

MARY D. FAN

The paradigm of the armed and dangerous mass killer in public opin-ion and gun control legislation is a homicidal-suicidal stranger hunting in crowded public places. Yet half of all incidents of firearms-related homicide take place in the home, typically among intimates and people known to the slain rather than strangers. Drawing on data from the National Violent Death Reporting System, this chapter shows that even in the context of extraordinary violence by the homicidal-suicidal, the major early red flags and risk factors involve seemingly ordinary smaller-scale assaults and domestic disturbances. Firearms possession laws prevent individuals convicted of crimes of domestic violence or placed under court-issued restraining orders from possessing firearms.[1] The problem is that many perpetrators never come to the attention of a court. [2] Based on these findings regarding what current legal screens miss, this chapter discusses how police discretion and scene-of-the-assault procedure for "ordinary" domestic violence can help prevent escalation to fatal violence, including the feared extraordinary violence of homicidal-suicidal mass killings.

I. Introduction

In the nation's nightmares come true, a man with a gun hunts and kills outside the home.[3] A stranger or disgruntled coworker to many of his victims, he is mentally disturbed or ideologically radical. Suicidal as well as homicidal, the threat of future penalties is no deterrent because he does not envision a future.[4] From Orlando to San Bernardino to Charleston to Aurora to Newtown and other communities across the United States, he—and sometimes they—have struck again and again, catapulting the nation into fractious debates over firearms regulation.

The perpetrators' faces and crimes change forms on a rapid reel. He is Omar Mateen, perpetrator of the deadliest mass killing by a single shooter in U.S. history, leaving forty-nine dead and fifty-three wounded at a gay Orlando nightclub before killing himself.[5] They are Syed Rizwan Farook and Tashfeen Malik, married parents of an infant daughter, who killed fourteen and wounded seventeen at Farook's workplace before killing themselves.[6] He is Dylann Storm Roof, who fatally shot nine people who welcomed him to their historically Black church.[7] He is Adam Lanza massacring twenty-six people—twenty of them children—at Sandy Hook Elementary School in Newtown, Connecticut.[8]

Many of the mass killings that have rocked the nation in recent years have a commonality: they are homicide-suicides.[9] Also referred to as dyadic death or murder-suicide, homicide-suicides generally involve a two-stage act in which the perpetrator kills one or more people and commits suicide shortly thereafter.[10] The interval between homicide and suicide is often brief—just twenty-four hours or less—though some definitions include an interval of up to a week to be more complete.[11] The shooter kills himself or commits "suicide by cop" by shooting it out with police officers.[12] Homicide-suicides are especially horrifying because they defy the usual constraints on carnage, such as self-interest in avoiding detection or heightened penalties for wreaking greater harm.[13] Salient cases of homicide-suicide are so branded into the national memory and discourse that they can be invoked with just one or two words, becoming part of our national vocabulary of horror: Orlando, Newtown, Columbine, Virginia Tech, Navy Yard.[14]

Salient mass killings have sparked recurrent abortive efforts to address the paradigmatic public nightmare of the heavily armed, mentally disturbed mass killer.[15] Proposed legislation in Congress would ban semiautomatic assault weapons and high-capacity ammunition magazines, expand background checks, and raise penalties for firearms crimes.[16] Among the flurry of proposed state legislation in the year after the Newtown killings, the most successfully passed were restrictions upon, and monitoring of, people with mental and behavioral health issues.[17] The public also fixated on mental illness: according to a national Gallup poll, 80% of Americans believed that the failure of the mental health system to identify dangerous individuals is a "great deal" or "fair deal" to blame for mass shootings.[18]

The attention to firearms violence prevention is salutary and important. In guiding both law and executive action, however, two important empirical questions need to be addressed: (1) who are the dangerous individuals that the law's current screens miss and (2) why do the screens miss them? This chapter draws on data from the National Violent Death Reporting System (NVDRS) to answer the crucial questions of who poses a danger and why the dangerous slip through current legal screens. The chapter also shows that prevention of both extraordinary homicidal-suicidal violence and firearms homicides generally calls for attention to how the nation addresses "ordinary" violence. Ordinary violence refers to violence viewed as "normal" or mundane everyday altercations, such as domestic disturbances or assaults, especially in the home among family members, friends, and intimates.[19]

While the current regulatory focus is on preventing violence from the armed, deranged stranger hunting in schools, businesses, and on the street, nearly half of all incidents of firearms-related homicide take place in the home.[20] The majority of firearms homicides with known victim-perpetrator circumstances are perpetrated by people the victim knew.[21] Even when it comes to the seemingly most extreme form of extraordinary violence—the homicidal-suicidal—the clearest warning signs entail incidents of ordinary violence. This chapter presents data revealing that a substantial proportion of high-risk actors who go on to commit homicide-suicides have a history of prior assaults or domestic disturbances but have never been in court. In contrast, a much smaller proportion of homicidal-suicidal shooters could have been caught by focusing on mental health red flags. Additionally, based on findings regarding what current legal screens miss, this chapter discusses how law enforcement procedures at the scenes of assaults can help prevent seemingly "ordinary" violence from erupting into homicidal violence.

Passing new firearms laws is excruciatingly hard.[22] For example, federal firearms regulations stalled amid a fierce hailstorm of opposition by gun proponents and the National Rifle Association (NRA) despite public support for universal background checks and a sharp spike in support for stricter gun laws after Newtown.[23] Implementing scene-of-assault procedure can improve firearms violence prevention regardless of whether new laws are added to the books.

II. The Homicidal-Suicidal Stranger Paradigm of Danger

Proposals to reform firearms regulation are frequently shaped by fears of a mentally disturbed individual targeting public places such as schools, parking lots, and workplaces.[24] The mass shooting at Sandy Hook Elementary School in Newtown, Connecticut, epitomized the paradigm of fear.[25] Shortly after school started on December 14, 2012, Adam Lanza shot his way into the school through the plate glass panel next to the school's locked front doors.[26] Lanza, age twenty, "was undoubtedly afflicted with mental health problems," according to the people who knew him.[27] That morning, Lanza had executed his mother with four shots to the head before proceeding to the elementary school. He was heavily armed with a Bushmaster rifle, Glock 20 10-mm pistol, Sig Sauer 9-mm pistol, and many rounds of ammunition. In just eleven minutes, Lanza murdered twenty children and six adults. He then shot and killed himself.

Responding to national outcry over the violence, President Barack Obama released a plan to reduce gun violence through a package of new laws introduced in 2013.[28] The president's three-pronged approach would have (1) expanded and improved background checks of gun purchasers, (2) banned military-style assault weapons and high-capacity ammunition magazines, and (3) heightened penalties for illegal firearms trafficking while directly criminalizing the use of "straw purchasers" to buy guns for prohibited persons or purposes.[29] In addition, the president announced twenty-three executive actions to improve enforcement and data sharing regarding mental health issues and other matters.[30] The president also directed the attorney general "to review the laws governing who is prohibited from having guns and make legislative and executive recommendations to ensure dangerous people aren't slipping through the cracks."[31]

By presidential memorandum, Obama also lifted the freeze on funding for gun violence research that had impoverished the gun debate of data.[32] The freeze had been in place since 1996, when Congress eliminated gun violence research funds from the budget of the Centers for

Disease Control and Prevention (CDC) and added a rider that "none of the funds made available for injury prevention and control at the Centers for Disease Control and Prevention may be used to advocate or promote gun control."[33] While the scope of the congressional limitation was unclear, funding for gun violence research was effectively eliminated because funding officials would not risk losing their jobs or budgets by testing the freeze's limits.[34] President Obama's presidential memorandum directed the CDC to fund gun violence research, thereby removing some of the risk and doubt while providing cover to open up funding.[35]

Change by executive action is swifter and surer than change by seeking new laws—especially in the firearms context. Firearms regulation is a perilous area for legislators to venture into because of deep cultural conflicts over the scope and meaning of the right to bear arms.[36] A gun is a powerful shape-shifting metaphor in the patchwork of American cultures—a symbol of self-defense, self-sufficiency, empowerment, and virility as well as an implement of mass violence, death, mortal threat, and danger.[37] Whether firearms regulation prevents violence or hinders people in self-protection is also fiercely debated on the rhetorical, anecdotal, and sometimes (despite the deprivation of research funding) empirical level.[38]

The scope of permissible regulation in light of the Second Amendment's guarantee of the right to bear arms is also contested and was narrowed after the Supreme Court's decisions in *McDonald v. City of Chicago* and *District of Columbia v. Heller*.[39] Addressing the more extreme pole of firearms restrictions, *McDonald* and *Heller* invalidated near-absolute bans on handgun possession.[40] As with other constitutional rights, however, the Second Amendment is not absolute.[41] The Supreme Court emphasized that the decisions did not put in doubt "longstanding prohibitions on the possession of firearms by felons and the mentally ill, or laws forbidding the carrying of firearms in sensitive places such as schools and government buildings, or laws imposing conditions and qualifications on the commercial sale of arms."[42]

Because gun control opponents tend to be rugged individualists who value self-sufficiency and oppose government interference, attempts to enact federal firearms restrictions are particularly fractious.[43] An example comes from one of the last major federal firearms restrictions enacted, the aging 1993 Brady Bill.[44] The Brady Bill requires background checks on gun purchasers from commercial sellers, who must be federally licensed.[45] The NRA and other gun control opponents waged a fierce campaign to punish legislators who voted in favor of the Brady Bill, ultimately shifting the balance of power in Congress from Democratic control to Republican.[46] Because of such intense political difficulties, much of the action in experimenting with firearms restrictions in recent years has been piecemeal at the state level, despite the need for data sharing and uniformity to improve screens for the dangerous.[47]

After Newtown, however, numerous firearms bills implementing the president's three-pronged plan were introduced in Congress.[48] One piece of legislation introduced would extend the Brady Bill's background check requirement to gun shows and private, as well as commercial, gun sellers, thus closing a major gap in screening purchasers.[49] Another bill heightened penalties for using "straw purchasers" to illegally buy firearms for prohibited persons, such as felons, or for prohibited purposes, such as to commit drug-trafficking crimes.[50] The legislation that sparked the most debate was an attempt to ban the sale, manufacturing, and importation of military-style assault weapons and large-capacity ammunition magazines, with exceptions for weapons used by military or law enforcement officials.[51] An earlier law, enacted around the time of the Brady Bill, had imposed a partial assault weapons ban, but the law sunset without renewal in 2004.[52]

The bill's cosponsor, Senator Carl Levin spoke about shootings in malls, movie theaters, and schools, urging, "We must not wait for the next madman to easily and legally purchase a military-style assault weapon and a high-capacity magazine."[53] Introducing the assault weapons bill on the Senate floor, Senator Feinstein invoked the memory of the mass shootings in schools and movie theaters, stating, "Let me say it as plainly as I can: weapons of war do not belong on our streets, in our schools, in our malls, in our theaters, or in our workplaces. We know the common denominator in these deadly massacres and these daily shootings: easy access to killing machines designed for the battlefield."[54]

Speaking for opponents, Senator Ted Cruz rebutted that the assault weapons legislation merely banned "scary-looking guns" and was "ineffective show legislation—sound and fury signifying nothing."[55] Senator Cruz stated that the focus should be on enforcing existing laws to keep guns out of the hands of the dangerous—violent criminals and individuals with dangerous mental illnesses.[56] Similarly, another opponent of the proposed firearms restrictions, Representative Mike Rogers, argued that the better discussion should be, "How do we target people with mental illness who use firearms?"[57]

Despite the deep fracture over whether new gun restriction laws are needed, what is striking is the common paradigm of danger in the debates—a heavily armed, mentally ill individual stalking public places. When evaluating risks and danger, people tend to focus on emotion-laden salient events.[58] By focusing on the salient rather than prevalent risks, regulatory strategies become framed around the high-horror event rather than harms that are more likely to occur.[59] This is a particular challenge when it comes to firearms-violence prevention law and policy because reform efforts are often jolted into action by gripping horror stories.[60] The deep divide over firearms regulation intensifies this effect, driving reformers to use emotionally resonant imagery to try to build a coalition for reform.[61]

This focus on the salient rather than prevalent source of danger may lead to blind spots and missed opportunities for more achievable firearms-violence prevention. Addressing these blind spots, the next section presents data on risk factors for firearms violence in general, and for the extraordinary violence of homicide-suicides in particular. Understanding the risk factors can help identify dangers that current and proposed regulations miss. The sections following show that potentially dangerous actors slip through legal screens because a substantial amount of violence that would trigger restrictions if adjudicated never makes it into the legal system.

III. To Prevent Extraordinary Violence, Focus on "Ordinary" Violence

To effectively address firearms violence, it is important to understand perpetration patterns and risk factors. Until the establishment of the National Violent Death Reporting System (NVDRS) in 2003, an accurate national picture of the context of firearms violence was difficult to attain because the U.S. lacked a national violent death surveillance system.[62] In public health parlance, "surveillance" means systematic aggregation and dissemination of timely data to people charged with protecting the nation's health and safety.[63] While the NVDRS does not yet cover the entire United States, its approach of mining official reports from contributing states is still a major advance.[64] Recognizing the need for data-guided violence prevention efforts, the NVDRS compiles information from death certificates, medical examiner or coroner records, law enforcement records, and crime laboratory records in participating states.[65]

The collection of data permits a closer look at the circumstances surrounding violent death, such as place of death and victim-perpetrator relationship. This enables the identification of risk factors to improve the aim and focus of law and policy crafted in hopes of preventing firearms violence. NVDRS data can also be supplemented with information from the FBI's Uniform Crime Reports (UCR) and the CDC's Web-Based Injury Statistics Query and Reporting System (WISQARS).[66] FBI data come from more than 18,000 law enforcement agencies voluntarily participating in the crime-reporting program.[67] WISQARS fatal-injury data come from death certificates reported to the National Vital Statistics System.[68] WISQARS nonfatal-injury data come from reports by U.S. hospitals and emergency departments submitted to the National Electronic Injury Surveillance System.[69] Both data sources have the advantage of national coverage but the disadvantage of less finely grained detail than data offered through the NVDRS. The richest nationally based source of data is the FBI's National Incident-Based Reporting System, which includes information on victim-offender relationships and crime locations by crime category, albeit not by weapon type.[70] The sections below present data from the NVDRS contextualizing firearms violence, supplemented with WISQARS and FBI data.

A. Firearms Violence at Home, among Family and Friends

While recent firearms-restrictions legislation and debates have focused on violence from deranged strangers hunting in public, NVDRS data reveal that firearms homicides tend to take place at home, among friends and family. Table 11.1 presents data on the victim-perpetrator relationship in firearms homicides for the most recently available four years, 2011 through 2014, from the eighteen NVDRS states with publicly available data.[71] The victim-perpetrator relationship data were derived

TABLE 11.1. Victim-perpetrator relationship, firearms homicides, seventeen NVDRS states, 2011–2014

	Count	Percent (%) of N with Specified Category*
Perpetrator known to victim (family, intimate, friend, acquaintance)	3,238	79%
Family or intimate	1,858	45%
Spouse or other intimate partner	1,153	28%
Parent or child	348	9%
Other relative or intimate partner of other relative	357	9%
Acquaintance or friend	1,380	34%
Rival gang member	101	2%
Stranger	777	19%
Other or unknown	4,175	
Total categorized**	8,291	
Total with specified category (excluding other, unknown)	4,116	

* The denominator for the percentage is the 4,116 deaths with a specified category, excluding other, unknown, and uncategorized. Relationships are listed as unknown or not categorized if the suspected perpetrator relationship is not listed in the reports, investigations are pending, or due to differences in data-reporting practices.
** While the total number of firearms homicides was 11,952 for this time period and sample of states, the total categorized by victim-perpetrator relationship is a subset, 8,291. While death due to law enforcement is a category, no data are supplied for this category in the NVDRS public portal.

from examining all cases with known circumstances of homicide by each perpetrator relationship type, and in combination.

As summarized in Table 11.1, killings by family, intimates, friends, or acquaintances accounted for at least 79% of all the firearms homicides in the seventeen NVDRS states for which victim-perpetrator relationship was specifically categorized. More than a quarter of the cases with known specified victim-perpetrator relationships involve spouse or intimate partner perpetrators.

Table 11.2 presents data on the place of firearms homicide by all relationship types based on NVDRS data. As summarized below, half of all firearms-related homicides between 2011 and 2014 in the seventeen NVDRS states occurred in the home. Indeed, the adage "home is where the violence is"[72] proves to be true among violent crime cases generally. National FBI data show that 55% of all homicides in 2014 occurred in a home or residence.[73] Among assaults, 63% occurred in a home or

TABLE 11.2. Place of firearms homicides, seventeen NVDRS states, 2011–2014

	Count	Percent (%) of Total Categorized
Home/curtilage*	5,780	50%
Highway, street, road	2,765	24%
Other transportation†	1,156	10%
Recreational/cultural/public building or area	117	1%
Commercial area	945	8%
Natural area/countryside	208	2%
Other‡	215	2%
Unknown	402	3%
Total Categorized	11,588§	100%

* Includes house or apartment and the curtilage (driveway, porch, or yard) as well as the interior of the home
† Includes the interior of motor vehicles
‡ Other specified place, including school, sports fields, or athletics arena
§ The total number of deaths is 11,952, but the categorized deaths total to 11,588 because some places were not categorized and the numbers of deaths in residential institutions, including a shelter or prison, were suppressed because they are fewer than ten.

residence.[74] Among sex offenses, forcible and nonforcible, 71% occurred in a home or residence.[75]

Nationally, firearms were used in about 68% of all homicides between 2010 and 2014.[76] While much debate has centered on military-style assault weapons, the main type of firearm used in homicide between 2010 and 2014 was the less lurid but nonetheless deadly handgun.[77] Among firearms homicides, 70% of the killings were committed using a handgun.[78] Most often, homicide by firearm occurs in the context of an argument.[79]

The data and discussion presented thus far have focused on firearms-related violence generally. As discussed in section II, a motivating concern in the recent spate of firearms legislation has been a particular form of extraordinary firearms violence—mass killings, often by a homicidal-suicidal perpetrator.[80] The NVDRS provides an even closer look at the risk factors for homicide-suicides, one form of extraordinary violence, because data on the history of persons who commit suicide are also collected. Even when it comes to the extraordinary violence of homicide-suicides, a major red flag is seemingly mundane "ordinary" violence. Many of these altercations never make it into the criminal justice system, thus evading existing screens for removing firearms from people convicted of certain offenses.

B. Rare but Devastating Harm: Homicide-Suicide

Newtown, Navy Yard, Virginia Tech, Santa Monica College—these site names that turned into shorthand for mass killings share a commonality. All of these mass shootings and many other mass killings that have shocked the nation into concern over firearms violence prevention involve homicide-suicides.[81] Homicide-suicides strike particular fear because criminal law's traditional artillery for deterring crime, such as higher penalties for causing more harm, are immaterial to someone who plans on dying after killing others.[82] Perpetrators who kill multiple people rather than one expose themselves to heavier penalties, including the death penalty, in many jurisdictions.[83] But someone who thinks he will die tomorrow only goes out in a greater blaze of fame and glory—a motivation among many rampage shooters—if more people are killed.[84]

Despite salient events that may lead to overestimation of probability, homicide-suicide rates have been low and generally stable over time.[85] Estimates of homicide-suicide prevalence in the United States vary, ranging from 0.2 per 100,000 up to 0.5 per 100,000 of the population.[86] In the United States, homicide-suicides constitute about 5–6% of homicides.[87] Homicide-suicides claim an estimated 1,000 to 1,500 American lives per year, averaging about twenty to thirty violent deaths per week.[88] The homicide-suicide mortality figure is similar to the numbers of American lives lost due to afflictions such as tuberculosis, viral hepatitis, Hodgkin's lymphoma, influenza, or meningitis.[89]

The incidence rates seem to suggest that homicide-suicide is a relatively rare, aberrant event. Yet the impact of homicide-suicides has been devastating for communities and individuals with long-term traumatic effects.[90] Homicide-suicides are more likely than general homicides to involve multiple victims.[91] Firearms are even more likely to be used in homicide-suicides than homicides in general—89% compared to 65%, according to one estimate.[92] The United States—which provides ready availability to firearms—has higher homicide-suicide rates than peer countries such as England and Wales, the Netherlands, and Switzerland.[93]

While research into the treatment of diseases with similar mortality rates as homicide-suicides is advanced, homicide-suicide prevention research remains in the earlier stage of assessing the scope of the problem.[94] What is known from homicide-suicide research to date is that this extreme form of violence particularly impacts women and children.[95] In contrast, homicides generally disproportionately impact adult men because of the predominance of male-on-male violence resulting in homicide.[96] The vast majority of homicide-suicides are "family affairs" involving killings of family members.[97] Studies indicate that 42–69% of homicide-suicides involve intimate partners, 18–47% involve familicide or filicide, and 12–26% involve extrafamilial homicide.[98] Thus, like firearms violence generally, most homicide-suicides are perpetrated by family and intimates.

Prior studies have found that intimate-partner conflict and domestic violence history are major risk factors for homicide-suicides.[99] Several studies indicate that the typical perpetrator of homicide-suicide is male, married, and a domestic abuser.[100] Even perpetrators of homicide-suicides involving nonpartners frequently had a history of intimate-partner conflicts.[101] A woman ending a relationship with a man may be at heightened risk for being the victim of a homicide-suicide by her former partner.[102] These conclusions are consistent with studies finding separation to be a risk factor for lethal violence, and a heightened risk of violence among separated women.[103] Studies have posited that pathological possessiveness and proprietariness, particularly over a woman attempting to leave, may give rise to the extraordinary violence of homicide-suicide.[104]

Existing federal law already prohibits the possession of firearms by individuals convicted of domestic violence or under a restraining order protecting an intimate partner or child.[105] The 1996 Lautenberg Amendment added the specific prohibition on individuals convicted of a state or federal domestic violence misdemeanor from possessing firearms.[106] In addition, many state laws also have similar or broader prohibitions on firearms possession by individuals convicted of domestic violence offenses or under a permanent restraining order.[107]

The nation has democratically agreed that batterers should not be armed because of the risk of escalation of violence to homicide. So what is the problem? The next subsection examines recent NVDRS data regarding the prior history of perpetrators of homicide-suicides to assess why high-risk persons may be slipping through the system's screens.

C. Unadjudicated Violence: Risks Current Legal Screens Miss

To explore risk factors, this chapter examines homicide-suicide data from NVDRS states from 2005 onward. The time period from 2005 onward was chosen because the last major survey of NVDRS homicide-suicide data was for the years 2003 through 2005.[108] Table 11.3 shows that from 2005 to 2011 in these states, between 50% and 85% of persons suspected of a recent homicide-suicide had perpetrated interpersonal violence in the past month before escalating to their final killing. The proportion with a documented past history of interpersonal violence has apparently declined over the period. This is a heartening potential trend to investigate further, particularly in conjunction with the spread of domestic violence interventions.[109]

Even with the decline over time, a substantial proportion of perpetrators still have a known history of interpersonal violence—half of the homicide-suicide perpetrators in 2011. Yet the rates of criminal legal

TABLE 11.3. Prevalence of interpersonal violence and legal system contacts among homicide-suicide perpetrators, NVDRS states, 2005–11

	2005	2006	2007	2008	2009	2010	2011†
Persons with known circumstances	193 97%	178 98%	182 98%	176 97%	196 94%	193 96%	207 96%
Past history of violence							
Interpersonal violence past month	164 85%	136 76%	140 77%	111 66%	112 57%	106 55%	103 50%
Legal system contacts							
Recent criminal legal problem	38 20%	37 21%	37 20%	24 14%	42 21%	38 20%	38 18%
Other legal problem	12 6%	7 4%	7 4%	10 6%	5 3%	11 6%	18 9%

Percentages will not add up to 100% because each case may have a different combination of circumstances.
† In 2011, the number of states for which data were publicly available changed from sixteen to seventeen. The increase in totals beginning in 2011 reflect the additional state(s), rather than a sudden jump.

system contacts are much lower, at between 14% and 21% during the same time period. The data suggest that red-flag violence is slipping through the cracks—coming to light too late during police investigations or coroners' inquests into a death that might have been prevented.

Table 11.4 summarizes perpetrator problem histories. Between 69% and 81% of homicide-suicide perpetrators had a history of intimate partner problems. In contrast, far fewer had a history of job, financial, other relationship, school, or physical health problems. As for mental health issues, strikingly few of the homicide-suicide perpetrators had ever been treated for a mental problem or had a current mental health problem. Table 11.5 summarizes known mental health circumstances of perpetrators. Only a small fraction of the perpetrators had ever been treated for mental health

TABLE 11.4. History of problems by type and percentage among homicide-suicide perpetrators, sixteen NVDRS states, 2005–14

	2005	2006	2007	2008	2009	2010	2011	2012†	2013†	2014†
N with known circumstances	193 97%	178 98%	182 98%	176 97%	196 94%	193 96%	207 96%	210 95%	216 96%	219 99%
Intimate partner problem	156 81%	124 70%	144 79%	125 71%	140 71%	137 71%	159 77%	148 70%	167 77%	152 69%
Crisis in two weeks before killing	169 88%	153 86%	163 90%	142 81%	150 77%	140 73%	142 69%	125 60%	144 67%	155 71%
Other relationship problem	19 10%	20 11%	24 13%	29 16%	21 11%	32 17%	30 14%	16 8%	10 5%	5 2%
Job problem	11 6%	10 6%	6 3%	14 8%	8 4%	12 6%	22 11%	9 4%	7 3%	8 4%
Financial problem	18 9%	17 10%	7 4%	15 9%	20 10%	18 9%	17 8%	9 4%	11 5%	14 6%
School problem	0 0%	0 0%	1 0.5%	0 0%	0 0%	0 0%	0 0%	0 0%	1 0.5%	0 0%
Physical health problem	19 10%	8 4%	12 7%	6 3%	16 8%	14 7%	16 8%	16 8%	21 10%	17 8%

Percentages will not add up to 100% because each case may have a different combination of circumstances.
† In 2011, the number of states for which data were publicly available changed from sixteen to seventeen and in 2014 it changed to eighteen. The increase in totals beginning in 2011 reflects the additional state(s), rather than a sudden jump.

TABLE 11.5. Mental health history of homicide-suicide perpetrators, sixteen NVDRS states, 2005–14

	2005	2006	2007	2008	2009	2010	2011	2012†	2013†	2014†
N, known circumstances	193 97%	178 98%	182 98%	176 97%	196 94%	193 96%	207 96%	210 95%	216 96%	219 99%
Current depressed mood	32 17%	23 13%	15 8%	25 14%	20 10%	27 14%	33 16%	25 12%	28 13%	30 14%
Current mental health problem	28 15%	9 5%	13 7%	28 16%	27 14%	29 15%	32 15%	19 9%	45 21%	36 16%
Current treatment for mental illness	20 10%	7 4%	7 4%	19 11%	18 9%	24 12%	22 11%	13 6%	32 15%	16 7%
Ever treated mental problem	24 12%	9 5%	13 7%	25 14%	23 12%	29 15%	27 13%	20 10%	40 19%	22 10%
Disclosed suicidal intent	32 17%	22 12%	10 5%	15 9%	22 11%	22 11%	31 15%	26 12%	24 11%	22 10%
Suicide attempt history	8 4%	5 3%	3 2%	4 2%	5 3%	5 3%	17 8%	4 2%	7 3%	4 2%
Alcohol dependent	8 4%	5 3%	9 5%	11 6%	15 8%	15 8%	19 9%	10 5%	17 8%	17 8%
Other substance problems	12 6%	9 5%	16 9%	11 6%	12 6%	18 9%	21 10%	16 8%	19 9%	20 9%

Percentages will not add up to 100% because each case may have a different combination of circumstances.
† In 2011, the number of states for which data were publicly available changed from sixteen to seventeen and in 2014 it changed to eighteen. The increase in totals beginning in 2011 reflects the additional state(s), rather than a sudden jump.

illness—ranging from 5% to 19% of the homicide-suicide perpetrators each year. Only a similarly small proportion of perpetrators were known to have had a current mental health problem. If mental health problems were used as the definition of the dangerous, the data indicate the criterion would miss the vast majority of perpetrators who escalate to homicide-suicide. Of course, mental health issues may fester unidentified in some cases. This low prevalence of a known history of mental health issues in homicide-suicide perpetrators is precisely why mental health issues are a substantially less suitable screen for the dangerous than the much more prevalent known circumstance of perpetration of interpersonal violence.

In sum, the data on perpetrator history summarized in Tables 11.3 through 11.5 above suggest that the perpetration of interpersonal violence and intimate partner relationship problems are major risk factors among homicide-suicide perpetrators. As discussed in section III.B, existing federal and state laws already reflect the democratic decision to disarm high-risk perpetrators of intimate partner violence. As the data on perpetrator history reveal, the problem is that a substantial number of perpetrators who committed interpersonal violence in the month before escalating to homicide-suicide had apparently not entered into the criminal legal system. Without a conviction or at least a protection order, potentially dangerous individuals evade legal screens meant to disarm the dangerous.

IV. Preventing Firearms Violence through Scene-of-the-Assault Procedure

The drive for new laws has proved difficult—even perilous. Attempts to pass federal legislation have faltered in Congress after fierce campaigns with influential interventions by the National Rifle Association (NRA).[110] Many state efforts have also stalled—and backlash has led to loosening firearms restrictions in several states.[111] Moreover, the majority of Americans have preferred stricter enforcement of existing laws rather than passing new gun laws—even when support for passing new gun laws spiked to a record high of 47% after Newtown.[112] Thus, this proposal focuses on executive action steering enforcement discretion at the scene of an assault rather than enacting more laws.

Despite revolutionary reforms to try to improve responses to assaults within the family in recent decades, many cases never proceed because of underreporting and victim reluctance.[113] Policies that mandate proceeding even if victims refuse to cooperate have proved immensely controversial, beset with allegations of coercing victims and exposing them to more violence.[114] In many cases, the only chance law enforcement has to intervene in a case of assault by someone familiar to the victim is when responding to an emergency call to stop the immediate assault.

There is a strong body of scholarship on how to improve procedures for disarming batterers after a legal system intervention, such as the issuance of a protective order or a criminal conviction.[115] But what happens if a perpetrator of interpersonal violence never makes it into the legal system, as the data presented in section III revealed is a problem among those who escalate to homicide-suicide? The best alternative intervention point is during the police response to the emergency call.

But what should police do? At least eighteen states allow police to confiscate firearms at the scene of a domestic violence assault.[116] Several of the laws use mandatory rather than permissive language requiring police to confiscate firearms.[117] The idea seems excellent. Unfortunately, however, studies evaluating the impact of such confiscation laws on homicide rates have generally found no statistically significant impact.[118] Whether this lack of effect is due to low enforcement or other reasons is not known.[119]

Worse, a leading study found that the existence of a confiscation law is associated with higher assault and burglary rates.[120] This finding raises the concern that the confiscation of weapons at the scene leads batterers to retaliate through nonlethal violence.[121] The available evidence suggests that, though confiscation-at-the-scene laws seem like a compelling approach, such laws may bring more pain without reducing firearms homicide rates.

More promisingly, studies have found that laws disarming batterers under criminal restraining orders have a significant impact in reducing intimate partner homicides.[122] Obtaining a civil protection order also substantially reduces the risk of future violence.[123] Obtaining a restraining order and then securing weapons removal based on the order has the advantage of imposing a legally mandated distance between perpetrator and victim before the weapons are removed. This is a safer approach than confiscating weapons at the scene while leaving the enraged perpetrator—freshly bereft of expensive property—in proximity to the target of violence.

Because a protective order proceeding is civil rather than criminal, there is a lesser standard of proof and process, thus exacting less of a toll on victims.[124] Still, many people experiencing intimate partner violence do not obtain a protective order: surveys have found that only between 17% and 34% of people experiencing intimate partner violence obtained a protective order.[125] Many victims of assault who call police to stop the immediate violence do not go on to access social services available to abuse victims.[126] Reasons for not seeking further help and protective orders include fear of retaliation for going to court to get a protective order, lack of resources to secure an order, mistrust of the justice system, and a misperception regarding the effectiveness of protection orders.[127]

Among those who do seek a protection order, advice from police about this potential avenue of protection plays an important role in enabling help-seeking.[128] For many people subject to violence within the home, an officer intervening to stop the immediate violence during an emergency call may be the only opportunity for exposure to outside counsel. Thus, police can play a crucial role in dispensing information about protection orders. Systematizing police advice to assault victims regarding how to obtain a protection order may bring more potentially dangerous individuals to the attention of legal screens for firearms possession. Police officers can also play an important role in informing potentially at-risk victims about the availability of protective orders and provide information about community resources to help people through the process.

V. Conclusion

One in five Americans polled by the Kaiser Health Tracking Poll reported knowing someone who fell victim to gun violence—often a close loved one.[129] Four in ten Americans expressed at least some worry about being affected by gun violence personally.[130] Since 2013, after the mass slaughter of school children and teachers in Newtown, more than 1,500 gun bills have been introduced in Congress and state legislatures.[131]

The high-horror events that jolted the nation to address firearms violence may misguide the focus of attention, however, because of the tendency to emphasize the salient and overlook the prevalent. The paradigm of the dangerous in public opinion and legislative proposals is the heavily armed, mentally disordered stranger hunting in public. Yet as the data presented in section III showed, there was a low prevalence of known mental issues among perpetrators of homicide-suicides. Mental health problems may have been festering but went unidentified. This means that using mental health problems as the key criterion for discerning the potentially dangerous would miss the majority of those at risk for committing homicide-suicides.

Instead, the main risk factors for both firearms homicides generally and extraordinary homicidal-suicidal violence feared by the public involve seemingly mundane violence at home and among people who know one another. Examining the history of perpetrators who escalate to extraordinary violence reveals that early warning signs often involve interpersonal violence. In many cases, such incidents of violence are never addressed in the legal system, thereby evading existing firearms restrictions triggered by adjudication. This chapter proffers a proposal focused on scene-of-the-assault procedure that can be achieved through police policy regardless of whether new laws survive the formidable gauntlet for adding new firearms restrictions.

Author's Note

This chapter was adapted, with permission and updates, from *Disarming the Dangerous: Preventing Extraordinary and Ordinary Violence*, 90 IND. L.J. 151 (2015).

NOTES

1 *See* 18 U.S.C. § 922(g)(1), (8)–(9) (2012) (forbidding firearms possession by felons, persons convicted of domestic violence misdemeanors, or persons subject to restraining orders for harassing, stalking, or threatening an intimate partner).

2 *See infra* section II.C and Table 11.3.

3 E.g., *From al-Shabaab to al-Nusra: How Westerners Joining Terror Groups Overseas Affect the Homeland: Hearing Before the H. Comm. on Homeland Sec.*, 113th Cong. 38 (2013) (statement of Stephanie Sanok Kostro, Senior Fellow and Acting Director, Homeland Security and Counterterrorism Program, Center for Strategic and International Studies) (noting that attackers "need a soft target, such as shopping malls, theaters, concerts, sporting events, or transportation systems"); WHITE HOUSE, NOW IS THE TIME: THE PRESIDENT'S PLAN TO PROTECT OUR CHILDREN AND OUR COMMUNITIES BY REDUCING GUN VIOLENCE 2–3 (2013), https://obamawhitehouse.archives.gov (discussing galvanizing incidents in public places) [hereinafter WHITE HOUSE, GUN VIOLENCE REDUCTION PLAN].

4 *See, e.g.,* Jeffrey Fagan, *Death and Deterrence Redux: Science, Law and Causal Reasoning on Capital Punishment*, 4 OHIO ST. J. CRIM. L. 255, 277 (2006) (noting limited possibility of deterrence among murder-suicides).

5 Dan Barry, Serge Kovaleski, Alan Blinder, & Mujib Mashal, *From Troubled Child to Aggrieved Killer*, N.Y. TIMES (June 19, 2016), at A1.

6 Adam Nagourney, Ian Lovett, & Richard Pérez-Peña, *Shooting Rampage Sows Terror in California*, N.Y. TIMES (Dec. 3, 2015), at A1.

7   Nick Corasaniti, Richard Pérez-Peña, & Lizette Alvarez, *Charleston Massacre Suspect Held as City Grieves*, N.Y. TIMES (June 19, 2015), at A1.

8   James Barron, *Gunman Massacres 20 Children at School in Connecticut; 28 Dead, Including Killer*, N.Y. TIMES (Dec. 15, 2012), at A1.

9   *See, e.g.*, Bonnie Berkowitz et al., *The Math of Mass Shootings*, WASH. POST (Jan. 8, 2017), www.washingtonpost.com (noting that of the 129 deadliest mass shootings evaluated, more than half of the shooters "died at or near the scene of the shooting, often by killing themselves").

10 Marieke Liem et al., *Homicide-Suicide and Other Violent Deaths: An International Comparison*, 207 FORENSIC SCI. INT'L 70, 70–71 (2011).

11 Yekeen A. Aderibigbe, *Violence in America: A Survey of Suicide Linked to Homicides*, 42 J. FORENSIC SCI. 662, 663 (1997). *Compare* Craig Campanelli & Thomas Gilson, *Murder-Suicide in New Hampshire, 1995–2000*, 23 AM. J. FORENSIC MED. & PATHOLOGY 248, 248–49 (2002) (up to one week), *with* Donna Cohen, Maria Llorente, & Carl Eisdorfer, *Homicide-Suicide in Older Persons*, 155 AM. J. PSYCHIATRY 390 (1998) (within twenty-four hours).

12 Dee Wood Harper & Lydia Voigt, *Homicide Followed by Suicide: An Integrated Theoretical Perspective*, 11 HOMICIDE STUD. 295 (2016); Kris Mohandie, J. Reid Meloy, & Peter I. Collins, *Suicide by Cop among Officer-Involved Shooting Cases*, J. FORENSIC SCI. 456 (2009).

13 *See* Fagan, *supra* note 4 and accompanying text.

14 September 11—another homicide-suicide—has a similar economy of meaning in our national vocabulary. The Orlando nightclub shooter Omar Mateen was shot by SWAT officers as he exited the building but there is evidence he had prepared for death before the rampage. This is thus classified as a form of "suicide by cop."

15 *See, e.g.*, 159 CONG. REC. S6496 (daily ed. Sept. 17, 2013) (statement of Sen. Richard Blumenthal) ("Let us make a mental health initiative a centerpiece of this renewal and reinvigoration of our effort to stop gun violence."); 159 CONG. REC. S288–89 (daily ed. Jan. 24, 2013) (statement of Sen. Feinstein) ("The one common thread running through all of these shootings is that the gunman used a semiautomatic assault weapon or large capacity ammunition magazine or drum.").

16 *E.g.*, Fix Gun Checks Act of 2013, S. 374, 113th Cong. (2013) (expanding background check requirement to private sellers); Gun Trafficking Prevention Act of 2013, S. 179, 113th Cong. (2013) (criminalizing sale of firearms for prohibited purposes); Assault Weapons Ban of 2013, H.R. 437, 113th Cong. (2013) (prohibiting the importation, sale, manufacture, transfer, or possession of a semiautomatic assault weapon or large-capacity ammunition-feeding device); Assault Weapons Ban of 2013, S. 150, 113th Cong. (2013) (prohibiting the importation, sale, manufacturing, transfer, or possession of semiautomatic assault weapons or large-capacity ammunition-feeding devices); Stop Illegal Trafficking in Firearms Act of 2013, S. 54, 113th Cong. (2013) (directly criminalizing straw purchases of firearms for prohibited persons or activities); Fix Gun Checks Act of 2013, H.R. 137, 113th Cong. (2013) (expanding background checks to cover sales by private actors).

17 *E.g.,* CAL. WELF. & INST. CODE §§ 8100, 8105 (West 2014) (requiring psycho-therapists to report credible violent threats and extending the prohibition on firearms ownership by persons making such threats to five years); N.Y. CRIM. PROC. LAW §§ 330.20, 380.96 (McKinney 2014) (adding procedures restricting firearms possession by mentally ill individuals and the certain criminally convicted individuals); TEX. HEALTH & SAFETY CODE ANN. § 573.001 (West 2014) (providing for firearms seizures from the mentally ill). For an overview of the laws passed in the states since Newtown, see *State Gun Laws Enacted in the Year Since Newtown,* N.Y. TIMES (Dec. 10, 2013), www.nytimes.com [hereinafter *State Gun Laws Report*].

18 *Poll on Factors To Blame in Mass Shootings,* GALLUP (Sept. 17–18, 2013), www.gallup.com.

19 *See, e.g.,* S. REP. NO. 103-108, at 37–38 (1993) (discussing reluctance to intervene in violence within the home); S. REP. NO. 102-197, at 35–46 (1991) (summarizing testimony on trivialization of violence within the home); S. REP. NO. 101-545, at 31–34 (1990) (documenting problems with neglect of familial violence). For an excellent history of normalization of the violence, *see, e.g.,* Reva Siegel, *"The Rule of Love": Wife Beating as Prerogative and Privacy,* 105 YALE L.J. 2117, 2150–205 (1996).

20 For the data, see *infra* Table 11.2.

21 For the data, see *infra* Table 11.1.

22 For an account of the pitched warfare over attempts to regulate firearms, *see, e.g.,* Philip J. Cook, *The Great American Gun War: Notes from Four Decades in the Trenches,* 42 CRIME & JUST. 19, 27–28 (2013). For a history, *see, e.g.,* ADAM WINKLER, GUNFIGHT: THE BATTLE OVER THE RIGHT TO BEAR ARMS IN AMERICA 253–58 (2011).

23 *See, e.g.,* 159 CONG. REC. S291 (daily ed. Jan. 24, 2013) (statement of Sen. Dianne Feinstein) ("Do we let the gun industry take over and dictate policy to this country?"); Robert Draper, *Inside the Power of the N.R.A.,* N.Y. TIMES MAG. 48 (Dec. 12, 2013) (discussing the NRA's role in blocking firearms legislation despite national momentum after mass shootings); see also *Americans Wanted Gun Background Checks To Pass Senate,* GALLUP (Apr. 29, 2013), www.gallup.com (showing that 65% of Americans polled supported the universal background checks measure); *Poll on Public Opinion Regarding Strictness of Gun Laws,* GALLUP (Dec. 19–22, 2012), www.gallup.com (finding a sharp, albeit ultimately temporary, spike in support for strict gun laws after the Newtown killings).

24 *See, e.g.,* 159 CONG. REC. S288–91 (daily ed. Jan. 24, 2013) (statement of Sen. Dianne Feinstein) (invoking memory of mass shootings at Sandy Hook; Aurora, Colorado; Virginia Tech; and Tucson, Arizona, in presenting assault-weapons ban bill).

25 Philip Rucker & Sari Horwitz, *Newtown Seen as "Tipping Point" for the President,* WASH. POST (Dec. 24, 2012), at A1.

26 STATE OF CONN., DIV. OF CRIMINAL JUSTICE, REPORT OF THE STATE'S ATTORNEY FOR THE JUDICIAL DISTRICT OF DANBURY ON THE SHOOT-INGS AT SANDY HOOK ELEMENTARY SCHOOL AND 36 YOGANANDA STREET, NEWTOWN, CONNECTICUT ON DECEMBER 14, 2012, at 5, 9 (2013).

27 *Id.* at 29.

28 WHITE HOUSE, GUN VIOLENCE REDUCTION PLAN, *supra* note 3; *see also* Fix Gun Checks Act of 2013, S. 374, 113th Cong. (2013) (expanding background checks requirement to private sellers); Gun Trafficking Prevention Act of 2013, S. 179, 113th Cong. (2013) (criminalizing sale of firearms for prohibited purposes); Assault Weapons Ban of 2013, H.R. 437, 113th Cong. (2013) (prohibiting the importation, sale, manufacture, transfer, or possession of a semiautomatic assault weapon or large-capacity ammunition-feeding device); Assault Weapons Ban of 2013, S. 150, 113th Cong. (2013) (prohibiting the importation, sale, manufacturing, transfer, or possession of semiautomatic assault weapons or large-capacity ammunition-feeding devices); Stop Illegal Trafficking in Firearms Act of 2013, S. 54, 113th Cong. (2013) (directly criminalizing straw purchases of firearms for prohibited persons or activities); Fix Gun Checks Act of 2013, H.R. 137, 113th Cong. (2013) (expanding background checks to cover sales by private actors).

29 WHITE HOUSE, GUN VIOLENCE REDUCTION PLAN, *supra* note 3, at 4–8.

30 *Id.*

31 *Id.* at 4–5.

32 Presidential Memorandum from the White House to the Secretary of Health and Human Services, Engaging in Public Health Research on the Causes and Prevention of Gun Violence, 78 Fed. Reg. 4295 (Jan. 16, 2013); *see also* WHITE HOUSE, GUN VIOLENCE REDUCTION PLAN, *supra* note 3, at 8 (discussing history of freeze); Arthur L. Kellermann & Frederick P. Rivara, *Silencing the Science on Gun Research*, 309 J. AM. MED. ASS'N 549, 549–50 (2013) (discussing research consequences of the funding freeze).

33 Department of Health and Human Services Appropriations Act, 1997, Pub. L. No. 104-208, tit. II, 110 Stat. 3009, 3009-244 (1996).

34 Kellermann & Rivara, *supra* note 32, at 549–50.

35 *See, e.g.,* Press Release, Nat'l Institute of Health, NIH Calls for Research Projects Examining Violence: Particular Consideration to Be Given to Firearm Violence (Sept. 27, 2013), www.nih.gov; *Research on the Health Determinants and Consequences of Violence and Its Prevention, Particularly Firearm Violence (R01), Funding Opportunity Announcement Number PA-13-363,* DEP'T OF HEALTH & HUMAN SERVS. (Sept. 27, 2013), http://grants.nih.gov.

36 *See, e.g.,* Dan M. Kahan, *The Cognitively Illiberal State*, 60 STAN. L REV. 115, 134–36 (2007) (discussing rifts in worldviews from a cultural cognition perspective).

37 *See, e.g.,* GARY KLECK, TARGETING GUNS: FIREARMS AND THEIR CONTROL 82–85 (1997).

38 *See, e.g.,* DAVID HEMENWAY, PRIVATE GUNS, PUBLIC HEALTH 1203–81 (2004) (discussing contested data); Ian Ayres & John J. Donohue III, *Shooting*

Down the "More Guns, Less Crime" Hypothesis, 55 STAN. L. REV. 1193, 1203–95 (2003) (summarizing controversies and empirically evaluating the "more guns, less violence" claim).

39 McDonald v. City of Chicago, 561 U.S. 742, 790-91 (2010); District of Columbia v. Heller, 554 U.S. 570, 628-29, 636 (2008).

40 McDonald, 130 S. Ct. at 3048; Heller, 554 U.S. at 626.

41 Heller, 554 U.S. at 626.

42 *Id.* at 626–27; *accord* McDonald, 130 S. Ct. at 3047 (plurality opinion).

43 Dan M. Kahan, *The Gun Control Debate: A Culture-Theory Manifesto*, 60 WASH. & LEE L. REV. 3, 6 (2003).

44 Omnibus Consolidated Appropriations Act of 1997, Pub. L. 104-208, § 658, 110 Stat. 3009, 3009-371 to 3009-372 (codified at 18 U.S.C. §§ 921–22, 925 (2012)).

45 *Id.*

46 *See* Reva B. Siegel, *Dead or Alive: Originalism as Popular Constitutionalism in Heller*, 122 HARV. L. REV. 191, 227–28 (2008) (providing history).

47 Jessica Bulman-Pozen, *Partisan Federalism*, 127 HARV. L. REV. 1077, 1128 (2014); Philip J. Cook, *The Great American Gun War: Notes from Four Decades in the Trenches*, 42 CRIME & JUST. 19, 27 (2013).

48 Fix Gun Checks Act of 2013, S. 374, 113th Cong. (2013) (expanding background checks requirement to private sellers); Gun Trafficking Prevention Act of 2013, S. 179, 113th Cong. (2013) (criminalizing sale of firearms for prohibited purposes); Assault Weapons Ban of 2013, H.R. 437, 113th Cong. (2013) (prohibiting the importation, sale, manufacture, transfer, or possession of a semiautomatic assault weapon or large-capacity ammunition-feeding device).

49 Fix Gun Checks Act of 2013, S. 374, 113th Cong. (2013); Stop Illegal Trafficking in Firearms Act of 2013, S. 54, 113th Cong. (2013); Gun Checks Act of 2013, H.R. 137, 113th Cong. (2013).

50 Gun Trafficking Prevention Act of 2013, S. 179, 113th Cong. (2013).

51 Assault Weapons Ban of 2013, S. 150, 113th Cong. (2013).

52 Violent Crime Control and Law Enforcement Act of 1994, Pub. L. No. 103-322, tit. XI, 108 Stat. 1796, 1996 (1994) (codified at 18 U.S.C. § 921–22 (1994)); *see also* 159 CONG. REC. S289 (daily ed. Jan. 24, 2013) (statement of Sen. Dianne Feinstein) (discussing criticisms of the earlier assault-weapons ban); Sheryl Gay Stolberg, *Effort To Renew Weapons Ban Falters on Hill*, N.Y. TIMES (Sept. 9, 2004), at A1 (discussing how intense lobbying by the NRA during an election year led to the demise of attempts to extend the assault weapons ban).

53 159 CONG. REC. S757–58 (daily ed. Feb. 14, 2013) (statement of Sen. Carl Levin).

54 159 CONG. REC. S288–91 (daily ed. Jan. 24, 2013) (statement of Sen. Dianne Feinstein).

55 *What Should America Do About Gun Violence?: Hearing Before the S. Comm. on the Judiciary*, 113th Cong, ¶ 5 (2013) (statement of Sen. Ted Cruz, Member, S. Comm. on the Judiciary), http://judiciary.senate.gov.

56 *Id.*

57 Richard A. Friedman, *In Gun Debate, a Misguided Focus on Mental Illness*, N.Y. TIMES (Dec. 18, 2012), at D5.

58 *See, e.g.*, Paul Slovic et al., *Risk as Analysis and Risk as Feelings: Some Thoughts About Affect, Reason, Risk, and Rationality*, 24 RISK ANALYSIS 311 (2004).

59 Cass R. Sunstein, *Probability Neglect: Emotions, Worst Cases, and Law*, 112 YALE L.J. 61, 62–70 (2002).

60 *See, e.g.*, Mary D. Fan, *Beyond Budget-Cut Criminal Justice: The Future of Penal Law*, 90 N.C. L. REV. 581, 627–30 (2012) (discussing how criminal-justice legislation is jolted by tragedies).

61 For discussions of the deep rift in cultural worldviews that polarize firearms debates, *see, e.g.*, WINKLER, *supra* note 22, at 8–14; Donald Braman & Dan M. Kahan, *Overcoming the Fear of Guns, the Fear of Gun Control, and the Fear of Cultural Politics: Constructing A Better Gun Debate*, 55 EMORY L.J. 569, 570–72, 577–87 (2006); Kahan, *supra* note 43, at 4–10.

62 Liem et al., *supra* note 10, at 70–71.

63 *See, e.g.*, Stephen B. Thacker, *Historical Development, in* PRINCIPLES AND PRACTICE OF PUBLIC HEALTH SURVEILLANCE 1, 1–8 (2d ed. 2000).

64 *See* Catherine W. Barber et al., *Suicides and Suicide Attempts Following Homicide*, 12 HOMICIDE STUD. 285, 286–87 (2008) (discussing the genesis and utility of the NVDRS).

65 L. J. Paulozzi et al., *CDC's National Violent Death Reporting System: Background and Methodology*, 10 INJURY PREVENTION 47, 49 (2004).

66 *Uniform Crime Reports*, FED. BUREAU OF INVESTIGATION, www.fbi.gov; *Injury Prevention & Control: Data & Statistics (WISQARS)*, CDC, www.cdc.gov.

67 *Uniform Crime Reports, supra* note 66.

68 *Injury Prevention & Control: Data & Statistics (WISQARS), supra* note 66.

69 *Id.*

70 *Uniform Crime Reports, supra* note 66.

71 The NVDRS currently has 42 participating states. *State by State*, NAT'L VIO-LENCE PREVENTION NETWORK, www.preventviolence.net. However, the most recently available four-year period is from 2011–2014 and includes data from eighteen states: Alaska, Colorado, Georgia, Kentucky, Maryland, Massachusetts, Michigan, New Jersey, New Mexico, North Carolina, Oklahoma, Ohio, Oregon, Rhode Island, South Carolina, Utah, Virginia, and Wisconsin.

72 JEANNINE BELL, HATE THY NEIGHBOR: MOVE-IN VIOLENCE AND THE PERSISTENCE OF RACIAL SEGREGATION IN AMERICAN HOUSING 4 (2013) (illustrating adage in the context of move-in violence).

73 *See* FED. BUREAU OF INVESTIGATION, CRIMES AGAINST PERSONS OF-FENSES BY OFFENSE CATEGORY BY LOCATION, 2014, http://ucr.fbi.gov (last visited Feb. 3, 2018) (giving offense counts; percentages are calculated from the counts).

74 *See id.*

75 *See id.*

76 See *Uniform Crime Reports, Expanded Homicide Data Table 8, Murder Victims by Weapon, 2010–2014*, FED. BUREAU OF INVESTIGATION, https://ucr.fbi.gov (last visited Feb. 3, 2018) (providing counts from which percentages are calculated).

77 *Id.*

78 *See id.* (providing counts; percentages are calculated from the counts).

79 See *Uniform Crime Reports, Expanded Homicide Data Table 11, Murder Circumstances by Weapon, 2014*, FED. BUREAU OF INVESTIGATION, https://ucr.fbi.gov (last visited Feb. 3, 2018).

80 *See supra* notes 1–12, 24 and accompanying text.

81 *Id.*

82 BRYAN VOSSEKUIL ET AL., THE FINAL REPORT AND FINDINGS OF THE SAFE SCHOOL INITIATIVE 11, 22 (2004) (noting that 78% of schoolhouse attackers studied had considered or attempted suicide).

83 *See, e.g.*, ALA. CODE § 13A-5-40(a)(10) (2005) (defining murder "wherein two or more persons are murdered by the defendant" as a capital offense); KAN. STAT. ANN. § 21–5401(6) (Supp. 2013) (defining "intentional and premeditated killing of more than one person" as a ground for capital murder); VA. CODE ANN. § 18.2-31(7) (2014) (defining the "willful, deliberate, and premeditated killing of more than one person as a part of the same act or transaction").

84 *See, e.g.*, Roger W. Byard, *Murder-Suicide*, 3 FORENSIC PATHOLOGY REV. 337, 343 (2005) (discussing "blaze-of-glory" as a type of motivation among murder-suicides); Adam Lankford & Nayab Hakim, *From Columbine to Palestine: A Comparative Analysis of Rampage Shooters in the United States and Volunteer Suicide Bombers in the Middle East*, 16 AGGRESSION & VIOLENT BEHAV. 98, 99, 105 (2011) (discussing fame and glory as a motivation among many rampage shooters).

85 Scott Eliason, *Murder-Suicide: A Review of the Recent Literature*, 37 J. AM. ACAD. PSYCHIATRY & L. 371, 371–73 (2009).

86 *E.g.*, R. M. Bossarte, T. R. Simon, & L. Barker, *Characteristics of Homicide Followed by Suicide Incidents in Multiple States, 2003–04*, 12 INJURY PREVENTION ii33, ii33, ii35 (2006) (noting prevalence estimates of between 0.2 and 0.38 per 100,000 persons annually and reporting homicide rate due to homicide-suicide of 0.238 per 100,000 persons in 2004); F. Stephen Bridges & David Lester, *Homicide-Suicide in the United States, 1968–1975*, 206 FORENSIC SCI. INT'L 185, 185–86 (2011) (noting reports of between 0.2 to 0.38 per 100,000 persons and finding 0.134 per 100,000 persons per year from 1968 to 1975); Julie E. Malphurs & Donna Cohen, *A Newspaper Surveillance Study of Homicide-Suicide in the United States*, 23 AM. J. FORENSIC MED. & PATHOLOGY 142, 142–43 (2002) (noting reports of between 0.2 to 0.3 per 100,000 persons and up to 0.4 to 0.5 per 100,000 persons).

87 Barber et al., *supra* note 64, at 286.

88 *Id.* at 285; Liem et al., *supra* note 10, at 70–71; J. Logan et al., *Characteristics of Perpetrators in Homicide-Followed-by-Suicide Incidents: National Violent Death*

Reporting System—17 US States, 2003–2005, 168 AM. J. EPIDEMIOLOGY 1056, 1056 (2008).

89 Barber et al., *supra* note 64, at 285; Liem et al., *supra* note 10, at 70–71.

90 Barber et al., *supra* note 64, at 285; Logan et al., *supra* note 88, at 1056.

91 Liem et al., *supra* note 10, at 70–75.

92 Bridges & Lester, *supra* note 86, at 186.

93 *Id.* at 186–88 (nearly double the rate of England and Wales).

94 *See, e.g.,* Aderibigbe, *supra* note 11, at 662–63 (discussing "severely limited" research on murder-suicides, in part for lack of a national surveillance system); Liem et al., *supra* note 10, at 70–71 (discussing challenges in studying homicide-suicide).

95 Liem et al., *supra* note 10, at 70–73; *accord* Bridges & Lester, *supra* note 86, at 186.

96 *See, e.g.,* Janet L. Lauritsen & Karen Heimer, *The Gender Gap in Violent Victimization, 1973–2004,* 24 J. QUANTITATIVE CRIMINOLOGY 125, 133 fig.1 (2008) (graphing disparity in violence victimization between genders).

97 Bridges & Lester, *supra* note 86, at 186–87.

98 Logan et al., *supra* note 88, at 1056.

99 Mary Cooper & Derek Eaves, *Suicide Following Homicide in the Family,* 11 VIOLENCE & VICTIMS 99 (1996); Jane Koziol-McLain et al., *Risk Factors for Femicide-Suicide in Abusive Relationships: Results from a Multisite Case Control Study,* 21 VIOLENCE & VICTIMS 3 (2006); Logan et al., *supra* note 88.

100 *E.g.,* Aderibigbe, *supra* note 11, at 663; Barber et al., *supra* note 64, at 290–92; Liem et al., *supra* note 10, at 70–76; Logan et al., *supra* note 88, at 1058–60.

101 Logan et al., *supra* note 88, at 1060, 1062.

102 Aderibigbe, *supra* note 11, at 663; Eliason, *supra* note 85, at 371–73; Koziol-McLain et al., *supra* note 99, at 8, 15 tbl.2; Peter M. Marzuk, Kenneth Tardiff, & Charles S. Hirsch, *The Epidemiology of Murder-Suicide,* 267 J. AM. MED. ASS'N 3179, 3179–80 (1992).

103 *E.g.,* Douglas A. Brownridge, *Violence Against Women Post-Separation,* 11 AGGRESSION & VIOLENT BEHAVIOR 514 (2006); Jacquelyn C. Campbell et al., *Risk Factors for Femicide in Abusive Relationships: Results from a Multi-Site Case Control Study,* 93 AM. J. PUB. HEALTH 1089 (2003); Martha R. Mahoney, *Legal Images of Battered Women: Redefining the Issue of Separation,* 90 MICH. L. REV. 1, 11, 63–64 (1991).

104 Campanelli & Gilson, *supra* note 11; Cooper & Eaves, *supra* note 99, at 99–112; M. Rosenbaum, *The Role of Depression in Couples Involved in Murder-Suicide and Homicide,* 147 AM. J. PSYCHIATRY 1036 (1990).

105 18 U.S.C. §§ 921–22, 925 (2012).

106 Pub. L. No. 104-208, § 658, 110 Stat. 3009, 3009-371 to 3009-372 (codified at 18 U.S.C. §§ 921–22, 925 (2012)). A qualifying domestic violence offense must involve use or attempted use of physical force or threatened use of a deadly weapon against an intimate partner. 18 U.S.C. § 921(a)(33) (2012).

107 For a summary, *see* April M. Zeoli et al., *Removing Firearms from Those Prohibited from Possession by Domestic Violence Restraining Orders: A Survey and Analysis of*

State Laws, TRAUMA, VIOLENCE, & ABUSE, e-publication ahead of print (Feb. 22, 2017), http://journals.sagepub.com/doi/abs/10.1177/1524838017692384.

108 Logan et al., *supra* note 88, at 1057.

109 *See, e.g.*, Virginia A. Moyer, *Screening for Intimate Partner Violence and Abuse of Elderly and Vulnerable Adults: U.S. Preventative Services Task Force Recommendation Statement*, 158 ANN. INTERN. MED. 478–86 (2013); Carla Smith Stover, Amy Lynn Meadows, & Joan Kaufman, *Interventions for Intimate Partner Violence: Review and Implications for Evidence-Based Practice*, 40 PROF'L PSYCHOL., 223–33 (2009).

110 Ed O'Keefe & Philip Rucker, *Gun-Control Overhaul Is Defeated in Senate*, WASH. POST (Apr. 17, 2013), at A1.

111 See, e.g., *State Gun Laws Report*, *supra* note 17 (reporting in the year after Newtown, seventy of the 109 state firearms laws passed—64%—loosened rather than tightened restrictions and only 36% of legislation successfully passed in the states tightened restrictions); Jack Healy, *Colorado Lawmakers Ousted in Recall Vote Over Gun Law*, N.Y. TIMES (Sept. 11, 2013), at A1 (reporting that two legislators in Colorado—site of two infamous mass shootings—who passed new firearms laws lost their jobs after a recall campaign bolstered by the NRA).

112 Lydia Saad, *Americans Want Stricter Gun Laws, Still Oppose Bans*, GALLUP (Dec. 27, 2012), www.gallup.com.

113 *See, e.g.*, David Hierschel & Ira W. Hutchison, *The Relative Effects of Offense, Offender, and Victim Variables on the Decision to Prosecute Domestic Violence Cases*, 7 VIOLENCE AGAINST WOMEN 46, 47–49, 51–55 (2001) (discussing policies to try to improve criminal-justice enforcement in the domestic-violence context and continuing barriers to prosecution, including victim reluctance to proceed).

114 *See, e.g.*, David A. Ford, *Coercing Victim Participation in Domestic Violence Prosecutions*, 18 J. INTERPERSONAL VIOLENCE 669, 669–70 (2003); Cheryl Hanna, *No Right to Choose: Mandated Victim Participation in Domestic Violence Prosecutions*, 109 HARV. L. REV. 1849, 1865–97 (2006).

115 *E.g.*, Emily J. Sack, *Confronting the Issue of Gun Seizure in Domestic Violence Cases*, 6 J. CENTER FOR FAM., CHILD. & CTS. 3 (2005); Katherine A. Vittes et al., *Removing Guns from Batterers: Findings from a Pilot Survey of Domestic Violence Restraining Order Recipients in California*, 19 VIOLENCE AGAINST WOMEN 602 (2013); Daniel W. Webster et al., *Women with Protective Orders Report Failure to Remove Firearms from their Abusive Partners: Results from an Exploratory Study*, 19 J. WOMEN'S HEALTH 93 (2010).

116 For a list of states, *see* Elizabeth Richardson Vigdor & James A. Mercy, *Do Laws Restricting Access to Firearms by Domestic Violence Offenders Prevent Intimate Partner Homicide?*, 30 EVAL. REV. 313, 318 (2006). *See, e.g.*, ARIZ. REV. STAT. § 13-3601(C) (West 2014); CAL. PENAL CODE § 13730(c)(3) (West 2014); HAW. REV. STAT. ANN. §§ 134-7.5(a) (West 2008); IND. CODE § 35-33-1-1.5(b) (West 2012).

117 *Id.*

118 *Id.* at 337; April M. Zeoli & Daniel W. Webster, *Effects of Domestic Violence Policies, Alcohol Taxes and Police Staffing Levels on Intimate Partner Homicide in Large US Cities*, 16 INJURY PREVENTION 90, 92 (2010).

119 Vigdor & Mercy, *supra* note 116, at 340.

120 *Id.* at 335.

121 *Id.*

122 *Id.* at 337; Zeoli & Webster, *supra* note 118, at 92.

123 Victoria L. Holt et al., *Civil Protection Orders and Risk of Subsequent Police-Reported Violence*, 288 J. AM. MED. ASS'N 589, 593 (2002) [hereinafter *Civil Protection Orders*]; Victoria L. Holt et al., *Do Protection Orders Affect the Likelihood of Future Partner Violence and Injury?*, 24 AM. J. PREVENTATIVE MED. 16, 18 (2003); TK Logan & Robert Walker, *Civil Protective Order Effectiveness: Justice or Just A Piece of Paper?*, 25 VIOLENCE & VICTIMS 332, 344–45 (2010).

124 TK Logan et al., *Protective Orders: Questions and Conundrums*, 7 TRAUMA VIOLENCE & ABUSE 175, 180 (2006).

125 *E.g.,* PATRICIA TJADEN & NANCY THOENNES, EXTENT, NATURE, AND CONSEQUENCES OF INTIMATE PARTNER VIOLENCE 52 (2000), www.ncjrs. gov (finding that only 17.1% of women physically assaulted by their intimate partners obtained a protection order); CDC, *Use of Medical Care, Police Assistance, and Restraining Orders by Women Reporting Intimate Partner—Massachusetts, 1996–1997*, 49 MORBIDITY & MORTALITY WKLY. REP. 485, 486 (2000) (34% of people reporting partner violence in the preceding five years obtained a protective order); *Civil Protection Orders, supra* note 123, at 593 (12% of women reporting partner violence to police received a protective order in the twelve-month follow-up period).

126 Daniel Brookoff et al., *Characteristics of Participants in Domestic Violence: Assessment at the Scene of Domestic Assault*, 277 J. AM. MED. ASS'N 1369, 1371–72 (1997).

127 Logan et al., *supra* note 124, at 185.

128 *Id.* at 180.

129 *Kaiser Health Tracking Poll*, KAISER FAMILY FOUNDATION (Feb. 27, 2013), www.kff.org.

130 *Id.*

131 *State Gun Laws Report, supra* note 17.

PART V

Moving Forward with a Critical Lens

12

Is Domestic Violence Politicized Too Narrowly?

JAMIE R. ABRAMS

This chapter explores whether domestic violence is politicized too narrowly for next generation law reforms to *end* domestic violence. First generation political framings of domestic violence—which still dominate today—achieved critical successes in bringing domestic violence into the public frame and shaping critical state interventions. Yet there are modern limits to their efficacy. First generation political framings collaterally immunized the state from accountability by paradoxically positioning the crisis of domestic violence and accountability for effective interventions squarely on victims and victim support networks. The chapter concludes that next generation law reforms should expand the politicization of domestic violence to include the larger ecosystem in which it occurs. Discussions of next generation political framings of domestic violence are a critical—albeit uncomfortable—move from *intervening* in domestic violence on behalf of victims to *ending* domestic violence.

Introduction

Imagine if domestic violence activists could reframe its politicization and present the issue for public response anew. How would this issue be framed and described? What legal solutions would be identified? Who would be accountable for effective results?

This chapter explores whether the domestic violence movement is politicized too narrowly in ways that collaterally restrain efforts to *end* domestic violence.[1] Its historic framing, which this chapter describes as its "first generation politicization," considered domestic violence to be internal to the relationship with two primary actors: the victim and the perpetrator. First generation politicization grew out of consciousness-raising, which gave powerful voice to a grave issue historically confined in the family without state intervention or response.[2] This approach positions law enforcement, social support services, and lawyers to intervene on demand, but the problem and legal responses to it are understood and defined as an internally contained unit: How can *this* victim be protected? How at risk is *this* victim for future violence? How will the perpetrator be prevented from contact with *this* victim? This political framing achieved critical law reform successes criminalizing domestic violence and setting up a network of victim support services.

Yet this chapter explores whether this enduring politicization should be broadened. Missing from the politicization of domestic violence are the ways in which interconnected factors external to the relationship also exacerbate, trigger, and facilitate domestic violence. Some examples of relevant context systemically excluded from our politicization of domestic violence are economic distress, the perpetrator's *own* history of prior abuse, job loss or dissatisfaction, bankruptcies, mental illness, larger gender inequality and cultural norms, and changes in custody/parenting status. Ignoring the larger ecosystem of domestic violence compromises the extent of state interventions, fictionalizes the family as an isolated unit separated from other political and social systems, and reveres state actors.

Domestic violence's first generation politicization presents a paradox. Victims gain autonomy by shaping law reform approaches and framing domestic violence in the public arena, but, in turn, they assume accountability for the *effectiveness* of interventions. Victim autonomy paradoxically immunizes the state and perpetrators from accountability, undermining political goals of the movement. This politicization creates insider-outsider politics that positions the victim as the insider party accountable for effective interventions and risk assessments. The state merely holds a supporting role, coming to her aid as an outsider. This framework ignores how actors in the judicial system and law enforcement might provoke or exacerbate risks of family violence. It also ignores how state actors might hold more accountability for more effective or earlier interventions. It disregards how larger systemic complexities will likely lead the perpetrator to recidivist behaviors with a new partner even if the state were able to successfully break the cycle of violence in the preceding relationship.

Women Victims Shape and Direct the Domestic Violence Movement Using Feminist Approaches

Women victims led the domestic violence movement in powerful and impactful ways. Feminists addressed the historic subordination of women by men and by the state.[3] The domestic violence movement[4] emerged uniquely from a consciousness-raising methodology iconic to the feminist movement.[5] Consciousness-raising brought women together to voice their collective experiences with domestic violence. The movement then positioned these experiences in a distinctly feminist lens as a political, social, and personal phenomenon.[6]

The movement came to name and frame the experiences of women as victims of domestic violence in the legal and political landscape.[7] Critically, the quest in the early feminist movement was to understand women's shared experiences *within* their relationships. These individual experiences were then connected to the larger women's equality project engaging the state.[8] The movement achieved unprecedented political success in making visible and defining domestic violence,[9] which reflects an additional success of feminist methodologies, but it also shaped early politicizations of domestic violence.

Eventually, the naming and framing of domestic violence moved to state interventions and law reform efforts. What began as a grassroots movement became a robust infrastructure of federal and state responses across legal, criminal, civil, mental health, and social service systems.[10] Advocates successfully constructed an expansive shelter and victims'-services model nationwide to provide safety.[11] The movement developed community education programs and secured a range of protections and services for domestic violence victims.[12]

These services have provided critical refuge and support, yet services for victims are still in grave need[13] and under great funding threats,[14] and domestic violence is still endemic.[15] Forty years after the birth of the domestic violence movement, intimate partner violence persists in systemic and gendered ways despite these interventions. The movement's success is often measured by the extent and volume of these victim interventions. For example, a survey of state coalitions to end domestic violence self-identified the following types of successful achievements in the survey period: increased or maintained revenue to domestic violence services, provided case support to victims, strengthened coalition-building within communities, provided training programs, developed health initiatives, provided pro bono referral networks, strengthened programs for domestic violence victims, and launched public relations campaigns.[16]

As much political mileage has come out of the domestic violence movement's first generation politicization, if the goal is to *end* domestic violence, then it may be time to revisit its politicization for next generation law reforms.[17]

A Narrow Politicization of Domestic Violence Dominates

Domestic violence is politicized narrowly in ways that were historically effective, but might be too limited looking forward. In the past, domestic violence was politicized as an issue defined by and contained within each individual relationship in which it occurred. The iconic cycle of violence coined by Lenore Walker is an example of this point.[18] The cycle of violence was developed from the voiced experiences of women victims of male violence,[19] and is used regularly in trainings worldwide to help individuals understand domestic violence and the responses that victims have to it. The cycle depicts a tension-building phase, involving minor battering or abuse; an acute battering and abuse phase; and a honeymoon phase in which the abuser shows remorse.[20] Imagery depicts the violence as self-contained in the relationship and disconnected from community, prior generations, job loss, or other context. The cycle of violence explains how women experience victimization and the complexities of leaving abusive relationships, but it has also been used to explain domestic violence itself.[21] Its imagery implicitly communicates that abuse starts and ends within the couple. This is a myopic view of domestic violence. It suggests that the political response begins only when the victim seeks to exit the insular cycle.

Lethality assessment models are another example of the narrowness of first generation politicization.[22] Risk assessment describes an intervention in which responders measure dangerousness to make better decisions.[23] Although there are many different models,[24] lethality assessments are now commonly used throughout the country.[25] The Maryland Model, for example, uses a two-pronged intervention model in which first responders conduct an initial screening with the victim.[26] Depending on the screening results, the victim may be referred to a hotline where she will be advised that other victims in her situation have been in danger and have been killed following comparable assessments.[27] Victims often complete a checklist exploring facts within the following clusters: prior victimization, the abuser's past drug and alcohol problems, the abuser's jealousy and obsessive behaviors, threats made by the abuser, the abuser's access to weapons, the abuser's previous violence toward others, any suicidal ideation of the abuser, and the status of the relationship between the victim and abuser (separated, separating, etc.).[28] These assessments seek to prevent homicides and recidivism and encourage victims to access domestic violence interventions.[29]

Lethality assessments further reveal the narrowness of first generation politicization. The victim is the insider providing internal information relevant to the narrow relationship between the victim and the perpetrator. The state's role and its potential effectiveness are entirely shaped by the victim interaction. Yet recidivism research is clear that if the victim successfully exits this abusive relationship, a new victim of the same abuser will emerge.[30] In that sense alone, this politicization is insufficient to end domestic violence.

There is so much missing from this politicized lens, such as culture, community, institutions, family history, and gender norms. Researcher Lori Heise, for example, concluded that domestic violence occurs based on personal history, the microsystem, the exosystem, and the macrosystem.[31] For the personal history level, risk factors for committing acts of domestic violence include prior childhood witnessing of domestic violence, prior childhood victimization, and the absence of a father figure during childhood.[32] On the microsystem level, situational risk factors are relevant, such as male decision-making domination, marital conflict, male economic control, and alcohol use.[33] On the exosystem level, which addresses "factors within the formal and informal social structures and institutions that impact the situation," risk factors such as low socioeconomic status, social isolation, and "delinquent peer association" are relevant factors.[34] On the macrosystem level, cultural values and beliefs are relevant. Beliefs in male dominance, traditional gender roles, and male entitlement over women can also be risk factors. Heise explains that no one factor is dispositive. Her approach reveals the narrowness of the first generation politicization of domestic violence.

Likewise, adding a masculinities perspective to the politicization of domestic violence further reveals the narrow scope of modern politicization. Masculinities theory explains how men wield and retain power over women and over other men, men have power over women as a group, and certain practices "maintain group power."[35] Masculinities scholarship critically examines how men as individuals do not feel privileged even though men may be dominant and powerful as a group.[36]

Masculine violence, in particular, operates on multiple systematic levels, many of which are not adequately contemplated in existing framings. These responses "generally fail to extinguish masculine violence because their ameliorative efforts usually focus on a single system level of action, whereas masculine violence has roots in multiple system levels."[37] When men fail to conform to unachievable masculine imperatives, it can trigger hypermasculinity, a theory of exaggerated masculinity expressed as a manifestation of insecurities shaped by external forces.[38] When individual men feel their masculinity has been threatened or masculine norms are unattainable, they might feel "guilty, ashamed and—critically—hostile."[39] Perceptions of masculine inadequacy triggered by externalities such as job loss or economic distress can lead to hyper-masculine expressions of violence, such as domestic violence and sexual assault.[40] The next section explores the collateral consequences of this first generation politicization.

The Consequences of Domestic Violence's Limited Politicization

A. The Narrow Lens of "Crisis"

Historic political framings politicize a faulty narrative that domestic violence has a beginning and an end and includes a decisive, transformative moment in time. Yet domestic violence is more systemic and interconnected.

Domestic violence is politicized as a one-dimensional crisis involving victims. Imagine instead politicizing *batterers* as the crisis in need of urgent legal, political, and social intervention. Unfortunately, decades of push back and co-optation by the men's rights movement make this thought exercise nearly impossible.[41] The troubled and complex history of men's rights advocacy in domestic violence leaves readers with a cognitive dissonance at the mere thought of focusing on batterers.

Remember, however, that the goal is to *end* family violence. With that in mind, imagine that batterers were relocated to alternate housing to focus intensively on their violence immediately, rather than to an incarceration setting that encourages silence and delay. Imagine if evaluators could intervene with batterers to assess their *own* lethality and likelihood to abuse. What if employees had to report their *own* acts of domestic violence to their employers to put them on notice of their propensity toward violence? Each of these scenarios would undoubtedly involve concerns of due process, self-incrimination, politics, and pragmatism. Yet, in a provocative thought exercise, they reveal just how heavily the politicization of domestic violence relies on victims and narrowly politicizes domestic violence around victims in ways that might impede progress and stifle innovation.

Domestic violence is often addressed and framed as a crisis,[42] but, importantly, that crisis framing politicizes the need for outside victim support. Only secondarily—or not at all—are perpetrators politicized as the root of the crisis itself. There were pragmatic, historic, and public health reasons to politicize the crisis around victims. The historic domestic violence movement included a powerful construction of community crisis interventions to help the victim assess risks and receive safe housing, legal representation, and medical care.[43] From the perspective of public health and safety, that approach is correct; victims often need to be immediately removed from the dangerous situation for legal and medical interventions.[44]

Yet there are also collateral consequences. The word "crisis" can be traced back to the Greek word "kpisis," which means discrimination or decision.[45] A crisis in this political sense is normally invoked in an attempt to "create a rupture in an existing discourse . . . that creates room for alternative discourses to enter."[46] This meaning aligns with the battered women's movement's transformative role in moving domestic violence onto the law reform agenda in the 1970s.[47] The battered women's movement ruptured the discourse and revealed a crisis in need of a public response.

The Oxford English Dictionary also uses a medical definition for "crisis": "the turning-point of a disease for better or worse; [or] . . . any marked or sudden variation occurring in the progress of a disease."[48] This medicalized understanding of the term might align consistently with the individual harms that victims suffer from domestic violence, but it might also distort the depth and longevity of domestic violence harms. Domestic violence causes short- and long-term effects in physical, psychological, financial, and social capacities.[49] It causes post-traumatic stress disorder, depression, and extended negative physical and mental health outcomes.[50] Women in abusive relationships are more likely to be unemployed, receive public assistance, and suffer from health problems.[51] These harms extend to victims directly and to their children,[52] employers,[53] and other community members, such as friends and family.[54] Thus, the medical meaning of "crisis" might actually diminish or complicate efforts to address domestic violence harms.

Crisis terminology is often used in a hybrid of these framings. Victims call crisis hotlines, they receive crisis interventions, and communities deploy crisis-response approaches. Such urgency is understandable and necessary, given the safety needs of victims. Might it also, however, minimize state accountability to play a role in victims' longer-term recovery and wellness and to address perpetrators more proactively and urgently? By framing crisis around victims, the burden is left to social services and nonprofits to meet those needs, yet they are contingent on victims' willingness to accept services and on service providers' ability to meet the needs.

The one-dimensional crisis framing obscures development of effective and accountable batterer's intervention. Batterers are notably not framed as part of the crisis. Rather, the interventions applied to perpetrators, such as incarceration and batterer's intervention programs, are normalized within the criminal justice system and are not framed as a *crisis* worthy of *state* response imminently and decisively.[55] For example, batterer's intervention programs are often voluntary,[56] participants can often terminate participation without sanction,[57] compliance is rarely monitored,[58] and their efficacy is highly contested and mixed.[59]

B. Weak State Accountability for Prevention

The political focus on victims also weakens state accountability. The politicization of domestic violence creates a paradox of victim accountability that implicitly immunizes the state. First generation political framings of domestic violence position the victim as the initiator, investigator, and information-provider accountable for *effective* domestic violence responses. This immunizes the state from developing effective responses to domestic violence and obscures and diminishes the role of the perpetrators. It paradoxically takes an autonomy and empowerment model and politicizes it around victim accountability for the effectiveness of the responses. It suggests that the movement successfully positioned domestic violence on the public agenda, but it did not shift accountability for its resolution to the state.[60]

Other than budgetary questions of properly funding the services model,[61] the state is left largely unaccountable for *ending* the crisis itself. For example, some states have enacted laws that prohibit discrimination against domestic violence victims,[62] require reasonable accommodations for victims,[63] or provide unpaid leave for victims,[64] but this is different from requiring the state to be accountable for interventions or framing the crisis around an urgent and decisive need to address the behavior of perpetrators. Only in rare cases, such as where a protective order was denied before a subsequent act of escalated violence, do state interventions consider state accountability.[65] Absent these events, accountability remains with the victim.

This creates a unique tension whereby the laudable goal of achieving victim autonomy is politicized so as to leave victims uniquely accountable for their own safety. Victim autonomy is a critical, but complex, goal in the domestic violence movement.[66] Achieving it in the context of law reforms and social and political responses, however, has proven much more difficult.[67] Rather, many victims feel like an object during the process of legal interventions, "nonexistent and invisible."[68] This, as many critical feminist accounts have noted, transforms the victim experience into a "glossed, patriarchal, legal narrative that may adequately function within the legal system, and more often than not fails to meet not only her need for personal safety, but her emotional need for justice and healing."[69]

The lethality assessments described above demonstrate this paradox in action. These assessment tools question victims about the risks they face rather than question perpetrators about the risks they pose.[70] They ask if a weapon has been used against the victim, if the perpetrator has threatened to kill the victim or the victim's children, whether the victim thinks the perpetrator might kill the victim, whether there were constant jealousy and control over daily activities, whether the perpetrator is unemployed, whether the perpetrator spied on the victim, and whether the victim has a child that the perpetrator knows is not his.[71] Although less common, other surveys also ask the victim about the perpetrator's mental health, harm to pets, her beliefs about his capabilities, and his level of access to her location.[72] These surveys critically rely on victim information that the evaluator uses to score the assessment and evaluate risks.[73]

This framework positions the effectiveness of the evaluator's lethality assessment on the victim's answers from which the evaluator then makes recommendations.[74] These assessment programs are distinctly intended to empower victims to gain autonomy over next steps.[75] They are heralded for providing support to women and working to protect them without "impos[ing] on them."[76] Yet these tools critically "presuppose a population of women who will complete questionnaires"[77] and implicitly shift accountability for proper interventions to the victim, instead of the state.[78]

Lethality assessments are effective only if the victim is reporting objectively and accurately, which may be difficult.[79] This is particularly noteworthy from an intersectional perspective. Women of color may be less comfortable disclosing personal information to the criminal justice system.[80] Risk assessments may not translate into same-sex relationships or assessing the likelihood of women abusers to kill their partners.[81] The assessment surveys have been criticized as "consistent with a broader patriarchal cultural ethic that silences, devalues, and dismisses women's intuitive and subjective ways of knowing."[82] They reflect an "economy of power which involves the fast and frugal screening and classification of women to 'efficiently' weed out those at greatest risk of lethal interpersonal violence with the minimum amount of effort on the part of overworked agency personnel."[83]

The assessments relieve law enforcement of accountability because high-risk cases are referred for *victim's* interventions and safety planning. If the assessment is faulty, it is seemingly because the victim did not adequately sense the risks or she did not avail herself of the services that were provided.[84] This disempowers the state from tracking efficacy, developing better responses, or critically assessing its role. The service provider then steps in to gain the trust of the victim, reinforce the officer's assessment of risk, educate the victim about safety planning, and encourage the victim to seek services.[85] It allows law enforcement to defer to victims' services to protect the victim without direct accountability.[86] These tools implicitly immunize the state from accountability for investigating lethality risks and making objective determinations.

Common wisdom on these preventative issues is that external indicators of domestic violence are rare and not clear enough.[87] Yet the question becomes: how is it that we are comfortable leaving victims solely accountable for that uncertainty? The state, importantly, has a crucial power of inquiry in judicial proceedings that need not be transferred to victims. There are professionals who could screen cases and evaluate how respondents are psychologically handling the process and assess risks objectively.[88] The state could play a larger role in preventing further domestic violence by intervening sooner and more positively.

The National Football League's (NFL's) response to domestic violence provides a good example of the limits of first generation politicization and the expansive and transformative power of next generation framings. In August 2014, NFL Commissioner Roger Goodell announced a new Personal Conduct Policy.[89] The policy was adopted after a high-profile case of domestic abuse came to light involving player Ray Rice and his then-fiancée Janay Rice.[90] Commissioner Goodell faced harsh criticism for his handling of the matter, such as giving Rice an inappropriately light punishment and attempting to cover up the scandal by ignoring the existence of the security camera footage until the media released it.[91] The revised policy stated that assault, battery, domestic violence, or sexual assault involving physical force would result in a suspension of six games without pay for the first offense.[92] The suspension would apply regardless of whether the player was formally charged, and a second qualifying offense would lead to a lifetime ban from professional football.[93] The NFL sought to ensure a "fair and consistent process for player and employee discipline" that would "set a higher standard."[94]

When understood in a broader context, the NFL could have dramatically reframed its approach by using its power as the NFL to *change* behaviors and by seeing its own institutional culture as a relevant component of domestic violence itself. The NFL camaraderie and team dynamics could have instead been leveraged to create positive peer associations and stronger cultural values and beliefs about healthy relationships. The NFL might play a role supporting its players who are prior victims or witnesses of abuse or who hold other risk factors. With the power and resources of the NFL expanded to a broader lens, perhaps stronger, lasting change could have been achieved.

Expanding the frame with which we politicize domestic violence reveals the limits of existing frames. The NFL policy depends on victims coming forward to report allegations of physical and sexual assault committed by prominent athletes. It adds an additional punitive and professional outcome to the existing criminal and civil consequences, which can harmfully affect the victim and children in common. This approach is inherently limited in its efficacy and insulates the NFL (which is a proxy for the state in this example) from accountability for its role in domestic violence and its ability to achieve change. For example, in a highly masculine environment, might the publicity, threatened job loss, and income loss embedded in the NFL policy—particularly when initiated by the victim—actually exacerbate the risk of domestic violence and stifle help-seeking? Might the NFL work to change its culture of masculinity in ways that effectively address the medical, social, and statistical risks of domestic violence that are unique to NFL culture? The next section explores more systemic examples of re-envisioned responses.

Re-envisioning Next Generation Responses

A. Greater State Accountability for Prevention

The state, broadly defined, could be empowered more creatively to prevent acts, beyond the carceral state. The state is stagnant in its role intervening in domestic violence and is overly reliant on the criminal justice system.[95] State interventions in domestic violence are more often symbolic, educational, or supportive, but do not carry the accountability of state action.[96] They are also narrowly limited to criminal justice and incarceration responses.

Effective programs should focus on both the perpetrator and the victim and the state should commit to evaluating the effectiveness of various interventions.[97] As noted by the Canton, Ohio, police chief, for example, "focusing on the offender, as a way to decrease the likelihood of a repeat offense, is a newer approach in law enforcement. There is no template for this yet."[98] The more the perpetrator believes himself to be losing control, "he may be more dangerous and extreme in his attempts to retain control."[99] This is something that trained law enforcement could be actively empowered to screen and intervene in more proactively and productively.

This is true for recidivist offenders particularly. State statutes, for example, allow the state to learn about the prior criminal and protective order history of offenders, but these permissive approaches do not impose accountability on the state or the batterer.[100] Rather, the goal of the "cessation of violence" to "provide for the safety of victims and their children" sits squarely in the batterer's intervention program, which is often optional.[101]

When the state does get involved, it frequently lacks accountability.[102] An example of the state's lack of accountability is its role assessing domestic violence in child custody proceedings. The state is statutorily required to consider domestic violence in some child custody cases, but it remains largely unaccountable for the results of those decisions. For example, twenty-seven states require judges to "consider" domestic violence allegations when making custody and visitation decisions.[103] The "consider" statutes, however, are permissive only. In contrast, twelve states and the District of Columbia have a rebuttable presumption that physical custody with the abusive parent is not in the best interests of the child. Are these approaches effective, though? The state lacks accountability for making effective custody decisions that contemplate the impact of domestic violence. When considering that impact, preventative and supportive interventions may be appropriate.

The state's role is further limited beyond criminal law or family law. Consider, for example, the story of Tuan Dao, who killed himself and his family one Easter morning. Before the tragic killings, he had suffered a home foreclosure, bankruptcy filing, domestic violence–related arrest, and separation from his wife.[104] Of those events, only the domestic violence arrest would trigger any state risk assessment. Although the foreclosure, bankruptcy filing, and separation all involve critical state action and are all potential risk factors in domestic violence, no existing political or legal framework exists to conduct risk assessments in these other contexts.

Yet a larger ecosystem approach or even an additional masculinities lens would reveal how economic circumstances, family law court interventions, and job loss might all trigger hyper-masculine violence. They would also explore how relational masculinities in employment, community, neighborhood, and family are relevant to shaping more effective responses. Masculinities theory can add greater dimensions to our efforts to end domestic violence.[105]

The state might also play a larger role in protecting future victims. For instance, in the context of adult caregivers who have been found to be abusive, some states acknowledge that these workers move from one job to another and that this creates liability. Similarly, the documentation is clear that perpetrators are recidivists. For caregivers who have abused or neglected the clients they were caring for, state have created "Vulnerable Adult Services Providers" registries to empower employers and contractors to inspect the database.[106] This reflects a starkly different politicization of safety in which the state is empowered to prevent future acts instead of accepting the normalization of future acts.

The state might also impose a greater role on lawyers. Lawyers representing victims are encouraged to prepare a safety plan with their clients leaving abusive relationships, conduct a lethality assessment, and ensure workplace safety.[107] Yet, for perpetrators, rarely is such planning and complex client counseling advised, although such duties and liabilities are not entirely unfamiliar in our legal system.

Tort law imposes liabilities on individuals with special relationships to warn of particular risks faced by known victims. Lawyers have ethical obligations to maintain confidential communications, but those ethical obligations still leave some room for lawyers to take more active roles.[108] Under Rule 1.6 of the Model Rules of Professional Conduct, for example, a lawyer may reveal information to the extent the lawyer "reasonably believes necessary to prevent reasonably certain death or substantial bodily harm" or to "comply with other law or a court order."[109] Under Rule 3.3 of the Model Rules of Professional Conduct, disclosure of some criminal activities are not only allowed, but required: "(b) A lawyer who represents a client in an adjudicative proceeding and who knows that a person intends to engage, is engaging or has engaged in criminal . . . conduct related to the proceeding shall take reasonable remedial measures, including, if necessary, disclosure to the tribunal."[110] The state could impose stronger ethical requirements on the respondent's counsel to monitor and assess risks of escalated violence.[111]

The state could also hold greater preventative accountability in the context of child welfare to prevent and mitigate future domestic abuse. Child welfare systems are vastly underfunded. Children exposed to domestic violence are likely to suffer longstanding harms, a critical opportunity for intervention for the domestic violence movement.[112] The child welfare system has a complicated relationship with the domestic violence movement because of "failure to protect" laws. How might we better identify the children in need of treatment or at risk of becoming abusers? This section urges a deepened conversation around state accountability for prevention. The next section considers the benefits of greater vigilance to the state as a provoker of domestic violence.

B. More Vigilance to the State as Provoker

One component of next generation domestic violence politicization is a new vigilance to the state as "provoker" of domestic violence in all state-perpetrator interactions, not just domestic violence proceedings. A consequence of framing domestic violence around the insular couple is that the state is always positioned as an outsider coming to the aid and response of the victim. This ignores the ways in which the state—broadly defined—can actually play a role in creating or stoking the culture of hyper-masculinity and provoking hyper-masculine acts of violence, as indicated above. It also ignores the ways in which incarceration-based approaches can actually *increase* the risk for domestic violence.[113]

This itself is a paradox. A model of increased state intervention must be vigilant to arguments that hyper-incarceration actually provokes and exacerbates domestic violence, as scholar Donna Coker urges.[114] Because hyper-incarceration harms defendants and their families economically, imposes trauma on those incarcerated, and undermines the role of neighborhood and social controls, greater incarceration strategies are not the answer.[115]

Instead, the state's interactions with family law or domestic violence litigants should be entirely reexamined. Training models might also be revisited and expanded. Judges and law enforcement already undergo training in domestic violence generally to be aware of the cycle of violence, barriers victims face, and lethality risks.[116] Traditional curricula do not train state actors, however, to consider whether it might be provoking hyper-masculine acts of violence. These state actors play a different role from victims' advocates in that they interface with *both* the victim and the accused. Broader political framings might extend to bankruptcy proceedings, custody, visitation, and public benefits offices in which an adverse outcome of the proceeding might increase the risk for domestic violence.[117] It could also extend to more situational role-plays as a judge or state official, in lieu of more scripted training materials. The infrastructure is already there to design, implement, and assess this type of training module. Already, law enforcement officials, health care workers, teachers, and judges often participate in domestic violence training.[118] A new training model might consider masculinities theory, community ecosystems, etc.[119]

C. Aligning with Modern Political Movements

It is also time for more candid and reflective conversations on the trajectory of the movement toward *ending* domestic violence. Advocates leading domestic violence organizations also recognize the challenge of "creating room for innovative ideas and collaborations without compromising core values and goals."[120] Some advocates, though anecdotally, describe a "fortress mentality" within the domestic violence movement that can compromise the work and constrain innovation.[121] As one advocate candidly voiced in a survey of domestic violence workers, "[We] need a revolution . . . in this movement. I think that we are not giving ourselves the opportunity to change the way we did things years ago, because we gotta do it different—we are looking at different times . . . And when, 20 years from now, when somebody writes the history, they'll say 'Oh, these people just let it happen, . . .' cuz they were not more revolutionary.'"[122]

This chapter seeks to expand the political framing of responses to domestic violence. One critical piece of the conversation is how the domestic violence movement connects to and aligns with larger social and political movements in modern times. As discussed in my prior article, *The Feminist Case for Acknowledging Women's Acts of Violence*,[123] there is a risk that the domestic violence movement could lose its collective identity by essentializing itself around the who (gendered binary) and the what (victims' services) of domestic violence.[124] While first generation framings achieved important goals, a more contextual political framing may be necessary going forward.[125] Many domestic violence advocates already distance themselves from the women's movement, instead viewing their work as providing services to women and children "as a depoliticized, degendered phenomenon" outside of a conscious movement.[126]

Moving forward toward a more expansive politicization might include aligning with movements for more systemic social change and reform.[127] It is critical that the movement remains relevant to and engaged with diverse communities and not entrenched in a framework that is unnecessarily exclusionary, narrow, or outdated.[128] As Donna Coker advocates, "What is needed now, more than ever, is a broad-based coalition that understands gender violence as deeply connected to the structural inequalities of race, class, immigration status, homophobia, and other oppressions."[129]

Domestic violence leaders self-report that they *do* want the movement to "include openness to new strategies and approaches, better inclusion of communities of color, a rethinking of community engagement and collaboration, and attention to mentoring the next generation of advocates."[130] Feminist scholars, such as Leigh Goodmark, have previously advocated strongly for this directional shift. Goodmark has concluded that the "time has come to reevaluate the legal system's responsiveness to the complex and variable needs of women," particularly focusing on a need for intersectional responses that avoid essentializing.[131] Deborah Weissman has likewise argued that stripping out attention to socioeconomic factors from domestic violence has "narrowed the scope for addressing structural determinants of gender-based violence."[132]

It is time to consider the synergies between the goals of the domestic violence movement and other social justice causes. The modern political climate invites and demands new solutions and new ideas. Holistic solutions and ideas are needed, particularly those that align with other modern political movements.

Conclusion

This chapter urges a candid examination of how domestic violence is politicized so as to move toward next generation framings. Existing approaches insulate the state and perpetrators from accountability for effective solutions. It creates a power paradox that saddles victims uniquely with the accountability for effective interventions. Consistent with the larger mission of the University of California, Irvine's Initiative to End Family Violence, this chapter urges next generation politicizations of domestic violence.

Author's Note

The author extends her deepest thanks to the University of California, Irvine's Initiative to End Family Violence's Politicization of Safety Conference for its support and feedback on this project. Thanks also to participants in the Law & Society Feminist Legal Theory Collaborative Research Network, Srimati Basu, Elizabeth MacDowell, Jane Stoever, and Mary Pat Treuthart for thoughtful feedback and engagement with this project. Thanks to Kristin Birkhold, Aleisha Cowles, Abigail Lewis, and Jennifer Reynolds for their research support.

NOTES

1 The terms "politicized" or "politicization" are used throughout the chapter to refer to the ways in which the social movement to end domestic violence has taken on a political tone or character in both intended and unintended ways.

2 LEIGH GOODMARK, A TROUBLED MARRIAGE: DOMESTIC VIOLENCE AND THE LEGAL SYSTEM 1 (2012) (explaining that advocates sought state interventions on behalf of women abuse victims). "Historically, domestic violence was treated as a private affair, an extension of the husband's right to control the behavior of his wife, to be handled within the confines of the home." *Id.* (highlighting how advocates pushed the state to acknowledge abuse and to use the legal system as a primary response). "That there is a legal response to domestic violence at all is, for some, a victory in and of itself." *Id.*

3 *See e.g.,* MARTHA CHAMALLAS, INTRODUCTION TO FEMINIST LEGAL THEORY 1 (2d. ed. 2003) (explaining that the root of feminist criticism is the

"belief that women are currently in a subordinate position in society and that the law often reflects and reinforces this subordination").

4 The movement was historically known as the battered women's movement. It emerged as a movement within the larger feminist project, which itself was intertwined with the civil rights and antiwar movements of the time. Amy Lehrner & Nicole E. Allen, *Still a Movement After All These Years?: Current Tensions in the Domestic Violence Movement,* 15 VIOLENCE AGAINST WOMEN 656, 656 (2009).

5 CHAMALLAS, *supra* note 3, at 4–6 (explaining that a core move of feminist thinkers is to begin by understanding women's experience consistent with the historical work of "consciousness-raising" in which women "were encouraged to express their subjective responses to everyday life and discovered that their personal problems also had a political dimension").

6 Lehrner & Allen, *supra* note 4, at 657.

7 *See* Kimberly D. Bailey, *Lost in Translation: Domestic Violence, "The Personal is Political," and the Criminal Justice System,* 100 J. CRIM. L. & CRIMINOLOGY 1255, 1256–57 (2010) (criticizing the criminal justice system for not prioritizing victim autonomy); *see also* Deborah M. Weissman, *The Personal Is Political— and Economic: Rethinking Domestic Violence,* 2007 BYU L. REV. 387, 389 (2007) (arguing that domestic violence discourse should expand "beyond the parameters of criminal justice to include the political economy of everyday experiences of households").

8 PATRICIA GAGNE, BATTERED WOMEN'S JUSTICE 11 (1998) (explaining that there was little understanding of the complexities of the problem, just an understanding that there was a need).

9 See *What is Domestic Violence?*, NAT'L COAL. AGAINST DOMESTIC VIOLENCE, www.ncadv.org. *See generally* LAWYER'S MANUAL ON DOMESTIC VIOLENCE, REPRESENTING THE VICTIM (Mary Rothwell Davis et al. eds., 6th ed. 2015) (chronicling the successes of the domestic violence movement in building out responses).

10 *See* Julie Goldscheid, *Domestic and Sexual Violence as Sex Discrimination: Comparing American and International Approaches,* 28 T. JEFFERSON L. REV. 355, 363–73 (2006) (cataloging reforms, including eliminating formal inequalities, enhancing criminal justice responses, expanding social services, and civil justice responses). *See generally* Albert R. Roberts, *Myths, Facts, and Realities Regarding Battered Women and Their Children: An Overview, in* HANDBOOK OF DOMESTIC VIOLENCE INTERVENTION STRATEGIES 17 (Albert Roberts ed., 2002) (explaining the historic development of legal interventions).

11 Lehrner & Allen, *supra* note 4, at 656–57 (concluding that today there are more than 2,000 domestic violence shelters nationwide).

12 Patricia Brownell & Albert Roberts, *National Organizational Survey of Domestic Violence Coalitions, in* HANDBOOK OF DOMESTIC VIOLENCE INTERVENTION STRATEGIES 31 (Albert Roberts ed., 2002).

13 An average of three women a day are killed by their current or former partner. NAT'L NETWORK TO END DOMESTIC VIOLENCE, DOMESTIC AND SEXUAL VIOLENCE FACT SHEET, www.nnedv.org [hereinafter DOMESTIC AND SEXUAL VIOLENCE FACT SHEET]. A 24-hour survey of domestic violence programs in 2013, for example, revealed that on a single day, 66,581 adults and children received refuge from intimate violence and an additional 9,641 requests for services were unmet due to lack of resources. NAT'L NETWORK TO END DOMESTIC VIOLENCE, DOMESTIC VIOLENCE COUNTS 2013: A 24-HOUR CENSUS OF DOMESTIC VIOLENCE SHELTERS AND SERVICES (2014), http:// nnedv.org; *see also* Marisa Kwiatkowski, *Central Indiana Domestic Violence Shelters Turn Away 1,743*, INDY STAR (Nov. 12, 2015), www.indystar.com.

14 *See, e.g.,* A. G. Sulzberger, *Facing Cuts, A City Repeals its Domestic Violence Law*, N.Y. TIMES A11 (Oct. 12, 2011) (describing a Topeka cost-saving measure repealing a local law criminalizing domestic violence). Importantly, the men's rights groups argue that gender symmetry requires states to defund services available to victims rather than expand services to men. *See* Kelly Alison Behre, *Digging Beneath the Equality Language: The Influence of the Fathers' Rights Movement on Intimate Partner Violence Public Policy Debates and Family Law Reform*, 21 WM. & MARY J. WOMEN & L. 525, 535 (2015); *see also* Molly Dragiewicz & Yvonne Lindgren, *The Gendered Nature of Domestic Violence: Statistical Data for Lawyers Considering Equal Protection Analysis*, 17 AM. U. J. GENDER SOC. POL'Y & L. 159, 234 (2009) ("The history of anti-feminist fathers' rights litigation across the country on this issue points to a systematic attempt to, at the very least, divert already inadequate and scarce resources away from women's shelters and, at worst, impede battered women's efforts to secure safety, accurate information, and services.").

15 The National Network to End Domestic Violence reports that more than one in three women have experienced rape, physical violence, and/or stalking by an intimate partner in their lifetime. This violence is "inextricably linked" to economic security. DOMESTIC AND SEXUAL VIOLENCE FACT SHEET, *supra* note 13. Many victims will struggle with food and housing insecurity. *Id.* The Centers for Disease Control reports that an estimated 5.4 million acts of intimate partner violence occur among women eighteen and older each year, resulting in nearly 2 million injuries and requiring 550,000 victims to seek medical help. Victims of intimate partner violence lose a combined total of 8 million paid work days and 5.6 million days of household productivity. *See* CTRS. FOR DISEASE CONTROL & PREVENTION, COSTS OF INTIMATE PARTNER VIOLENCE AGAINST WOMEN IN THE UNITED STATES (2003), www.cdc.gov.

16 Brownell & Roberts, *supra* note 12, at 31.

17 *See, e.g.,* HOME TRUTHS ABOUT DOMESTIC VIOLENCE; FEMINIST INFLUENCES ON POLICY AND PRACTICE—A READER 1 (Jalna Hanmer & Catherine Itzin eds., 2000) ("Change requires new conceptual frameworks.").

18 *See generally* LENORE WALKER, THE BATTERED WOMAN 61 (1979).

19 *Id.* at 55–77 (describing the "striking discoveries" of a "definite battering cycle" that women experience).

20 *Id.*

21 *Id.*

22 *See generally* EDWARD W. GONDOLF, THE FUTURE OF BATTERER PRO-GRAMS (2012). These assessment tools are often called "lethality assessments," but some scholars critique that the research underlying these tools more accurately supports calling them "dangerousness assessments," not lethality assessments. *See, e.g.,* NEIL WEBSDALE, NAT'L ONLINE RESOURCE CTR. ON VIOLENCE AGAINST WOMEN, LETHALITY ASSESSMENT TOOLS: A CRITICAL ANALYSIS 4 (2000) (explaining that most of the assessment tools "derive from a generalized appreciation or commonsense analysis of what questionnaire writers have gleaned from the research literature on domestic violence in general"). The author notes that the line between lethal and non-lethal is hard to establish and is heavily influenced by the availability of emergency medical procedures to treat the victim. *Id.*

23 D. Kelly Weisberg, *Risk Assessment in Context,* 21 DOMESTIC VIOLENCE REP. 69, 69 (June–July 2016).

24 JILL THERESA MESSING ET AL., POLICE DEPARTMENTS' USE OF THE LETHALITY ASSESSMENT PROGRAM: A QUASI-EXPERIMENTAL EVALUATION 19–21 (2014) (describing the Danger Assessment and the Lethality Screen).

25 *Attorney General Mark R. Herring,* VIRGINIA.GOV, www.oag.state.va.us (last visited Feb. 15, 2017) (referencing and linking to many other programs throughout the country); *Lethality Assessment Program (LAP),* UTAH DOMESTIC VIOLENCE COALITION, http://udvc.org (last visited Feb. 15, 2017); *Lethality Assessment Program,* NEW HAMPSHIRE DEPARTMENT OF JUSTICE: OFFICE OF THE ATTORNEY GENERAL, www.doj.nh.gov (last visited Feb. 15, 2017); *Lethality Assessment Program,* INDIANA COALITION AGAINST VIOLENCE, www.icadvinc.org (last visited Feb. 15, 2017).

26 MARYLAND NETWORK AGAINST DOMESTIC VIOLENCE, LETHALITY ASSESSMENT PROGRAM MARYLAND MODEL FOR FIRST RESPONDERS (2005). It was used by thirty states as of 2013.

27 *Id.* (explaining that this lethality assessment should happen when there is an intimate relationship involved, when the first responder believes an assault has occurred, when the first responder believes the potential for danger is high, when the first responder is in a repeat response situation, and when the first responder believes one should be run).

28 *See, e.g.,* WEBSDALE, *supra* note 22, at 2.

29 MARYLAND NETWORK AGAINST DOMESTIC VIOLENCE, *supra* note 26.

30 There is overwhelming consensus in the research community that there is a pattern of domestic abusers engaging in domestic abuse in multiple relationships, so most literature on the subject focuses on how to decrease recidivism, not on the mere existence of a recidivism problem with domestic abusers. *See generally*

Robert M. Sartin et al., *Domestic Violence Treatment Response and Recidivism: A Review and Implications for the Study of Family Violence*, 11 AGGRESSION & VIOLENT BEHAVIOR 425 (2006); Katreena Scott et al., *Intervening to Prevent Repeat Offending Among Moderate-to-High-Risk Domestic Violence Offenders: A Second-Responder Program for Men*, 59 INT'L J. OFFENDER THERAPY & COMP. CRIMINOLOGY 273 (2015).

31 Mary P. Brewster, *Domestic Violence Theories, Research, and Practice Implications*, *in* HANDBOOK OF DOMESTIC VIOLENCE INTERVENTION STRATEGIES 35 (Albert Roberts ed., 2002).

32 *Id.*

33 *Id.*

34 *Id.* (explaining that delinquent peer association involves attaching to others who "legitimize violence against women").

35 Nancy Dowd, Ann C. McGinley, & Nancy Levit, *Feminist Legal Theory Meets Masculinities Theories*, *in* MASCULINITIES AND THE LAW: A MULTIDIMENSIONAL APPROACH 26 (Frank Rudy Cooper & Ann C. McGinley eds., 2012).

36 *See, e.g.*, Nancy Dowd, *Masculinities and Feminist Legal Theory*, 23 WIS. J.L. GENDER & SOC. 213 (2008).

37 Lee H. Bowker, *On the Difficulty of Eradicating Masculine Violence*, *in* MASCULINITIES AND VIOLENCE 1 (Lee H. Bowker ed., 1998) (proposing an approach to attacking masculine violence across five systems, including economics, social, cultural, and personality systems).

38 JOSEPH H. PLECK, THE MYTH OF MASCULINITY 96 (1981).

39 Harris O'Malley, *Defining a Modern Masculinity*, THE GOOD MEN PROJECT (Feb. 9, 2014), http://goodmenproject.com.

40 *See generally* Angela P. Harris, *Gender, Violence, Race, and Criminal Justice*, 52 STAN. L. REV. 777 (Apr. 2000) (describing how men use violence as a way of "providing individual or collective masculinity, or in desperation when they perceive their masculine self-identity to be under attack"). Hyper-masculinity has been used to explain some acts of male violence, extreme conservative viewpoints, and bodybuilding behaviors, to name a few. PLECK, *supra* note 38, at 96. "The risk of domestic violence in relationships rises when the man feels that he's no longer the primary breadwinner, especially when his wife earns equal or greater income—thus losing a critical aspect of his masculine identity." O'Malley, *supra* note 39.

41 *See, e.g.*, Jamie R. Abrams, *The Feminist Case for Understanding Women's Acts of Violence*, 27 YALE J.L. & FEMINISM 101 (2016) (describing the ways in which the men's rights movement has shaped feminist framings of domestic violence).

42 *See, e.g.*, DOMESTIC VIOLENCE RESOURCE CENTER, www.dvrc-or.org (providing "crisis support, intervention, and resource referrals to victims and survivors of domestic violence").

43 Brewster, *supra* note 31, at 38.

44 CHRISTINE SHEARER-CREMAN & CAROL L. WINKELMANN, SURVIVOR RHETORIC: NEGOTIATIONS AND NARRATIVITY IN ABUSED WOMEN'S LANGUAGE 7 (2004) (explaining how, "before any other work can be accomplished," "the trauma victim needs to find a sense of safety from harm"). *See generally* Rebecca Morley, *Domestic Violence and Housing, in* HOME TRUTHS ABOUT DOMESTIC VIOLENCE: FEMINIST INFLUENCES ON POLICY AND PRACTICE—A READER 228–45 (Jalna Hanmer & Catherine Itzin eds., 2001).

45 J. B. Shank, *Crisis: A Useful Category of Post-Social Scientific Historical Analysis?*, 113 AM. HIST. REV. 1090, 1090 (2008).

46 Laura Henderson, *What It Means to Say "Crisis" in Politics and Law* (Mar. 5, 2014), www.e-ir.info.

47 *But see* Jayne Mooney, *Revealing the Hidden Figure of Domestic Violence, in* HOME TRUTHS ABOUT DOMESTIC VIOLENCE: FEMINIST INFLUENCES ON POLICY AND PRACTICE—A READER 24 (Jalna Hanmer & Catherine Itzin eds., 2001) ("There is, of course, a great deal of historical evidence to show that women have always suffered violence from their husbands and partners.").

48 *Id.* (noting that French and Italian dictionaries reveal similar language).

49 Brewster, *supra* note 31, at 35–36 (explaining for example the high rate of PTSD among battered women).

50 MESSING ET AL., *supra* note 24, at 11.

51 *Id.*

52 *See generally* Patrick T. Davies & Melissa L. Sturge-Apple, *The Impact of Domestic Violence on Children's Development, in* FAMILY INTERVENTIONS IN DOMESTIC VIOLENCE 165 (John Hamel & Tonia L. Nichols eds., 2007) (explaining the ways in which children from homes in which domestic violence occurred are five to seven times more likely to suffer from psychological harms).

53 JULIE GOLDSCHEID & ROBIN RUNGE, EMPLOYMENT LAW AND DOMESTIC VIOLENCE 3 (ABA Comm'n on Domestic Violence ed., 2009) (explaining how domestic violence can affect the workplace in a variety of ways because survivors may need time off for injuries or court dates, family members may need to care for loved ones, and employees may face workplace dangers of abuse or stalking).

54 Brewster, *supra* note 31, at 35.

55 GONDOLF, *supra* note 22, at 14 (noting that most programs still rely on "linkages, especially with courts and probation").

56 Brewster, *supra* note 31, at 41.

57 *See, e.g.,* David Adams, *Decreasing the Violence of Men, in* HOME TRUTHS ABOUT DOMESTIC VIOLENCE: FEMINIST INFLUENCES ON POLICY AND PRACTICE—A READER 320 (Jalna Hanmer & Catherine Itzin eds., 2000).

58 GONDOLF, *supra* note 22, at 219 (describing the results of a survey giving a "disappointing picture of the most basic aspect of a system intervention" when less than two-thirds of courts required monitoring of batterer program compliance).

59 *See, e.g.,* GONDOLF, *supra* note 22, at 46–81 (analyzing the debate about the effectiveness of BIPs). "Most of the reviews of available instruments conclude that

there is no one overwhelming winner among the validated instruments. They assess different risks (for example, of committing a new assault, severe assault, or homicide), and they have different approaches (actuarial checklist versus structured ratings) and primary sources (police and court records, batterer interviews, and victim responses)." *Id.* at 195. Brewster, *supra* note 31, at 41 (noting, for example, that court-ordered treatment yielded a lower response rate than voluntary participation).

60 *See generally* Donna Coker, *Why Opposing Hyper-Incarceration Should be Central to the Work of the Anti-Domestic Violence Movement*, 5 MIAMI RACE & SOC. JUST. L. REV. 585 (2015) (explaining that criminal justice reforms were never the only subject of feminist activism, but these reforms achieved political traction in revealing domestic violence as a crime); Jane H. Aiken, *The Perils of Empowerment*, 20 CORNELL J.L. & PUB. POL'Y 139, 170 (2010) (noting that "advocates of the empowerment approach also did not appreciate that the focus on autonomy even as it supposed empowerment, nonetheless still supported the public/private distinction," thus "retaining all the isolation and individualizing that characterize the so-called private realm").

61 *See, e.g.*, Emily Allen, *Domestic Violence Advocates, Survivors Concerned About President Trump's Budget Blueprint*, FOX31 DENVER (Mar. 16, 2017), http://kdvr.com.

62 GOLDSCHEID & RUNGE, *supra* note 53, at 7 (noting, for example, a New York City law prohibiting employers from firing victims when they are residing in domestic violence shelters).

63 *Id.* at 8 (noting New York City and Illinois as examples).

64 *Id.* at 9 (explaining that more than half of states have general "crime-victim leave laws").

65 *See, e.g.*, Jennifer Smolo, *March Intended to Honor Shooting Victim, Stop Domestic Violence*, THE COLUMBUS DISPATCH (May 25, 2017) (describing a march in Ohio after a woman was fatally shot after obtaining three court protection orders against her abuser); Chris Ingalls, *King County Fails to Ensure Abusers Surrender Guns*, KING5.COM NEWS (May 3, 2017) (concluding that nearly half of defendants accused of domestic violence never surrendered their guns as legally required); *Judicial Shortcomings for Domestic Violence Victims*, SHARE, INC. (May 13, 2016), https://sharemorgancounty.org.

66 *See generally* Jane H. Aiken, *The Perils of Empowerment*, 20 CORNELL J.L. & PUB. POL'Y 139 (2010).

67 *See id.* at 142 ("The very changes that were ostensibly meant to empower battered women have instead paved the way for the state—indeed, for all of us—to put responsibility for ending domestic violence in the hands of its victims and avoid dealing with the problem ourselves.").

68 Christine Shearer-Cremean, *Epistemology of Police Science and the Silencing of Battered Women*, *in* SURVIVOR RHETORIC: NEGOTIATIONS AND NARRATIVITY IN ABUSED WOMEN'S LANGUAGE 173 (Christine Shearer-Cremean & Carol L. Winkelman eds., 2004) (explaining that this status of the woman as sub-

ject can be seen in the documents describing interviews and injuries). The woman moves through the process as a body upon which the abuse is inflicted and then an object of investigation, but "when her personhood is distilled into several key characteristics noted in a police report, she is still rendered less powerful and voiceless." *Id.* at 174.

69 *Id.*

70 *See, e.g.,* WEBSDALE, *supra* note 22, at 1.

71 MARYLAND NETWORK AGAINST DOMESTIC VIOLENCE, *supra* note 26 (also including an open-ended question for the victim to elaborate on safety worries).

72 *See, e.g.,* WEBSDALE, *supra* note 22, at 2.

73 UNITED COMMUNITY SERVICES OF JOHNSON COUNTY, AN ANALYSIS OF THE DOMESTIC VIOLENCE LETHALITY ASSESSMENT IN JOHNSON COUNTY, KANSAS 6 (2014) (explaining how the officer separates the victim and the abuser and then administers a series of calculations, and scores the assessment); GONDOLF, *supra* note 22, at 195 (explaining that *who* exactly administers the risk assessment varies from jurisdictions to jurisdiction).

74 MESSING ET AL., *supra* note 24, at 9.

75 GONDOLF, *supra* note 22, at 184–85.

76 *Id.* at 184–85 (explaining that this process replicates the "formulating assessments" that victims are already doing on their own).

77 *See, e.g., id.* at 5 (noting, however, that some women are more likely to provide this kind of private information to the court).

78 Katie McDevitt, *Dads as Killers: Valley Epidemic: 4 Kids have Died at Fathers' Hands in Custody Disputes,* EAST VALLEY TRIBUNE (Nov. 22, 2007). For example, in one 2007 case in Arizona, an engineer and business owner shot his six-year-old son and four-year-old daughter. While he had previously threatened the children's mother with the same hunting rifle and threatened to kill her when she brought up divorce, nonetheless the wife told police in a screening that her husband would not hurt himself, her, or the children.

79 *See, e.g.,* MESSING ET AL., *supra* note 24, at 19 ("Indeed, research has found that survivors are more likely to underestimate than overestimate their risk, possibly as a coping strategy in an effort to maintain a normal life. . . ."); Ed Balint, *Special Report: Trying to Predict the Risk of Domestic Abuse,* INDEONLINE.COM (Mar. 30, 2016), www.indeonline.com.

80 *See, e.g.,* WEBSDALE, *supra* note 22, at 5 (explaining the results of a focus group at a Nashville domestic violence center in which women of color reported a sensitivity to reporting domestic violence within their community).

81 *See, e.g., id.*

82 *See, e.g.,* WEBSDALE, *supra* note 22, at 5.

83 *See, e.g., id.* at 5–6 (noting, however, that agency personnel who administer these tools can mitigate this concern by using "warmer and supportive body language" and "adapt[ing] the instrument to the experiences and emotional affect of women").

84 *See, e.g.,* MESSING ET AL., *supra* note 24, at 19 (summarizing the results of one study in which "approximately 50% of the women who were killed or almost killed by their intimate partner did not accurately assess him (or her) as capable of homicide").

85 *Id.* at 24.

86 *See, e.g., id.* at 24 ("At the core of the LAP Process is a willing partnership between law enforcement and a local domestic violence service provider."). High danger victims are advised of the assessment and then encouraged to speak to a hotline worker. *Id.*

87 Troy Wayrynen, *Experts: Father Likely Sought Control,* COLUMBIAN (May 1, 2011), at A1 (explaining that experts believe red flags are rare and also revealing that his own lawyer "detected nothing out of the ordinary about his client").

88 Janet and Ricardo Weinstein, *"I Know Better Than That": The Role of Emotions and the Brain in Family Law Disputes,* 7 J. L. & FAM. STUD. 351, 397 (2005).

89 NATIONAL FOOTBALL LEAGUE, PERSONAL CONDUCT POLICY (Dec. 10, 2014), http://static.nfl.com [hereinafter NFL CONDUCT POLICY].

90 Don Van Natta Jr. & Kevin Van Valkenburg, *Rice Case: Purposeful Misdirection by Team, Scant Investigation by NFL,* ESPN.COM (Sept. 19, 2014), www.espn.com.

91 *Id.*

92 NFL CONDUCT POLICY, *supra* note 89.

93 *Id.*

94 *Id.*

95 For example, every Congress since 1995 has considered, but failed to pass, a bill providing employment-related protections to victims of domestic violence. GOLDSCHEID & RUNGE, *supra* note 53, at 13 (casting these state interventions as the "next frontier in protecting victims of domestic violence").

96 *Id.* at 6 (explaining, for example, that states often disseminate information about domestic violence and train human resource professionals).

97 *Id.* at 43 ("The challenge for researchers will be to identify which programs, parts of programs, and/or combinations of services provide the most effective approaches for dealing with victims, batterers, and their children.").

98 Balint, *supra* note 79 (quoting Police Chief Bruce Lawver).

99 Peter Jaffe, Claire Crooks, & Samatha Poisson, *Common Misconceptions in Addressing Domestic Violence in Child Custody Disputes,* JUVENILE & FAM. CT. J. 57, 59 (2003).

100 KY. REV. STAT. § 403.741 (2010) (allowing the court to review and consider the respondent's criminal history, particularly past violence and non-compliance with orders).

101 KY. REV. STAT. § 403.7505 (2005).

102 *See, e.g.,* Town of Castle Rock v. Gonzales, 574 U.S. 748 (2005) (disallowing suit under 42 U.S.C. 1983 when a police department failed to enforce a restraining order).

103 *See* NATIONAL COUNCIL FOR JUVENILE AND FAMILY COURT JUDGES, www.ncjfcj.org.

104 Wayrynen, *supra* note 87.

105 *Judicial Shortcomings for Domestic Violence Victims*, SHARE, INC. (May 13, 2016), https://sharemorgancounty.org (explaining that "the next step in domestic violence prevention is 'shifting the community conversation to the unhealthy aspects of masculinity'").

106 *See, e.g.,* Hon. MaryLee Underwood, Heidi Schissler, & Sen. Sara Beth Gregory, *Adult Protection Legislation*, supporting the enactment of KY REV. STAT. 209.032 (2014) (noting that the listing only gets finalized after an appeal or a time period for appeal). The Kentucky Adult Protective Services Caregiver Misconduct Registry is available online at https://prdweb.chfs.ky.gov. This registry allows free searching for validated and substantiated findings of adult abuse, neglect, or exploitation, but the registry only dates back to 2014 because of its recent creation.

107 John Marchlowska, *A Lawyer's Role in Safety Planning for Victims of Domestic Violence*, PREVENTATIVE L. REP. 13–15 (2001–2002) (noting that the lethality assessment considers the abuser's access to the victim, threats made to the victim, weapons, severity of past abuse, possessive behaviors, and mental health concerns, while the safety plan considers the victim's fears, home security, documentation, and connectivity).

108 *See, e.g.,* MODEL RULES OF PROF'L CONDUCT r. 1.6(b)(6) (AM. BAR ASS'N 1983).

109 MODEL RULES OF PROF'L CONDUCT r. 1.6(b)(1), 1.6(b)(6) (AM. BAR ASS'N 1983). Of course there are state variations of these specific rules as codified.

110 MODEL RULES OF PROF'L CONDUCT r. 3.3(b), 3.3(c) (AM. BAR ASS'N 1983) ("The duties stated in paragraph . . . (b) continue to the conclusion of the proceeding, and apply even if compliance requires disclosure of information otherwise protected by Rule 1.6.").

111 *See generally* John M. Burman, *Lawyers and Domestic Violence: Raising the Standard of Practice*, 9 MICH. J. GENDER & L. 207 (2003).

112 *See generally* Davies & Sturge-Apple, *supra* note 52, at 184.

113 *See generally* Coker, *supra* note 60.

114 *Id.* at 598.

115 *Id.* (explaining the collateral consequences of hyper-incarceration, including the toxic masculinity dimensions of incarceration).

116 *The Verdict Is In: Mandate Domestic Violence Training for Judges*, THE MARY BYRON PROJECT (July 8, 2015). *See generally* Deborah Epstein, *Effective Interventions in Domestic Violence Cases: Rethinking the Roles of Prosecutors, Judges, and the Court System*, 11 YALE J. L. & FEMINISM 1, 44 (1999).

117 Epstein, *supra* note 116, at 44.

118 *Id.* The National Judicial Institute on Domestic Violence, for example, reflects a partnership with the U.S. Department of Justice's Office on Violence Against Women, the National Council of Juvenile and Family Court Judges, and Futures

Without Violence. NATIONAL JUDICIAL INSTITUTE ON DOMESTIC VIO-
LENCE, https://njidv.org (last visited Nov. 14, 2016). The organization's mission is
to assist judges in handling domestic violence, being leaders on these issues, and
"advancing the state of knowledge about how the justice system can intervene in
and prevent violence against women and children, adolescents and elders."

119 Such training would need to be mandatory to be effective, which is a source of
some tension in the field. *The Verdict Is In, supra* note 116 (critiquing a decision by
Kentucky judges to shift a mandatory domestic violence training to voluntary).
This approach combats the "'preaching to the choir' phenomenon" and ensures
that the judges most in need of the training are able to receive it. *Id.*

120 *Id.* at 669. And there are strong examples of innovative models within the domestic violence movement that are interconnected to other systemic community
conversations. For example, INCITE! is an organization that "sets out to end
violence against women, gender-nonconforming, and trans people of color and
their communities." Zai, *Social Justice Approach to Ending Domestic Violence in
Context*, BCRW BLOG (Apr. 7, 2014), http://bcrw.barnard.edu. This organization
acknowledges the dangerous intersections of violence by race, class, and gender.
It understands that "increasing law enforcement is actually not helpful in the fight
to end domestic and sexual violence against women of color." *Id.* These conversations bring the law reform responses involving victims and perpetrators together.
Other examples exist of collaboration between anti-violence groups in communities generally and initiatives to end domestic violence. *See id.* (describing collaboration among NY-based anti-violence groups and domestic violence groups,
which sought to "explore the challenges of building a broader anti-violence movement within a social and gender justice framework").

121 *See* Lehrner & Allen, *supra* note 4, at 671 ("A failure to engage with local communities constrains both the nature of interventions with victims and the possibilities for creative new approaches to social change.").

122 *Id.* at 657.

123 Jamie Abrams, *The Feminist Case for Acknowledging Women's Acts of Violence*, 27
YALE J. LAW & FEMINISM 101 (2016).

124 *See, e.g.,* Alex Williams, *How to Spot a Member of Generation Z*, N.Y. TIMES
(Sept. 18, 2015) ("'This group seems much less attached to traditional gender
binaries or linear definitions of sexuality,' said Lucie Greene, a trend forecaster
at J. Walter Thompson, the advertising giant. 'It's all about individualism and the
right to be whatever you want.'").

125 *See generally* Lynne N. Henderson, *The Wrongs of Victim's Rights*, 37 STAN. L.
REV. 937 (1995) (critiquing and considering the impact of victim's rights approaches). *See also* Weissman, *supra* note 7, at 231. Weissman is specifically concerned with the inattention given to socioeconomic structures.

126 Lehrner & Allen, *supra* note 4, at 662.

127 *See generally* Priya Kandaswamy, *"You Trade in a Man for the Man": Domestic
Violence and the U.S. Welfare State*, AM. Q. 253, 260 (2010) ("A structural problem

is reframed as a question of cultivating individual skills and responsibility, and reform of the individual is seen as a means of moving women from dependency (whether on the state or on an abusive partner) to independence. . . .").

128 *See* Lehrner & Allen, *supra* note 4, at 673.

129 Coker, *supra* note 60, at 596 (advocating for greater coalitions with the prison abolition movement and work to end hyper-incarceration).

130 *Id.* at 669.

131 GOODMARK, *supra* note 2, at 4–5.

132 Weissman, *supra* note 7, at 231 (explaining that the causes of violence are varied and complex and are often interconnected with considerations of historic and structural context).

13

Harm Reduction in the Domestic Violence Context

COURTNEY CROSS

I. Introduction

Domestic violence in the United States has long been recognized as a public health crisis.[1] Yet it is the legal response to domestic violence— more specifically, efforts to criminally prosecute batterers—that receives the lion's share of national funding to combat this epidemic.[2] Over the last half century, domestic violence has been transformed from a painful secret that women were only beginning to discover was not theirs alone to bear, to a broadly condemned phenomenon for which survivors are able to invoke the power of the law for protection. The availability of non-legal services, including domestic violence shelters (the long-time bulwark of the domestic violence moment), therapeutic programs, and a wide variety of educational courses, has also expanded dramatically since the early 1970s.[3] Yet despite near-universal public censure and the undeniable progress embodied in the resources and remedies now available to many survivors,[4] rates of domestic violence have remained fairly steady.[5]

Law and public health both attempt to prevent domestic violence and mitigate its impact on survivors and communities. The legal system does so primarily by employing different theories of punishment: deterrence to prevent future violence, retribution to punish the batterer, and incapacitation to protect the public.[6] Survivors are also able to seek civil protection orders, which can include civil remedies ranging from stay-away orders to financial damages.[7] The legal system is, by its very nature, limited to measures provided for by law and attainable through court.[8]

The public health field, on the other hand, is grounded in developing interdisciplinary, community-based, data-driven programs.[9] Public health approaches to domestic violence are thus able to be significantly more flexible and adaptable than are legal responses. Moreover, public health programs are able to expeditiously implement lessons learned across myriad global initiatives while the law moves at a far slower pace. Despite the insights from the public health field that could be utilized by lawyers in different contexts, lawyers are rarely informed about public health developments that could be beneficial to their practice.[10]

One public health philosophy that has yet to be explicitly transferred into the U.S. domestic violence context is that of harm reduction. Harm reduction is a cluster of principles developed in the context of working with individuals engaging in high-risk behavior.[11] Rather than demand that an individual abstain from such behavior, which may not be realistic, harm reduction focuses on mitigating collateral dangers associated with the behavior. Depending on the individual, this may include strategies to decrease or ultimately cease the high-risk behavior, or it may simply consist of maintenance strategies.[12] One example of this approach is the long-term prescription of methadone to heroin users: rather than insist on the dangerous process of "cold-turkey" withdrawal, heroin users are instead prescribed a controlled opiate derivative that mimics some effects of opioids while curbing cravings and minimizing withdrawal symptoms.[13] At its core, harm reduction accepts the inevitability of high-risk behavior and prioritizes individuals' own assessments of their needs and goals over normative assumptions.

In many ways, harm reduction has a great deal in common with the early domestic violence movement: both focus on individuals' and communities' holistic needs and empowerment. The domestic violence movement, like contemporary harm reduction practitioners, initially placed great credence in survivors being able to define their own goals and determine their own methods for achieving them.[14] This chapter argues that the domestic violence movement should explicitly incorporate principles of harm reduction into its mission, and section II discusses harm reduction in greater depth, using examples from the illicit drug and sex work contexts. Section III explores the overlap between harm reduction and the early domestic violence movement and highlights the compatibility of harm reduction with other practices serving survivors. Section IV suggests one specific area where harm reduction could be incorporated into the domestic violence movement: working with survivors who have not left their abusive partners. This section analyzes the potential harm survivors face in staying or leaving abusive relationships and argues that harm reduction policies would better serve survivors than the legal system's current emphasis on separation. Section V closes by acknowledging the political challenges of explicitly incorporating harm reduction techniques into the domestic violence movement, but concludes by arguing that doing so would benefit survivors and reinvigorate the movement.

II. Harm Reduction

A. The Basic Principles of Harm Reduction

The modern harm reduction movement got its start in Great Britain in the 1920s, a time when misuse of and addiction to opium and cocaine were becoming increasingly widespread.[15] Rather than criminalize all possession of these substances, the British government, in consultation with the medical profession, crafted a policy in which medical professionals were allowed to prescribe and administer opium derivatives and cocaine to patients who were struggling with addiction and the harmful side effects of withdrawal.[16] This model of treating addiction as a disease and allowing medical professionals to incorporate illegal substances into addiction treatment programs rather than requiring complete and immediate cessation was not without controversy, but nonetheless represents a harm reduction approach that is still being practiced to this day.[17]

While this early example of harm reduction illuminates harm reduction's commitment to compassionate and pragmatic solutions to public health challenges,[18] it by no means encompasses the entirety of the movement. Rather than a dogmatic set of rules, harm reduction is grounded in principles of dignity and empathy.[19] Its nebulous boundaries make harm reduction challenging to define—and, indeed, there are many different definitions used within the public health field.[20] Yet this same intentional imprecision is what renders harm reduction philosophies relevant both across the many different public health contexts[21] and within myriad public health strategies.[22] Exact definitions of harm reduction are developed within the very settings that they are meant to operate in: that is, every context where harm reduction measures are being designed and implemented has a project-specific definition that is determined by the culture, goals, and barriers that exist in that situation.[23]

Yet despite both the breadth and idiosyncrasy necessary to produce an exacting definition of harm reduction, it is nonetheless characterized by certain hallmarks. Harm reduction interventions focus on improving quality of life as determined by the individuals or groups affected by them.[24] Moreover, intervention outcomes are evaluated in terms of any positive changes made rather than merely whether significant change was accomplished.[25] In their book *Harm Reduction: Pragmatic Strategies for Managing High-Risk Behaviors*, psychology and psychiatry professors G. Alan Marlett, Mary E. Larimer, and Katie Witkiewitz identify eight principles underlying all harm reduction efforts: (1) the level of risk of a certain behavior is rather socially constructed; (2) high-risk behaviors are unlikely to be eradicated; (3) high-risk behaviors do not exist in a vacuum; (4) high-risk behaviors should not be pathologized but rather treated pragmatically; (5) harm exists on a spectrum and can be mitigated through numerous methods; (6) high-risk behaviors should be addressed at both the individual and system-wide level; (7) harm reduction strategies should be driven by the realities of the situation they operate in; and (8) harm reduction is an ethical practice committed to addressing the reality of choices rather than the morality thereof.[26] As such, harm reduction focuses on increasing quality of life and decreasing risk without requiring abstinence from the behaviors in question.[27] It is important to note, however, that harm reduction practices are compatible with abstinence so long as cessation has been identified as a feasible strategy or goal by the individual mapping her or his own path to success.[28]

B. Examples of Harm Reduction in Action

Harm reduction practices have been implemented to mitigate high-risk behaviors across the field of public health. Exploring how harm reduction has influenced responses to intravenous drug use and sex work will shed light on the potential for such practices in other contexts.

1. INTRAVENOUS OPIOID USE

As noted above, the first contemporary application of harm reduction principles occurred nearly a century ago in response to opium and cocaine abuse in Great Britain. Since then, global rates of opiate consumption have decreased.[29] Yet opiate addiction remains widespread and has been declared an epidemic in the United States,[30] where nearly 13,000 people died from overdosing on heroin and over 20,000 people died from overdosing on painkillers in 2015.[31] Although no opiate abuse is free from negative side effects,[32] injection comes with a host of health risks from both the substances themselves and the method of delivery.[33] Harm reduction practices have been prevalent in the public health response to this crisis. Needle exchange programs reduce the risk that injection drug users will contract HIV or hepatitis,[34] while various forms of medically overseen drug maintenance programs provide opioid users with safer, non-injectable, less potent products.[35] Peer-led outreach and education efforts have been effective means for reaching and engaging with members of drug-using communities.[36]

These practices have a positive impact on individuals by reducing the risk of infection and disease, on communities by reducing the burden on law enforcement and emergency services, and on society by reducing overall rates of infection and disease.[37] Moreover, each of these programs can be implemented in an individually and culturally sensitive manner with a focus on increased quality of life rather than a mandate of total drug abstention.

2. SEX WORK

Although harm reduction is most commonly associated with drug use programs, its application is far broader and includes work in areas closer to domestic violence than drug use. Harm reduction has proven valuable in reducing the spread of HIV/AIDS among sex workers—a vulnerable population with extremely high rates of HIV.[38] To reduce the spread of HIV and other sexually transmitted infections to sex workers from individuals paying for sex, harm reduction–informed programs have focused on peer-to-peer education and outreach programs, distribution of condoms and other forms of protection, and social and relational support.[39] Some programs have had sex workers provide health education to men who pay for sex, with beneficial results.[40]

In addition to reducing the risk of exposure to disease on an individual level, these programs also reduce visits to emergency services providers within the community. On a policy level, harm reduction programs are also advocating for the decriminalization of sex work, expansion of employment policies to include and cover sex workers, and implementation of programs to better serve low-income women more broadly.[41] Harm reduction policies in the sex-work context exemplify how harm reduction can positively impact vulnerable individuals in often coercive situations.

III. Harm Reduction and Domestic Violence

A. Similarities between the Movements

In the United States, the domestic violence movement preceded the first harm reduction programs by over a decade. Yet both began as grassroots initiatives to respond to widespread, yet only recently recognized, harms. In the late 1960s, activists already involved in the feminist movement came to recognize that substantial numbers of women were being abused by their partners.[42] In response, early domestic violence activists, many of whom were survivors themselves, opened their homes to fleeing survivors and established battered women's shelters.[43] These shelters prioritized empowerment and self-determination, focusing on supporting survivors as they identified and worked towards their own goals.[44] Shelters were run without hierarchy and there was little differentiation between shelter workers—many of whom were survivors—and residents.[45] In addition to providing safe places for survivors and their children to stay, domestic violence activists and their coalitions also fought for both legal and social change, focusing on measures that would both upend women's subordination to men and promote women's independence and stability.[46]

Similarly, harm reduction efforts in the United States directly resulted from the recognition that the HIV/AIDS crisis in America was far more widespread than initially understood. Although government agencies were slow to respond to the AIDS epidemic, grassroots organizations were started by individuals in the gay community to educate, protect, and treat members of their communities.[47] For example, the Gay Men's Health Crisis started the first AIDS hotline in 1982, the same year it distributed 50,000 copies of its first newsletter, created a "Buddy" program, and opened an office in San Francisco—all before the federal government provided any funding for medical research.[48] In addition to com-

munity members providing services directly to individuals with HIV/
AIDS and at-risk communities, HIV-focused organizations pressured
the government and medical agencies to take HIV/AIDS research more
seriously and make treatment more widely available.[49]

Both the domestic violence movement and the response to the HIV/
AIDS crisis were born out of the realization that oppressed individuals
(women and gay men, respectively) were experiencing significant harm
that was being overwhelmingly ignored by policy and community responses centered around the interests of heterosexual white men. Both
movements were focused on achieving individual stability, community
resilience, and broader social change. Both relied on and believed in the
voices of those most impacted and were able to achieve concrete success
despite eradicating neither domestic violence nor HIV/AIDS.

B. Harm Reduction in the Domestic Violence Movement

Although activists, advocates, and practitioners in the domestic violence
movement share a commitment to reducing intimate partner violence
at the individual, community, and societal levels, harm reduction
approaches have not been explicitly integrated into mainstream anti-
domestic violence practices in the United States.

Despite this lack of explicit integration, it is worth noting that the
movement does implicitly employ practices that resonate with harm
reduction principles. For example, harm reduction practices include
providing fleeing survivors with access to food, clothing, housing, and
social support, since the services will reduce the risks survivors encounter both while in abusive relationships and later if they do choose to
leave.[50] Likewise, providing client-centered counseling where clients can
make their own decisions about how to proceed with legal cases, and
providing legal services to survivors who may have dropped their cases
in the past also constitute harm reduction practices in the legal sphere,
because they honor a client's ability to know what will, and will not, help
the survivor achieve her or his own goals.[51]

Although the domestic violence movement has strayed from its grassroots beginnings and has traded its more radical politics for mainstream
staying power,[52] it nonetheless remains infused with many of the same
principles that inform harm reduction practices to this day.

C. Where to Apply the Framework

When considering the application of harm reduction principles in the domestic violence context, it may initially be tempting to envision this public health framework applied to batterers rather than to survivors. After all, it is the abusive partner who is committing the harmful acts and who is more in control of stopping the abuse. It is important to note, however, that in as much as battering may negatively impact the actor, it is the survivor who is being more significantly harmed by this behavior—physically, psychologically, and often financially. This chapter focuses on these harms experienced by survivors in violent relationships while nonetheless recognizing that harm reduction programs for batterers are needed to reduce violence.

IV. Survivors Who Stay and the Need for Harm Reduction–Informed Approaches

Given the critical overlap between the domestic violence movement and harm reduction principles, an explicit incorporation of harm reduction frameworks into the everyday work and long-term goals of the movement would improve outcomes for survivors and their communities without undermining the integrity of the movement.[53] Survivors who stay in abusive relationships would particularly benefit. These survivors are often pressured by the legal system to end their relationships and punished when they do not, despite the fact that staying may be a better choice for them and may better allow them to accomplish their goals both within and beyond the relationship. Because choosing to stay puts survivors at risk of experiencing harm at the hands of both the state and their partner, staying can be conceptualized as a high-risk behavior that is fraught with the potential for both direct and indirect harm to some survivors. As such, it presents an opportunity for applying harm reduction principles.

A. Leaving Is the Law

1. THE CRIMINAL RESPONSE TO DOMESTIC VIOLENCE
The legal response to domestic violence puts a great deal of pressure on survivors to end abusive relationships and permanently separate from

their partners.[54] This phenomenon is most apparent in the criminal context once law enforcement begins investigating potential domestic violence. Due to widely implemented mandatory arrest laws, if a police officer has probable cause to believe that domestic violence has occurred, that officer must arrest the alleged abusive partner—*regardless* of the wishes of the survivor.[55] These policies were put in place in response to the legitimate outcry by domestic violence activists over law enforcement's refusal to hold batterers accountable for their actions.[56] Yet the pendulum has swung too far in the opposite direction, as the very individuals these policies were intended to protect have been stripped of their agency and autonomy.[57] Additionally, under mandatory arrest policies, survivors face increased rates of arrest themselves,[58] without necessarily experiencing increased safety from continued abuse.[59]

In conjunction with mandatory arrest policies, many jurisdictions have also adopted policies to encourage or ensure the prosecution of alleged batterers.[60] Because of the widespread adoption of no-drop prosecution policies, prosecutors are more likely to pursue domestic violence cases: in jurisdictions with "hard" no-drop policies, prosecutors will go forward regardless of the survivor's wishes and often without her or his involvement, while prosecutors in jurisdictions with "soft" no-drop policies will focus more on what kind of support a survivor needs to stay separated and involved in the prosecution.[61] Like mandatory arrest policies, no-drop prosecution policies were enacted to ensure that batterers were brought to justice.[62] Yet, like mandatory arrest policies, no-drop prosecution policies also override individual survivors' actual needs with the blanket assumption that separation and criminalization will best serve all survivors.[63]

Once a criminal case is filed, most prosecutors will either seek pretrial detention or pretrial conditions of release that prohibit the defendant from coming near the survivor, communicating with her or him in any way, and returning to their potentially shared home.[64] Under these circumstances, the defendant and the survivor cannot legally resume their relationship, nor can they jointly determine whether or how to restructure their relationship in light of recent events—the criminal case has essentially mandated that their relationship come to a complete and final end.[65] Moreover, if the defendant violates these conditions of release, even with the survivor's full consent, the defendant may nonetheless be charged with a new crime that will come with the same requirements and consequences.[66] Those survivors who abide by these conditions of release but decide not to testify against their partner are not immune from punishment as they may be arrested on material witness bench warrants and forced to testify.[67] Similarly, survivors who apply for or receive funding from their state's victims' compensation fund may be denied or forced to forfeit funds if they cease cooperating with law enforcement.[68]

For survivors who are willing and able to engage the criminal legal response to domestic violence from start to finish, these policies and practices may no doubt prove to be both desirable and beneficial.[69] Survivors who are unwilling or unable to pursue criminal intervention will find themselves silenced and without options, forced to either comply with the criminal system's one-size-fits-all approach or risk their partner's, or even their own, liberty by defying it. Many survivors instead attempt to avoid the criminal system altogether to prevent unwanted, unhelpful, or unsafe intervention.[70]

2. THE CIVIL RESPONSE TO DOMESTIC VIOLENCE

Survivors who decide to seek protection from the civil legal response to domestic violence or who are pressured to do so by the child welfare system will also encounter pressure to end their abusive relationships.[71] Survivors who seek civil protection orders against their abusive partners may find, for example, that a judge is unwilling to craft the order in a manner that would allow the couple to stay together or remain in contact.[72] This may be in part because judges have long seen civil protection orders as a tool for judges, and not survivors, to address domestic violence,[73] and in part because judges struggle to understand or empathize with a survivor's desire to have any kind of relationship with an abusive partner.[74] When it comes to domestic violence, judges often substitute their own values and goals for those of survivors, resulting in protection orders that do not meet survivors' needs.[75] This could include ordering unrequested remedies like a physical stay-away order, no-contact order, eviction order, order to pay restitution, order to drug test, or an order to complete mental health counseling or batterer's intervention treatment.[76] While some survivors may not have requested these remedies because they feel they are unnecessary, others may have avoided them strategically if they believe such requirements imposed on their abusive partner will make them *less* safe. Because survivors often seek protection orders to regain control in their relationships and put their abusive partners on notice that they will no longer tolerate abusive behavior,[77] judges who override survivors' wishes are denying survivors the opportunity to dictate their future on their own terms.[78]

Moreover, once a civil protection order is in place, survivors may also struggle to have it vacated or modified.[79] A survivor may seek to vacate an order that is no longer necessary or modify an order to allow for more robust co-parenting, less restrictive communication, or even reconciliation. While a judge may be wary of how such changes may impact a survivor's safety, the decision to ignore a litigant's unopposed motion is highly unusual in other civil contexts.[80] Yet in the domestic violence context, survivors must overcome judges' assumptions and biases in order to modify or vacate their protection orders as they see fit.[81] For survivors who are unable to accomplish their goals in court, the parties must either abide by the court's structuring of the relationship or risk the criminal consequences of violating a protection order.[82]

The civil legal system is critically important for many survivors who are able to obtain their desired results. Survivors who choose to opt out of the criminal system may instead be able to fully accomplish their goals with a civil protection order.[83] Yet as important as it is to acknowledge the successes generated by the civil legal response to domestic violence, it is also imperative to call attention to those who experience resistance or rejection from that same system.

B. When Staying Makes More Sense

1. SEPARATION VIOLENCE AND RETALIATION

The legal system's push to separate survivors from their abusive partners is grounded in the desire to provide survivors with immediate, albeit short-term, safety.[84] But separation itself may not result in safety; it is well known that the threat of violence increases for many survivors at the time of separation.[85] This violence may be physical—in fact, homicide rates are highest among survivors after they have left the relationship.[86] The violence may also intentionally exploit vulnerable aspects of a survivor's identity. For example, an abusive partner may threaten to interfere with a non-citizen survivor's immigration status or threaten to get a survivor's parole or probation revoked.[87]

Survivors who fear this kind of retaliation or who have experienced it after previous attempts to leave may thus make a strategic decision to stay in a violent relationship in order to stay safer.[88] Yet strategic decisions around safety, while important, are not the only reasons survivors may elect to stay in unsafe relationships.

2. FROM LOVE TO LOGISTICS

Many survivors are not ready to end abusive relationships, whether because they love their partners, want to give their partners another chance, or want their children to maintain their relationship with their other parent.[89] Others believe that they can and should salvage the relationship and heal and protect their partners.[90] While it should come as no surprise that love plays a significant role in individuals' calculations about ending even a violent relationship,[91] the law nonetheless ignores this dynamic completely, with legal actors even going so far as interpreting survivors' expressions of love and commitment as symptoms of mental illness and proof of unworthiness.[92]

In addition to fear of separation violence or love for the partner or the relationship, survivors may simply not be able to afford to leave.[93] For survivors who rely on their abusive partner financially, housing, childcare, transportation, food, and basic necessities may all be unattainable without their partners' involvement.[94] For survivors whose culture or family discourages or forbids separation, the social cost of leaving may also be too high.[95] Further, many survivors from underrepresented communities fear—not incorrectly—that they will not be able to obtain culturally sensitive services to help them navigate the process of leaving an abusive relationship.[96]

3. LOSSES AND TRADE-OFFS

These concerns about the cost of leaving are not speculative. In 2015, social work professor Kristie A. Thomas, psychology professor Lisa Goodman, and social worker Susan Putnins explored both the upsides and downsides of leaving a violent relationship.[97] They distributed a written survey to over 300 survivors seeking domestic violence services across the Northeast, probing participants' thoughts and fears related to obtaining physical safety by leaving the relationship.[98] Their first question was, "To what extent and how does working toward safety affect other life demands?"[99] In response, 62% of respondents said they had to give up too much to be safe, and more than half of the respondents expressed that keeping safe did or would create new problems for themselves and/or loved ones.[100] Over half the participants also said that they experienced or anticipated experiencing problems in seeking safety.[101] These problems were primarily related to loss—loss of physical and emotional safety for themselves and loved ones and loss of the survivor's social support, financial stability, home and "rootedness," parenting control, and freedom.[102]

The survey then asked survivors to what extent they anticipated these challenges before taking action to acquire safety.[103] Of those survivors who reported new problems, respondents were nearly equally split in terms of whether they had or had not anticipated the problems.[104] Survivors who did leave were then asked to reflect on that choice.[105] Twenty-eight percent of survivors who left to seek safety reported that, in hindsight, they would have made a different decision. Among this group, 15% said they would have stayed with their abusive partner and worked on the relationship, 12% said they would have avoided formal support systems and services, and only 6% said they would have sought help sooner.[106] Participants also noted that they wished they had gotten more information about what it would be like to enter a shelter and how hard it would be to maintain safety.[107]

These findings validate survivors' fears of leaving to seek safety and highlight the barriers to maintaining safety in the face of unexpected challenges. The authors refer to these sacrifices in the name of safety as "trade-offs" and note that, for many survivors, "gains in one domain [lead] to losses in another."[108] The authors also make clear that, while not safety-related, many of the domains where survivors experienced loss are extremely important to survivors' well-being, which is why nearly two-thirds reported that they had to "give up too much to be safe."[109]

The many intersecting realities that constrain survivors' choices when navigating abusive relationships also expose survivors to the risk of harm from both their abusive partners and from the state. As such, there are many ways in which applying harm reduction principles would benefit survivors who are in, or have returned to, violent relationships.

C. The Potential Impact of Harm Reduction

While survivors who remain in violent relationships may very well experience continued abuse from their partners, as well as unwanted and potentially dangerous intrusions from the state, leaving may not only fail to solve survivors' problems, it may intensify existing challenges while creating new ones. For some survivors, then, staying may be a safer or more desirable choice—whether the choice is to remain temporarily or longer-term. As the challenges of leaving become more widely known, some in the domestic violence movement are questioning the movement's prioritization of physical safety; many activists and advocates now argue that the movement must move away from physical safety toward a broader conception of stability that would be less adamant about separation.[110] One way to catalyze this shift is for both community-based organizations and the broader domestic violence movement to embrace the principles of harm reduction, especially in the context of survivors who stay in abusive relationships.

1. THE ADVANTAGES OF HARM REDUCTION OVER SEPARATION-BASED STRATEGIES

For several reasons, harm reduction approaches are advantageous to abstinence-based programs, the latter of which are embodied in the current legal response to domestic violence and require complete separation. First, harm reduction is compatible with abstinence without requiring it.[111] Thus, survivors who have left and are struggling, survivors who want to leave but face specific challenges, and survivors who are not ready or able to leave would be equally eligible to receive services and assistance from harm reduction-informed domestic violence organizations. Next, harm reduction supports human rights, especially for individuals who have been marginalized due to their high-risk behaviors.[112] Survivors who do not leave have certainly been stigmatized and marginalized as less credible and less worthy victims. Moreover, domestic violence activists have long advocated for a human rights approach to domestic violence that would directly address the oppression of all victims generally,[113] and this demand has intensified over the last decade.[114]

Third, harm reduction is grounded in culturally competent, flexible strategies that are specifically tailored to the individuals and communities they serve.[115] Rather than a one-size-fits-all approach, harm reduction strategies are formed around individuals' and communities' goals, needs, strengths, and deficits. Such strategies would reduce the likelihood that individual survivors who cannot leave violent relationships fall outside the ambit of domestic violence services. Survivors from underserved communities who stay in their relationships would nonetheless be able to access culturally competent and welcoming services should they choose to seek them out. Next, harm reduction strategies can be empowering.[116] Because individuals and communities rather than service providers or law enforcement dictate their own goals and identify feasible ways of achieving them, they are treated as competent and important agents. Rather than replicating the oppressive dynamic of abusive partners,[117] domestic violence organizations employing harm reduction strategies would begin rebuilding survivors' agency and autonomy.

Finally, harm reduction strategies have widely efficacious outcomes.[118] Not only are harm reduction strategies effective at reducing the harms associated with high-risk behaviors, they are often effective at reducing the high-risk behaviors themselves.[119] In the domestic violence context, this could mean that a byproduct for some survivors in abusive relationships might include less violence and less state intrusion, and actually less commitment to the relationship itself.

2. SPECIFIC HARM REDUCTION STRATEGIES AND THEIR IMPACT

Harm reduction strategies can be implemented at individual, community, and societal levels. In addition to making harm reduction psychotherapy more available at the individual level,[120] other innovative harm reduction–influenced strategies employed by non-legal and legal service providers could include safety planning around staying, as well as having frank conversations and brainstorming sessions around the real challenges of leaving.[121] Currently much safety planning revolves around planning how to leave or how to stay safe after leaving. While these plans are critically important, planning around staying in the relationship would be valuable to survivors who are not yet contemplating leaving.[122] This could involve anything from attempting to avoid triggers or deflect anger to taking self-defense classes—all while underscoring that the abuse is not the survivor's fault but can perhaps nonetheless be mitigated. Discussions around the very real challenges of leaving would serve not to dissuade a survivor from seeking safety but to ensure that, should she or he make this decision, the survivor is prepared to both leave and maintain her or his departure.

Additionally, more holistic services to help the survivor achieve stability and independence, even while in the relationship, would render her or him better able to leave the relationship if so desired.[123] Services including employment and/or public benefits assistance, housing assistance, physical and behavioral health services, and financial management courses would help survivors become more stable and better able to assess and achieve their goals before having to leave a relationship they are not ready to leave. Significantly, these services, if made available to both parties in the relationship, could also reduce battering that may be exacerbated or triggered by socio-economic factors.[124]

Domestic violence programs targeted at the community level might include outreach campaigns that would educate community members on topics including healthy relationships, early signs of abuse, how to best support survivors, and why it is hard for survivors to leave and stay separated from their abusers. Not only would such a campaign foster stronger connections between survivors and their support networks,[125] it would also reduce the stigma felt by survivors about both being abused and not being ready to seek help.

Finally, at the societal level, harm reduction principles would mandate revisiting laws and policies that oppress rather than empower survivors. Laws and policies that constrain survivors' choices must be reworked to maximize their agency. Reform should occur regarding both the direct legal response to domestic violence as well as policies in related fields, like family law and child protection law, that also serve to diminish survivors' choices.[126] In order to achieve these goals, the domestic violence movement must return to its grassroots political origins in which tackling gender-based subordination and the oppression of women take priority over collaborating with the criminal legal system.

V. Challenges and Conclusion

A. *The Political Risks of the Harm Reduction Label*

Despite being an increasingly implemented approach to addressing public health crises, harm reduction has by no means received
mainstream—let alone universal—approval.[127] Politicians have traditionally espoused a "zero-tolerance policy" on domestic violence,
which leaves little room to explore more nuanced, survivor-centered
approaches.[128] Domestic violence activists considering adopting harm
reduction principles should be aware of this reality and the potential
for conflict specifically in the domestic violence context in order to best
craft feasible, successful, and widely supported policies.

1. CONTROVERSY OVER HARM REDUCTION PRACTICES

Although harm reduction originated in and has made positive contributions to the conversation around substance use, it is also in this context
that it has generated the most controversy. Despite widely reported
effectiveness,[129] the U.S. Congress did not repeal its ban against federal
funding for needle exchange programs until late 2015, and recipients of
federal funding are still not allowed to spend federal money on syringes
themselves.[130] In 2016, then-Governor Mike Pence was slow to lift a ban
against needle exchange programs in Indiana despite the state's opioid
injection–related HIV outbreak.[131] In the face of an unprecedented
spread of HIV among drug users in southern Indiana, Pence initially
stood firm against needle exchange programs while new cases of HIV
soared; once he relented and allowed programs to distribute clean
needles, the rate of new infections declined drastically.[132] Like other politicians who opposed needle exchange programs, Pence saw such efforts
as enabling drug use and viewed them as morally wrong.[133] Although he
changed his position, there are still many who believe that harm reduction is too soft on drug users and enables illegal habits.[134]

While America increasingly accepts needle exchange programs, it has
not embraced other drug-related harm reduction approaches employed
in Europe and Canada. One example of a more hands-on harm reduction approach that has been met with opposition in the U.S. is that of
supervised injection sites, where intravenous drug users can bring drugs
and inject them with clean needles under the supervision of a nurse who

can administer overdose medication if necessary.[135] While more common in Europe,[136] until 2017, the only safe injection facilities in North America were located in British Columbia, Canada.[137] In January 2017, Seattle approved the first safe injection site in the United States despite strong opposition.[138] As with needle exchange programs, opponents of safe injection sites posit that they are dangerous and support drug use over treatment.[139] While several states and municipalities are considering similar action, safe injection sites are neither popular nor legal under federal law, and individuals coming and going would not receive immunity from arrest from federal agents.[140]

While harm reduction's greatest gains in terms of visibility have been made in the substance use context, these developments have not been without opposition and critique. The most consistent complaint is that these measures are actually putting drug users in harm's way rather than helping them live drug-free lives. It is not hard to imagine similar, if not more vociferous, objections to policies that aim to support survivors who stay in unsafe relationships. Domestic violence activists and advocates must combat this claim by focusing on the long-term goal of stability rather than the short-term goal of temporary safety, which may not actually produce real safety.

2. THE POTENTIAL FOR INAPPROPRIATE ANALOGIES

Another potential criticism of incorporating harm reduction approaches into working with survivors in abusive relationships is the claim that they are being likened to addicts, which would certainly be an unfair and inaccurate analogy. To employ harm reduction techniques is not to insist that the recipient is in a situation akin to drug addiction. Rather, incorporating harm reduction techniques acknowledges that survivors may have valid reasons for making choices that expose them to risks— risks that can and should be mitigated even if the original decision to stay remains the same. The analogy may actually be more apt on the governmental response side. Survivors are not analogous to drug users, but the state's response to survivors' decisions to stay is about as realistic and effective as Nancy Reagan's "just say no" solution to drug abuse.[141]

Domestic violence advocates and activists must guard against such an analogy being used either as a critique of harm reduction in this context or as shorthand used to explain it. One of harm reduction's core tenets is to avoid pathologizing individuals,[142] which would include any type of assumption or implication that survivors want or need abuse. It is thus doubly critical that proponents of domestic violence harm reduction commit to educating survivors, practitioners, and the public about the nuanced and individualized risks inherent in both being in and leaving abusive relationships.

3. THE FATE OF HARM REDUCTION POLICIES DURING THE TRUMP PRESIDENCY

While it is too soon to predict the place of harm reduction policies in the Trump administration, there is reason to believe that the movement's momentum may slow or cease in the illegal drug-use context. Despite President Trump promising "great compassion" as he signed an executive order establishing a commission to combat drug addiction, that commission has been slow to take action or propose solutions.[143] Additionally, former Health and Human Services Secretary Tom Price referred to medication-assisted treatment, like methadone, for drug addiction as "substituting one opioid for another," a statement squarely at odds with harm reduction philosophies.[144] Attorney General Jeff Sessions has also repeatedly made statements that directly contradict harm reduction philosophies and practices: in addition to praising the abstinence-only drug program D.A.R.E.,[145] he has also long supported tougher criminal sentences, as opposed to non-criminal intervention or treatment, for drug addicts.[146]

Moreover, Jeff Sessions has linked drug use and abuse with violent crime in order to promote his "tough on crime" agenda.[147] This commitment to harsh sentences and one-size-fits-all criminal intervention, combined with Sessions's opposition to reauthorizing the Violence Against Women Act in 2013,[148] suggests that harm reduction policies, especially those aimed at revisiting domestic violence policy, may not be well received by the Department of Justice. Nor does it seem like the president himself, a man who has bragged about committing sexual violence in several contexts, will engage in any meaningful reform of how domestic violence is understood or responded to in the United States.[149]

Nevertheless, as the current administration politicizes safety to promote regressive, "tough on crime" policies, it is of dire importance that the domestic violence movement reject these approaches in favor of evidence-based, trauma-informed, and survivor-centered practices. In addition to resisting these shifts in federal policy, domestic violence activists and advocates must seek to incorporate harm reduction–infused practices at the local level, where they will be most effective at both serving individual survivors and responding to new community needs that may arise out of changes at the federal level.

B. Conclusion

Harm reduction techniques have been gaining momentum as tools to combat public health crises both globally and domestically. Recognizing that high-risk behaviors are unlikely to be eradicated, harm reduction techniques focus on minimizing risk without insisting that the behavior itself must stop. This approach has launched successful initiatives in the substance use context as well as in lesser-known contexts such as sex work. In both cases, individuals are offered education, support, and tools to promote safety so that they can decide how to best achieve their personal goals. Survivors of domestic violence are not typically provided with the same breadth of options. Rather, they are told to leave the abusive relationship and are provided with insufficient resources to maintain this separation.

Explicitly incorporating harm reduction into domestic violence work would entail expanding our conception of how survivors actually respond to domestic violence to include possibly staying in the relationship. Survivors who cannot or do not want to leave their relationship should be able to access support, education, and resources from domestic violence organizations that would enable them to achieve their goals, even if that goal is not separation. It may be that helping survivors achieve stability will encourage them to seek safety, but this cannot be a precondition to working with survivors who are in abusive relationships.

Embracing harm reduction in the domestic violence context may be a politically difficult choice, as it would require the movement to reevaluate its longstanding relationship with law enforcement and its prioritization of the legal system as the most effective response to domestic violence. Yet, in so doing, the movement would not be making a radical departure so much as it would be returning to its more politicized roots, which were grounded in the same individualized goals and holistic needs that are central to harm reduction. Now more than ever, survivors need thoughtful, individually tailored remedies both within and outside of the legal system: harm reduction principles, which value survivors' dignity, autonomy, and experiences, should be at the forefront of this reform.

Author's Note

Thanks are due to Jane Stoever for organizing the Politicization of Safety Conference as well as to all the incredible panelists and participants. Thanks also to Tamara Kuennen for insights into this piece.

NOTES

1 *See, e.g.,* CTRS. FOR DISEASE CONTROL & PREVENTION, COST OF INTI-MATE PARTNER VIOLENCE AGAINST WOMEN IN THE UNITED STATES 3 (2003); Jane H. White, *Violence: A Public Health Epidemic,* HEALTH PROGRESS (Jan.–Feb. 1994), at 18–20.

2 Deborah M. Weissman, *Law, Social Movements, and the Political Economy of Domestic Violence,* 20 DUKE J. GENDER L. & POL'Y 221, 226–28 (2013); ANANNYA BHATTACHARJEE, WHOSE SAFETY?: WOMEN OF COLOR AND THE VIO-LENCE OF LAW ENFORCEMENT 27 (2001); LEIGH GOODMARK, A TROUBLED MARRIAGE 21 (2012).

3 *See, e.g,* LISA GOODMAN & DEBORAH EPSTEIN, LISTENING TO BATTERED WOMEN: A SURVIVOR-CENTERED APPROACH TO ADVOCACY, MENTAL HEALTH, AND JUSTICE 34 (2008) (discussing the rapid expansion of shelters and services for battered women).

4 It is important to note that existence of programs does not necessarily imply ac-cess. For survivors from underrepresented communities, the presence of nearby services or programs may not render these services culturally appropriate or available. Moreover, for rural survivors, resources and programming may be prohibitively far.

5 GOODMARK, *supra* note 2, at 21.

6 *See generally* JEFFREY FAGAN, THE CRIMINALIZATION OF DOMESTIC VIO-LENCE: PROMISES AND LIMITS (1996).

7 Margaret E. Johnson, *Redefining Harm, Reimagining Remedies, and Reclaiming Domestic Violence Law,* 42 UC DAVIS L. REV. 1107, 1111 (2009) [hereinafter John-son, *Redefining Harm*].

8 Camille M. Davidson, *What's Love Got to Do with It?: Examining Domestic Vio-lence as a Public Health Issue Using* Their Eyes Were Watching God, 81 UMKC L. REV. 867, 869 (2013) (discussing examples of survivors who would not encounter the legal system during the navigation of their abusive relationships).

9 CTRS. FOR DISEASE CONTROL & PREVENTION, THE PUBLIC HEALTH AP-PROACH TO VIOLENCE PREVENTION 1 (2015).

10 Linda L. Chezem, *Public Health Law & Equal Access to Justice in Rural America*, 59 S.D. L. REV. 529, 529 (2014).

11 Susan E. Collins et al., *Current Status, Historical Highlights, and Basic Principles of Harm Reduction, in* HARM REDUCTION: PRAGMATIC STRATEGIES FOR MANAGING HIGH-RISK BEHAVIORS 1, 6–10 (G. Alan Marlat et al. eds., 2d ed. 2012).

12 HARM REDUCTION COALITION, PRINCIPLES OF HARM REDUCTION, available at http://harmreduction.org (last visited Mar. 20, 2017).

13 *See, e.g.,* Miranda W. Langendam et al., *The Impact of Harm-Reduction-Based Methadone Treatment on Mortality Among Heroin Users*, 91 A. J. OF PUB. HEALTH 775 (2001).

14 GOODMAN & EPSTEIN, *supra* note 3, at 35.

15 Collins et al., *supra* note 11, at 10.

16 *Id.* at 11.

17 *See, e.g.,* Gavin Bart, *Maintenance Medication for Opiate Addiction: The Foundation of Recovery*, 31 J. ADDICTIVE DISEASES 2017 (2012) (discussing long-term opiate maintenance medications as successful in addiction treatment). *See also* DRUG POL'Y ALLIANCE, HEROIN-ASSISTED TREATMENT (HAT) (2016) (exploring the positive outcomes achieved in Europe and Canada through the administration of pharmacological heroin to addicts who have struggled with other maintenance medications).

18 *See* Collins et al., *supra* note 11, at 6–7 (describing the ways in which compassion and pragmatism comprise omnipresent components of harm reduction strategies).

19 *Id.* ("Harm reduction is more of an 'attitude' than a fixed set of rules and regulations, and has described this attitude as a humanitarian stance that accepts the inherent dignity of life and facilitates the ability to 'see oneself in the eyes of others.'").

20 *See, e.g.,* Andrew Lee Ball, *HIV, Injecting Drug Use and Harm Reduction: A Public Health Response*, 102 ADDICTION 684, 686 (2007) (noting that, even a decade ago, "there is still no universally accepted definition for, and use of, the term 'harm reduction'. This is not through lack of interest or debate").

21 Harm reduction strategies have proven beneficial in many contexts including but not limited to HIV/AIDS (*see, e.g.,* Ball, *supra* note 20); tobacco usage (*see, e.g.,* Zachary Chan & Michael Siegel, *Electronic Cigarettes As a Harm Reduction Strategy for Tobacco Control: A Step Forward or a Repeat of Past Mistakes?*, 32 J. OF PUB. HEALTH POL'Y 16 (2011)); heroin addiction (*see, e.g.,* Langendam et al., *supra* note 13); alcohol consumption (*see, e.g.,* Mary E. Larimer et al., *Harm Reduction for Alcohol Problems, in* HARM REDUCTION: PRAGMATIC STRATE-GIES FOR MANAGING HIGH-RISK BEHAVIORS 63 (G. Alan Marlat et al. eds., 2d ed. 2012); and risky sexual behavior (*see, e.g.,* Michael Peake Andrasik & Ty W. Lostutter, *Harm Reduction for High-Risk Sexual Behavior and HIV, in* HARM

REDUCTION: PRAGMATIC STRATEGIES FOR MANAGING HIGH-RISK BE-
HAVIORS (G. Alan Marlat et al. eds., 2d ed. 2012).

22 *See* Collins et al., *supra* note 11, at 3 (noting harm reduction's presence in multiple types of public health responses "including public health policy, prevention, intervention, education, peer support, and advocacy").

23 *Id.* at 8 ("Defining harm depends on various factors, including the culture, the level (e.g., individual, community, and societal), and the constellation of targeted behaviors in the context of which harm is considered.").

24 *Id.* at 9.

25 *Id.*

26 *Id.* at 18–21.

27 *Id.* at 22.

28 *Id.*

29 UNITED NATIONS OFFICE ON DRUGS & CRIME, A CENTURY OF INTER-
NATIONAL DRUG CONTROL 3 (2009) ("In 1906, 25 million people were using opium in the world (1.5% of the world population) compared with 16.5 [million] opiate users today (0.25% of the world population).").

30 HEALTH & HUMAN SERVS., THE OPIOID EPIDEMIC: BY THE NUMBERS (2016).

31 AM. SOC'Y OF ADDICTION MED., OPIOID ADDICTION: 2016 FACTS & FIGURES 1 (2016).

32 *See, e.g.,* TAITE ADAMS, OPIATE ADDICTION: THE PAINKILLER ADDICTION EPIDEMIC, HEROIN ADDICTION AND THE WAY OUT 21 (2013).

33 See, e.g., *Overall Life-Threatening Risks of Abusing Painkillers*, NARCONON, www .narconon.org (last visited Feb. 6, 2018) (noting that the additives often included in injectable heroin and pain killers may cause serious health problems, as can injection with dirty syringes).

34 Anna Maria Barry-Jester, *It Took 20 Years For The Government To Pay For An Obvious Way To Prevent HIV*, FIVETHIRTYEIGHT.COM (Jan. 8, 2016, 2:10 PM), https://fivethirtyeight.com.

35 Jason R. Kilmer et al., *Reducing Harm Associated with Illicit Drug Use: Opiates, Amphetamines, Cocaine, Steroids, and Other Substances, in* HARM REDUCTION: PRAGMATIC STRATEGIES FOR MANAGING HIGH-RISK BEHAVIORS 170, 172–79 (G. Alan Marlat et al. eds., 2d ed. 2012) (discussing several types of maintenance drugs prescribed to opioid users).

36 *Id.* at 184 (noting that "innovative outreach programs, such as those using peer health advocates, may be an effective way to provide information to users who might not otherwise receive information" and providing an example of one such program that improved outcomes among both the community and the peer leaders themselves).

37 Collins et al., *supra* note 11, at 8.

38 Adrasik & Lostutter, *supra* note 21, at 214 (describing HIV rates among sex workers as "some of the highest HIV rates in the world").

39 *Id.* at 214–15. An example of a program providing these services to sex workers in District of Columbia is the nonprofit HIPS which provides counseling, HIV and hepatitis testing, and safer sex materials—which are available both on-site and via a van that takes products to areas frequented by sex workers. Recognizing the high overlap between sex work and drug use, HIPS provides needle exchange services, linkages to care, and treatment adherence and counseling services. For more information, see www.hips.org.

40 Adrasik & Lostutter, *supra* note 21, at 215.

41 *Id.*

42 GOODMAN & EPSTEIN, *supra* note 3, at 31 (noting that these discoveries of widespread abuse were made by women participating in feminist consciousness-raising groups).

43 *Id.* at 33.

44 Johnson, *Redefining Harm, supra* note 7, at 1125.

45 G. Kristian Miccio, *A House Divided: Mandatory Arrest, Domestic Violence, and the Conservatization of the Battered Women's Movement,* 42 HOUS. L. REV. 237, 259 (2005).

46 *Id.* at 261–62.

47 Collins et al., *supra* note 11, at 16.

48 *GMHC/HIV/AIDS Timeline,* GAY MEN'S HEALTH CRISIS, www.gmhc.org (last visited Feb. 6, 2018).

49 Collins et al., *supra* note 11, at 16.

50 BRITISH COLUMBIA SOC'Y OF TRANSITION HOUSES, REDUCING BARRIERS TO SUPPORT FOR WOMEN FLEEING VIOLENCE: A TOOLKIT FOR SUPPORTING WOMEN WITH VARYING LEVELS OF MENTAL WELLNESS AND SUBSTANCE USE 3–4 (2011).

51 *Id.*

52 *See generally* Miccio, *supra* note 45, at 248–65; Courtney Cross, *Reentering Survivors: Invisible at the Intersection of the Criminal Legal System and the Domestic Violence Movement,* 31 BERKELEY J. GENDER L. & JUST. 60, 87–102 (2016).

53 In fact, such evolution could reinvigorate the movement by returning it to its political and politicized roots.

54 GOODMARK, *supra* note 2, at 9; Margaret E. Johnson, *Balancing Liberty, Dignity, and Safety: The Impact of Domestic Violence Lethality Screening,* 32 CARDOZO L. REV. 519 (2010). Non-legal domestic violence advocacy also prioritizes separation. *See, e.g.,* JILL DAVIES, WHEN BATTERED WOMEN STAY . . . ADVOCACY BEYOND LEAVING 5–6 (2008).

55 Miccio, *supra* note 45, at 265; Cheryl Hanna, *No Right to Choose,* 109 HARV. L. REV. 1849, 1859–60 (1996).

56 Miccio, *supra* note 45, at 265; Aya Gruber, *The Feminist War on Crime,* 92 IOWA L. REV. 741, 757–58 (2007).

57 Miccio, *supra* note 45, at 293–94; Leigh Goodmark, *Autonomy Feminism: An Anti-Essentialist Critique of Mandatory Interventions in Domestic Violence Cases,*

37 FLA. ST. U. L. REV. 1, 4 (2009) [hereinafter Goodmark, *Autonomy Feminism*]; Tamara L. Kuennen, *Analyzing the Impact of Coercion on Domestic Violence Victims: How Much is Too Much?*, 22 BERKELEY J. GENDER L. & JUST. 2, 6 (2007) [hereinafter Kuennen, *Analyzing the Impact of Coercion*].

58 Gruber, *supra* note 56, at 813; Ellen L. Pence & Melanie F. Shepard, *An Introduction: Developing a Coordinated Community Response, in* COORDINATING COMMUNITY RESPONSES TO DOMESTIC VIOLENCE: LESSONS FROM DULUTH AND BEYOND 7 (Melanie F. Shepard & Ellen L. Pence eds., 1999); Donna Coker, *Shifting Power for Battered Women: Law, Material Resources, and Poor Women of Color*, 33 UC DAVIS L. REV. 1009, 1043 (2000) [hereinafter Coker, *Shifting Power for Battered Women*]; Andrea Richie, *Law Enforcement Violence against Women of Color, in* THE COLOR OF VIOLENCE: THE INCITE! ANTHOLOGY 140 (IN-CITE! ed. 2006); Myrna S. Raeder, *Preserving Family Ties for Domestic Violence Survivors and Their Children by Invoking a Human Rights Approach to Avoid the Criminalization of Mothers Based on the Acts and Accusations of Their Batterers*, 17 J. GENDER RACE & JUST. 105, 114 (2014).

59 Donna Coker, *Crime Control and Feminist Law Reform in Domestic Violence Law: A Critical Review*, 4 BUFF. CRIM. L. REV. 801, 824 (2001) [hereinafter Coker, *Crime Control*]; Coker, *Shifting Power for Battered Women*, *supra* note 58, at 1009, 1041; GOODMAN & EPSTEIN, *supra* note 3, at 75.

60 Angela Corsilles, *No-Drop Policies in the Prosecution of Domestic Violence Cases: Guarantee To Action or Dangerous Solution?*, 63 FORDHAM L. REV. 853, 855–57 (1994).

61 Miccio, *supra* note 45, at 266–67; Goodmark, *Autonomy Feminism*, *supra* note 57, at 12–13; Margaret E. Johnson, *Changing Course in the Anti-Domestic Violence Legal Movement: From Safety to Security*, 60 VILL. L. REV. 145, 158–59 (2015) [hereinafter Johnson, *Changing Course*].

62 Miccio, *supra* note 45, at 265–67.

63 Goodmark, *Law Is the Answer? Do We Know That for Sure?: Questioning the Efficacy of Legal Interventions for Battered Women*, 23 ST. LOUIS U. PUB. L. REV. 7, 8 (2004) [hereinafter Goodmark, *Law Is the Answer?*].

64 Jeannie Suk, *Criminal Law Comes Home*, 116 YALE L.J. 2, 8 (2006).

65 *Id.* at 8.

66 *Id.* at 21.

67 *See, e.g.*, Alex Barber, *Prosecutor Orders Arrest of Woman as Material Witness to Testify Against Her Alleged Abuser*, BANGOR DAILY NEWS (Sept. 20, 2013, 9:38 PM), https://bangordailynews.com; Jodie Fleischer, *Innocent Victim Speaks Out About Being Jailed for 17 Days*, WSB-TV 2 ATLANTA (May 1, 2012, 8:50 PM), www.wsbtv.com. *See also* Myrna S. Raeder, *Remember the Ladies and the Children Too: Crawford's Impact on Domestic Violence and Child Abuse Cases*, 71 BROOK. L. REV. 311, 328–29 (2005); Goodmark, *Law Is the Answer?*, *supra* note 63, at 17; GOODMAN & EPSTEIN, *supra* note 3, at 76.

68 S. Greer, *A Transatlantic Perspective on the Compensation of Crime Victims in the United States*, 85 J. CRIM. L. & CRIMINOLOGY 333, 367 (1994).

69 Sue Osthoff, *But, Gertrude, I Beg to Differ, a Hit Is Not a Hit Is Not a Hit: When Battered Women Are Arrested for Assaulting Their Partners*, 8 VIOLENCE AGAINST WOMEN 1521, 1533 (2002).

70 T. K. LOGAN & ROB VALENTE, NATIONAL DOMESTIC VIOLENCE HOT-LINE: WHO WILL HELP ME?: DOMESTIC VIOLENCE SURVIVORS SPEAK OUT ABOUT LAW ENFORCEMENT RESPONSES 4 (2015).

71 For a discussion of the ways the child welfare system pressures abused mothers into leaving or seeking protection, *see, e.g.,* Margo Lindaur, *Damned if You Do, Damned if You Don't: Why Multi-Court-Involved Battered Mothers Just Can't Win*, 20 AM. U. J. GENDER SOC. POL'Y & L. 797, 798 (2012).

72 Sally F. Goldfarb, *Reconceiving Civil Protection Orders for Domestic Violence: Can Law Help End the Abuse Without Ending the Relationship?*, 29 CARDOZO L. REV. 1487, 1488–89 (2008); Johnson, *Redefining Harm, supra* note 7, at 1150; Tamara L. Kuennen, *Love Matters*, 56 ARIZ. L. REV. 977, 991 (2014).

73 Johnson, *Redefining Harm, supra* note 7, at 1150.

74 *Id.*

75 *Id.*; GOODMAN & EPSTEIN, *supra* note 3, at 81.

76 Johnson, *Redefining Harm, supra* note 7, at 1111.

77 *Id.* at 1151; Goldfarb, *supra* note 72, at 1510.

78 Goldfarb, *supra* note 72, at 1503.

79 Johnson, *Redefining Harm, supra* note 7, at 1149; Laurie S. Kohn, *The Justice System and Domestic Violence: Engaging the Case but Divorcing the Victim*, NYU REV. L. & SOC. CHANGE 191, 233–34 (2008).

80 Kohn, *supra* note 79, at 234. *See generally* Tamara L. Kuennen, *"No-Drop" Civil Protection Orders: Exploring the Bounds of Judicial Intervention in the Lives of Domestic Violence Victims*, 16 UCLA WOMEN'S L.J. 39 (2007).

81 Kohn, *supra* note 79, at 234; Johnson, *Redefining Harm, supra* note 7, at 1149.

82 Kohn, *supra* note 79, at 230.

83 Goldfarb, *supra* note 72, at 1508.

84 Johnson, *Changing Course, supra* note 61, at 149.

85 ELIZABETH SCHNEIDER, BATTERED WOMEN AND FEMINIST LAWMAK-ING 77 (2000); Johnson, *Changing Course, supra* note 61, at 170; GOODMAN & EPSTEIN, *supra* note 3, at 76; DAVIES, *supra* note 54, at 11; Martha R. Mahoney, *Legal Images of Battered Women: Redefining the Issue of Separation*, 90 MICH. L. REV. 1, 5 (1991); *see also* Martha Mahoney, *Victimization or Oppression?: Women's Lives, Violence, and Agency, in* THE PUBLIC NATURE OF PRIVATE VIOLENCE 59, 79 (Martha Albertson Fineman & Roxanne Mayktiuk eds., 1994).

86 GOODMAN & EPSTEIN, *supra* note 3, at 76.

87 Cross, *supra* note 52, at 85.

88 Goldfarb, *supra* note 72, at 1502.

89 Kuennen, *Love Matters, supra* note 72, at 991; SCHNEIDER, *supra* note 85, at 77; Leigh Goodmark, *Reframing Domestic Violence Law and Policy: An Anti-Essentialist Proposal*, 31 WASH. U. J.L. & POL'Y 39, 55 (2009).

90 BETH RICHIE, COMPELLED TO CRIME: THE GENDER ENTRAPMENT OF BATTERED BLACK WOMEN 75 (1996); DAVIES, *supra* note 54, at 7.

91 Goldfarb, *supra* note 72, at 1500.

92 Kuennen, *Love Matters, supra* note 72, at 978–79.

93 Kohn, *supra* note 79, at 200–202; SCHNEIDER, *supra* note 85, at 77; Jody Raphael, *Battering through the Lens of Class*, 11 J. GENDER, SOC. POL'Y & L. 368, 372 (2003); DAVIES, *supra* note 54, at 6.

94 Coker, *Crime Control, supra* note 59, at 832; Kuennen, *Analyzing the Impact of Coercion, supra* note 57, at 4–5.

95 LINDA G. MILLS, INSULT TO INJURY: RETHINKING OUR RESPONSES TO INTIMATE ABUSE 61 (2003).

96 *See, e.g.,* Valli Kalei Kanuha, *Compounding the Triple Jeopardy: Battering in Lesbian of Color, in* DOMESTIC VIOLENCE AT THE MARGINS: READINGS ON RACE, CLASS, GENDER, AND CULTURE 71, 77 (Natalie J. Sokoloff ed., 2006); RICHIE, *supra* note 90, at 94–95; GOODMARK, *supra* note 2, at 72.

97 Kristie A. Thomas, Lisa Goodman, & Susan Putnins, *"I Have Lost Everything": Trade-Offs of Seeking Safety from Intimate Partner Violence*, AM. J. OF ORTHO-PSYCHIATRY 1 (2015).

98 *Id.* at 4–5.

99 *Id.* at 5.

100 *Id.*

101 *Id.*

102 *Id.*

103 *Id.* at 7.

104 *Id.*

105 *Id.*

106 *Id.*

107 *Id.*

108 *Id.*

109 *Id.*

110 *See, e.g.,* Johnson, *Redefining Harm, supra* note 7, at 111–14; DAVIES, *supra* note 54, at 8.

111 Collins et al., *supra* note 11, at 23.

112 *Id.* at 24.

113 *See, e.g.,* Niel Websdale & Byron Johnson, *Reducing Woman Battering: The Role of Structural Approaches*, 24 SOC. JUST. 67, 76 (1997); Rhonda Copelon, *Recognizing the Egregious in the Everyday: Domestic Violence as Torture*, 25 COL. HUM. RTS. L. REV. 291 (1994).

114 *See generally* Caroline Bettinger-Lopez, *Human Rights at Home: Domestic Violence as a Human Rights Violation*, 40 COLUM. HUM RTS. L. REV. 19 (2008); Cheryl

Hanna, *The Violence Against Women Act and Its Impact on the U.S. Supreme Court and International Law: A Story of Vindication, Loss, and a New Human Rights Paradigm*, 52 DUQ. L. REV. 415 (2014); Ethan Kate & Max Siegel, *A "Supremer" Court?: How an Unfavorable Ruling in the Inter-American Commission on Human Rights Should Impact United States Domestic Violence Jurisprudence*, 28 WIS. INT'L L.J. 430 (2010); Lenora M. Lapidus, *The Role of International Bodies in Influencing U.S. Policy to End Violence Against Women*, 77 FORDHAM R. REV. 529 (2008); Sandra S. Park, *Equal Protection for Survivors of Gender Based Violence: From Criminalization to Law Enforcement Accountability*, 5 U. MIAMI RACE & SOC. JUST. L. REV. 401 (2015).

115 Collins et al., *supra* note 11, at 24.

116 *Id.* at 25.

117 Kuennen, *Analyzing the Impact of Coercion, supra* note 57, at 6; Miccio, *supra* note 45, at 242.

118 Collins et al., *supra* note 11, at 26.

119 *Id.*

120 Andrew Tatarsky & Scott Kellog, *Harm Reduction Psychotherapy, in* HARM REDUCTION: PRAGMATIC STRATEGIES FOR MANAGING HIGH-RISK BE- HAVIORS 36, 39–40 (G. Alan Marlat et al. eds., 2d ed. 2012) (describing the core ideas of harm reduction psychotherapy as meeting the patient as an individual and starting wherever the patient currently is, recognizing the patient's strengths, accepting small changes in the right direction as progress, not imposing any pre- conditions like abstinence on working with the patient, developing a collaborative and empowering relationship with the client, and destigmatizing drug use).

121 DAVIES, *supra* note 54, at 8–9.

122 The "stages of change" model is especially valuable in this context, as survivors' state of mind in relation to their readiness to leave is not static. *See, e.g.,* Jane Stoever, *Freedom from Violence: Using the Stages of Change Model to Realize the Promise of Civil Protection Orders*, 72 OHIO ST. L.J. 303, 322–32 (2011).

123 *See, e.g.,* DAVIES, *supra* note 54, at 9–10.

124 *See, e.g.,* Weissman, *supra* note 2, at 229 (arguing the importance of recognizing the "political economic circumstances of the perpetrator"); DAVIES, *supra* note 54, at 12 ("What happens to men who batter affects their partners emotionally, financially, and may affect their physical safety as well—including partners who leave, but especially those who say and those who are living in poverty.").

125 Survivors' social and emotional networks are extremely important to their evalu- ation of their own success. *See, e.g.,* THE FULLFRAME INITIATIVE, HOW DO SURVIVORS DEFINE SUCCESS?: A NEW PROJECT TO ADDRESS AN OVER- LOOKED QUESTION 36 (2014).

126 *See generally* Rona Kaufman Kitchen, *Constrained Choices: Mothers, the State, and Domestic Violence*, 24 TEMP. POL. & CIV. RTS. L. REV. 375 (2015); Lindaur, *supra* note 71, at 797.

127 Collins et al., *supra* note 11, at 27.

128 *See, e.g.,* Kuennen, *Love Matters, supra* note 72, at 995 (discussing politicians' commitment to "zero-tolerance" domestic violence policies).

129 *See, e.g.,* THE FOUNDATION FOR AIDS RESEARCH, FACT SHEET: PUBLIC SAFETY, LAW ENFORCEMENT, AND SYRINGE EXCHANGE (2013).

130 All Things Considered, *Congress Ends Ban on Federal Funding for Needle Exchange Programs,* NATIONAL PUBLIC RADIO (Jan. 8, 2016); Laura Ungar, *Funding Ban on Needle Exchange Effectively Lifted,* USA TODAY (Jan. 7, 2016), www .usatoday.com.

131 Paul Demko, *How Pence's Slow Walk on Needle Exchange Helped Propel Indiana's Health Crisis,* POLITICO (Aug. 7, 2016, 7:09 AM), www.politico.com; Erin Schumaker, *Mike Pence's Defining Moment as Governor? Enabling an HIV Outbreak,* HUFFINGTON POST (Oct. 5, 2016).

132 Megan Twohey, *Mike Pence's Response to H.I.V. Outbreak: Prayer, Then a Change of Heart,* N.Y. TIMES (Aug. 7. 2016), www.nytimes.com.

133 *Id.*

134 *See, e.g.,* Seth Barron, *Harm-Reduction Fantasies: New York City Opts for an Enabling Approach to Drug Addiction,* CITY JOURNAL (Summer 2016), www.city -journal.org.

135 John Knefel, *The Controversial Answer to America's Heroin Surge,* BUZZFEED NEWS (May 15, 2014, 9:26 PM), www.buzzfeed.com.

136 EUROPEAN MONITORING CENTRE FOR DRUGS AND DRUG ADDICTION, PERSPECTIVES ON DRUGS: DRUG CONSUMPTION ROOMS: AN OVERVIEW OF PROVISION AND EVIDENCE 2 (2016).

137 Andrea Woo, *British Columbia Opens Drug Injection Sites Amid Opioid Crisis,* THE GLOBE AND MAIL (Dec. 9, 2016); CBC News, *Insite Supervised Injection Site Marks 10-Year Milestone,* CBC NEWS (Sept. 20, 2013), www.cbc.ca.

138 Katie Zezima, *Awash in Overdoses, Seattle Creates Safe Sites for Addicts to Inject Illegal Drugs,* WASH. POST (Jan. 27, 2017).

139 John P. Walters, *Heroin Injection Sites Perpetuate Harm: Opposing View,* USA TODAY (May 16, 2016), www.usatoday.com.

140 Zezima, *supra* note 138.

141 Aviva Shen, *The Disastrous Legacy of Nancy Reagan's "Just Say No" Campaign,* THINK PROGRESS (Mar. 6, 2016, 9:45 PM), https://thinkprogress.org; Collins et al., *supra* note 11, at 20.

142 Collins et al., *supra* note 11, at 20.

143 Sarah Gabrielli & Stephen Rex Brown, *Schumer Slams Feds for Delay in Fighting Opioid Crisis,* DAILY NEWS (July 24, 2017), www.nydailynews.com.

144 Jake Harper, *Price's Remarks on Opioid Treatment Were Unscientific and Damaging, Experts Say,* NATIONAL PUBLIC RADIO (May 16, 2017, 11:57 AM), www.npr. org.

145 Matt Ferner, *Jeff Sessions Wants to Bring Back D.A.R.E.,* HUFFINGTON POST (July 12, 2017) (noting studies that disputed the effectiveness of the program).

146 Grant Smith, *Jeff Sessions Will Double Down on the Failed Drug War*, THE HILL (Feb. 2, 2017, 3:40 PM), http://thehill.com.

147 Jeff Sessions, *Being Soft on Sentencing Means More Violent Crime. It's Time to Get Tough Again.*, WASH. POST (June 16, 2017). *See also* Rebecca R. Ruiz, *Attorney General Orders Tougher Sentences, Rolling Back Obama Policy*, N.Y. TIMES (May 12, 2017); Sari Horwitz, *How Jeff Sessions Wants to Bring Back the War on Drugs*, WASH. POST (April 8, 2017).

148 P. J. Lockhart, *Jeff Sessions Is In Charge of Enforcing the Violence Against Women Act, and Victims' Advocates Are Worried*, MOTHER JONES (Feb. 22, 2017, 11:00 AM), www.motherjones.com.

149 Gillian Chadwick, *Predator in Chief: President Trump and the Glorification of Sexual Violence*, HUFFINGTON POST (Nov. 30, 2016, 3:34 PM).

14

Developing a National Plan of Action on Violence against Women and Gender Violence

A Human Rights Approach

CAROLINE BETTINGER-LÓPEZ

I. Introduction

On October 15, 2017, the hashtag #MeToo inundated U.S. social media. "If all the women who have been sexually harassed or assaulted wrote 'Me too.' as a status, we might give people a sense of the magnitude of the problem," wrote the actor Alyssa Milano on Twitter,[1] building upon the "Me Too" movement founded by activist Tarana Burke a decade earlier.[2] Over the next month, millions of women—and many men—posted #MeToo on their social media accounts, many with painful accompanying stories.[3] The hashtag campaign came on the heels of multiple shocking allegations of sexual and intimate partner violence against women committed by high-profile men—Harvey Weinstein, Bill O'Reilly, Roger Ailes, Bill Cosby, Ray Rice, and Donald Trump, to name a few. Subsequent revelations of sexual violence by powerful men followed, and sexual harassment and assault stories dominated news headlines.[4]

Many have described this moment in our country—indeed in our world—as a "tipping point" on gender violence.[5] Malcolm Gladwell defines a tipping point as "the moment a social trend passes a threshold and starts to spread like wildfire."[6] Sexual assault, sexual harassment, domestic violence, dating violence, and stalking have increasingly become regular topics of conversation in schools, in the media and public spaces, and in law and policymaking—due largely to survivors, advocates, and institutional champions stepping up and speaking out. An estimated three to five million people participated in women's marches in hundreds of cities and towns across the United States (and hundreds of thousands more worldwide) on January 21, 2017.[7] Approximately 440,000 people have taken the *It's on Us* pledge online to be a part of the solution to ending sexual assault, and students have hosted over 3,000 It's On Us events on 575 college campuses nationwide.[8] Domestic violence, once a footnote in public policy discussions, has become a leading focus in our national discourse about gun safety[9] and "sanctuary cities" that refuse to enforce immigration law.[10] State and local governments, much like the Obama-Biden administration (in which I had the honor of serving as the White House Advisor on Violence Against Women),[11] are taking unprecedented action to ramp up prevention and response efforts to gender violence.[12] If there ever was a tipping point on sexual and intimate partner violence in the United States, it is arguably now.

Tipping points do not inevitably result in systemic change, however. A coordinated and systematic national response to violence against women and gender violence in the United States—one which builds upon the decades of advocacy and the collective outpouring of energy, angst, and experience in the current moment, and one that pulls together the public and private sectors and government at all levels (federal, state, and local)—is needed to create lasting change.

A national plan of action on violence against women and gender violence in the United States can be a catalyst for such lasting change. UN Women, the United Nations organization dedicated to gender equality and the empowerment of women, has urged all countries to adopt such plans, and approximately 50 countries—located on every continent except Antarctica—have adopted national plans of action on violence against women and/or gender-based violence.[13]

The United States does not have a national plan of action on violence against women or gender violence. That makes it a global outlier. Many of the countries that have adopted national plans—including Canada, the United Kingdom, Australia, Germany, Spain, and Ireland—are considered "sister countries" to the United States, due to shared legal, political, and cultural traditions. While the Violence Against Women Act in the United States is a landmark piece of legislation and has many of the hallmarks of a national action plan on violence against women, it does not constitute a whole-of-government, goal-oriented, community-informed, forward-looking national plan of action, for the reasons discussed below.

While the United States should develop a national plan of action on violence against women and gender violence, that plan should not (and, presumably, will not) come from the Trump administration. This administration has rolled back important protections for women, girls, and gender-nonconforming individuals,[14] and has ended important White House initiatives on gender equality and violence launched by the Obama-Biden administration.[15]

But women's rights are human rights, and human rights start at home, as Eleanor Roosevelt once famously said.[16] A national plan of action on violence against women and gender violence should ultimately be a product of activism that is cultivated locally and then coordinated nationally. Two ways of engaging in local mobilization include the Cities for CEDAW campaign[17] and the dozens of municipalities that have passed resolutions declaring that "freedom from domestic violence is a fundamental human right."[18]

II. National Plans of Action on Violence against Women: An Overview

Over the past two decades, international human rights treaties and monitoring bodies have called upon governments to formulate and implement national plans of action to eliminate violence against women.[19] Such action plans constitute strategic, long-term, multi-sectoral "blueprints" or programs of activity designed to address the underlying causes of violence against women and strengthen the systems that respond to it—as opposed to more reactive approaches.

Many countries have heeded these calls and have adopted dedicated plans on violence against women. In some countries, plans focus on a particular form of violence, such as domestic violence, human trafficking, female genital mutilation/cutting, and forced marriage. Many national action plans on violence against women set out measures in relation to support for victims/survivors; prevention, including awareness-raising, education, and engaging men and boys; training and capacity-building efforts; prosecution, punishment, and rehabilitation of perpetrators; and research.[20]

Some countries have even developed second- or third-generation action plans, which contain lessons learned or impact assessments of earlier efforts. These subsequent plans often focus attention on specific groups of women or different forms of violence not addressed in the first plan. Action plans and strategies to address violence against women are also increasingly adopted at the provincial and local levels, as well as by independent public and private institutions, such as universities. Additionally, many countries have incorporated targets and activities to combat violence against women in other existing national action plans on, e.g., health, HIV/AIDS, development/social inclusion, and integration/migration.[21]

Guiding Principles

UN Women has recommended that national action plans on violence against women should reflect several guiding principles, described below.

1. Embrace a *human rights–based approach* that acknowledges that violence against women is a violation of human rights, defines violence against women according to international human rights norms, and responds explicitly to State obligations under relevant human rights treaties.
2. Recognize that *violence against women is a form of sex discrimination* and a manifestation of historically unequal power relations between men and women.
3. Identify the *different forms of violence against women*: physical, sexual, psychological/emotional, and financial; domestic violence, sexual violence, marital rape, stalking, sexual harassment, trafficking and sexual exploitation, child marriage, female genital mutilation, and other practices; violence that happens across the life course; violence in public and private spheres; and violence in national and transnational contexts.
4. Address the *root causes, prevalence, and impact of violence against women,* and identify gaps for future work.

5. Take account of *multiple and intersecting forms of discrimination and disadvantage,* and tailor strategies and action that recognize how women's experience of violence is shaped by factors such as their race, color, religion, political or other opinion, national or social origin, property, marital status, sexual orientation, HIV/AIDS status, migrant or refugee status, age, or disability. [22]

Developing and Implementing Plans of Action

UN Women has emphasized[23] that developing national plans of action "is not just about drafting actions, but setting up the structures and engaging stakeholders necessary for its effective implementation."[24] Governmental agencies, non-governmental organizations, communities, and individuals must engage on these issues, work in cooperation, and act and advocate together to realize the plan's intentions, which then must also be sustained.[25] UN Women instructs that "structures for coordination, information sharing and networking, and for the ongoing communication of, and advocacy for, the plan's messages, are just as important as the plan itself."[26] Thus, the development and implementation phases of national action plans should include:

1. Developing a coherent, comprehensive, and sustained program of activity that includes cross-cutting actions to establish and build the capacity of governance structures; a focus on primary prevention and meaningful response systems to violence against women; an articulation of concrete goals, actions, timelines, implementing entities; designated funding sources; and evaluation, monitoring, and reporting mechanisms.
2. Establishing and fortifying a mechanism to facilitate direct, ongoing, and meaningful engagement with civil society.
3. Creating effective and accountable governance structures that ensure leadership, oversight, support, and engagement at the highest political levels and across all levels of government in all aspects of the plan.
4. Ensuring the creation of a whole-of-government implementing institution that includes a high-level board or steering committee

(lead institution), comprised of senior government officials across all government departments and other stakeholders, and which makes high-level decisions and coordinates activities concerning implementation of the plan. This body should be adequately resourced and have substantive expertise along with a strategic mandate to drive action.

5. Supporting community organizations and networks to drive activity at the local level and ensure coordinated action across geographical locations.

6. Ensuring coherent, comprehensive, and consistent approaches to legislation and policy related to violence against women.

7. Building capacity of professionals involved in the prevention of, and response to, violence against women.

8. Supporting independent research on emerging issues and regularly collecting, communicating, and analyzing comprehensive statistical and qualitative data, disaggregated by sex, race, age, ethnicity, and other relevant characteristics, on the nature, prevalence, and impact of all forms of violence against women.

9. Developing primary prevention programs that address social and cultural norms, including awareness-raising strategies and sensitization of the media; that are established in key educational, organizational, and community settings; that target and engage specific groups, such as men and boys, parents, children, and young people; and that address associated factors which can exacerbate or intensify violence against women.

10. Establishing an effective, integrated response system that provides care, support, and empowerment of survivors; provides measures of protection and justice for victims; coordinates and integrates key systems; and provides for universal coverage across geographical locations and for all women.

11. Providing sufficient and ongoing funding for the plan's cross-cutting actions (including training, collection and analysis of data, legislative and policy reviews, and the establishment and activity of institutions and mechanisms (i.e., research and monitoring bodies) necessary for the plan's effective implementation).

12. Supporting broader law, policy, and social efforts to support gender equality.

Evaluation, Monitoring, and Reporting

As UN Women explains in their report, effective and independent monitoring[27]"is a cornerstone of human rights based policy-making and democratic principles" that can foster improved implementation of national plans of action over time, "by identifying successful initiatives/ programmes [sic] for further development, and problem areas for timely management."[28] Key features of regular and comprehensive evaluation, monitoring and reporting of implementation progress include the following elements:

1. Clearly defined indicators and targets that are closely linked to the goals and objectives of the national action plan to monitor progress and evaluate effectiveness.
2. A multi-sectoral mechanism to monitor implementation of the plan that (1) gathers and analyzes information; (2) monitors progress in attaining the plan's objectives; (3) identifies good practices and obstacles; and (4) proposes measures for future action.
3. Ensuring meaningful participation of civil society and other stakeholders in all phases of the plan.
4. Comprehensive and regular evaluation of projects, programs of action, and whole systems.
5. Regular and accountable reporting procedures on implementation and progress of the plan.

III. The United States' National Response to Violence against Women

Despite being a global leader in the violence against women arena, the United States has never developed a national plan of action to combat violence against women. When pressed on this point in a case before the Inter-American Commission on Human Rights, the United States responded that the Violence Against Women Act (VAWA), originally passed in 1994 and reauthorized three times—in 2000, 2005, and 2013—is effectively our national action plan, since VAWA constitutes "a comprehensive legislative package"[29] that has invested billions of dollars toward protecting victims and preventing and responding to violence against women.

Indeed, the 2013 reauthorization of VAWA took the legislation in an increasingly progressive direction that addressed multiple and intersecting forms of discrimination and disadvantage.[30] Despite VAWA's substantial contributions, however, it does not contain some of the core features of a national action plan—such as a strategic vision for ending violence against women in the United States, or a declaration that violence against women is a human rights violation and a form of sex discrimination, or a set of goals or benchmarks to measure progress. VAWA also does not identify the many laws, policies, and programs that, whether explicitly or not, affect survivors' lives.

Another shortcoming is that since VAWA is primarily focused on the criminal justice response,[31] it does not sufficiently take into consideration other important aspects that should be included in a national action plan, such as: economic justice issues, access to affordable housing, health care, workplace polices on domestic violence and sexual assault, the public health perspective, education, prevention initiatives, youth dating violence, children who witness violence, children in the juvenile justice system, the "sexual assault to prison pipeline," access to public benefits for low-income survivors, institutional accountability, and gender-based violence (a more expansive term than "violence against women"). These issues are scattered across various pieces of legislation and different agencies without a coordinated approach. The value of a national action plan is that it would look more comprehensively at all these different issues as important aspects of preventing and addressing intimate partner violence and sexual violence, with a lens of intersectionality and with a more coordinated approach across sectors, along with benchmarks.

IV. The United States' National Action Plans on Global Violence against Women

By contrast, the United States has developed national action plans on violence against women *outside* the U.S. and in other thematic areas within the U.S. Take, for instance, the *United States National Action Plan on Women, Peace, and Security* ("WPS Strategy"), enacted pursuant to a United Nations Security Council Resolution 1325, and whose goal is "to empower half the world's population to act as equal partners in preventing conflict and building peace in countries threatened and affected by war, violence, and insecurity."[32] The plan contains five high-level objectives: National Integration and Institutionalization, Participation in Peace Processes and Decision-making, Protection from Violence, Conflict Prevention, and Access to Relief and Recovery. It also contains a detailed Action Framework for inter-agency coordination; an implementation, monitoring, and reporting strategy; and a call to action.[33]

Another example is the *United States Strategy to Prevent and Respond to Gender-Based Violence Globally* ("GBV Strategy"), whose goal "is to strengthen and marshal U.S. expertise and capacity to prevent and respond to gender-based violence globally."[34] The GBV Strategy contains four laudable objectives:

1. Institutionalize coordination of gender-based violence prevention and response efforts among U.S. government departments and agencies and with other stakeholders;
2. Integrate gender-based violence prevention and response efforts into existing U.S. government work;
3. Collect, analyze, and use data and research to enhance U.S. government's gender-based violence prevention and response efforts; and
4. Expand U.S. government programming that addresses gender-based violence.[35]

The GBV Strategy does exactly what a national action plan should do: it memorializes United States commitments to strengthen gender-based violence prevention and response through inter-agency coordination in accordance with human rights principles. However, there is a catch: it only applies to U.S. foreign policy—that is, to the U.S. government's efforts *in other countries*.

Both the GBV Strategy and the WPS Strategy were developed pursuant to Executive Orders signed by President Obama. They are detailed, proactive, and aspirational, and recognize the national security benefits of a thoughtful approach to gender violence.

V. National Action Plans in the United States

The United States has adopted at least two national action plans to address human rights issues within the U.S., one of which relates directly to violence against women. In 2014, in commemoration of the 150th anniversary of the Emancipation Proclamation, President Obama released a *Federal Strategic Action Plan on Services for Victims of Human Trafficking in the United States,* co-chaired through an inter-agency process by the Departments of Justice (DOJ), Health and Human Services (HHS) and Homeland Security (DHS).[36] This five-year plan (2013-2017) was designed to "reaffirm[] the American values of freedom and equality by asking federal agencies to develop a plan to strengthen services for victims of human trafficking in the United States."[37] The plan featured four key goals, each with accompanying objectives:

1. *Align efforts* by promoting strategic and coordinated services for victims at the federal, regional, state, territorial, tribal, and local levels.
2. *Improve understanding* by expanding and coordinating human trafficking–related research, data, and evaluation to support evidence-based victim services.
3. *Expand access to services* by providing outreach, training, and technical assistance to increase victim identification and expand availability of services.
4. *Improve outcomes* by promoting effective, culturally appropriate, trauma-informed services that improve the short- and long-term health, safety, and well-being of victims.[38]

The Trafficking Plan of Action contained a detailed timeline for future action, specifying federal agency participation in specific actions tied to each objective.[39]

In December 2015, the White House released a *National HIV/ AIDS Strategy/Federal Action Plan for the United States: Updated to 2020.*[40] The plan contains a vision statement, an implementation strategy, action items, and goals that were both prevention- and response-oriented:

1. Reducing New HIV Infections
2. Increasing Access to Care and Improving Health Outcomes for People Living With HIV
3. Reducing HIV-Related Disparities and Health Inequities
4. Achieving a More Coordinated National Response to the HIV Epidemic

Interestingly, five of the plan's core policy recommendations address the intersection of HIV/AIDS, violence against women and girls, and gender-related health disparities. This intersectional approach stemmed directly from a 2012 Presidential Memorandum establishing a Working Group on the Intersection of HIV/AIDS, Violence Against Women and Girls, and Gender-related Health Disparities—an example of the power of high-level leadership on this issue.[41]

As we make the case for why the United States should have a national action plan on violence against women and gender violence, one cannot resist highlighting one of the most recent White House national action plans: the 2015 *National Action Plan for Combating Antibiotic-Resistant Bacteria*.[42] Surely if we can have a national action plan on bacteria, we can have one on violence against women![43]

VI. Proposal: Developing a Locally Driven National Action Plan on Violence against Women and Gender Violence

As discussed at the outset of this chapter, while the United States should develop a national plan of action on violence against women and gender violence, that plan should not come from the current administration. This is a moment for states and municipalities to rise to the challenge of developing locally driven action plans that can, collectively, form a national action plan on violence against women and gender violence.

One vehicle to accomplish this might be in the more than thirty municipalities across the United States that have adopted local resolutions or proclamations recognizing that freedom from domestic violence is a fundamental human right.[44] Another vehicle is the Cities for CEDAW campaign, a grassroots effort that provides tools and leadership to empower local women's civil and human rights organizations and municipalities to effectively initiate the Convention on the Elimination of All

Forms of Discrimination Against Women (CEDAW) in cities and towns across the United States.[45]

These "freedom from DV" resolutions and the Cities for CEDAW campaign have inspired legislation and reporting in some municipalities.[46] But few, if any, of the municipalities have adopted a local action plan of the type described in the UN Women Handbook.[47] Especially in progressive jurisdictions, such plans could, both individually and collectively, capture a vision that is both proactive and reflective of what freedom from gender violence truly looks like, and could also prioritize the populations who are being erased, or undermined, by federal policymaking in the Trump era.

Author's Note

The author wishes to thank the following individuals for their contributions to this chapter: Filiz Akkaya, Cailin Crockett, Bea Hanson, Rosie Hidalgo, and Lynn Rosenthal.

NOTES

1 Alyssa Milano, Twitter post (Oct. 15, 2017), https://twitter.com/alyssa_milano/status/919659438700670976.

2 Tarana Burke, a Black woman from Harlem, founded the grassroots "Me Too" movement in 2006 to spur "mass healing" for sexual violence survivors in underprivileged communities. Zahara Hill, *A Black Woman Created the "Me Too" Campaign Against Sexual Assault 10 Years Ago*, EBONY MAGAZINE (Oct. 18, 2017), www.ebony.com; ME TOO MOVEMENT, https://metoomvmt.org (last visited Feb. 6, 2018).

3 "In the first 24 hours following Milano's invitation to women to share their personal experiences by replying 'Me Too' to her Facebook post, the social media platform received 4.5 million posts. On Twitter, her tweet drew 70,000 replies, while another 1.7 million tweets on the topic have been posted, according to the social media platform. More than 85 countries have registered more than 1,000 tweets with the 'MeToo' hashtag." Sintia Radu, *How #MeToo Has Awoken Women Around the World*, U.S. NEWS AND WORLD REPORT (Oct. 25, 2017), www.usnews.com. *See also* Emanuella Grinberg & Jennifer Agiesta, *One-Fifth of Americans Know Someone Who Said #MeToo*, CNN (Nov. 9, 2017), www.cnn.com ("1 in 5 Americans said close friends or family members shared stories about sexual harassment or assault on social media, according to a CNN poll.").

4 Doug Criss, *The (Incomplete) List of Powerful Men Accused of Sexual Harassment After Harvey Weinstein*, CNN (Nov. 1, 2017), www.cnn.com. While most advocates

have praised the #MeToo movement for bringing much-needed attention to an issue that has historically been swept under the rug, some have criticized the mainstream manifestation of the "MeToo" movement and the "Weinstein effect" for
primarily focusing on high-profile, white, cis-gender women, not on those most
vulnerable to violence: women of color, gender-nonconforming individuals, and
women who work in service industries, low-wage industries, and in industries
dominated by men. Others have criticized #MeToo for being a "trauma-driven
spectacle" that promotes a hierarchy of trauma, and still others have expressed
caution that a public battle against sexual assault can become a moral panic
against sex. *See, e.g.,* Harry Lewis, *When "Me Too" is Too Much (And Not Enough),*
HUFFINGTON POST (Nov. 10, 2017), www.huffingtonpost.com; Masha Gessen,
When Does a Watershed Become a Sex Panic, NEW YORKER (Nov. 14, 2017), www
.newyorker.com; Annie Lowrey, *The Inequality Beneath the Sexual-Harassment
Headlines,* ATLANTIC (Oct. 26, 2017), www.theatlantic.com.

5 CNN, *Tipping Point: Sexual Harassment in America,* YOUTUBE (Nov. 9, 2017),
www.youtube.com/watch?v=67ITJuCQets.

6 MALCOM GLADWELL, THE TIPPING POINT: HOW LITTLE THINGS CAN
MAKE A BIG DIFFERENCE (2002).

7 *Sister Marches,* WOMEN'S MARCH, www.womensmarch.com; Erica Che-
noweth & Jeremy Pressman, *This is What We Learned by Counting the Women's
Marches,* WASH. POST (Feb. 7, 2017), www.washingtonpost.com.

8 IT'S ON US, www.itsonus.org; personal correspondence with Tracey Vitchers, It's
on Us Executive Director, Nov. 16, 2017 (on file with author).

9 See, e.g., *Guns and Domestic Violence,* EVERYTOWN FOR GUN SAFETY, https://
everytownresearch.org (last visited Feb. 6, 2018).

10 *Officials Worry Trump's Vow to Squeeze 'Sanctuary Cities' Could Hurt Health
Programs,* PBS NEWSHOUR (May 1, 2017), www.pbs.org; P. R. Lockhart, *Women
Are Now Living With the Fear of Deportation If They Report Domestic Violence,*
MOTHER JONES (May 25, 2017), www.motherjones.com.

11 THE UNITED STATE OF WOMEN WHITE HOUSE SUMMIT, THE COUNCIL
ON WOMEN AND GIRLS: VIOLENCE AGAINST WOMEN ACCOMPLISH-
MENTS (June 2016), https://obamawhitehouse.archives.gov [hereinafter WHITE
HOUSE SUMMIT].

12 *See, e.g.,* Jessie Schlacks, *Illinois Attorney General Issues Sexual Assault Response
Guidelines,* ILLINOIS PUBLIC MEDIA NEWS (July 14, 2017), https://will.illinois
.edu; Richard Winton, *L.A. Prosecutors Form Special Hollywood Sexual Assault
Task Force,* L.A. TIMES (Nov. 9, 2017), www.latimes.com; Brandon Carter, *20 Attorneys General Urge DeVos to Keep College Sexual Assault Protections,* HILL (July
20, 2017 2:56 PM), http://thehill.com.

13 UN WOMEN, HANDBOOK FOR NATIONAL ACTION PLANS ON VIOLENCE
AGAINST WOMEN (2012), www.unwomen.org.

14 *See, e.g.,* Tara Palmeri, *White House Council for Women and Girls Goes Dark
under Trump,* POLITICO (June 30, 2017), www.politico.com; Sunny Frothing-

ham & Shilpa Phadke, *100 Days, 100 Ways the Trump Administration Is Harming Women and Families*, CENTER FOR AMERICAN PROGRESS (Apr. 25, 2017), www.americanprogress.org; Brittany Levine Beckman, *8 Things Trump's Done to Hurt Girls Since Taking Office*, MASHABLE (Oct. 11, 2017), http://mashable.com.

15 Among the many initiatives in the Obama-Biden administration to combat violence against women were: the establishment of the position of White House Advisor on Violence Against Women, the White House Council on Women and Girls, the White House Task Force to Protect Students from Sexual Assault, the Sexual Assault Kit Initiative, the White House Interagency Working Group on Violence Against Women. WHITE HOUSE SUMMIT, *supra* note 11. These significantly expanded upon initiatives established by President Bill Clinton, including the President's Interagency Council on Women and the White House Office of Women's Initiatives and Outreach. See *Records of the President's Interagency Council on Women*, CLINTON DIGITAL LIBRARY (June 2, 2011), https://clinton.presidentiallibraries.us.

16 *Lesson Plan: "Where Do Human Rights Begin? In Small Places Close to Home,"* NATIONAL PARK SERVICE, www.nps.gov (last visited Feb. 6, 2018).

17 CITIES FOR CEDAW, http://citiesforcedaw.org (last visited Feb. 6, 2018).

18 *Freedom from Domestic Violence as a Fundamental Human Right Resolutions, Presidential Proclamations, and Other Statements of Principle*, CORNELL, www.lawschool.cornell.edu (last visited Feb. 6, 2018) [hereinafter *Freedom from Domestic Violence*].

19 These treaties and monitoring bodies include, *inter alia*: the UN Committee on the Elimination of Discrimination against Women, the UN Committee on Human Rights, the Beijing Platform for Action (adopted by the Fourth World Conference on Women in 1995), the UN Declaration on the Elimination of Violence against Women, the UN General Assembly, the Inter-American Convention on the Prevention, Punishment and Eradication of Violence against Women ("Convention of Belem do Para"), the Mechanism to follow-up the Convention Belem do Para (MESECVI), the Council of Europe, and the European Parliament of the European Union. See UN WOMEN, HANDBOOK FOR NATIONAL ACTION PLANS ON VIOLENCE AGAINST WOMEN 5–8 (2012).

20 *Id.*

21 *Id.*

22 *Id.* at 10–15.

23 *Id.* at 16–68.

24 *Id.* at 16.

25 *Id.*

26 *Id.*

27 *Id.* at 69–73.

28 *Id.* at 69.

29 Lenahan v. United States, Case 12.626, Inter-Am. Comm'n H.R., Report No. 80/11, P 168 (2011), U.S. Government merits brief response 27 (2008) (on file with author). For information on the Lenahan case, *see* www.law.miami.edu.

30 Violence Against Women Reauthorization Act of 2013, 42 U.S.C. §§ 13701–14135 (2013), available at www.gpo.gov.

31 VAWA grantmaking by the Department of Justice Office on Violence Against Women (OVW) from 2008–2016 increasingly focused on social and economic justice issues, but the primary focus and funding remained on the criminal justice system. *See, e.g.,* U.S. DEPARTMENT OF JUSTICE, OFFICE ON VIOLENCE AGAINST WOMEN, 2016 BIENNIAL REPORT, www.justice.gov.

32 THE WHITE HOUSE, THE UNITED STATES NATIONAL ACTION PLAN ON WOMEN, PEACE, AND SECURITY 2 (2016), www.usaid.gov.

33 *Id.*

34 DEP'T OF STATE, UNITED STATES STRATEGY TO PREVENT AND RESPOND TO GENDER-BASED VIOLENCE GLOBALLY 17 (2016), www.state.gov.

35 *Id.*

36 OFFICE FOR VICTIMS OF CRIME (OVC), FEDERAL STRATEGIC ACTION PLAN ON SERVICES FOR VICTIMS OF HUMAN TRAFFICKING IN THE UNITED STATES 2013–2017 (2017), www.ovc.gov.

37 *Id.* at 1.

38 *Id.* In September 2015, the United States was one of the 193 Member States of the United Nations that committed to the Sustainable Development Goals (SDGs), which includes, among seventeen areas of global action, a priority to "eliminate all forms of violence against all women and girls in the public and private spheres, including trafficking and sexual and other types of exploitation" (Goal 5, Target 5.2). Given the requirements for data monitoring to measure country-level implementation of the SDGs, the absence of a national plan of action on violence against women may be a challenge for the US. The lack of an NAP also impedes our ability to meaningfully, and credibly, engage with other countries in multilateral contexts.

39 OFFICE FOR VICTIMS OF CRIME (OVC), *supra* note 36, at 46 (Appendix B: Timeline).

40 THE WHITE HOUSE, NATIONAL HIV/AIDS STRATEGY FOR THE UNITED STATES: UPDATED TO 2020 (2015), www.hiv.gov.

41 Memorandum from President Barack Obama to the Heads of Executive Departments and Agencies, Establishing a Working Group on the Intersection of HIV/AIDS, Violence Against Women and Girls, and Gender-related Health Disparities (Mar. 30, 2012), https://obamawhitehouse.archives.gov.

42 The White House, *National Action Plan for Combating Antibiotic-Resistant Bacteria* (Mar. 2015), https://obamawhitehouse.archives.gov.

43 Moreover, as detailed in the report *The Spirit of Houston*, the idea of a U.S. national action plan on women's rights is not new. With the blessings of Presidents Ford and Carter, 20,000 people gathered in Houston for the first National Women's Conference in 1977. This government-sponsored national gathering included first ladies, activists, artists, writers, and more to focus on issues of concern to women. Conference attendees ultimately proposed a national action

plan with twenty-six planks that ran the gamut of issues that touch women's lives—employment, violence, disabled women, women in prison, abortion, and more—and a statement urging final ratification of the Equal Rights Amendment. THE SPIRIT OF HOUSTON: THE FIRST NATIONAL WOMEN'S CONFERENCE (Mim Kelber ed., 1978).

44 See *Freedom from Domestic Violence, supra* note 18.

45 CEDAW is a United Nations treaty that promotes all women's equality. The United States is one of only a handful of countries in the world that has not ratified CEDAW. For more information on the Cities for CEDAW campaign, *see* http://citiesforcedaw.org.

46 For example, the Miami-Dade County Commission amended its anti-discrimination ordinance in July 2014, adding victims of domestic violence, dating violence, or stalking to the list of protected classes regarding discrimination in employment, family leave, public accommodations, credit and financing practices, and housing accommodations. In Austin, the resolution tasked the local Family Violence Task Force to provide biennial reports on the challenges faced by survivors of domestic violence and recommendations on how to improve services to those survivors.

47 The City of San Francisco's CEDAW Ordinance and establishment of the San Francisco Department on the Status of Women have taken meaningful steps toward establishing a local action plan. *See* CITY AND COUNTY OF SAN FRANCISCO, http://sfgov.org.

ABOUT THE EDITOR

Jane K. Stoever, Professor and Director, Domestic Violence Clinic and UCI Initiative to End Family Violence, University of California, Irvine School of Law. Professor Stoever has extensive experience teaching domestic violence clinics and engaging in scholarship in the areas of domestic violence law, family law, feminist legal theory, and clinical legal theory. As Director of the UCI Law Domestic Violence Clinic, she supervises law students representing abuse survivors in civil, criminal, and immigration interventions in abuse. She is also Director of the UCI Initiative to End Family Violence, which unites faculty from over twenty departments at UCI with community partners in research, education, and clinical care endeavors. Stoever additionally teaches Family Law, Domestic Violence Law, and Legal Profession at UCI Law; has a faculty appointment in the UCI Center for Psychology & Law; and co-chairs the Orange County Domestic Violence Death Review Team. Her scholarship has appeared in the *Vanderbilt Law Review*, *Washington Law Review*, *North Carolina Law Review*, and *Harvard Journal of Law & Gender*, among other journals. She previously taught at Georgetown University Law Center; American University, Washington College of Law; and Seattle University School of Law. Stoever received her J.D. from Harvard Law School and her LL.M. from Georgetown University Law Center.

Jamie R. Abrams, Professor, University of Louisville Brandeis School of Law. Professor Abrams teaches Torts, Family Law, Legislation, and Women and the Law. Her research focuses on reproductive and birthing decision-making, gendered citizenship, legal protections for immigrant victims of domestic violence, and legal education pedagogy. Her most recent law review articles include "Debunking the Myth of Universal Male Privilege," published as the lead article in the *University of Michigan Journal of Law Reform*, and "The Feminist Case for Acknowledging Women's Acts of Violence" in the *Yale Journal of Law & Feminism*. Her chapter in *Feminist Judgments* (Cambridge University Press) provides historical commentary on *Rostker v. Goldberg*, a U.S. Supreme Court case considering the constitutionality of women's exclusion from the draft. She co-directs the Brandeis Human Rights Advocacy Program, which works actively with other nonprofits and community members to advance the human rights of immigrants, refugees, and noncitizens. Current initiatives focus on language access, access to education and health care, and media rhetoric.

Caroline Bettinger-López, White House Advisor on Violence Against Women (March 2015–January 2017), Professor and Director of the Human Rights Clinic at the University of Miami School of Law, and lead counsel on *Jessica Lenahan (Gonzales) vs. United States (Inter-American Commission on Human Rights, 2011)*. Caroline Bettinger-López is a Professor of Clinical Legal Education and Director of the Human Rights Clinic at the University of Miami School of Law. She recently completed a two-year term in the Obama administration as the White House Advisor on Violence Against Women and Senior Advisor to Vice President Joe Biden. In fall 2014, she was a Visiting Associate Clinical Professor and Acting Director of the International Human Rights Clinic at the University of Chicago Law School. Bettinger-López's scholarship, practice, and teaching concern international human rights law and policy advocacy, violence against women, gender and race discrimination, immigrants' rights, and clinical legal education. She focuses on the implementation of human rights norms at the domestic level, principally in the United States and Latin America. Bettinger-López regularly litigates and engages in other forms of advocacy before the Inter-American Human Rights system, the United Nations, and federal and state courts and legislative bodies.

Alisa Bierria, Associate Director, Center for Race and Gender, University of California, Berkeley, and Graduate Student, Stanford University. Alisa Bierria is the Associate Director of the Center for Race and Gender at UC Berkeley and a Ph.D. candidate in the Department of Philosophy at Stanford University. Her dissertation explores the role of social and political recognition in human agency. She is the recipient of the Diane J. Middlebrook Prize for Graduate Teaching and has years of experience writing, teaching, and organizing on issues of violence and redress. Other research interests include social ontology, critical legal studies, feminist of color theory, speculative theory of the body, and popular culture. Bierria is a member of INCITE!, the Free Marissa Now Mobilization Campaign, and the Survived And Punished project. She is co-editor of *Community Accountability: Emerging Movements to Transform Violence,* a special issue of *Social Justice: A Journal of Crime, Conflict, and World Order.*

Donna Coker, Professor, University of Miami School of Law. Professor Coker examines the connection between economic vulnerability and intimate partner violence; restorative justice approaches to intimate partner violence and sexual assault; gender, race, and class bias; and criminal justice policy and law. She is a leading critic of the disproportionate focus on criminal justice responses that characterizes U.S. domestic violence policy. Her widely cited research illustrates the negative impact of this focus on women marginalized as a function of poverty, race, or immigration status. Her empirical study of the adjudication of domestic violence cases in Navajo Peacemaking Courts has influenced work in the fields of restorative justice and domestic violence in the United States and abroad.

Courtney Cross, Assistant Professor of Clinical Legal Instruction and Director of the Domestic Violence Law Clinic, University of Alabama School of Law. Prior to teaching in the Civil Litigation Clinic at Sturm College of Law, Courtney Cross was a Clinical Teaching Fellow in the Domestic Violence Clinic at Georgetown University Law Center. During this fellowship, she taught and supervised law students representing indigent survivors of domestic violence while earning her LL.M. in Advocacy and participating in the Women's Law and Public Policy Fellowship Program. Before she began teaching, Cross was an Equal Justice Works Fellow and staff attorney at a women's reentry organization in the District of Columbia where she represented formerly incarcerated women in domestic violence and family court proceedings and represented incarcerated women in parole revocation hearings. She also conducted legal clinics and legal education classes at D.C.'s women's jail and provided advice and assistance on matters including housing, public benefits, and record sealing.

Mary D. Fan, Henry M. Jackson Professor of Law, University of Washington School of Law. Professor Fan's research and teaching are informed by her experiences as a federal prosecutor and as an associate legal officer at a United Nations criminal tribunal. Fan's expertise includes U.S. and international criminal law and procedure, evidence, privacy, immigration, and epidemiological criminology. She also collaborates on interdisciplinary violence prevention research as a core faculty member at Harborview Medical Center's Injury Prevention & Research Center. Fan was elected to the American Law Institute (ALI) in 2012 and is an Advisor to the ALI's Model Penal Code: Sexual Assault and Related Crimes Project. She was elected as a fellow of the American Bar Association in 2014. She is a two-time recipient of the Dean's Medal for excellence in teaching, scholarship, and service.

Cynthia Godsoe, Professor, Brooklyn Law School. Cynthia Godsoe teaches courses in family law, criminal law, children and the law, professional responsibility, and public interest lawyering. Her scholarship centers on the regulation of intimate behavior and gender roles through family and criminal law, encompassing topics including the path to marriage equality, the designation of victims and offenders in intimate violence, and the criminalization of non-conforming girls. Her recent work has appeared in the *Yale Law Journal Forum, Washington and Lee Law Review, Tulane Law Review,* and *California Law Review Circuit,* among others. The media, including *The New York Times* and *Time Magazine,* have consulted Godsoe on juvenile justice and family law issues. She was chair of the Juvenile Justice Committee of the New York City Bar from 2008 to 2011 and continues to participate in pro bono work on a variety of children's rights issues.

Leigh Goodmark, Professor and Director, Gender Violence Clinic, University of Maryland Carey School of Law. Leigh Goodmark is a Professor of Law at the University of Maryland Carey School of Law. Goodmark directs the Gender Violence Clinic, which provides direct representation in matters involving intimate partner abuse, sexual assault, and trafficking, and teaches Family Law and Gender and the Law. Goodmark's scholarship focuses on domestic violence. She is the co-editor of *Comparative Perspectives on Gender Violence: Lessons from Efforts Worldwide* (Oxford 2015) and the author of *A Troubled Marriage: Domestic Violence and the Legal System* (New York University 2012), which was named a *CHOICE* Outstanding Academic Title of 2012. Goodmark is a graduate of Yale University and Stanford Law School.

Mimi E. Kim, Professor of Social Work, California State University, Long Beach. Dr. Kim joined the CSU, Long Beach School of Social Work faculty as an Assistant Professor in fall 2014. Kim's research is in the area of social movements and community organizing with an emphasis on domestic violence and sexual assault in communities of color. She is a long-time anti-domestic violence advocate in Asian immigrant and refugee communities and remains active in the promotion of community organizing, community accountability, and transformative justice approaches to violence intervention and prevention. Kim currently teaches social work policy and supervises MSW thesis projects.

Colby Lenz, Graduate Student, American Studies and Ethnicity Department, University of Southern California. Colby Lenz is a legal advocate with the California Coalition for Women Prisoners. Lenz has been working with people imprisoned in California women's prisons for the past fourteen years. This work includes survival and release support, building leadership power with currently and formerly imprisoned people, and developing community-based responses to violence that do not rely on or reinforce the prison-industrial complex. Lenz organizes with the Survived And Punished project, a national organizing effort to end the criminalization of survivors of sexual and domestic violence. Lenz is a Ph.D. candidate in American Studies and Ethnicity at the University of Southern California, where she studies criminalization, imprisonment, and social movements against life and death sentencing. Lenz is committed to collaborative scholarship focused on refining and strengthening social movement strategy.

Elizabeth L. MacDowell, Professor and Director, Family Justice Clinic, William S. Boyd School of Law, University of Nevada, Las Vegas. Professor MacDowell is Director of the Family Justice Clinic, a legal clinic focusing on the intersection of family law with criminalization, child welfare, and other forms of state intervention into families. Her research concentrates on intersectional issues of race, class, and gender; domestic violence; and access to justice. She recently received a Fulbright Scholar Award to study access to justice for domestic violence survivors in Turkish family courts, and was a Senior Researcher at Anadolu University in Eskişehir, Turkey, from 2017 to 2018. Previously, the American Association of Law Schools named her a Bellow Scholar for her empirical study of domestic violence self-help clinics in the United States. MacDowell joined the UNLV faculty from Chapman University School of Law, where she developed and taught a clinical course in the Chapman Family Violence Clinic and taught courses on family law and domestic violence law and policy.

Amy M. Magnus, Graduate Student, University of California, Irvine School of Social Ecology. Amy Magnus is a Ph.D. candidate in Criminology, Law and Society at UC Irvine. Her research interests include: critical and feminist criminology and socio-legal studies, social inequality, specialized/alternative justice initiatives and their collateral consequences, access to justice, social control, and the carceral net.

Natalie Nanasi, Professor and Director, Hunter Legal Center for Victims of Crimes Against Women, Southern Methodist University Dedman School of Law. Professor Nanasi is Director of the Judge Elmo B. Hunter Legal Center for Victims of Crimes Against Women. Her work involves teaching and supervising students who represent survivors of gender-based violence in a broad range of legal areas, including immigration claims, family law matters, and post-conviction relief. Prior to joining the faculty at SMU, Nanasi was the Director of the Domestic Violence Clinic at American University, Washington College of Law and a Senior Attorney at the Tahirih Justice Center, where she represented immigrant women and girls fleeing human rights abuses such as female genital mutilation, domestic violence, human trafficking, forced marriage, honor crimes, and sexual abuse. Nanasi's research interest is at the inter-section of immigration, gender, and feminist legal theory. She received her J.D. from Georgetown University Law Center.

Deborah M. Weissman, Reef C. Ivey II Distinguished Professor of Law, University of North Carolina School of Law. Professor Weissman was Director of Clinical Programs at the UNC School of Law from January 2001 through July 2010. Weissman teaches the Human Rights Policy Lab, Gender Violence and the Law, and the Lawyer as Public Citizen. She has taught the Immigration/Human Rights Policy Clinic, Civil Lawyering Process, and the Civil Litigation Clinic. She serves as an executive com-mittee member for The Consortium in Latin American Studies at UNC at Chapel Hill and Duke University, and as a member of the advisory board with The Institute for the Study of the Americas at UNC. In 2013, she received the Frank Porter Graham Award from the North Carolina American Civil Liberties Union for outstanding civil rights work.

INDEX

access to justice: challenges to, 66–68; empowerment and, 62; gender-based violence and, 80; self-help programs and, 62, 69, 71–73; specialized courts and, 159–60

accountability: alternative, 25–26; autonomy and, 304, 311; community, 27; hyper-incarceration and, 317; state, 304, 311–14, 315, 317–18; victim, 20, 304, 311, 313

Adelman, Madelaine, 233–34

advocacy, 363, 366; Asian Americans and, 118n56; children's, 111; empowerment and, 62–66; gender-based violence, 54, 62; gun safety, 10, 246, 252–54; law enforcement and, 229; men's rights, 309; politics of, 1, 9; racism and, 155–56; resources, 70–71, 77–78; self, 75; self-help programs and, 70–71, 77–78; survivor-centered, 66, 67; systemic, 69; victim-blaming and, 9; victim rights, 21. *See also* domestic violence advocates; feminist advocacy

Affordable Care Act, 261

agency, 64, 81n7, 340, 347; battered women's movement and, 63; BCS and, 108; collective, 47; failure to protect and, 92; harm reduction and survivor, 346; law enforcement and, 218; model victim and, 46; privacy and, 49; protection orders and, 65; self-help programs and, 68, 73–74; survivor, 46–47, 346; victimhood and, 46–48, 54. *See also* autonomy

Alexander, Marissa, 28

alternative justice, 152; classist, 154–55, 158; as gendered, 154, 158; as racialized, 154–56, 158; therapeutic jurisprudence as, 160. *See also* restorative justice

anti-carceral movement, 8, 17; anti-domestic violence movement and, 23–25, 29–31; Critical Resistance and, 24; organizations supporting, 24–25

anti-domestic violence movement, 1, 6–8, 10–11, 15, 318; anti-carceral movement and, 23–25, 29–31; carceral actors and organizations in, 19–20; collective identity of, 319; community accountability and, 27; counter-hegemonic movement and, 24–25, 32–33, 34n6; criminalization and, 17–22, 32, 137, 228, 304, 332, 340–41; criminal justice and, 54–55, 314; failure to protect litigation and, 18; feminist social movements and, 19–20, 21, 305; grassroots strategies and, 25–27; harm reduction and, 337–38; Lautenberg and, 246; mainstream conferences and, 30–31; NCADV and, 18, 20; NCDBW and, 22; Reagan, R., and, 20–22; second wave and, 17–18; self-defense campaigns and, 27–29; timeline of, 16, 17–24; Transformative Justice for, 25, 27, 30–31; VAWA and, 22–23, 229; victim rights and, 20–21

anti-police brutality movement, 55

anti-rape movement, 17

anti-violence movement: crime control approach of, 15; current pivots in mainstream, 31–32; feminists of color critique of, 23; immigrant communities and, 30; Richie critique of, 29; timeline of, *16*

asylum protection, 3

autonomy, 2, 47, 312; accountability and, 304, 311; harm reduction and, 340, 346, 352; model victim and, 46; privacy and, 49; VAWA and, 6. *See also* agency

background checks, 259, 260–61, 274

Barkley, Charles, 133

BATJC. *See* Bay Area Transformative Justice Collective

Battered Immigrant Women Protection Act of 2000 (BIWPA), 205

battered women's movement, 8, 321n4; achievements of, 66; agency and, 63; crisis and, 309–10; empowerment and, 62; law reform agenda and, 309; lawyers in, 65; LEAA funding and, 18–19; *National Communication Network Newsletter* of, 19; self-help and, 68, 76

battered women's syndrome: mitigating factors and, 103, 107; structural critique of failure to protect and, 92–93

Battering Court Syndrome (BCS), 92; agency and, 108; culpability and, 108–9; as judicial collusion, 107, 108–10; principles of, 107–8; recommendations for, 109–10; structural critique of failure to protect and, 107

Bay Area Transformative Justice Collective (BATJC), 27

BCS. *See* Battering Court Syndrome

BIWPA. *See* Battered Immigrant Women Protection Act of 2000

Black Lives Matter movement, 54; Martin and, 28

Blackstone, William, 119, 123, 138n1

Bloomberg, Michael, 254

Brady Law, 256, 276–77

Braxton, Robert, 104

Breall, Susan, 42–43

Brenner, Alletta, 176

Brown, Jennifer, 233

Bumiller, Kristin, 66

Burke, Tarana, 6–7, 362

Bush, George W., 3

campus climate: hate crimes and, 181; intersectionality and, 181–82; rape myth endorsement and, 183; school reporting mechanisms and, 182; sexual assault and, 174–75, 181; surveys on, 171, 183; Trump impacting, 173

Campus Climate Survey Validation Study, 171

campus sexual assault: alcohol and, 175–76, 179, 190; campus climate and, 174–75, 181; choice and, 176; *Crime Logic* and, 174–79, 190; DCL for, 171–72, 185–86; DOE and, 171; federal funding for, 174; feminist advocacy and, 172, 173–74; gender bias and, 172, 173; hostile masculinity and, 179–80; implicit bias and, 184–86; intersectional framework for, 174–75, 180–83, 190; LGBTQ students and, 182, 183, 185; marginalized students and, 181–83; Obama administration and, 171–72, 173, 181; peer networks in sexual aggression and, 180; public health approach to, 176, 179; racism in, 173, 181–83, 184–85; Rape Myth instrument and, 183; restorative justice approaches to, 9, 186–90, 200n140; sexual dominance and, 179; social determinants of, 179–80; Title IX policies and, 173–74; Trump administration and, 172–73, 174; Turner and, 175–76

CARA. *See* Communities Against Rape and Abuse

carceral feminism, *16*, 19–20; anti-carceral movement and, 17, 23–25, 29–31; critiques of, 26–27; mass incarceration and, 15; VAWA and, 22–23

caregivers, 316

Carter, Jimmy, 18–19

CDC. *See* Center for Disease Control and Prevention

CEDAW. *See* Convention on the Elimination of all Forms of Discrimination Against Women

Center for Disease Control and Prevention (CDC), 120, 275–76

Center for Juvenile Justice Reform (CJJR), 161

Chicago juvenile courts, 154, 156–58

child abuse and neglect: abuse cycle of, 120; corporal punishment and, 124, 135; criminalization of, 120, 121; criminalization of child survivors of, 96–97; crossover youth and, 162; cycle of violence and, 120; institutionalized neglect and, 155; *parens patriae* doctrine and, 157–58; poverty and, 5; specialized courts for, 153. *See also* failure to protect

Child Protective Services, 5

child-saving movement, 161, 165

child welfare system: foster care system and, 161–62; homelessness and, 163, 211; juvenile justice and, 162; next generation reforms of domestic violence and, 317

Christie, Chris, 258

Chung, Sandra, 94

Cities for CEDAW campaign, 372–73

CJJR. *See* Center for Juvenile Justice Reform

Clinton, Bill, 22

Coates, Ta-Nehisi, 132–33

Communities Against Rape and Abuse (CARA), 25

community: accountability, 27; assessments in Mirkarimi-López case,

39–40, 50–54; crisis interventions, 309; harm reduction and, 347; organizations on sexual assault, 26; restorative justice and, 187

community response programs: coordinated community response, 229–30; Family Justice Centers and, 230; mandatory arrest policies and, 229–30

concealed-carry laws, 257–58

congressional intent, 203

Constitution, U.S., 276

Convention on the Elimination of all Forms of Discrimination Against Women (CEDAW), 364; Cities for CEDAW campaign, 372–73

Convention on the Rights of the Child, 135

coordinated community response, 229–30

corporal punishment, 138n2, 140n21; anger and stress during, 126–28, 146n78; banning of, 120, 136, 137–38, 142n35; Blackstone on, 119, 123, 138n1; child abuse and, 124, 135; countries banning, 124; criminalization and, 136, 139n13; disabilities and, 132, 147n93; educational, 124; efficacy of, 120; harms of, 124–25, 142n40; insults and, 134; IPV and, 125, 135; power structures and, 121; race and, 132–34; rationales for, 123; slavery and, 119, 133–34. *See also* parental discipline privilege

Corrigan, Rose, 176

counter-hegemonic movement: anti-domestic violence movement and, 24–25, 32–33, 34n6; empowerment and, 74–75, 77

Creative Interventions, 25–26, 30

Crenshaw, Kimberlé, 23

Crime Logic, 190; criminal justice discourse and, 175; predator narrative and, 174, 176–79 criminalization, 1, 2; anti-domestic violence movement and, 17–22, 32, 137, 228, 304, 332, 340–41; BCS and, 92, 107, 108–10; of child abuse, 120, 121; of child survivors, 96–97; corporal punishment and, 136, 139n13; failure to protect and, 94, 97; family violence and, 96, 136; gender-based violence and, 108, 110; of immigrants, 202; of IPV, 228; of LG-BTQI individuals, 96; sex work and, 336–37; state accountability and hyperincarceration and, 317; of survivors, 9, 91, 111, 120; VAWA and, 15, 23, 31–32, 229, 369; victim rights and, 20–21, 54; of women of color, 28. *See also* Battering Court Syndrome

criminal justice: anti-domestic violence movement and, 54–55, 314; *Crime Logic* and discourse on, 175; critical race theory and, 38; infrastructural reach of, 164–65; justice industrial complex and, 159, 164, 165; multisystem involvement and, 152, 153, 158–59, 161–64; prison abolitionism and, 24, 25, 30, 36n34, 331n129; prison industrial complex and, 23–24, 164; public and procedural fairness in, 39–40; punishment ideologies and, 160–61; race and, 54

Crips-Blood truce, 30

crisis: battered women's movement and, 309–10; definitions of, 309, 310; narrow framing of, 308–9; terminology, 310

critical race theory, 23; criminal justice response in, 38

Critical Resistance, 24

crossover youth: child abuse and neglect and, 162; juvenile justice and, 162, 163; specialized justice and, 163

Cruz, Ted, 277–78

custody: domestic violence and, 66, 84n35; immigration status and, 41; state accountability and, 315

cycle of violence and abuse, 148n17; child abuse and, 120; judges and law enforcement on, 318; phases in, 306; recidivism and, 304–5

Dao, Tuan, 315–16

Davis, Angela, 23, 30; prison abolitionism and, 24

Dear Colleague Letter (DCL) (2011), 171; debate over, 172; POE and, 185–86

Defense of Battered Women (NCDBW), 22

Department of Education (DOE), 171

Department of Homeland Security (DHS), 216

deportation: consequences of, 209; immigrant survivors of IPV and, 206, 208–10, 216; offenses causing, 210–11

DeVos, Betsy, 172

DHS. *See* Department of Homeland Security

discrimination, 158–59; children and, 121, 132, 133; crisis and, 309; domestic violence victims and, 311; juvenile justice and, 156; law enforcement and, 207; race and, 132, 133, 135, 156; Title IX, 172, 173–74; Trump and lawsuits on gender, 4; VAWA and, 2, 369; violence against women and, 365–66

DOE. *See* Department of Education

domestic violence, 8, 120, 320n2; abstinence-based programs and, 345, 350; Alexander and, 28; asylum protection and, 3; caregivers and, 316; criminalization of survivors of, 9, 91, 120; cultural shifts for, 218–19; custody and, 66, 84n35; cycle of violence in, 306; discrimination and, 311; early politicizations of, 305; ecosystem of, 304; gay couples and, 5; gun safety and, 1–2, 74, 258, 260, 262–65, 283; homelessness and, 211; human rights and, 372; interventions, 18–19, 304–7,

310, 312–13; judicial collusion and, 105–6, 107; law enforcement and, 6, 351; lawyers and, 316–17; leaving, 212–14, 283, 306; LGBTQI individuals and, 34n7, 312; Mateen and, 249; mental health issues and, 47; model victim of, 46; next generation reforms of, 303, 306, 313–18; NFL policies on, 313–14; no-drop prosecution policies for, 217, 340; power and, 249; public health approaches to, 332–33; rates of, 332; recidivism and, 304–5, 307; risk assessments, 315–16; risk factors of, 306–8, 315–16; service providers for, 230–31; shelters for, 305, 337, 344; types of, 52; victim accountability and, 20, 304, 311, 313; workplace policies on, 313–14, 369; zero tolerance and, 53, 348. *See also* first generation politicization, of domestic violence; intimate partner violence; Mirkarimi-López case; survivors

domestic violence advocates: anti-police brutality movement and, 55; Mirkarimi-López case and, 48–49, 51, 52–54; shelter and victims'-services model of, 305; victimhood and, 48–49, 51. *See also* feminist advocacy

domestic violence services organization (DVSO), 70–71

drug use, 351; heroin and, 333; HIV and, 336, 348; needle exchange programs and, 336, 348; opioids and, 334, 335–36; Reagan, N., and, 349; supervised injection sites and, 348–49; Trump and, 350

DVSO. *See* domestic violence services organization

economic justice issues, 369
elite feminism, 5–6
emergency protective order (EPO), 42
empowerment: access to justice and, 62; advocacy and, 62–66; battered women's movement and, 62; collective sharing and, 63; continuum, 67–68, 79; counter-hegemonic movement and, 74–75, 77; feminist advocacy and, 62–66, 64, 67, 70–71; goals, 67, 71, 76; gun ownership and, 250; harm reduction and, 346; mandatory law enforcement engagement and, 218; multidimensional, 8, 63–64, 68, 69, 74, 79, 80; protection orders and, 64–65, 86n60; race and class and, 67; self-help programs and, 62–63, 68, 71

ending domestic violence, 303
EPO. *See* emergency protective order

failure to protect, 317; agency and, 92; anti-domestic violence movement and, 18; battered women's syndrome and, 92–93, 103, 107; BCS and, 92, 107–10; charges pursued for, 98; coalition building and, 111; criminalization and, 94, 97; criminalized reproduction and, 115n25; culpability inflation and, 105; disappearance of survivors and, 111; felony murder convictions and, 97–98, 115n27; gender bias in, 94, 104; habeas corpus and, 100–104, 116n35; Hall and, 104–9, 117n55, 118n58; hyper-culpable motherhood and, 92, 95, 98; institutionalization of, 97; LGBTQI individuals and, 113n3; matrix of violence and, 91–94; mitigating circumstances model and, 91, 94, 103, 107; patriarchy and, 94; political ideology of, 92, 94–99; racialized differences in, 104–5, 117n44; recommendations for, 109–13; reframing, 111–12; Savage, K., and, 99–104, 109; structural critique of, 92–94, 104, 107, 112

family court, 81n5; DVSO and, 70–71; protection orders and, 66

family justice, 153, 155–56, 164

Family Justice Centers, 153; coordinated community response programs and, 230

family law: harm reduction and, 347; self-help and, 69

family violence, 2, 6, 16, 151; criminalization and, 96, 136; ending, 309; firearms and, 246–47, 260; gun bans and, 264; as inevitable, 11; interventions, 5, 8; juvenile justice and, 96, 154, 162; law enforcement and, 18, 21, 304; mass shootings and, 254; mens rea of, 120; parental discipline privilege and, 9; police-perpetrated, 10; specialized courts and, 153; surveillance and, 154; Task Force Against Family Violence, 21, 22

Family Violence Prevention Services Act (FVPSA), 20, 22

Farook, Syed Rizwan, 273

Federal Strategic Action Plan on Services for Victims of Human Trafficking in the United States, 371

Feinstein, Dianne, 277

felony murder law, 97–98, 115n27

feminism. See anti-domestic violence movement; carceral feminism; elite feminism; social movements

feminist advocacy, 22; anti-domestic violence movement and, 19–20, 21, 305; anti-violence movement as, 32; campus sexual assault and, 172, 173–74; decision-making of survivors and, 65–66; empowerment and, 62–64, 64, 67, 70–71; IPV narrative and, 238–39; López and, 45; professionalization of, 66; protection orders and, 64–65, 86n60; resources and self-help programs, 77–78; survivor-centered and collaborative methods in, 63–64

Firearm Owners' Protection Act (FOPA), 256

firearms, 10; family violence and, 246–47, 260; homicide-suicide and, 282; illegal access to, 251–52; Lautenberg Amendment and, 236. See also gun ownership; gun safety; guns in the home; gun violence

first generation politicization, of domestic violence, 305, 319; cycle of violence and, 306; framing of crisis in, 308–10; lethality assessment models and, 306–7, 312; masculinities theory and, 308; NFL and, 313–14; risk factors and, 306–8; state accountability and, 311–14; victim accountability and, 20, 304, 311, 313; victim autonomy in, 304, 311

FOPA. See Firearm Owners' Protection Act

foster care system, 161–62

frontier masculinity, 249

Fugate, Jeanne, 94

FVPSA. See Family Violence Prevention Services Act

Garland, David, 23

Gay Men's Health Crisis, 337

GBV Strategy. See Strategy to Prevent and Respond to Gender-Based Violence Globally, U.S.

GCA. See Gun Control Act

Gejdenson, Sam, 205

gender-based violence, 5, 66, 319, 369; access to justice for, 80; advocacy, 54, 62; criminalization and, 108, 110; as intersectional, 27, 67; protection orders and, 65; tipping point for, 362–63. See also self-defense campaigns

gender bias, 1; campus sexual assault and, 172, 173; failure to protect and, 94, 104; institutional, 104; racialized, 184–85; Trump and lawsuits on, 4

generationFIVE, 24; Transformative Justice and, 27

Gladwell, Malcolm, 362

Glenn, Evelyn Nakano, 95
Global Gag Rule, 4–5
Goldberg, Whoopi, 254
Goodell, Roger, 313
Goodman, Lisa, 343
Goodmark, Leigh, 47, 137, 319, 320n2
Gottschalk, Marie, 45
Gun Control Act (GCA), 256
gun ownership: adolescents and, 251; empowerment and, 250; gendered, 248–49; gendered gap in knowledge of, 249–51; income and, 248; masculinity and, 248–49, 252; political sales and, 248; racism and, 248; subcultures of, 248; teen dating violence and, 251–52; women and, 250–51
gun rights, 246; open-carry groups and, 252–54
gun safety: advocacy, 10, 246, 252–54; assault weapons and, 277; Brady Law and, 256, 276–77; concealed-carry laws and, 257–58; confiscation-at-the-scene laws as, 288; court cases on, 257–59; doctors and, 250, 259, 261–62; domestic abusers and, 1–2, 74, 258, 260, 262–65, 283; enforcement efforts for, 264–65; executive action and, 276; FOPA, 256; GCA, 256; homicide-suicide and, 1–2; Lautenberg Amendment and, 236, 263; legislation, 246, 256–60, 272, 273, 277, 279, 281, 287, 298n11; magazine capacity and, 264, 277; Obama and, 248, 259–60, 275–76; politics and, 246, 248, 255–60, 277–78; public opinion on, 254–55; registry for, 261, 262; Sandy Hook Elementary School shooting and, 289, 298n111; Second Amendment and, 276; state laws on, 256, 257–59, 264–65; Supreme Court and, 257–58, 276; terrorism and, 260; universal background checks and, 259, 260–61, 274; VAWA and, 262, 264

guns in the home: gender gap and, 249–51; racism and, 248; self-help programs and, 74
gun violence: annual deaths from, 252; children and, 247; data sources for, 278–79; homicides and, 246–47, 260–61, 263, 280–81, *280–81*; law enforcement and, 262, 263; mass shootings as, 10, 249, 254–57, 272; public health and, 258–59; strangers and, 247; victim-perpetrator relationship for, 279–81, *280–81*; youth and lethality of, 251. *See also* homicide-suicide

habeas corpus, 116n35; Savage, K., and, 100–103; structural interpretation of, 103–4
Hall, Tondalao, 108, 109, 117n55, 118n58; body language of, 105–7; culpability of, 104–5; sentence of, 104, 106–7; victim-blaming of, 104–5, 117n55
Harcourt, Bernard, 54–55
harm reduction, 332; abstinence and, 335, 345, 350; advantages of, 345–46; agency and, 346; analogies of, 349–50; anti-domestic violence movement and, 337–38; autonomy and, 340, 346, 352; batterers and, 339; client-centered counseling and, 338; community level, 347; critique of, 348–50; drug use and, 333, 334, 335–36, 348–51; empowerment and, 346; flexibility of, 345–46; high-risk behavior and, 333, 335, 346; HIV/AIDS and, 336–38; human rights and, 345; origins of, 334; politics and, 334, 348, 350–51; principles of, 334–35; psychotherapy, 346, 359n120; public health and, 10, 333; quality of life and, 335; safety planning and, 346–47; sex work and, 335–37, 351, 355n39; stability and, 249, 347; staying in abusive relationships and, 339–45, 351; Trump and, 350

Harm Reduction: Pragmatic Strategies for Managing High-Risk Behaviors (Witkiewitz, Larimer and Marlett), 335

Harris, Angela, 232

Hart, Barbara, 22

hate crimes: anti-LGBTQ bias and, 182; campus climate and, 181; racism and, 181–82

hegemonic masculinity: militarism and, 233; police-perpetrated domestic abuse and, 232–33

Heidensohn, Frances, 233

Heise, Lori, 307

heroin, 333, 336

Higate, Paul, 233

high-risk behavior: harm reduction and, 333, 335, 346; staying in abusive relationships as, 339

HIV/AIDS, 338; drug use and, 336, 348; Gay Men's Health Crisis and, 337; National HIV/AIDS Strategy/Federal Action Plan, 371–72; sex work and, 336

Hollander-Blumoff, Rebecca, 128

homelessness: child welfare system and, 163, 211; delinquent youth and, 160–61; domestic violence and, 211

homicide: gun violence and, 246–47, 260–61, 263, 280–81, *280–81*; IPV and, 246–47, 280–81, *280–81*; separation violence and, 213–14, 342

homicide-suicide: confiscation-at-the-scene laws and, 288; Dao and, 315–16; firearms and, 282; gun safety and, 1–2; interpersonal violence and, 274, 281–85, *284*, 288, 290; IPV and, 283, 285, *285*; Lanza and, 273, 275; law enforcement and, 274; Mateen and, 249, 273; mental health and, 273, 274–75, 285–86, *286*, 289; national memory and, 273, 291n14; paradigm of danger for, 272, 273, 275, 278, 289; rates of, 282; research on, 283; risk factors for, 281, *284–86*, 284–88, *290*; Sandy Hook Elementary School, 273, 274–75, 277,

287, 289, 298n111; scene-of-assault procedure and, 272, 274–75, 288–90; separation violence and, 283; September 11 as, 291n14; stranger paradigm for, 275–78; two-stage act of, 273

Hopton, John, 233

hostile masculinity, 176, 179–80. *See also* masculinity

human rights: domestic violence and, 372; harm reduction and, 345; violence against women and, 364, 365, 369

human trafficking, 202

hyper-culpable motherhood, 92, 95; prosecutorial culpability inflation and, 98

hyper-incarceration, 317

hypermasculinity: law enforcement and, 231–32, 240; militarism and, 233, 235; state accountability and, 317–18; triggers for, 316, 324n40. *See also* masculinity

ICE. *See* Immigration and Customs Enforcement

immigrants: anti-violence organizations and, 30; criminalization of, 202; intra-family violence and, 205. *See also* immigrant survivors, of IPV

immigrant survivors, of IPV: asylum protection and, 3; congressional intent and, 203; deportation and, 206, 208–10, 216; DHS and, 216; economic abuse and, 211; home country and, 207; Immigrant Power and Control Wheel for, 209, 222n35; immigration enforcement and, 202, 208; INS and, 209; language barriers for, 205, 221n23; law enforcement and, 206–10, 212; legislation on, 205; lethality of abuse and, 206; mandatory interventions and, 217–19; partner deportation and, 210–11; power imbalance and, 208–9; prevalence of, 205–6; separation violence and, 212–14; solutions for, 214–17; state legislatures and, 216–17; T-Visa and, 214–15; USCIS and, 204, 210, 214–16; VAWA and, 214. *See also* U visa program

Immigration and Customs Enforcement (ICE), 5, 209–10, 221n28

Immigration and Naturalization Service (INS), 209

immigration enforcement: deportation as, 206, 208–11, 216; immigrant survivors of IPV and, 202, 208; Sanctuary Cities and, 208, 363; Trump administration and, 202, 208

immigration status: custody disputes and, 41; of López, 39, 41, 42–43, 48; separation violence and, 342–43

implicit bias, of campus sexual assault: heteronormative, 185; in investigation and adjudication, 185–86; racialized gender and, 184–85

INCITE!, 24, 26, 27, 330n120; founding of, 29

INS. *See* Immigration and Naturalization Service

institutionalized neglect, 155

International Association of Chiefs of Police, 207

intersectionality, 6, 9, 33, 180–81; campus climate and, 181–82; campus sexual assault and, 174–75, 180–83, 190; Crenshaw and, 23; gender-based violence and, 27, 67; implicit bias and, 184–86; lethality assessments and, 312; national action plan and, 369; National HIV/AIDS Strategy/Federal Action Plan and, 372; race-related criminal justice violence and, 28; research and scholarship and, 2, 183; restorative justice and, 175; state violence and, 24

interventions, 314; community crisis, 309; domestic violence, 18–19, 304–7, 310, 312–13; family violence, 5, 8; lethality assessment, 306–7; perpetrator focused, 315; police-perpetrated domestic abuse, 239–40; scene-of-assault procedure as homicide-suicide, 272, 274–75, 288–90; voluntary, 310. *See also* mandatory interventions; restorative justice; specialized justice

intimate partner violence (IPV), 322n13, 322n15; corporal punishment and, 125, 135; criminalizing, 228; feminist narratives on, 8, 238–39; gender and, 247; homicide and, 246–47, 280–81, *280–81*; homicide-suicide and, 283, 285, *285*; Lautenberg Amendment and, 236; law enforcement and, 227, 240; lethality assessment programs and, 230; mandatory arrest and, 217–19; no-drop prosecution and, 217, 340; police-perpetrated domestic abuse rates compared to, 238, 244n63; power and, 212; protection order for, 288–89; resources for, 227; separation violence as, 212–14, 283. *See also* immigrant survivors, of IPV; survivors

intra-family violence, 119; corporal punishment and, 125; immigrants and, 205; mandatory interventions and, 217; rule of thumb and, 135

IPV. *See* intimate partner violence

It's on Us pledge, 363

Jo, Nan-Hui, 28

Johnson, Leanor, 235, 238

Johnson, Lyndon B., 234

justice industrial complex, 164, 165

juvenile courts, 154, 156–58. *See also* juvenile justice

juvenile justice: in Chicago, 155–56; child-saving movement and, 161, 165; cross-over youth and, 162, 163; discrimination and, 156; family violence and, 96, 154, 162; first courts for, 157; foster care system and, 161–62; girls in, 155; Mountain Crest as, 151–52; *parens patriae* doctrine and, 157–58, 161, 165; surveillance and social control and, 153–54

Kennedy, Anthony, 247–48
Know Your IX, 198n126
Kraska, Peter, 233

Lanza, Adam, 273; mental health issues
of, 275
LAPD. See Los Angeles Police Department
Larimer, Mary E., 335
Lautenberg, Frank, 246
Lautenberg Amendment, 236, 263
Lave, Tamara, 185
law enforcement: advocacy groups and,
229; agency and, 218; cycle of violence
training for, 318; discrimination and,
207; distrust of, 207–8; domestic
violence and, 6, 351; domestic violence
service providers and, 230–31; empowerment and mandatory engagement
with, 218; family violence and, 18, 21,
304; gun violence against, 262, 263;
hegemonic masculinity and, 232–33;
homicidal-suicides and, 274; hyper-
masculine environment of, 231–32,
240; immigrant survivors of IPV
and, 206–10, 212; IPV and, 227, 240;
LAPD as, 236–37; lethality assessments and, 230, 312–13; mandatory
arrest policies of, 6, 20, 66–67, 217–19,
229–30, 340; militarism and, 233–35,
240; in Mirkarimi-López case, 41–42;
ordinary violence and, 274; protection
orders and, 289; PRPD as, 237; racism
and, 207–8; scene-of-assault procedure
for, 272, 274–75, 288–90; separation
violence and cooperation with, 213; U-
Visa program and cooperation with,
203, 204, 206–7, 214–18; VAWA and,
229, 231–32, 240; women and treatment by, 232
Law Enforcement Assistance Administration (LEAA), 18–19
lawyers, 316–17

LEAA. See Law Enforcement Assistance
Administration
leaving, domestic violence situations:
cycle of violence and, 306; separation
violence and, 212–14, 283
legal consciousness, 65; self-help and, 80
legislation, 21, 82n16, 216–17; in California, 100; Cities for CEDAW campaign
and, 373; environmental protection, 51;
gun safety, 246, 256–60, 272, 273, 277,
279, 281, 287, 298n11; on immigrant
survivors, 205; national action plan
and, 366, 369; on teen dating violence,
3. See also protection orders; Violence
Against Women Act (VAWA)
lesbian-gay-bisexual-transgender-queer-
intersex (LGBTQI) individuals, 34n7,
181; anti-carceral and community based
movements, 24–25, 29, 50; campus sexual assault and, 182, 183, 185; criminalization of, 96; domestic violence and,
34n7, 312; failure to protect and, 113n3;
hate crimes and, 182, 249; HIV/AIDS
and, 337–38; Mateen and, 249; parental
discipline privilege and, 132; race and,
24; sexual assault and, 174–75, 181–85
lethality assessments, 230, 306; intersectionality and, 312; law enforcement
and, 230, 312–13; Maryland Model of,
307; state accountability and, 312–13
Levin, Carl, 277
LGBTQI. See lesbian-gay-bisexual-
transgender-queer-intersex individuals
Liederbach, John, 239
Lisak, David, 176–79
López, Eliana: immigration status of, 39,
41, 42–43, 48; victimhood of, 47–50;
victim rights and, 53; "What is the
Scandal, ¿Cuál es el Escándolo?" by,
44–45
Lopez, Gerald, 68
Los Angeles Police Department (LAPD),
236–37

MADD. *See* Mothers Against Drunk Driving

Madison, Ivory, 41–42

Mahoney, Martha, 212

Malik, Tashfeen, 273

mandatory arrest policies, 6, 20; community response programs and, 229–30; critique of, 218; IPV and, 217–19; survivors and, 66–67, 340

mandatory interventions: immigrant survivors of IPV and, 217–19; no-drop prosecution as, 6, 217. *See also* mandatory arrest policies

Mann, Michael, 164–65

Marlett, G. Alan, 335

Martin, Trayvon, 27; Black Lives Matter movement and, 28

masculinity: campus sexual assault and hostile, 176, 179–80, 190; first generation politicization of domestic violence and, 308; frontier, 249; gun ownership and, 248–49, 252; hegemonic, 232–33; hypermasculinity, 231–33, 235, 240, 316–18, 324n40; NFL and, 314

mass incarceration, 23, 31, 164; carceral feminism and, 15

mass shootings, 10, 249, 255, 272; family violence and, 254; gun laws and, 256–57

Mateen, Omar, 249, 273

maternity leave, 5

matrix of violence, 91–94

MDA. *See* Moms Demand Action for Gun Sense in America

Meadows, Bresha, 96

mens rea, of parental discipline privilege, 121, 125–27; control and, 128–30; family violence and, 120; hierarchy of, 128

men's rights movement, 309, 322n14

mental health issues: domestic violence victim and, 47; homicide-suicides and, 273, 274–75, 285–86, 286, 289; Lanza and, 275

#MeToo movement, 6–8, 33; allegations during, 362; Burke starting, 6–7, 362; criticism of, 8, 373n4; Milano and, 7, 362, 373n3; Nassar and, 173; race and, 6–7

Michigan State, 173

Milano, Alyssa, 7, 362, 373n3

militarism: federal policy and, 235; hegemonic masculinity and, 233; hypermasculinity and, 233, 235; law enforcement and, 233–35, 240; patriarchal gender hierarchies and, 233–34; violence against women and, 233–34

Miller, Paul, 177

Miller, Susan, 232

Million Mom March, 252

minimizing victim, 44, 49

Mirkarimi, Ross, 39, 42

Mirkarimi-López case: argument in, 41; Breall and, 42–43; community assessments of, 39–40, 50–54; criminal charges in, 42; domestic violence advocates and, 48–49, 51, 52–54; EPO in, 42; Ethics Commission and Board of Supervisors hearings for, 39, 44–45, 53; feminists and, 45, 51; law enforcement intervening in, 41–42; López immigration status and, 39, 41, 42–43, 48; López statements in, 43–44; Madison and, 41–42; minimizing victim in, 44, 49; outcome of, 40; plea agreement in, 44; privacy rights in, 43, 49; procedural fairness in, 50–51; substantive fairness in, 40, 50, 52–54; victimhood construction in, 47–50; victim rights and, 40, 53; "What is the Scandal, ¿Cuál es el Escándolo?" on, 44–45

mitigating circumstances model: battered women's syndrome and, 103, 107; of failure to protect, 91, 94, 103, 107; Savage and, 103

Model Rules of Professional Conduct, 316–17

Moms Demand Action for Gun Sense in America (MDA), 252; open-carry groups and, 253–54

Morrison, Adele, 67–68

Morse, Stephen J., 129

motherhood, 109; constructions of, 94; hyper-culpable, 92, 95, 98; ideology, 95; MDA and, 252–54

Mothers Against Drunk Driving (MADD), 21, 252

Mountain Crest, 151

multidimensional empowerment, 8, 63–64; self-help and, 68, 69, 74, 79, 80

multi-system involvement, 153, 158–59; realities of, 161–64; specialized justice model and, 152

Nassar, Larry, 173

national action plan: coordination for, 366; developing and implementing, 366–67; Federal Strategic Action Plan on Services for Victims of Human Trafficking in the United States as, 371; GBV strategy and, 370; guiding principles for, 365–66; historical, 376n43; intersectionality and, 369; legislation and, 366, 369; local action plan and, 373; measures for, 364–65; monitoring and reporting in, 368; prevention and response for, 367; targets in, 365; Trump and, 364, 372; types of violence and, 364; UN Women and, 363; VAWA and, 363–64, 369

National Action Plan for Combating Antibiotic-Resistant Bacteria, 372

National Action Plan on Women, Peace, and Security, U.S. (WPS Strategy), 369–70

National Clearinghouse for the Defense of Battered Women (NCDBW), 22

National Coalition Against Domestic Violence (NCADV), 18, 20

National Football League (NFL), 313; masculinity culture and, 314

National HIV/AIDS Strategy/Federal Action Plan for the United States, 371; intersectionality and, 372

National Plan of Action, 10, 363–67. See also national action plan

National Rifle Association (NRA), 2, 260, 265, 287; member gender of, 254; politics and, 3, 246, 255; Trump supported by, 3, 255

National Violent Death Reporting System (NVDRS), 272, 274, 278, 280–81, 283–84; sources for, 279

NCADV. See National Coalition Against Domestic Violence

NCDBW. See Defense of Battered Women; National Clearinghouse for the Defense of Battered Women

needle exchange programs: harm reduction and, 336, 348; politics and, 348

Newtown. See Sandy Hook Elementary School shooting

next generation reforms, of domestic violence, 303, 306, 313, 314; caregivers and, 316; child welfare and, 317; lawyers and, 316–17; modern political movements and, 318–20; recidivism and, 315; state provoking domestic violence and, 317–18; training models for, 318

NFL. See National Football League

Nixon, Richard, 18

no-drop prosecution, 217, 340

Nourn, Ny, 109, 118n56

NRA. See National Rifle Association

NVDRS. See National Violent Death Reporting System

Oakley, Annie, 248

Obama, Barack, 5, 124, 363, 375n15; campus sexual assault and, 171–72, 173, 181; Federal Strategic Action Plan on Services for Victims of Human Trafficking in the United States and,

371; GBV Strategy and WPS Strategy and, 369–70; gender equality and, 364; gun safety and, 248, 259–60, 275–76; National HIV/AIDS Strategy/Federal Action Plan and, 371–72

Obergefell v. Hodges, 135

OCR. *See* Office of Civil Rights

Odem, Mary, 155

Office of Civil Rights (OCR), 171

Office on Violence Against Women (OVW), 23, 31, 231; grants for, 228; restorative justice and, 32

officer-perpetrated intimate partner violence. *See* police-perpetrated domestic abuse

Omnibus Crime Act, 228

open-carry groups, 253–54

opium, 334, 335–36

Osthoff, Sue, 22

OVW. *See* Office on Violence Against Women

parens patriae doctrine: child abuse and neglect and, 157–58; child-saving and, 161, 165

parental discipline privilege, 119, 144n53; abolition of, 121; cases of, 126–27, 128; control and, 128–29; elimination of, 137; family violence and, 9; as justification, 120, 122; LGBTQI children and, 132; medical experts on, 122–23; *mens rea* of, 120, 121, 125–30; normalizing violence through, 130–35; Peterson and, 126, 130–31, 133, 136; precedent for, 131; public approval of, 121; scope of, 122; sexual assault and, 132; social and familial hierarchies and, 131–32; as status-based exception, 122, 123

patriarchy: failure to protect and, 94; militarism and, 233–34

Patterson, Orlando, 134

Patton, Stacey, 133–34

Pence, Mike, 3, 348

Peterson, Adrian, 126, 136; prosecution of, 130–31; race justification and, 133

Philly Stands Up, 25–26

Planned Parenthood, 5

POE. *See* preponderance of the evidence

police discretion, 272

police-perpetrated domestic abuse, 227; authoritarian personalities and, 239; data on, 235–39; emotional and verbal, 238; family violence and, 10; female officers and, 236; hegemonic masculinity and, 232–33; intervention for, 239–40; IPV compared to, 238, 244n63; LAPD and, 236–37; policymakers and, 239; PRPD and, 237; Rivera Hernández and, 237; self-reporting of, 238

political ideology, of failure to protect, 92, 99; charges pursued and, 98; criminalization and, 96–97; gender bias and, 94; motherhood and, 95

politics: of advocacy, 1, 9; gender, 1; gun safety and, 246, 248, 255–60, 277–78; harm reduction and, 334, 348, 350–51; needle exchange programs and, 348; NRA and, 3, 246, 255; self-help programs and, 74–76; of victimhood, 47–50

power mapping, 3

predator narrative: *Crime Logic and*, 174, 176–79; Lisak on, 176–79; longitudinal study and, 178; repeat rapists in, 177–78

preponderance of the evidence (POE), 185

Price, Tom, 5, 350

prison abolitionism, 25, 36n34, 331n129; Davis and, 24, 30

prison industrial complex, 23–24, 164

procedural fairness, 39–40; in Mirkarimi-López case, 50–51

Project Nia, 27

prosecution: conditions of release for, 340–41; no-drop prosecution policies, 217, 340; victims' compensation fund and, 341 prosecutorial culpability inflation, 98

protection orders: agency and, 65; control through, 341–42; empowerment and, 64–65, 86n60; EPO as, 42; family court and, 66; gender-based violence and, 65; IPV and, 288–89; judges and, 341–42; law enforcement and, 289; racism and, 65

PRPD. *See* Puerto Rico Police Department

public health: campus sexual assault and, 176, 179; domestic violence and, 332–33; gun violence and, 258–59; harm reduction approach, 10, 333

Puerto Rico Police Department (PRPD), 237

Putnins, Susan, 343

racism: advocacy and, 155–56; alternative justice and, 154–56, 158; campus hate crimes and, 181–82; campus sexual assault and, 173, 181–83, 184–85; carceral state and, 51; gun ownership and, 248; hate crimes and, 181–82; law enforcement and, 207–8; protection orders and, 65; racialized gender bias, 184–85; scientific, 106

rape myth endorsement, 183

Reagan, Nancy, 349

Reagan, Ronald: anti-domestic violence movement and, 20–22; Task Force on Violent Crime report and, 21; VOCA and, 20–21

recidivism: cycle of violence and, 304–5; domestic violence and, 304–5, 307; next generation reforms for domestic violence and, 315; restorative justice and, 189

refugees. *See* Syrian refugees

restorative justice, 31, 37n44, 137, 158–60, 165; campus sexual assault and, 9, 186–90, 200n140; community-building circles and, 187; Conferencing, 187–88;

intersectionality and, 175; OVW and, 32; recidivism and, 189; reparative plan for, 188–89; theory of, 187; use-immunity agreement for, 200n140. *See also* Transformative Justice

Rhode, Deborah, 159

Rice, Janay, 313

Rice, Ray, 313

Richie, Beth, 29; on matrix of violence, 91–94

risk factors: domestic violence, 306–8, 315–16; homicide-suicide, 281, *284–86*, 284–88, *290*

Rivera Hernández, Heriberto, 237

Rogers, Mike, 278

Roof, Dylann Storm, 273

Roosevelt, Eleanor, 364

Sanctuary Cities, 208, 363

Sandy Hook Elementary School shooting, 274, 277, 287; gun safety and, 289, 298n111; Lanza and, 273, 275

Savage, Kelly Ann, 109; conviction of, 99, 102; culpability of, 104; habeas corpus for, 100–103; mitigating factors and, 103; structural critique of, 104

Savage, Mark, 99–102

#SayHerName, 28, 54

scene-of-assault procedure, 272, 274–75, 289–90; confiscation-at-the-scene laws and, 288

Schechter, Susan, 63, 66, 68

Schept, Judah, 159

SDGs. *See* Sustainable Development Goals

Second Amendment, of U.S. Constitution, 276

self-defense campaigns: anti-domestic violence movement and, 27–29; Transformative Justice and, 28

self-help programs, 8; access to justice and, 62, 69, 71–73; advocacy and, 70–71, 77–78; agency and, 68, 73–74; applicant decision-making and, 77;

battered women's movement and, 68, 76; disempowerment and, 71–73; empowerment and, 62–63, 68, 71; empowerment continuum and, 67–68, 79; family law and, 69; guns in the home and, 74; legal consciousness and, 80; method and, 71; multidimensional empowerment and, 68, 69, 74, 79, 80; political consciousness and, 74–76; research sites for, 69–71; stereotypes and, 76, 79; weak claims and, 72–73

separation violence: homicide as, 213–14, 342; homicide-suicide as, 283; immigrant survivors of IPV and, 212–14; immigration status and, 342–43; law enforcement cooperation and, 213

September 11 homicide-suicide, 291n14

Service-Training-Officers-Prosecutors (STOP) Program, 228, 229–30

Sessions, Jeff, 350

sexual assault, 2, 19, 31, 229, 308, 313; community-based organizations on, 26; *It's on Us* pledge and, 363; LGBTQI individuals and, 34n7; #MeToo movement and, 6–8, 33, 173, 362, 373n3; parental discipline privilege and, 132; social determinants of, 179; Trump committing, 4, 350, 362; youth, 176. *See also* campus sexual assault

sexual dominance, 179

sex work, 335, 351, 355n39; decriminalization of, 336–37; HIV/AIDS and, 336

shelters: for domestic violence, 305, 337, 344; shelter and victims' services model of, 305

Sherills, Aqeela, 30

Simon, Jonathan, 175

situational couple violence, 52, 53

slavery, 119, 133–34

social control, 154, 157, 164, 317

social movements, 1, 54; anti-war, 19; feminist, 4, 6–8, 10–11, 19–20, 21, 305; INCITE! and, 24

specialized justice: access to justice and, 159–60; Chicago's court of domestic relations as, 154; for child abuse and neglect, 153; crossover youth and, 163; multi-system involvement and, 152; purposes of, 154; socializing and, 153, 154–57, 160, 165; women's rights activists and, 155

state accountability, 314; autonomy and, 304, 311; custody proceedings and, 315; hyper-incarceration and, 317; hypermasculinity and, 317–18; lethality assessments and, 312–13; services model and, 311; training models for, 318

state violence. *See* self-defense campaigns

staying in abusive relationships, 350; civil response and, 341–42; harm reduction and, 339–45, 351; high-risk behavior and, 339; laws on, 339–41; losses deterring, 343–44; love and logistics for, 343; safety planning for, 346–47; separation violence and, 212–14, 283, 342–43; state harm and, 339, 345; stigmas of, 345

Stinson, Philip, 239

Stoll, Laurie Cooper, 183

Stoops, Nan, 31

STOP. *See* Service-Training-Officers-Prosecutors Program

Strategy to Prevent and Respond to Gender-Based Violence Globally, U.S. (GBV Strategy), 370

Straus, Murray, 124

structural critique, of failure to protect, 112; battered women's syndrome and, 92–93; BCS and, 107; matrix of violence and, 93–94; Savage, K., and, 104

substantive fairness, 40, 50, 52–54

Supreme Court, 3; gun control and, 257–58, 276

survivor-centered domestic violence protections, 4, 351

survivors, 113n2; autonomy of, 304, 311; child, 96–97, 111; criminalization of, 9, 91, 111, 120; mandatory arrest policies and, 66–67, 340; mental health and, 47; Nourn as, 109, 118n56; public benefits and, 369; victimhood and, 46–48, 93; victims' compensation fund for, 341. *See also* harm reduction; immigrant survivors, of IPV; staying in abusive relationships

Sustainable Development Goals (SDGs), 376n38

Swartout, Kevin, 178, 179

Syrian refugees, 5

Task Force Against Family Violence, 21, 22

teen dating violence: gun ownership and, 251–52; legislation on, 3

theory of victimhood. *See* victimhood theories

therapeutic jurisprudence, 160

Thomas, Kristie A., 343

#TimesUp movement, 33

Title IX policies, 172; campus sexual assault and, 173–74

Transformative Justice: anti-domestic violence movement and, 25, 27, 30–31; BATJC and, 27; generationFIVE and, 27; self-defense campaigns and, 28. *See also* restorative justice

Trump, Donald, 373; campus climate impacted by, 173; campus sexual assault and, 172–73, 174; criminalization of immigrants and, 202; drug use and, 350; gender-discrimination lawsuits and, 4; Global Gag Rule and, 4–5; harm reduction and, 350; hate crimes and, 182; immigration enforcement and, 202, 208; maternity leave and, 5; national action plan and, 364, 372; NRA supporting, 3, 255; Sanctuary Cities and, 208, 363; sexual assault by, 4, 350, 362; VAWA and, 4; Women's March and, 6

Turner, Brock, 175–76

Tuthill, Richard, 158

T-Visa, 214–15

TVPA. *See* Victims of Trafficking and Violence Prevention Act

United Nations (UN): CEDAW, 364, 372–73; Convention on the Rights of the Child, 135; SDGs of, 376n38; WPS Strategy and, 369–70

universal background checks, 259, 260–61, 274

UN Women, 373; on development and implementation of national action plans, 366–67; guiding principles for national action plans by, 365–66; on monitoring, 368; national action plans and, 363

U.S. Citizenship and Immigration Services (USCIS), 204, 216; Green Card application process and, 215; removal proceedings and, 210; T-Visa and, 214–15

U visa program, 9, 219, 222n37; aims of, 202–3; application process for, 203, 204; BIWPA and, 205; eligibility for, 204; law enforcement cooperation and, 203, 204, 206–7, 214–18; state legislatures and, 216–17; as voluntary, 209–10; work authorization for, 204–5

VAWA. *See* Violence Against Women Act

victim accountability, 20, 304, 311, 313

victim-blaming, 92, 93, 99–100, 117, 130, 188, 212–13; advocacy against, 9; battering principles and, 107–8; courts and, 104–5, 108–9; Hall and, 104–5, 117n55; state actors and, 65. *See also* failure to protect

victimhood: agency and, 46–48, 54; domestic violence advocates and, 48–49, 51; of López, 47–50; minimizing victim, 44, 49; political constructions of, 47–50; survivors and, 46–48, 93 victimhood theories, 39; guilt and, 45; victim narratives and, 45–46

victim rights, 45; advocacy, 21; anti-domestic violence movement and, 20–21; criminalization and, 20–21, 54; defendant rights and, 22; Marsy's law and, 43, 44; Mirkarimi-López case and, 40, 53; movement, 47

Victims of Crime Act (VOCA), 20–21

Victims of Trafficking and Violence Prevention Act (TVPA), 205

violence against women: discrimination and, 365–66; forms of, 365; as human rights violation, 364, 365, 369; It's on Us pledge and, 363; militarism and, 233–34; national response to, 368–69; race and, 93; tipping point for, 362–63

Violence Against Women Act (VAWA): anti-domestic violence movement and, 22–23, 229; autonomy and, 6; carceral feminism and, 22–23; Clinton and, 22; community response programs and, 229–30; criminalization and, 15, 23, 31–32, 229, 369; discrimination and, 2, 369; funding by, 228–29, 231, 240; gun safety and, 262, 264; immigrant survivors and, 214; law enforcement and, 229, 231–32, 240; national action plan and, 363–64, 369; Omnibus Crime Act and, 228; OVW and, 23, 31, 32, 228, 231; reauthorizations of, 2–3, 368–69; Sessions and, 350; STOP Program and, 228, 229–30; Trump administration budget cuts for, 4; TVPA and, 205; Violent Crime Control and Law Enforcement Act and, 6

Violent Crime Control and Law Enforcement Act, 6

VOCA. See Victims of Crime Act

Walker, Lenore, 306

Ward, Geoff, 155

Watts, Shannon, 253

Web-Based Injury Statistics Query and Reporting System (WISQARS), 278

Weissman, Deborah, 319

"What is the Scandal, ¿Cuál es el Escándolo?," 44–45

white supremacists, 134; hate crimes and, 182

WISQARS. See Web-Based Injury Statistics Query and Reporting System

Witkiewitz, Katie, 335

Women's March: participants of, 362–63; Trump inauguration and, 6

workplace policies: on domestic violence, 313–14, 369; NFL, 313–14

WPS Strategy. See National Action Plan on Women, Peace, and Security, U.S.

Wynn, Mark, 238

Young Women's Empowerment Project, 25

zero tolerance policies, 53, 348